LAN Switching and Wireless
CCNA Exploration Companion Guide

Wayne Lewis, Ph.D.

Cisco Press

800 East 96th Street

Indianapolis, Indiana 46240 USA

LAN Switching and Wireless
CCNA Exploration Companion Guide

Wayne Lewis, Ph.D.

Copyright© 2008 Cisco Systems, Inc.

Published by:
Cisco Press
800 East 96th Street
Indianapolis, IN 46240 USA

Printed in the United States of America

Fourth Printing March 2009

Library of Congress Cataloging-in-Publication Data

Lewis, Wayne, Ph.D.

  LAN switching and wireless : CCNA exploration companion guide / Wayne Lewis. -- 1st ed.

        p. cm.

  ISBN 978-1-58713-207-0 (hardcover w/cd)

1.   Telecommunication--Switching systems--Examinations--Study guides.
2.   Wireless LANs--Examinations--Study guides. 3.   Telecommunications engineers--Certification--Examinations--Study guides.   I. Cisco Networking Academy Program. II. Cisco Systems, Inc. III. Title.

  TK5103.8.L493 2008
  004.6'8--dc22

2008011633
ISBN-13: 978-1-58713-207-0
ISBN-10: 1-58713-207-9

This book is part of the Cisco Networking Academy® series from Cisco Press. The products in this series support and complement the Cisco Networking Academy curriculum. If you are using this book outside the Networking Academy, then you are not preparing with a Cisco trained and authorized Networking Academy provider.

For more information on the Cisco Networking Academy or to locate a Networking Academy, please visit www.cisco.com/edu.

Warning and Disclaimer

This book is designed to provide information about LAN Switching and Wireless of the Cisco Network Academy CCNA Exploration curriculum. Every effort has been made to make this book as complete and as accurate as possible, but no warranty or fitness is implied.

Publisher
Paul Boger

Associate Publisher
Dave Dusthimer

Cisco Representative
Anthony Wolfenden

Cisco Press Program Manager
Jeff Brady

Executive Editor
Mary Beth Ray

Production Manager
Patrick Kanouse

Development Editor
Andrew Cupp

Senior Project Editor
San Dee Phillips

Copy Editor
Barbara Hacha

Technical Editors
Martin S. Anderson
Samuel Bolaños
George Wong

Editorial Assistant
Vanessa Evans

Book and Cover Designer
Louisa Adair

Composition
TnT Design, Inc.

Indexer
Publishing Works

Proofreader
Mike Henry

The information is provided on an "as is" basis. The authors, Cisco Press, and Cisco Systems, Inc. shall have neither liability nor responsibility to any person or entity with respect to any loss or damages arising from the information contained in this book or from the use of the discs or programs that may accompany it.

The opinions expressed in this book belong to the author and are not necessarily those of Cisco Systems, Inc.

Trademark Acknowledgments

All terms mentioned in this book that are known to be trademarks or service marks have been appropriately capitalized. Cisco Press or Cisco Systems, Inc. cannot attest to the accuracy of this information. Use of a term in this book should not be regarded as affecting the validity of any trademark or service mark.

Corporate and Government Sales

The publisher offers excellent discounts on this book when ordered in quantity for bulk purchases or special sales, which may include electronic versions and/or custom covers and content particular to your business, training goals, marketing focus, and branding interests. For more information, please contact: **U.S. Corporate and Government Sales**   1-800-382-3419   corpsales@pearsontechgroup.com

For sales outside the United States please contact: **International Sales** international@pearsoned.com

Feedback Information

At Cisco Press, our goal is to create in-depth technical books of the highest quality and value. Each book is crafted with care and precision, undergoing rigorous development that involves the unique expertise of members from the professional technical community.

Readers' feedback is a natural continuation of this process. If you have any comments regarding how we could improve the quality of this book, or otherwise alter it to better suit your needs, you can contact us through e-mail at feedback@ciscopress.com. Please make sure to include the book title and ISBN in your message.

We greatly appreciate your assistance.

Americas Headquarters	Asia Pacific Headquarters	Europe Headquarters
Cisco Systems, Inc.	Cisco Systems, Inc.	Cisco Systems International BV
170 West Tasman Drive	168 Robinson Road	Haarlerbergpark
San Jose, CA 95134-1706	#28-01 Capital Tower	Haarlerbergweg 13-19
USA	Singapore 068912	1101 CH Amsterdam
www.cisco.com	www.cisco.com	The Netherlands
Tel: 408 526-4000	Tel: +65 6317 7777	www-europe.cisco.com
800 553-NETS (6387)	Fax: +65 6317 7799	Tel: +31 0 800 020 0791
Fax: 408 527-0883		Fax: +31 0 20 357 1100

Cisco has more than 200 offices worldwide. Addresses, phone numbers, and fax numbers are listed on the Cisco Website at **www.cisco.com/go/offices**.

©2007 Cisco Systems, Inc. All rights reserved. CCVP, the Cisco logo, and the Cisco Square Bridge logo are trademarks of Cisco Systems, Inc.; Changing the Way We Work, Live, Play, and Learn is a service mark of Cisco Systems, Inc.; and Access Registrar, Aironet, BPX, Catalyst, CCDA, CCDP, CCIE, CCIP, CCNA, CCNP, CCSP, Cisco, the Cisco Certified Internetwork Expert logo, Cisco IOS, Cisco Press, Cisco Systems, Cisco Systems Capital, the Cisco Systems logo, Cisco Unity, Enterprise/Solver, EtherChannel, EtherFast, EtherSwitch, Fast Step, Follow Me Browsing, FormShare, GigaDrive, GigaStack, HomeLink, Internet Quotient, IOS, IP/TV, iQ Expertise, the iQ logo, iQ Net Readiness Scorecard, iQuick Study, LightStream, Linksys, MeetingPlace, MGX, Networking Academy, Network Registrar, Packet, PIX, ProConnect, RateMUX, ScriptShare, SlideCast, SMARTnet, StackWise, The Fastest Way to Increase Your Internet Quotient, and TransPath are registered trademarks of Cisco Systems, Inc. and/or its affiliates in the United States and certain other countries.

All other trademarks mentioned in this document or Website are the property of their respective owners. The use of the word partner does not imply a partnership relationship between Cisco and any other company. (0609R)

About the Author

Wayne Lewis is the Cisco Academy Manager for the Pacific Center for Advanced Technology Training (PCATT), based at Honolulu Community College (HonCC), and the Legal Main Contact for the CCNA/CCNP/Network Security Cisco Academy Training Center at PCATT/HonCC. Since 1998, Wayne has taught routing and switching, wide area networking, network troubleshooting, network security, wireless networking, IP telephony, and quality of service to instructors from universities, colleges, and high schools in Australia, Canada, Mexico, Central America, South America, United States, American Samoa, Guam, China, Hong Kong, Taiwan, Indonesia, Singapore, Korea, Japan, Italy, Germany, Netherlands, Sweden, Poland, Hungary, and Great Britain, both onsite and at PCATT/HonCC.

Cisco Systems has sent Wayne to several countries to conduct inaugural Networking Academy teacher-training sessions to certify the initial cohorts of instructors and kick off the training centers for these countries. Before teaching networking, Wayne began teaching at age 20 at Wichita State University, followed by the University of Hawaii and HonCC. In 1992, Wayne received a Ph.D. in math, specializing in finite rank torsion-free modules over a Dedekind domain; he now works on algebraic number theory research in his spare time. Wayne works as a contractor for Cisco Systems, performing project management for the development of network security, CCNA, and CCNP curriculum. He and his wife, Leslie, also run a network consulting company. Wayne enjoys surfing the South Shore of Oahu in the summer and surfing big waves on the North Shore in the winter.

About the Technical Reviewers

Martin S. Anderson has been an instructor and program director for Computer Science Technology at BGSU Firelands since 2001. BGSU Firelands, located in Huron, Ohio, is a regional branch college of Bowling Green State University. He has more than 30 years of experience in network computing, which began with the computerization of his family's small business in the mid-1970s. He returned to college in the mid-1990s and earned an associate's, a bachelor's, and a master's degree in a five-year span. He has taught the CCNA curriculum at BGSU Firelands since 2002.

Samuel Bolaños became involved with the Cisco Networking Academy in 2001 when he participated in the promotion and establishment of the program at ITESO University in Guadalajara, Mexico. This work, and his firm beliefs in the benefits of the Cisco Networking Academy and the computer networking technology as an educational and career opportunity, led to his participation in the establishment of a four-year undergraduate engineering program in Computer Networks at ITESO University in 2003. In 2005 he started working for the Computer Networking Department at the College of the Canyons in Santa Clarita, California, where he happily continues teaching at the Regional Academy established in this institution. He is proud of the recent participation of the College of the Canyons Academy in the reviewing process of the new CCNA courses (version 4.0) where they had the opportunity of directly contributing to the growing success of the program. Samuel has a bachelor's degree in electronics from ITESO University and a master's degree in electrical engineering from Loyola Marymount University. Samuel lives with his wife, Eugenia, and his son, Jorge.

George Wong has been an instructor in the Computer, Networking and Emerging Technologies Department at Ohlone College in Fremont Ca. He received his MSEE from the University of Kentucky and worked as an electrical engineer for more than 35 years. He has been a Cisco Networking Academy instructor for both CCNA and CCNP for the past nine years.

Dedications

To my wife, Leslie, who has steadfastly supported me during eight years of authoring eight Cisco Press books. You have managed to work full time, get two college degrees, and provide the consummate nurturing environment for our daughters since 1991, as I was busy writing math papers and networking textbooks. Your serenity and grounding create an environment that enables me the luxury of intellectual pursuits. I am eternally grateful for your abiding love and support.

To my daughter and fellow freethinker, Christina, for providing me with inspiration in my day-to-day life. I never tire of seeing you explore your intellectual curiosity. The way that you support diversity in your friendships truly differentiates you as a leader and a role model.

To my daughter, Lenora, for being my hiking partner, Xbox 360 Halo teammate, and 15-year-old calculus student. You bring a smile to my face every day. I know your dreams will come true.

- Wayne Lewis

Acknowledgments

I would first like to thank Mary Beth Ray, Executive Editor, for her continued support of my Cisco Press writing projects over the years. I truly appreciate the unique opportunity to author networking texts. I know from my travels that readers across the planet are grateful for the availability of companion guides to the Academy curriculum, which often go far beyond the content in the online curriculum. It is a real joy to be able to synthesize one's experience in the creative form of the written word. Your commitment to quality provides the foundation for the continued benefit that the companion guides afford the readers.

Andrew Cupp, development editor for Cisco Press, has worked with me over the past several years on companion guides to the Academy curriculum. Drew has been extremely patient with me when I have stretched timelines, always putting quality first. Drew is a seasoned professional with the innate ability to assist authors in achieving milestones. I am grateful for his guidance along the path and his resolute commitment to getting it right.

Don Bourassa, previous director of PCATT, was the best boss I ever had. Don recently retired from PCATT/HonCC. I would like to thank Don for being so supportive during the years I worked for him. He has the rare ability to lead faculty, who are notoriously difficult to manage. He enabled me to grow and experiment, to succeed and to fail, and I am positive that PCATT and HonCC have made very significant advances in technology education as a result.

Scott Murakami, the current PCATT director, is carrying on the tradition begun by Don Bourassa. Scott has been very supportive of my writing efforts. I am also stoked because my boss is a fellow surfer!

Ramsey Pedersen, chancellor of HonCC, hired me in 1992 when he was but a dean. He has consistently encouraged me to strive to be my best while staying out of the way to allow that to happen. He has the professional confidence to permit his faculty to take risks so that our institution is able to keep up with the rapid pace of technology. As a result, HonCC has remained a beacon of excellence in the international arena of technology education.

Computer networking and math, the two subjects I've taught over the years, are dramatically different in that networking changes yearly and math is relatively fixed within the undergraduate curriculum. However, people are often surprised to find that math is not "done"—new math results are being made each day across the planet. Networking is a science in its embryonic stage, whereas math has been developing for thousands of years. Networking will one day be studied as a science, similar to genetics or environmental science, but it is now a continuously evolving disparate collection of concepts and technologies. My mathematics professors in undergraduate and graduate school provided me with a foundation that was perfect for computer networking. When it comes down to it, computer networking is logic, which is also the foundation of mathematics. So...I would like to acknowledge my math professors, especially my dissertation adviser, Adolf Mader, for providing a rock-solid foundation upon which networking is easily constructible, discernible, synthesizable, and teachable.

I would also like to thank the technical editors, Martin Anderson, Samuel Bolaños, and George Wong, for consistently providing intelligent feedback and suggestions. Part of the process at Cisco Press is to, without exception, carry out a thorough technical review of the contents of each book prior to publication. This is a key factor in the near 15-year primacy of Cisco Press networking books in the industry.

Last, I would like to acknowledge the students and instructors I have taught networking over the past 10 years. As is common among information technology professors, I learn as much from those populating the classrooms as I do from reading books and perusing websites. There is no professional joy that exceeds that of teaching a group of smart students or instructors.

Contents at a Glance

Contents

Icons Used in This Book

Router

Switch

PC

Server

Straight-Through
Ethernet Connection

Cross-Over
Ethernet Connection

Console
Connection

Serial Line
Connection

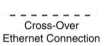
Network
Cloud

Access
Point

Command Syntax Conventions

The conventions used to present command syntax in this book are the same conventions used in the IOS Command Reference. The Command Reference describes these conventions as follows:

- **Boldface** indicates commands and keywords that are entered literally as shown. In actual configuration examples and output (not general command syntax), boldface indicates commands that are manually input by the user (such as a **show** command).

- *Italics* indicate arguments for which you supply actual values.

- Vertical bars (|) separate alternative, mutually exclusive elements.

- Square brackets [ ] indicate optional elements.

- Braces { } indicate a required choice.

- Braces within brackets [{ }] indicate a required choice within an optional element.

Introduction

The Cisco Networking Academy is a comprehensive e-learning program that provides students with Internet technology skills. A Networking Academy delivers web-based content, online assessment, student performance tracking, and hands-on labs to prepare students for industry-standard certifications. The CCNA curriculum includes four courses oriented around the topics on the Cisco Certified Network Associate (CCNA) certification.

LAN Switching and Wireless, CCNA Exploration Companion Guide is the official supplement textbook to be used with v4 of the CCNA Exploration LAN Switching and Wireless online curriculum of the Networking Academy.

This book goes beyond earlier editions of the Cisco Press Companion Guides by providing many alternative explanations and examples as compared with the course. You can use the online curriculum as normal and use this companion guide to help solidify your understanding of all the topics through the alternative examples.

The basis for this book, as well as the online curriculum, is to provide the reader with a thorough understanding of LAN switching and wireless technologies beyond that necessary for the CCNA certification exam. The commands and web-based GUI utilities for configuring LAN switching and wireless are not very difficult. The challenge is to understand the operation of these technologies and protocols and their role in the network.

The objective of this book is to explain LAN switching and wireless technologies. Every concept is methodically explained with no assumptions made of the reader's knowledge of LAN switching or wireless technologies. The only exceptions are if a concept is beyond the scope of this course or is covered in CCNP, and then it is noted within the text.

Readers are encouraged to peruse the resources managed by Wayne Lewis at cisco.honolulu.hawaii.edu. Please e-mail Wayne Lewis at waynel@hawaii.edu for more information about CCNP and network security instructor training and for access to more resources for this course and other CCNP, IP telephony, QoS, and network security courses.

Goal of This Book

First and foremost, by providing a fresh, complementary perspective on the content, this book is intended to help you learn all the required materials of the LAN Switching and Wireless course in the Networking Academy CCNA Exploration curriculum. As a secondary goal, the text is intended as a mobile replacement for the online curriculum for individuals who do not always have Internet access. In those cases, you can instead read the appropriate sections of the book, as directed by your instructor, and learn the same material that is covered in the online curriculum. Another secondary goal is to serve as your offline study material to prepare for the CCNA exam.

Audience for This Book

This book's main audience is anyone taking the CCNA Exploration LAN Switching and Wireless course of the Cisco Networking Academy curriculum. Many Academies use this textbook as a required tool in the course, and other Academies recommend the Companion Guides as an additional source of study and practice materials.

Book Features

The educational features of this book focus on supporting topic coverage, readability, and practice of the course material to facilitate your full understanding of the course material.

Topic Coverage

The following features give you a thorough overview of the topics covered in each chapter so that you can make constructive use of your study time:

- **Objectives:** Listed at the beginning of each chapter, the objectives reference the core concepts covered in the chapter. The objectives match the objectives stated in the corresponding chapters of the online curriculum; however, the question format in the Companion Guide encourages you to think about finding the answers as you read the chapter.

- **"How-to" feature**: When this book covers a set of steps that you need to perform for certain tasks, this book lists the steps as a how-to list. When you are studying, the icon helps you easily refer to this feature as you skim through the book.

- **Notes, tips, cautions, and warnings:** These are short sidebars that point out interesting facts, time-saving methods, and important safety issues.

- **Chapter summaries:** At the end of each chapter is a summary of the chapter's key concepts. It provides a synopsis of the chapter and serves as a study aid.

Readability

The author has compiled, edited, and in most cases rewritten the material so that it has a more conversational tone that follows a consistent and accessible college-reading level. In addition, the following features have been updated to assist your understanding of the networking vocabulary:

- **Key terms:** Each chapter begins with a list of key terms, along with a page-number reference from inside the chapter. The terms are listed in the order in which they are explained inside the chapter. This handy reference allows you to find a term, flip to the page where the term appears, and see the term used in context. The Glossary defines all the key terms.

- **Glossary:** This book contains an all-new Glossary with more than 150 terms.

Practice

Practice makes perfect. This new Companion Guide offers you ample opportunities to put what you learn to practice. You will find the following features valuable and effective in reinforcing the instruction that you receive:

- **Check Your Understanding questions and answer key:** Updated review questions are presented at the end of each chapter as a self-assessment tool. These questions match the style of questions that you see in the online course. The Appendix, "Check Your Understanding and Challenge Questions Answer Key," provides an answer key to all the questions and includes an explanation of each answer.

- **(NEW) Challenge questions and activities:** Additional—and more challenging—review questions and activities are presented at the end of chapters. These questions are purposefully designed to be similar to the more complex styles of questions you might see on the CCNA exam. This section might also include activities to help prepare you for the exams. The Appendix provides the answers.

- **Packet Tracer activities:** Interspersed throughout the chapters, you'll find many activities to work with the Cisco Packet Tracer tool. Packet Tracer allows you to create networks, visualize how packets flow in the network, and use basic testing tools to determine whether the network would work. When you see this icon, you can use Packet Tracer with the listed file to perform a task suggested in this book. The activity files are available in this book's CD-ROM; Packet Tracer software, however, is available through the Academy Connection website. Ask your instructor for access to Packet Tracer.

Labs and Study Guide

The supplementary book *LAN Switching and Wireless, CCNA Exploration Labs and Study Guide* (ISBN: 1-58713-202-8) by Cisco Press contains all the labs from the curriculum plus additional challenge labs and study guide material. The end of each chapter of this Companion Guide indicates with icons what labs, activities, and Packet Tracer activities are available in the Labs and Study Guide.

- **Lab references:** This icon notes the hands-on labs created for this chapter in the online curriculum. Within the *LAN Switching and Wireless, CCNA Exploration Labs and Study Guide* you will find additional study guide material created by the author of that book.

- **(NEW) Packet Tracer Companion activities:** Many of the Hands-on Labs include Packet Tracer Companion Activities where you can use Packet Tracer to complete a simulation of the lab. Look for this icon in the *LAN Switching and Wireless, CCNA Exploration Labs and Study Guide* for Hands-on Labs that have a Packet Tracer Companion.

- **(NEW) Packet Tracer Skills Integration Challenge activities:** These activities require you to pull together several skills learned from the chapter to successfully complete one comprehensive exercise. Look for this icon in the *LAN Switching and Wireless, CCNA Exploration Labs and Study Guide* for instructions on how to perform the Packet Tracer Skills Integration Challenge for this chapter.

A Word About Packet Tracer

Packet Tracer is a self-paced, visual, interactive teaching and learning tool developed by Cisco. Lab activities are an important part of networking education. However, lab equipment can be a scarce resource. Packet Tracer provides a visual simulation of equipment and network processes to offset the challenge of limited equipment. Students can spend as much time as they like completing standard lab exercises through Packet Tracer and have the option to work from home. Although Packet Tracer is not a substitute for real equipment, it allows students to practice using a command-line interface. This "e-doing" capability is a fundamental component of learning how to configure routers and switches from the command line.

Packet Tracer v4.x is available only to Cisco Networking Academies through the Academy Connection website.

The course includes essentially three types of Packet Tracer activities. This book uses an icon system to indicate which type of Packet Tracer activity is available. The icons are intended to give you a sense of the purpose of the activity and the amount of time you need to allot to complete it. The three types of Packet Tracer activities follow:

- **Packet Tracer Activity:** This icon identifies straightforward exercises interspersed throughout the chapters where you can practice or visualize a specific topic. The activity files for these exercises are available on this book's CD-ROM. These activities take less time to complete than the Packet Tracer Companion and Challenge activities.

- **Packet Tracer Companion:** This icon identifies exercises that correspond to the hands-on labs of the course. You can use Packet Tracer to complete a simulation of the hands-on lab or complete a similar "lab." The Companion Guide points these out at the end of each chapter, but look for this icon and the associated exercise file in *LAN Switching and Wireless, CCNA Exploration Labs and Study Guide* for hands-on labs that have a Packet Tracer Companion.

- **Packet Tracer Skills Integration Challenge:** This icon identifies activities that require you to pull together several skills learned from the chapter to successfully complete one comprehensive exercise. The Companion Guide points these out at the end of each chapter, but look for this icon and the associated exercise file in *LAN Switching and Wireless, CCNA Exploration Labs and Study Guide* for instructions on how to perform a Packet Tracer Skills Integration Challenge.

How This Book Is Organized

The book covers the major topic headings in the same sequence as the online curriculum for the CCNA Exploration LAN Switching and Wireless course. This book has seven chapters with the same numbers and names as the online course chapters.

For people reading this book without being in the CCNA Exploration LAN Switching and Wireless class, or just using this book for self-study, the sequence of topics in each chapter provides a logical sequence for learning the material presented.

Each chapter has a reference topology that is used to maintain a common framework from which to build upon the LAN switching and wireless concepts. The single topology per chapter allows for better continuity and easier understanding of switching commands, operations, and outputs, as well as web-based GUI utility mastery.

- **Chapter 1, "LAN Design,"** provides an overview of the switched LAN architecture for small- and medium-sized businesses. The concept of converged network services within hierarchical networking is emphasized. You also learn how to select the appropriate switch to implement at each hierarchical layer in the switched LAN topology.

- **Chapter 2, "Basic Switch Concepts and Configuration,"** reviews and reinforces the underlying concepts included within the IEEE 802.3 LAN standard and introduces the role of an Ethernet switch within a LAN. The basic configuration of switches to support voice, video, and data transmission is introduced, as well as basic network management options and rudimentary security measures.

- **Chapter 3, "VLANs,"** provides an introduction to types of VLANs, port membership within VLANs, and VLAN trunking. VLANs are the logical basis upon which switched LANs are built. Configuring, verifying, and troubleshooting VLANs are discussed.

- **Chapter 4, "VTP,"** examines the VLAN trunking protocol. VTP automates many of the VLAN configuration options in a switched LAN, but requires a good conceptual understanding of how the Layer 2 protocol operates. The underlying operation of VTP and VTP pruning are explored, followed by detailed guidance on VTP configuration.

- **Chapter 5, "STP,"** provides a detailed analysis of the original IEEE 802.1D spanning-tree protocol (STP) and the improved IEEE 802.1w rapid spanning-tree protocol (RSTP). The operation of STP is complex and requires a careful, measured approach, which is provided herein. Compared to the underlying operation of STP, the configuration of 802.1D and 802.1w is relatively straightforward. Both 802.1D and 802.1w result in a logical, loop-free, Layer 2 topology with physical redundancy.

- **Chapter 6, "Inter-VLAN Routing,"** explores three methods of inter-VLAN routing: one router interface per VLAN, router-on-a-stick, and multilayer switching. The configuration of the first two methods on access layer switches is detailed. Verification and troubleshooting inter-VLAN routing scenarios round out the chapter.

- **Chapter 7, "Basic Wireless Concepts and Configuration,"** provides a quick introduction to all the important elements necessary to understand wireless technologies and standards. A web-based GUI is used to configure wireless routers in constructing the LAN/WLAN reference topology for the chapter. Common troubleshooting issues specific to wireless LANs are explored.

- The **Appendix, "Check Your Understanding and Challenge Questions Answer Key,"** provides the answers to the Check Your Understanding questions that you find at the end of each chapter. It also includes answers for the Challenge Questions and Activities that conclude most chapters.

- The **Glossary** provides a compiled list of all the key terms that appear throughout this book.

About the CD-ROM

The CD-ROM included with this book provides many useful tools and information to support your education:

Packet Tracer
☐ Activity

- **Packet Tracer Activity files:** These are files to work through the Packet Tracer Activities referenced throughout the book, as indicated by the Packet Tracer Activity icon.

- **Taking Notes:** This section includes a .txt file of the chapter objectives to serve as a general outline of the key topics of which you need to take note. The practice of taking clear, consistent notes is an important skill not only for learning and studying the material but for on-the-job success as well. Also included in this section is "A Guide to Using a Networker's Journal" PDF booklet providing important insight into the value of the practice of using a journal, how to organize a professional journal, and some best practices on what, and what not, to take note of in your journal.

- **IT Career Information:** This section includes a student guide to applying the toolkit approach to your career development. Learn more about entering the world of Information Technology as a career by reading two informational chapters excerpted from *The IT Career Builder's Toolkit*: "Communication Skills" and "Technical Skills."

- **Lifelong Learning in Networking:** As you embark on a technology career, you will notice that it is ever-changing and evolving. This career path provides new and exciting opportunities to learn new technologies and their applications. Cisco Press is one of the key resources to plug into on your quest for knowledge. This section of the CD-ROM provides an orientation to the information available to you and tips on how to tap into these resources for lifelong learning.

About the Cisco Press Website for This Book

Cisco Press may provide additional content that can be accessed by registering your individual book at the ciscopress.com website. Becoming a member and registering is free, and you then gain access to exclusive deals on other resources from Cisco Press.

To register this book, go to www.ciscopress.com/bookstore/register.asp and log in to your account or create a free account if you do not have one already. Then enter the ISBN located on the back cover of this book.

After you register the book, it will appear on your Account page under Registered Products, and you can access any online material from there.

CHAPTER 1

LAN Design

Objectives

Upon completion of this chapter, you will be able to answer the following questions:

- How does a hierarchical network support the voice, video, and data needs of a small- or medium-sized business?

- What are the functions of each of the three layers of the hierarchical network design model?

- What are common examples of the effect of voice and video over IP on network design?

- What devices are recommended at each layer of the hierarchical design model?

- How are Cisco Catalyst switch product lines best positioned in the hierarchical design model?

Key Terms

This chapter uses the following key terms. You can find the definitions in the Glossary.

For small- and medium-sized businesses, digital communication with data, voice, and video is critical to performing day-to-day business functions. Consequently, a properly designed LAN is a fundamental requirement for doing business. You must understand what a well-designed LAN is and be able to select appropriate devices to support the network specifications of a small- or medium-sized business.

In this chapter, you begin exploring the switched LAN architecture and some of the principles that are used to design a hierarchical network. You learn about converged networks. You also learn how to select the correct switch for a hierarchical network and which Cisco switches are best suited for each hierarchical layer of the network.

Switched LAN Architecture

When building a switched LAN architecture that satisfies the needs of a small- or medium-sized business, your plan is more likely to be successful if a hierarchical design model is used. Compared to other network designs, a hierarchical network is easier to manage and expand, and problems are solved more quickly.

Hierarchical network design involves dividing the network into discrete layers. Each layer provides specific functions that define its role within the overall network. By separating the various functions that exist on a network, the network design becomes modular, which facilitates scalability and performance.

The typical hierarchical design model is broken into three layers:

- Access
- Distribution
- Core

An example of a three-layer hierarchical network design is displayed in Figure 1-1.

The Hierarchical Network Model

This section describes the access, distribution, and core layers in more detail. Following the introduction of the three-layer model, we explore the hierarchical model in medium-sized businesses. Finally, we delve into the benefits of hierarchical network design.

Access Layer

The *access layer* interfaces with end devices, such as PCs, printers, and IP phones, to provide access to the rest of the network. The access layer can include routers, switches, bridges, hubs, and wireless access points. The main purpose of the access layer is to provide a means of connecting devices to the network and controlling which devices are allowed to communicate on the network.

Figure 1-1   The Hierarchical Network Model

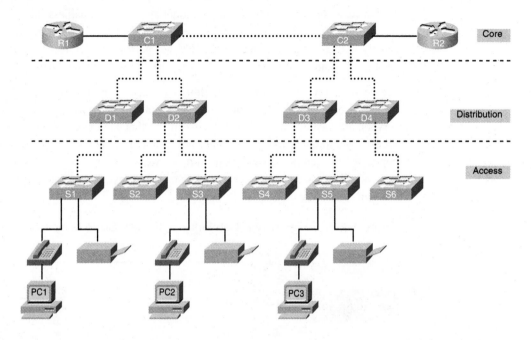

Distribution Layer

The *distribution layer* aggregates the data received from the access layer switches before it is transmitted to the core layer for routing to its final destination. The distribution layer controls the flow of network traffic using policies and delineates broadcast domains by performing routing functions between virtual LANs (VLANs) defined at the access layer. **VLANs** allow you to segment the traffic on a switch into separate subnetworks. For example, in a university you might separate traffic according to faculty, students, and guests. Distribution layer switches are typically high-performance devices that have high availability and redundancy to ensure reliability. You will learn more about VLANs, broadcast domains, and inter-VLAN routing later in this book.

Core Layer

The *core layer* of the hierarchical design is the high-speed backbone of the internetwork. The core layer is critical for interconnectivity between distribution layer devices, so it is important for the core to be highly available and redundant. The core area can also connect to Internet resources. The core aggregates the traffic from all the distribution layer devices, so it must be capable of forwarding large amounts of data quickly.

Note

In small networks, it is not unusual to implement a collapsed core model, where the distribution layer and core layer are combined into one layer.

A Hierarchical Network in a Medium-Sized Business

Now look at the hierarchical network model applied to a business. In Figure 1-1, the access, distribution, and core layers are separated into a well-defined hierarchy. This logical representation makes it easy to see which switches perform which function. It is much harder to see these hierarchical layers when the network is installed in a business.

Figure 1-2 shows two floors of a building. The user computers and network devices that need network access are on one floor. The resources, such as e-mail servers and database servers, are located on another floor. To ensure that each floor has access to the network, access layer and distribution switches are installed in the wiring closets of each floor and connected to each of the devices needing network access. The figure shows a small rack of switches. The access layer switch and distribution layer switch are stacked on top of each other in the wiring closet.

Figure 1-2   A Hierarchical Network in a Medium-Sized Business

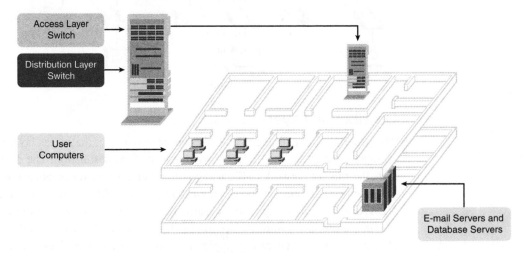

Although the core and other distribution layer switches are not shown, you can see how the physical layout of a network differs from the logical layout of Figure 1-1.

Benefits of a Hierarchical Network

Many benefits are associated with hierarchical network designs:

- *Scalability*
- *Redundancy*
- *Performance*

- *Security*
- *Manageability*
- *Maintainability*

Detailed descriptions of each of these benefits follow.

Scalability

Hierarchical networks scale very well. The modularity of the design allows you to replicate design elements as the network grows. Because each instance of the module is consistent, expansion is easy to plan and implement. For example, if your design model consists of two distribution layer switches for every 10 access layer switches, you can continue to add access layer switches until you have 10 access layer switches cross-connected to the two distribution layer switches before you need to add additional distribution layer switches to the network topology. Also, as you add more distribution layer switches to accommodate the load from the access layer switches, you can add additional core layer switches to handle the additional load on the core.

Redundancy

As a network grows, availability becomes more important. You can dramatically increase availability through easy redundant implementations with hierarchical networks. Access layer switches are connected to two different distribution layer switches to ensure path redundancy. If one of the distribution layer switches fails, the access layer switch can switch to the other distribution layer switch. Additionally, distribution layer switches are connected to two or more core layer switches to ensure path availability if a core switch fails. The only layer where redundancy is limited is at the access layer. Typically, end node devices, such as PCs, printers, and IP phones, do not have the capability to connect to multiple access layer switches for redundancy. If an access layer switch fails, just the devices connected to that one switch would be affected by the outage. The rest of the network would continue to function unaffected.

Performance

Communication performance is enhanced by avoiding the transmission of data through low-performing, intermediary switches. Data is sent through aggregated switch port links from the access layer to the distribution layer at near wire speed in most cases. The distribution layer then uses its high-performance switching capabilities to forward the traffic up to the core, where it is routed to its final destination. Because the core and distribution layers perform their operations at very high speeds, no contention for network bandwidth occurs. As a result, properly designed hierarchical networks can achieve near wire speed between all devices.

Security

Security is improved and easier to manage. Access layer switches can be configured with various port security options that provide control over which devices are allowed to connect to the network. You also have the flexibility to use more advanced security policies at the distribution layer. You may apply access control policies that define which communication protocols are deployed on your network and where they are permitted to go. For example, if you want to limit the use of HTTP to a specific user community connected at the access layer, you could apply a policy that blocks HTTP traffic at the distribution layer. Restricting traffic based on higher layer protocols, such as IP and HTTP, requires that your switches are able to process policies at that layer. Some access layer switches support Layer 3 functionality, but it is usually the job of the distribution layer switches to process Layer 3 data because they can process it much more efficiently.

Manageability

Manageability is relatively simple on a hierarchical network. Each layer of the hierarchical design performs specific functions that are consistent throughout that layer. Therefore, if you need to change the functionality of an access layer switch, you could repeat that change across all access layer switches in the network because they presumably perform the same functions at their layer. Deployment of new switches is also simplified because switch configurations can be copied between devices with very few modifications. Consistency between the switches at each layer allows for rapid recovery and simplified troubleshooting. In some special situations, configuration inconsistencies could exist between devices, so you should ensure that configurations are well documented so that you can compare them before deployment.

Maintainability

Because hierarchical networks are modular in nature and scale very easily, they are easy to maintain. With other network topology designs, maintainability becomes increasingly complicated as the network grows. Also, in some network design models, there is a finite limit to how large the network can grow before it becomes too complicated and expensive to maintain. In the hierarchical design model, switch functions are defined at each layer, making the selection of the correct switch easier. Adding switches to one layer does not necessarily mean there will not be a bottleneck or other limitation at another layer. For a full mesh network topology to achieve maximum performance, all switches need to be high-performance switches because each switch needs to be capable of performing all the functions on the network. In the hierarchical model, switch functions are different at each layer. You can save money by using less-expensive access layer switches at the lowest layer, and spend more on the distribution and core layer switches to achieve high performance on the network.

Principles of Hierarchical Network Design

Just because a network seems to have a hierarchical design does not mean that the network is well designed. These simple guidelines will help you differentiate between well-designed and poorly designed hierarchical networks. This section is not intended to provide you with all the skills and knowledge you need to design a hierarchical network, but it offers you an opportunity to begin to practice your skills by transforming a flat network topology into a hierarchical network topology.

Network Diameter

When designing a hierarchical network topology, the first thing to consider is network diameter, as depicted in Figure 1-3. Diameter is traditionally a measure of distance, but in the case of networking, we are using the term to measure the number of devices. Network diameter is the number of devices that a packet has to cross before it reaches its destination. Keeping the network diameter low ensures low and predictable latency between devices.

Figure 1-3   Network Diameter

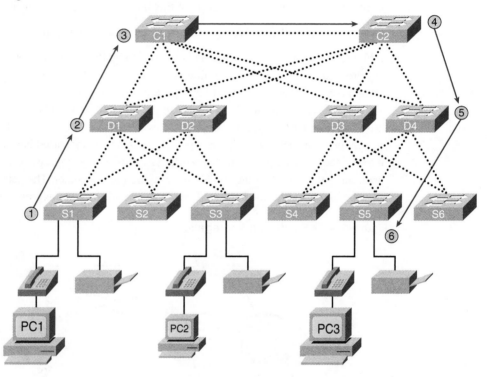

In Figure 1-3, PC1 communicates with PC3. Up to six interconnected switches could be between PC1 and PC3. In this case, the network diameter is six. Each switch in the path introduces some degree of latency. Network device latency is the time spent by a device as it processes a packet or frame. Each switch has to determine the destination MAC address of the frame, check its MAC address table, and forward the frame out the appropriate port. Even though that entire process happens in a fraction of a second, the time adds up when the frame has to cross many switches.

In the three-layer hierarchical model, Layer 2 segmentation at the distribution layer practically eliminates network diameter as an issue. In a hierarchical network, network diameter is always going to be a predictable number of hops between the source and destination devices.

Bandwidth Aggregation

Each layer in the hierarchical network model is a possible candidate for bandwidth aggregation. Bandwidth aggregation is the combining of two or more connections to create a logically singular higher bandwidth connection. After bandwidth requirements of the network are known, links between specific switches can be aggregated, which is called link aggregation. Link aggregation allows multiple switch port links to be combined so as to achieve higher throughput between switches. Cisco has a proprietary link aggregation technology called EtherChannel, which allows multiple Ethernet links to be consolidated. A discussion of EtherChannel is beyond the scope of this book. To learn more, visit

www.cisco.com/en/US/tech/tk389/tk213/tsd_technology_support_protocol_home.html.

In Figure 1-4, computers PC1 and PC3 require a significant amount of bandwidth because they are frequently used for streaming video. The network manager has determined that the access layer switches S1, S3, and S5 require increased bandwidth. Following up the hierarchy, these access layer switches connect to the distribution switches D1, D2, and D4. The distribution switches connect to core layer switches C1 and C2. Notice how specific links on specific ports in each switch are aggregated. In this way, increased bandwidth is provided for in a targeted, specific part of the network. As is customary, aggregated links are indicated in this figure by two dotted lines with an oval tying them together. The path PC1-S1-D1-C1-C2-D4-S5-PC3 enjoys the enhanced bandwidth resulting from aggregating links.

Figure 1-4   Bandwidth Aggregation

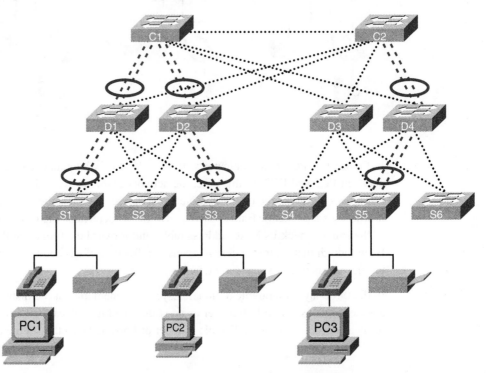

Redundancy

Redundancy is one part of creating a highly available network. Redundancy can be provided in a number of ways. For example, you can double up the network connections between devices, or you can double the devices themselves. This chapter explores how to employ redundant network paths between switches. A discussion on doubling up network devices and employing special network protocols to ensure high availability is beyond the scope of this book. For an interesting discussion on high availability, visit

www.cisco.com/en/US/products/ps6550/products_ios_technology_home.html.

Implementing redundant links can be expensive. Imagine if every switch in each layer of the network hierarchy had a connection to every switch at the next layer. It is unlikely that you will be able to implement redundancy at the access layer because of the cost and limited features in the end devices, but you can build redundancy into the distribution and core layers of the network.

In Figure 1-5, redundant links are shown at the distribution layer and core layer. At the distribution layer are four distribution layer switches; two distribution layer switches is the minimum required to support redundancy at this layer. The access layer switches, S1, S3, S4, and S6, are cross-connected to the distribution layer switches. The bolder dotted lines here indicate the secondary redundant uplinks. This protects your network if one of the distribution switches fails. In case of a failure, the access layer switch adjusts its transmission path and forwards the traffic through the other distribution switch.

Figure 1-5   Redundancy

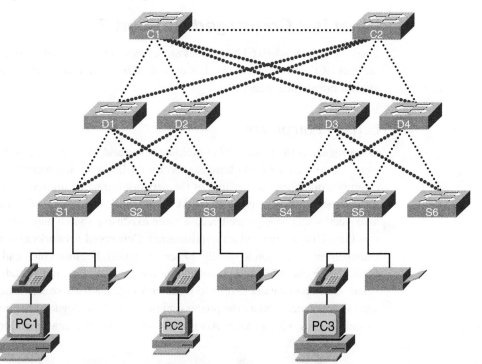

Some network failure scenarios can never be prevented—for example, if the power goes out in the entire city, or the entire building is demolished because of an earthquake. Redundancy does not attempt to address these types of disasters. To learn more about how a business can continue to work and recover from a disaster, visit

www.cisco.com/en/US/netsol/ns516/networking_solutions_package.html.

Imagine that a new network design is required. Design requirements, such as the level of performance or redundancy necessary, are determined by the business goals of the organization. After the design requirements are documented, the designer can begin selecting the equipment and infrastructure to implement the design.

When you start the equipment selection at the access layer, you can ensure that you accommodate all network devices needing access to the network. After you have all end devices accounted for, you have a better idea of how many access layer switches you need. The number of access layer switches, and the estimated traffic that each generates, helps you to determine how many distribution layer switches are required to achieve the performance and redundancy needed for the network. After you have determined the number of distribution layer switches, you can identify how many core switches are required to maintain the performance of the network.

A thorough discussion on how to determine which switch to select based on traffic flow analysis and how many core switches are required to maintain performance is beyond the scope of this book. For a good introduction to network design, an excellent reference is *Top-Down Network Design*, by Priscilla Oppenheimer, available at ciscopress.com.

What Is a Converged Network?

Small- and medium-sized businesses are embracing the idea of running voice and video services on their data networks. Let us look at how *voice over IP (VoIP)* and video over IP affect a hierarchical network.

Legacy Equipment

Convergence is the process of combining voice and video communications on a data network. Converged networks have existed for a while now, but were feasible only in large enterprise organizations because of the network infrastructure requirements and complex management that was involved to make them work seamlessly. High network costs were associated with convergence because more expensive switch hardware was required to support the additional bandwidth requirements. Converged networks also required extensive management in relation to *quality of service (QoS)*, because voice and video data traffic needed to be classified and prioritized on the network. Few individuals had the expertise in voice, video, and data networks to make convergence feasible and functional. In addition, legacy equipment hinders the process. Figure 1-6 shows legacy telephone company switches and a legacy wiring closet. Also, many offices still use analog phones, so they still have existing analog telephone wiring closets. Because analog phones have not yet been replaced, you will see equipment that has to support both legacy *private branch exchange (PBX)* telephone systems and IP-based phones. This sort of equipment will slowly be migrated to modern IP-based phone switches. IP phones replace analog phones and IP PBXs, such as Cisco CallManager, replace PBXs.

Figure 1-6   Legacy Equipment

Large Telephone Switches

Small PBX Systems

Wiring Closet Infrastructure

Advanced Technology

Converging voice, video, and data networks has become more popular recently in the small- to medium-sized business market because of advancements in technology. Convergence is now easier to implement and manage, and less expensive to purchase. Figure 1-7 shows a high-end IP phone and switch combination suitable for a medium-sized business of 250 to 400 employees. The figure also shows a Cisco Catalyst Express 500 switch and a Cisco 7906G phone suitable for small- to medium-sized businesses. This VoIP technology used to be affordable only to enterprises and governments.

Moving to a converged network can be a difficult decision if the business already invested in separate voice, video, and data networks. It is difficult to abandon an investment that still works, but there are several advantages to converging voice, video, and data on a single network infrastructure.

Figure 1-7   VoIP Equipment

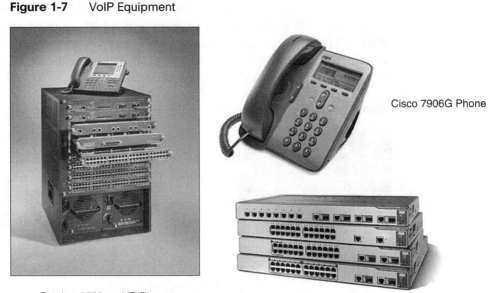

Cisco 7906G Phone

Catalyst 6500 and IP Phone

Catalyst Express 500 Switches

One benefit of a converged network is that there is just one network to manage. With separate voice, video, and data networks, changes to the network have to be coordinated across networks. Also, additional costs result from using three sets of network cabling. Using a single network means you have to manage just one wired infrastructure.

Other benefits are lower implementation and management costs. It is less expensive to implement a single network infrastructure than three distinct network infrastructures. Managing a single network is also less expensive. Traditionally, if a business has a separate voice and data network, it has one group of people managing the voice network and another group managing the data network. With a converged network, you have one group managing both the voice and data networks.

New Options

Converged networks give you options that had not existed previously. You can now tie voice and video communications directly into an employee's personal computer system, as shown in Figure 1-8.

Figure 1-8   Advanced Voice and Video Communications

There is no need for an expensive handset phone or videoconferencing equipment. You can accomplish the same function using special software integrated with a personal computer. Softphones, such as the Cisco Unified Personal Communicator for PC or Mac, offer a lot of flexibility for businesses. The person in the top left of Figure 1-8 is using a softphone on the computer. When software is used in place of a physical phone, a business can quickly convert to converged networks because there is no capital expense in purchasing IP phones and the switches needed to power the phones. With the addition of inexpensive webcams, videoconferencing can be added to a softphone. These are just a few examples provided by a broader communications solution portfolio that redefine business processes today.

Separate Voice, Video, and Data Networks

The new options for software and hardware for the purpose of integrating voice, video, and data, force the issue of redesigning existing networks to support these devices. It is no longer feasible to separate out the voice, video, and data networks.

As you see in Figure 1-9, a legacy voice network contains isolated phone lines running to a PBX switch to allow phone connectivity to the Public Switched Telephone Network (PSTN). When a new phone is added, a new line has to be run back to the PBX. The PBX switch is typically located in a Telco wiring closet, separate from the data and video wiring closets. The wiring closets are usually separated because different support personnel require access to each system. However, using a properly designed hierarchical network and implementing QoS policies that prioritize the audio data, voice data can be converged onto an existing data network with little to no impact on audio quality.

Figure 1-9   Voice Network

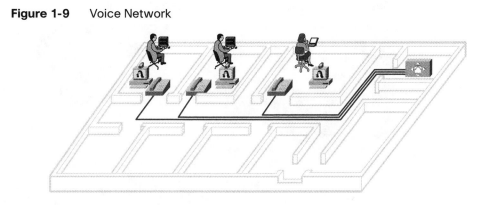

In Figure 1-10, videoconferencing equipment is wired separately from the voice and data networks. Videoconferencing data can consume significant bandwidth on a network. As a result, video networks were maintained separately to allow the videoconferencing equipment to operate at full speed without competing for bandwidth with voice and data streams. Using a properly designed hierarchical network and implementing QoS policies that prioritize the video data, video can be converged onto an existing data network with little to no impact on video quality.

Figure 1-10   Video Network

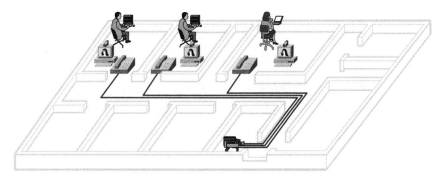

The data network, shown in Figure 1-11, interconnects the workstations and servers on a network to facilitate resource sharing. Data networks can consume significant data bandwidth, which is why voice, video, and data networks were kept separated for such a long time. Now that properly designed hierarchical networks can accommodate the bandwidth requirements of voice, video, and data communications at the same time, it makes sense to converge them all onto a single hierarchical network.

Figure 1-11   Data Network

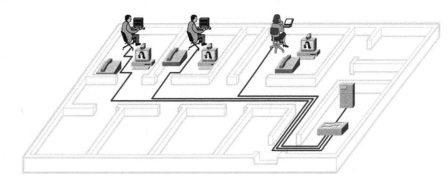

Matching Switches to Specific LAN Functions

To select the appropriate switch for a one of the hierarchical network layers, you need to
have specifications that detail the target traffic flows, user community, data stores, and data
servers. We continue our discussion of switched LAN design with an analysis of topology
diagrams, switch features, classification of switches, Power over Ethernet, Layer 3 functionality, and Cisco switch platforms appropriate for small- and medium-sized businesses.

Considerations for Hierarchical Network Switches

Companies need a network that can meet evolving requirements. A business may start with
a few PCs interconnected so that they can share data. As the business adds more employees,
devices such as PCs, printers, and servers are added to the network. Accompanying the new
devices is an increase in network traffic. Some companies are replacing their existing telephone systems with converged VoIP phone systems, which adds additional traffic.

When selecting switch hardware, determine which switches are needed in the core, distribution, and access layers to accommodate the bandwidth requirements of your network. Your
plan should take into account future bandwidth requirements. Purchase the appropriate
Cisco switch hardware to accommodate both current needs as well as future needs. To help
you more accurately choose appropriate switches, perform and record traffic flow analyses
on a regular basis.

Traffic Flow Analysis

Traffic flow analysis is the process of measuring the bandwidth usage on a network and analyzing the data for the purpose of performance tuning, capacity planning, and making hardware improvement decisions. Traffic flow analysis is done using traffic flow analysis software.
Although there is no precise definition of network traffic flow, for the purposes of traffic flow
analysis we can say that network traffic is the amount of data sent through a network for a
given period of time. All network data contributes to the traffic, regardless of its purpose or

source. Analyzing the various traffic sources and their impact on the network allows you to more accurately tune and upgrade the network to achieve the best possible performance.

Traffic flow data can be used to help determine just how long you can continue using existing network hardware before it makes sense to upgrade to accommodate additional bandwidth requirements. When you are making your decisions about which hardware to purchase, you should consider port densities and switch forwarding rates to ensure adequate growth capability. Port density is the number of ports per switch.

You can monitor traffic flow on a network in many ways. You can manually monitor individual switch ports to get the bandwidth utilization over time. When analyzing the traffic flow data, you want to determine future traffic flow requirements based on the capacity at certain times of the day and where most of the data is generated and sent. However, to obtain accurate results, you need to record enough data. Manual recording of traffic data is a tedious process that requires a lot of time and diligence. Fortunately, there are some automated solutions.

Analysis Tools

Many traffic flow analysis tools that automatically record traffic flow data to a database and perform a trend analysis are available. In large networks, software collection solutions are the only effective method for performing traffic flow analysis. Figure 1-12 displays sample output from Solarwinds Orion 8.1 NetFlow Analysis, which monitors traffic flow on a network. Using the included charts, you can identify traffic flow problems visually. This is much easier than having to interpret the numbers in a column of traffic flow data.

Figure 1-12 Traffic Flow Analysis

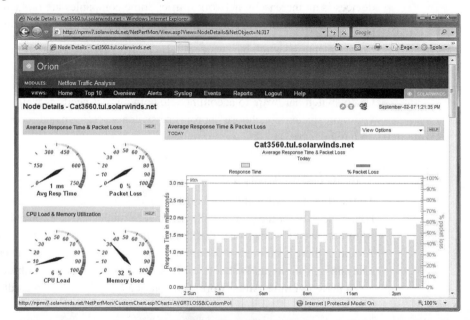

For a list of some commercial traffic flow collection and analysis tools, visit

www.cisco.com/warp/public/732/Tech/nmp/netflow/partners/commercial/index.shtml.

For a list of some freeware traffic flow collection and analysis tools, visit

www.cisco.com/warp/public/732/Tech/nmp/netflow/partners/freeware/index.shtml.

User Community Analysis

User community analysis is the process of identifying various groupings of users and their impact on network performance. The way users are grouped affects issues related to port density and traffic flow, which, in turn, influence the selection of network switches.

In a typical office building, end users are grouped according to their job function because they require similar access to resources and applications. You may find the Human Resource (HR) department located on one floor of an office building, whereas Finance is located on another floor. Each department has a different number of users and application needs and requires access to different data resources available through the network. For example, when selecting switches for the wiring closets of the HR and Finance departments, you would choose a switch that had enough ports to meet the department needs and was powerful enough to accommodate the traffic requirements for all the devices on that floor. Additionally, a good network-design plan factors in the growth of each department to ensure that there are enough open switch ports that can be utilized before the next planned upgrade to the network.

As shown in Figure 1-13, the HR department requires 20 workstations for its 20 users. That translates to 20 switch ports needed to connect the workstations to the network. If you were to select an appropriate access layer switch to accommodate the HR department, you would probably choose a 24-port switch, which has enough ports to accommodate the 20 workstations and the uplinks to the distribution layer switches.

But this plan does not account for future growth. Consider what will happen if the HR department grows by five employees, as shown on the bottom right of Figure 1-13. A solid network plan includes the rate of personnel growth over the past five years to be able to anticipate the future growth. With that in mind, you would want to purchase a switch that can accommodate more than 24 ports, such as stackable or modular switches that can scale.

As well as looking at the number of devices on a given switch in a network, you should investigate the network traffic generated by end-user applications. Some user communities use applications that generate a lot of network traffic, whereas other user communities do not. By measuring the network traffic generated for all applications in use by different user communities, and determining the location of the data source, you can identify the effect of adding more users to that community.

Figure 1-13   HR Department Analysis

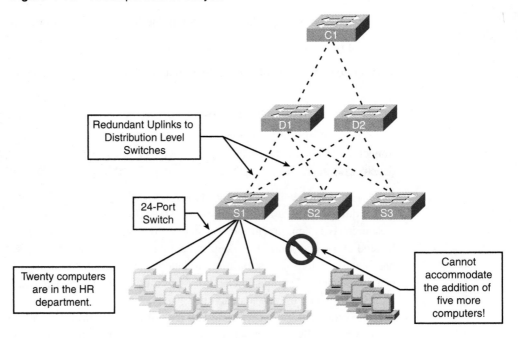

A workgroup-sized user community in a small business is supported by a couple of switches and is typically connected to the same switch as the server. In medium-sized businesses or enterprises, user communities are supported by many switches. The resources that medium-sized business or enterprise user communities need could be located in geographically separate areas. Consequently, the location of the user communities influences where data stores and server farms are located.

If the Finance users are using a network-intensive application that exchanges data with a specific server on the network, as shown in Figure 1-14, it may make sense to locate the Finance user community close to that server. By locating users close to their servers and data stores, you can reduce the network diameter for their communications, thereby reducing the impact of their traffic across the rest of the network. Note that spanning-tree protocol (STP), discussed in Chapter 5, is a determining factor in the displayed network diameters.

One complication of analyzing application usage by user communities is that usage is not always bound by department or physical location. You may have to analyze the impact of the application across many network switches to determine its overall impact.

Figure 1-14   Finance Department Analysis

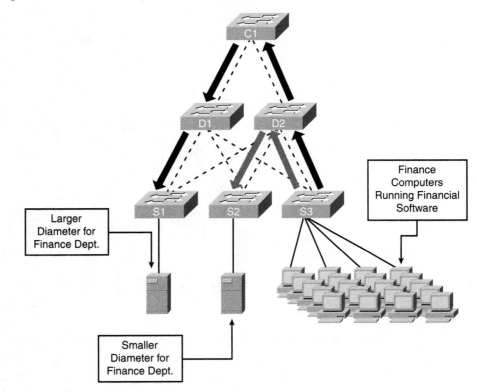

Data Stores and Data Servers Analysis

When analyzing traffic on a network, consider where the data stores and servers are located so that you can determine the impact of traffic on the network. Data stores can be servers, storage area networks (SANs), network-attached storage (NAS), tape backup units, or any other device or component where large quantities of data are stored.

When considering the traffic for data stores and servers, consider both client/server traffic and server/server traffic.

As you can see in Figure 1-15, client/server traffic is the traffic generated when a client device accesses data from data stores or servers. Client/server traffic typically traverses multiple switches to reach its destination. Bandwidth aggregation and switch forwarding rates are important factors to consider when attempting to eliminate bottlenecks for this type of traffic.

Figure 1-15   Client/Server Communication

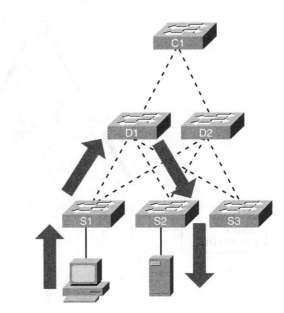

Server/server traffic, shown in Figure 1-16, is the traffic generated between data storage devices on the network. Some server applications generate very high volumes of traffic between data stores and other servers. To optimize server/server traffic, servers needing frequent access to certain resources should be located in close proximity to each other so that the traffic they generate does not affect the performance of the rest of the network. Servers and data stores are typically located in data centers within a business. A data center is a secured area of the building where servers, data stores, and other network equipment are located. A device can be physically located in the data center but represented in quite a different location in the logical topology. Traffic across data center switches is typically very high because of the server/server and client/server traffic that traverses the switches. As a result, switches selected for data centers should be higher-performing switches than the switches you would find in the wiring closets at the access layer.

By examining the data paths for various applications used by different user communities, you can identify potential bottlenecks where performance of the application can be affected by inadequate bandwidth. To improve the performance, you could aggregate links to accommodate the bandwidth, or replace the slower switches with faster switches capable of handling the traffic load.

Topology Diagrams

A topology diagram is a graphical representation of a network infrastructure. A topology diagram shows how all switches are interconnected, detailed down to which switch port interconnects the devices. A topology diagram graphically displays any redundant paths or aggregated ports between switches that provide for resiliency and performance. It shows where and how many switches are in use on your network, and identifies their configuration. Topology diagrams can also contain information about device densities and user communities. Having a topology diagram allows you to visually identify potential bottlenecks in network traffic so that you can focus your traffic analysis data collection on areas where improvements can have the most impact on performance.

Figure 1-16   Server/Server Communication

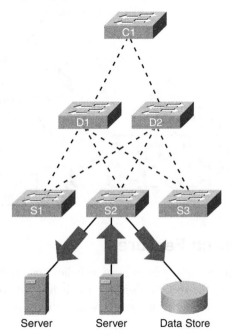

A network topology can be very difficult to piece together after the fact if you were not part of the design process. Network cables in the wiring closets disappear into the floors and ceilings, making it difficult to trace their destinations. And because devices are spread throughout the building, it is difficult to know how all the pieces are connected together. Constructing a topology diagram from the physical layout of the network becomes a tedious and time-consuming exercise; however, this is an important piece of network documentation that significantly enhances the maintenance and troubleshooting of the network and should be done regardless of the current health of the network.

Figure 1-17 displays a simple network topology diagram. Notice how many switches are present in the network, as well as how each switch is interconnected. The topology diagram identifies each switch port used for interswitch communications and redundant paths between access layer switches and distribution layer switches. The topology diagram also displays where different user communities are located on the network and the location of the servers and data stores.

Figure 1-17   Topology Diagrams

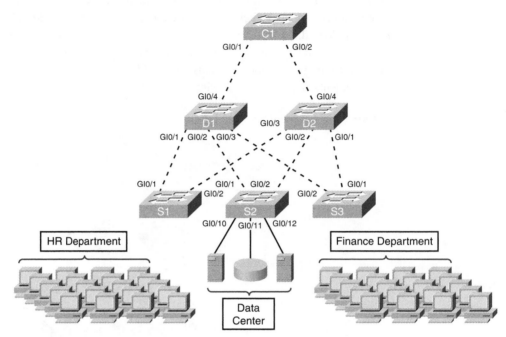

Switch Features

What are the key features of switches that are used in hierarchical networks? When you look up the specifications for a switch, what do all the acronyms and word phrases mean? What does "PoE" mean and what is "forwarding rate"? In this section, you will learn about these features.

Switch Form Factors

When you are selecting a switch, you need to decide between fixed configuration or modular configuration, and stackable or nonstackable. Another consideration is the thickness of the switch expressed in number of rack units. For example, the fixed configuration switches shown in Figure 1-18 are all 1 rack unit (1U). The physical size of the switches can be an important consideration when selecting switches to be deployed. Networking equipment in a hierarchical design is placed into central locations, such as the wiring closets; oftentimes, the space in these areas is limited, and switch form factors (physical configuration) becomes a significant issue.

Fixed Configuration Switches

Fixed configuration switches are just as you might expect, fixed in their configuration. What that means is that you cannot add features or options to the switch beyond those that originally came with the switch. The particular model you purchase determines the features and options available. For example, if you purchase a 24-port gigabit fixed switch, you cannot add additional ports when you need them. Typically, different configuration choices vary in how many and what types of ports are included.

Figure 1-18   Switch Form Factors

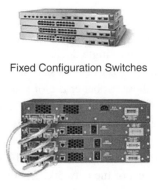

Fixed Configuration Switches

Modular Configuration Switches

Stackable Configuration Switches

Modular Switches

Modular switches offer more flexibility in their configuration. Modular switches come with different sized chassis that allow for the installation of different numbers of modular line cards. The line cards contain the ports. The line card fits into the switch chassis like expansion cards fit into a PC. The larger the chassis, the more modules it can support. As you can see in Figure 1-18, you can choose from many chassis sizes. If you bought a modular switch with a 24-port line card, you could easily add an additional 24-port line card to bring the total number of ports up to 48.

Stackable Switches

Stackable switches can be interconnected using a special backplane cable that provides high-bandwidth throughput between the switches. Cisco introduced StackWise technology in one of its switch product lines. StackWise allows you to interconnect up to nine switches using fully redundant backplane connections. As you can see in Figure 1-18, switches are stacked one atop of the other, and cables connect the switches in daisy-chain fashion. The stacked switches effectively operate as a single larger switch. Stackable switches are desirable where fault tolerance and bandwidth availability are critical and a modular switch is too costly to implement. Using cross-connected connections, the network can recover quickly if a single switch fails. Stackable switches use a special port for interconnections and do not use line ports for interswitch connections. The speeds are also typically faster than using line ports for connection switches.

Switch Performance

When selecting a switch for the access, distribution, or core layers, consider the capability of the switch to support the port density, forwarding rates, and bandwidth aggregation requirements of your network.

Port Density

Port density is the number of ports available on a single switch. Fixed configuration switches typically support up to 48 ports on a single device, with options for up to four additional ports for small form-factor pluggable (SFP) devices, as shown in the 48-port switch in Figure 1-19. High port densities allow for better use of space and power when both are in limited supply. If you have two switches that each contain 24 ports, you would be able to support up to 46 devices because you lose at least one port per switch to connect each switch to the rest of the network. In addition, two power outlets are required. On the other hand, if you have a single 48-port switch, 47 devices can be supported, with only one port used to connect the switch to the rest of the network, and only one power outlet needed to accommodate the single switch.

Figure 1-19   Port Density

24-Port Switch

48-Port Switch

Modular Switch with up to 1000+ Ports

Modular switches can support very high port densities through the addition of multiple switch port line cards, as shown in Figure 1-19. For example, the Catalyst 6500 switch can support in excess of 1000 switch ports on a single device.

Large *enterprise networks* that support many thousands of network devices require high density, modular switches to make the best use of space and power. Without using a high-density modular switch, the network would need many fixed configuration switches to accommodate the number of devices that need network access. This approach can consume many power outlets and a lot of closet space.

You must also address the issue of uplink bottlenecks. A series of fixed configuration switches may consume many additional ports for bandwidth aggregation between switches for the purpose of achieving target performance. With a single modular switch, bandwidth aggregation is less of an issue because the backplane of the chassis can provide the necessary bandwidth to accommodate the devices connected to the switch port line cards.

Forwarding Rates

As illustrated in Figure 1-20, forwarding rates define the processing capabilities of a switch by rating how much data the switch can process per second. Switch product lines are classified by forwarding rates. Entry-layer switches have lower forwarding rates than enterprise-layer switches. Forwarding rates are important to consider when selecting a switch. If the switch forwarding rate is too low, it cannot accommodate full wire-speed communication across all its switch ports. Wire speed is the data rate that each port on the switch is capable of attaining—either 100 Mbps Fast Ethernet or 1000 Mbps Gigabit Ethernet. For example, a 48-port gigabit switch operating at full wire speed generates 48 Gbps of traffic. If the switch supports a forwarding rate of only 32 Gbps, it cannot run at full wire speed across all ports simultaneously. Fortunately, access layer switches typically do not need to operate at full wire speed because they are physically limited by their uplinks to the distribution layer. This allows you to use less expensive, lower-performing switches at the access layer, and use the more expensive, higher-performing switches at the distribution and core layers, where the forwarding rate makes a bigger difference.

Figure 1-20   Forwarding Rates

24-Port Gigabit Ethernet Switch

48-Port Gigabit Ethernet Switch

Capable of Generating 24 Gbps of Traffic

Capable of Generating 48 Gbps of Traffic

Link Aggregation

As part of bandwidth aggregation, you should determine if there are enough ports on a switch to aggregate to support the required bandwidth. For example, consider a Gigabit Ethernet port, which carries up to 1 Gbps of traffic. If you have a 24-port switch, with all ports capable of running at gigabit speeds, you could generate up to 24 Gbps of network traffic. If the switch is connected to the rest of the network by a single network cable, it can forward only 1 Gbps of the data to the rest of the network. Due to the contention for bandwidth, the data would forward more slowly. That results in 1/24th wire speed available to each of the 24 devices connected to the switch. Wire speed describes the theoretical maximum data transmission rate of a connection.

Link aggregation helps to reduce these bottlenecks of traffic by allowing up to eight switch ports to be bound together for data communications, providing up to 16 Gbps of data throughput when Gigabit Ethernet ports are used. With the addition of multiple 10 Gigabit Ethernet uplinks on some enterprise-layer switches, 160 Gbps throughput rates can be achieved. Cisco uses the term EtherChannel when describing aggregated switch ports. Keep in mind that EtherChannel reduces the number of available ports to connect network devices.

As you can see in Figure 1-21, four separate ports on switches C1 and D1 are used to create a 4-port EtherChannel. EtherChannel technology allows a group of physical Ethernet links to create one logical Ethernet link for the purpose of providing fault tolerance and high-speed links between switches, routers, and servers. In this example, there is four times the throughput when compared to the single port connection between switches C1 and D2.

Figure 1-21 Link Aggregation

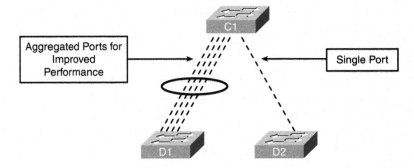

Power over Ethernet and Layer 3 Functionality

Two other characteristics you want to consider when selecting a switch are Power over Ethernet (PoE) and Layer 3 functionality.

Power over Ethernet

Power over Ethernet (PoE) allows the switch to deliver power to a device over the existing Ethernet cabling. As you can see in Figure 1-22, this feature can be used by IP phones and some wireless access points.

PoE ports on a switch, IP phone, access point, and wireless LAN controller look the same as any switch port, as shown in Figure 1-23. Check the model of the networking device to determine whether the port supports PoE.

PoE allows you more flexibility when installing wireless access points and IP phones because you can install them anywhere you can run an Ethernet cable. You do not need to consider how to run ordinary power to the device. You should select a switch that supports PoE only if you are actually going to take advantage of the feature because it adds considerable cost to the switch.

Figure 1-22   Power over Ethernet

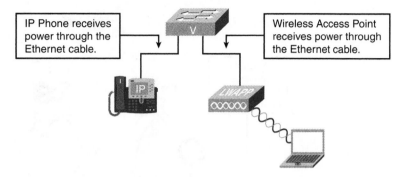

Figure 1-23   Appearance of Power over Ethernet Ports

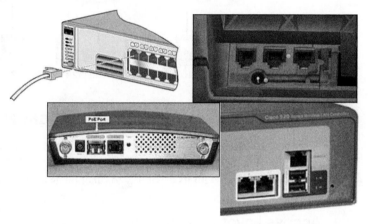

Layer 3 Functionality

Typically, switches operate at Layer 2 of the OSI reference model, where they deal primarily with the MAC addresses of devices connected to switch ports. Layer 3 switches offer advanced functionality that will be discussed in greater detail in the later chapters of this book. Layer 3 switches are also known as *multilayer switches*. Figure 1-24 illustrates some functions of Layer 3 switches.

Figure 1-24   Layer 3 Switch Functionality

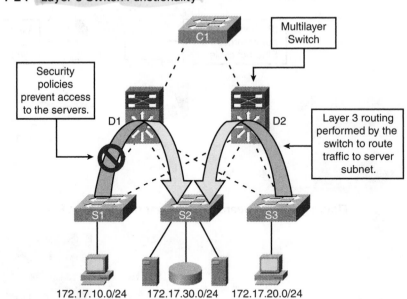

172.17.10.0/24   172.17.30.0/24   172.17.20.0/24

Switch Features in a Hierarchical Network

Now that you know which factors to consider when choosing a switch, let us examine which features are required at each layer in a hierarchical network. You will then be able to match the switch specification with its capability to function as an access, distribution, or core layer switch.

Access Layer Switch Features

Access layer switches facilitate the connection of end node devices to the network. For this reason, they need to support features such as port security, VLANs, Fast Ethernet/Gigabit Ethernet, PoE, and link aggregation, as shown in Figure 1-25.

Port security allows the switch to decide how many or what specific devices are allowed to connect to the switch. All Cisco switches support port layer security. Port security is applied at the access. Consequently, it is an important first line of defense for a network. You will learn about port security in Chapter 2, "Basic Switch Concepts and Configuration."

VLANs are an important component of a converged network. Voice traffic is typically given a separate VLAN. In this way, voice traffic can be supported with more bandwidth, more redundant connections, and improved security. Access layer switches allow you to set the VLANs for the end node devices on your network.

Port speed is also a characteristic you need to consider for your access layer switches. Depending on the performance requirements for your network, you must choose between Fast Ethernet and Gigabit Ethernet switch ports. Fast Ethernet allows up to 100 Mbps of traffic per switch port. Fast Ethernet is adequate for IP telephony and data traffic on most business networks; however, performance is slower than Gigabit Ethernet ports. Gigabit Ethernet allows up to 1000 Mbps of traffic per switch port. Most modern devices, such as workstations, notebooks, and IP phones, support Gigabit Ethernet. This allows for much more efficient data transfers, enabling users to be more productive. Gigabit Ethernet does have a drawback—switches supporting Gigabit Ethernet are more expensive.

Figure 1-25 Access Layer Switch Features

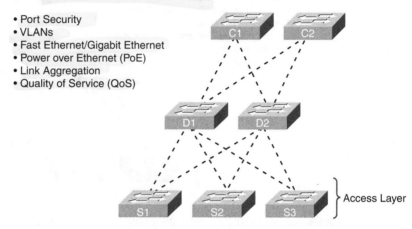

Another feature requirement for some access layer switches is PoE. PoE dramatically increases the overall price of the switch across all Cisco Catalyst switch product lines, so it should be considered only when voice convergence is required or wireless access points are being implemented, and power is difficult or expensive to run to the desired location.

Link aggregation is another feature that is common to most access layer switches. Link aggregation allows the switch to operate multiple links simultaneously as a logically singular high bandwidth link. Access layer switches take advantage of link aggregation when aggregating bandwidth up to distribution layer switches.

Although the uplink connection between the access layer and distribution layer switches can become a bottleneck, it does not present a significant bottleneck to the entire network, because the effect is localized to the devices connected to the switch. The uplink from the distribution layer to the core presents a much more significant bottleneck to the entire network because distribution layer switches collect the traffic of multiple network segments. Bottlenecks present a much more significant quality of service issue for voice and video data than they do for data; this is because voice and video cannot afford gaps and delays in transmissions for obvious reasons. In a converged network supporting voice, video, and data network traffic, access layer switches need to support QoS to maintain the prioritization of traffic. Cisco IP phones are types of equipment that are found at the access layer. When a Cisco IP phone is plugged into an access layer switch port configured to support voice traffic, that switch port tells the IP phone how to send its voice traffic. QoS needs to be enabled on access layer switches so that voice traffic from the IP phone has priority over, for example, data traffic.

Distribution Layer Switch Features

Distribution layer switches have a very important role on the network. Features of distribution layer switches are illustrated in Figure 1-26.

Figure 1-26   Distribution Layer Switch Features

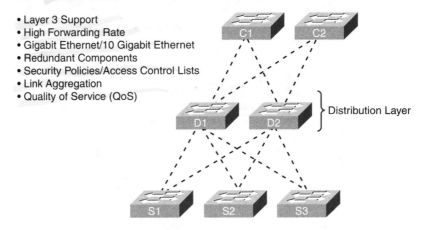

- Layer 3 Support
- High Forwarding Rate
- Gigabit Ethernet/10 Gigabit Ethernet
- Redundant Components
- Security Policies/Access Control Lists
- Link Aggregation
- Quality of Service (QoS)

Distribution layer switches receive the data from all the access layer switches and forward it to the core layer switches. As you will learn later in this book, traffic that is generated at Layer 2 on a switched network needs to be managed, or segmented into VLANs, so it does not needlessly consume bandwidth throughout the network. Distribution layer switches provide the inter-VLAN routing functions so that one VLAN can communicate with another on the network. This routing typically takes place at the distribution layer because distribution layer switches have higher processing capabilities than the access layer switches. Distribution layer switches alleviate the core switches from needing to perform that task, because the core is busy handling the forwarding of very high volumes of traffic. Because inter-VLAN routing is performed at the distribution layer, the switches at this layer need to support Layer 3 functions.

Another reason why Layer 3 functionality is required for distribution layer switches is because of the advanced security policies that can be applied to network traffic. Access lists are used to control how traffic flows through the network. An access control list (ACL) allows the switch to prevent certain types of traffic and permit others. ACLs also allow you to control which network devices can communicate on the network. Using ACLs is processing-intensive because the switch needs to inspect every packet to see if it matches one of the ACL rules defined on the switch. This inspection is performed at the distribution layer because the switches at this layer typically have the processing capability to handle the additional load, and it also simplifies the use of ACLs. Instead of using ACLs for every access layer switch in the network, they are defined on the fewer distribution layer switches, making management of the ACLs much easier.

The distribution layer switches are under high demand on the network because of the functions that they provide. It is important that distribution switches support redundancy for adequate availability. Loss of a distribution layer switch could have a significant impact on the rest of the network because all access layer traffic passes through the distribution layer switches. Distribution layer switches are typically implemented in pairs to ensure availability. It is also recommended that distribution layer switches support multiple, hot-swappable power supplies. Having more than one power supply allows the switch to continue operating even if one of the power supplies failed during operation. Having hot-swappable power supplies allows you to change a failed power supply while the switch is still running. This allows you to repair the failed component without impacting the functionality of the network.

Also, distribution layer switches need to support link aggregation. Typically, access layer switches use multiple links to connect to a distribution layer switch to ensure adequate band-width to accommodate the traffic generated on the access layer and provide fault tolerance in case a link is lost. Because distribution layer switches accept incoming traffic from multiple access layer switches, they need to be able to forward all that traffic as fast as possible to the core layer switches. As a result, distribution layer switches also need high-bandwidth aggregated links back to the core layer switches. Newer distribution layer switches support aggregated 10 Gigabit Ethernet (10GbE) uplinks to the core layer switches.

Finally, distribution layer switches need to support QoS to maintain the prioritization of traffic coming from the access layer switches that have implemented QoS. Priority policies ensure that audio and video communications are guaranteed adequate bandwidth to main-tain an acceptable quality of service. To maintain the priority of the voice data throughout the network, all the switches that forward voice data must support QoS; if not all the net-work devices support QoS, the benefits of QoS will be reduced. This results in poor per-formance and quality for audio and video communications.

Core Layer Switch Features

Core layer switches are responsible for handling the majority of data on a switched LAN. Core layer switch features are illustrated in Figure 1-27.

Figure 1-27   Core Layer Switch Features

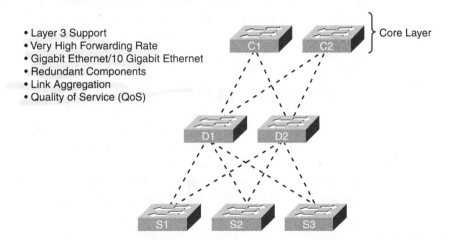

The core layer of a hierarchical topology is the high-speed backbone of the network and requires switches that can handle very high forwarding rates. The required forwarding rate is largely dependent on the number of devices participating in the network. You determine the necessary forwarding rate by conducting and examining various traffic flow reports and user community analyses. Based on your results, you can identify an appropriate switch to support the network. Take care to evaluate your needs for the present and near future. If you choose an inadequate switch to run in the core of the network, you face potential bottleneck issues in the core, slowing down all communications on the network.

The availability of the core layer is also critical, so you should build in as much redundancy as you can. Layer 3 redundancy typically has faster convergence than Layer 2 redundancy in the event of hardware failure. Convergence in this context refers to the time it takes for the network to adapt to a change, not to be confused with a converged network that supports data, audio, and video communications. With that in mind, you want to ensure that your core layer switches support Layer 3 functions. A complete discussion on the implications of Layer 3 redundancy is beyond the scope of this book. It remains an open question about the need for Layer 2 redundancy in this context. Layer 2 redundancy is examined in Chapter 5 when we discuss the spanning-tree protocol. Also, look for core layer switches that support additional hardware redundancy features, such as redundant power supplies that can be swapped while the switch continues to operate. Because of the high workload carried by core layer switches, they tend to operate hotter than access or distribution layer switches, so they should have more sophisticated cooling options. Many true core-layer-capable switches have the capability to swap cooling fans without having to turn the switch off.

For example, it would be disruptive to shut down a core layer switch to change a power supply or a fan in the middle of the day when the network usage is at its highest. To perform a hardware replacement, you could expect to have at least a 5-minute network outage, and that is if you are very fast at performing the maintenance. In a more realistic situation, the switch could be down for 30 minutes or more, which most likely is not acceptable. With hot-swappable hardware, there is no downtime during switch maintenance.

The core layer also needs to support link aggregation to ensure adequate bandwidth coming into the core from the distribution layer switches. Core layer switches should have support for aggregated 10 Gigabit Ethernet connections, which is currently the fastest available Ethernet connectivity option. This allows corresponding distribution layer switches to deliver traffic as efficiently as possible to the core.

QoS is an important part of the services provided by core layer switches. For example, service providers (who provide IP, data storage, e-mail, and other services) and enterprise wide-area networks (WANs) are adding more voice and video traffic to an already growing amount of data traffic. At the core and network edge, mission-critical and time-sensitive traffic such as voice should receive higher QoS guarantees than less time-sensitive traffic such as file transfers or e-mail. Because high-speed WAN access is often prohibitively expensive, adding bandwidth at the core layer is not an option. Because QoS provides a software-based solution to prioritize traffic, core layer switches can provide a cost-effective way of supporting optimal and differentiated use of existing bandwidth.

Switches for Small and Medium Sized Business (SMB)

Now that you know which switch features are used at which layer in a hierarchical network, you will learn about the Cisco switches that are applicable for each layer in the hierarchical network model. Today, you cannot simply select a Cisco switch by considering the size of a business. A small business with 12 employees might be integrated into the network of a large multinational enterprise and require all the advanced LAN services available at the corporate head office. The following classification of Cisco switches within the hierarchical network model represents a starting point for your deliberations on which switch is best for a given application. The classification presented reflects how you might see the range of Cisco switches if you were a multinational enterprise. For example, the port densities of the Cisco 6500 switch make sense as an access layer switch only where there are many hundreds of users in one area, such as the floor of a stock exchange. If you think of the needs of a medium-sized business, a switch that is typically known as an access layer switch, such as the Cisco 3560 switch, could be used as a distribution layer switch if it met the criteria determined by the network designer for that application.

Cisco currently has seven switch product lines. Each product line offers different characteristics and features, allowing you to find the right switch to meet the functional requirements of your network. The Cisco switch product lines are as follows:

- Catalyst Express 500

- Catalyst 2960

- Catalyst 3560

- Catalyst 3750

- Catalyst 4500

- Catalyst 4900

- Catalyst 6500

Catalyst Express 500

The Catalyst Express 500, shown in Figure 1-28, is the Cisco entry-layer switch.

The Catalyst Express 500 offers the following:

- Forwarding rates from 8.8 Gbps to 24 Gbps

- Layer 2 port security

- Web-based management

- Converged data/IP communications support

Figure 1-28   Catalyst Express 500

This switch series is appropriate for access layer implementations where high port density is not required. The Cisco Catalyst Express 500 series switches are scaled for small business environments ranging from 20 to 250 employees. The Catalyst Express 500 series switches are available in different fixed configurations:

- Fast Ethernet and Gigabit Ethernet connectivity

- Up to 24 10/100 ports with optional PoE or 12 10/100/1000 ports

Catalyst Express 500 series switches do not allow management through the Cisco IOS CLI. They are managed using a built-in web management interface, the Cisco Network Assistant or the new Cisco Configuration Manager developed specifically for the Catalyst Express 500 series switches. The Catalyst Express does not support console access.

To learn more about the Cisco Express 500 series of switches, go to www.cisco.com/en/US/products/ps6545/index.html.

Catalyst 2960

The Catalyst 2960 series switches enable entry-layer enterprise, medium-sized, and branch office networks to provide enhanced LAN services. The Catalyst 2960 series switches, shown in Figure 1-29, are appropriate for access layer implementations where access to power and space is limited. The CCNA Exploration 3 LAN Switching and Wireless labs are based on the features of the Cisco 2960 switch.

Figure 1-29   Catalyst 2960

The Catalyst 2960 series switches offer the following:

- Forwarding rates from 16 Gbps to 32 Gbps

- Multilayered switching

- QoS features to support IP communications

- Access control lists

- Fast Ethernet and Gigabit Ethernet connectivity

- Up to 48 10/100 ports or 10/100/1000 ports with additional dual purpose gigabit uplinks

The Catalyst 2960 series of switches does not support PoE.

The Catalyst 2960 series supports the Cisco IOS CLI, integrated web management interface, and Cisco Network Assistant. This switch series supports console and auxiliary access to the switch.

To learn more about the Catalyst 2960 series of switches, visit www.cisco.com/en/US/products/ps6406/index.html.

Catalyst 3560

The Cisco Catalyst 3560 series is a line of enterprise-class switches that include support for PoE, QoS, and advanced security features such as ACLs. These switches, shown in Figure 1-30, are ideal access layer switches for small enterprise LAN access or branch-office converged network environments.

Figure 1-30   Catalyst 3560

The Cisco Catalyst 3560 series supports forwarding rates of 32 Gbps to 128 Gbps (Catalyst 3560-E switch series).

The Catalyst 3560 series switches are available in different fixed configurations:

- Fast Ethernet and Gigabit Ethernet connectivity

- Up to 48 10/100/1000 ports, plus four small form-factor pluggable ports

- Optional 10 Gigabit Ethernet connectivity in the Catalyst 3560-E models

- Optional integrated PoE (Cisco prestandard and IEEE 802.3af); up to 24 ports with 15.4 watts or 48 ports with 7.3 watts

To learn more about the Catalyst 3560 series of switches, visit www.cisco.com/en/US/products/hw/switches/ps5528/index.html.

Catalyst 3750

The Cisco Catalyst 3750 series of switches, shown in Figure 1-31, is ideal for access layer switches in midsize organizations and enterprise branch offices. This series offers forwarding rates from 32 Gbps to 128 Gbps (Catalyst 3750-E switch series). The Catalyst 3750 series supports Cisco StackWise technology. StackWise technology allows you to interconnect up to nine physical Catalyst 3750 switches into one logical switch using a high-performance (32 Gbps), redundant, backplane connection.

Figure 1-31   Catalyst 3750

The Catalyst 3750 series switches are available in different stackable fixed configurations:

- Fast Ethernet and Gigabit Ethernet connectivity

- Up to 48 10/100/1000 ports, plus four SFP ports

- Optional 10 Gigabit Ethernet connectivity in the Catalyst 3750-E models

- Optional integrated PoE (Cisco prestandard and IEEE 802.3af); up to 24 ports with 15.4 watts or 48 ports with 7.3 watts

To learn more about the Catalyst 3750 series of switches, visit www.cisco.com/en/US/products/hw/switches/ps5023/index.html.

Catalyst 4500

The Catalyst 4500, shown in Figure 1-32, is the first midrange modular switching platform offering multilayer switching for enterprises, small- to medium-sized businesses, and service providers.

Figure 1-32   Catalyst 4500

With forwarding rates up to 136 Gbps, the Catalyst 4500 series is capable of managing traffic at the distribution layer. The modular capability of the Catalyst 4500 series allows for very high port densities through the addition of switch port line cards to its modular chassis. The Catalyst 4500 series offers multilayer QoS and sophisticated routing functions.

The Catalyst 4500 series switches are available in different modular configurations:

- Modular 3, 6, 7, and 10 slot chassis offering different layers of scalability

- High port density: up to 384 Fast Ethernet or Gigabit Ethernet ports available in copper or fiber with 10 Gigabit uplinks

- PoE (Cisco prestandard and IEEE 802.3af)

- Dual, hot-swappable internal AC or DC power supplies

- Advanced hardware-assisted IP routing capabilities

To learn more about the Catalyst 4500 series of switches, visit www.cisco.com/en/US/products/hw/switches/ps4324/index.html.

Catalyst 4900

The Catalyst 4900 series switches, shown in Figure 1-33, are designed and optimized for server switching by allowing very high forwarding rates. The Cisco Catalyst 4900 is not a typical access layer switch. It is a specialty access layer switch designed for data center deployments where many servers may exist in close proximity. This switch series supports dual, redundant power supplies and fans that can be swapped out while the switch is still running. This allows the switches to achieve higher availability, which is critical in data center deployments.

Figure 1-33   Catalyst 4900

The Catalyst 4900 series switches support advanced QoS features, making them ideal candidates for the back-end IP telephony hardware. Catalyst 4900 series switches do not support the StackWise feature of the Catalyst 3750 series, nor do they support PoE.

The Catalyst 4900 series switches are available in different fixed configurations:

- Up to 48 10/100/1000 ports with four SFP ports or 48 10/100/1000 ports with two 10 Gigabit Ethernet ports

- Dual, hot-swappable internal AC or DC power supplies

- Hot-swappable fan trays

To learn more about the Catalyst 4900 series of switches, visit www.cisco.com/en/US/products/ps6021/index.html.

Catalyst 6500

The Catalyst 6500 series modular switch, shown in Figure 1-34, is optimized for secure, converged voice, video, and data networks. The Catalyst 6500 is capable of managing traffic at the distribution and core layers. The Catalyst 6500 series is the highest-performing Cisco switch, supporting forwarding rates up to 720 Gbps. The Catalyst 6500 is ideal for very large network environments found in enterprises, medium-sized businesses, and service providers.

Figure 1-34   Catalyst 6500

The Catalyst 6500 series switches are available in different modular configurations:

- Modular 3, 4, 6, 9, and 13 slot chassis

- LAN/WAN service modules

- PoE up to 420 IEEE 802.3af Class 3 (15.4W) PoE devices

- Up to 1152 10/100 ports, 577 10/100/1000 ports, 410 SFP Gigabit Ethernet ports, or 64 10 Gigabit Ethernet ports

- Dual, hot-swappable internal AC or DC power supplies

- Advanced hardware-assisted IP routing capabilities

To learn more about the Catalyst 6500 series of switches, visit
www.cisco.com/en/US/products/hw/switches/ps708/index.html.

Comparing Switches

The following tool can help identify the correct switch for an implementation:

www.cisco.com/en/US/products/hw/switches/products_promotion0900aecd8050364f.html.

Last, the following guide provides a detailed comparison of current switch offerings from
Cisco:

www.cisco.com/application/pdf/en/us/guest/products/ps708/c2072/cdccont_0900aecd805f09
55.pdf.

Build a Hierarchical Topology (1.2.4)

Use the Packet Tracer Activity to build a topology representative of the switched LANs discussed in the book. You will add all the necessary devices and connect them with the correct cabling. Use file e3-1243.pka on the CD-ROM that accompanies this book to perform
this activity using Packet Tracer.

Summary

In this chapter, we discussed the hierarchical design model. Implementing this model improves the performance, scalability, availability, manageability, and maintainability of the network. Hierarchical network topologies facilitate network convergence by enhancing the performance necessary for voice and video data to be combined onto the existing data network.

The traffic flow, user community, data store and data server locations, and topology diagram analysis are used to help identify network bottlenecks. The bottlenecks can then be addressed to improve the performance of the network and accurately determine appropriate hardware requirements to satisfy the desired performance of the network.

We surveyed the different switch features, such as form factor, performance, PoE, and Layer 3 support, and how they relate to the different layers of the hierarchical network design. An array of Cisco Catalyst switch product lines are available to support any application or business size.

Labs

The labs available in the companion *LAN Switching and Wireless, CCNA Exploration Labs and Study Guide* (ISBN 1-58713-202-8) provide hands-on practice with the following topics introduced in this chapter:

Lab 1-1: Review of Concepts from Exploration 1 (1.3.1)

In this lab, you will design and configure a small routed network and verify connectivity across multiple network devices. This requires creating and assigning two subnetwork blocks, connecting hosts and network devices, and configuring host computers and one Cisco router for basic network connectivity. You will use common commands to test and document the network.

Lab 1-2: Review of Concepts from Exploration 1—Challenge (1.3.2)

In this lab, you will repeat the procedures in Lab 1.3.1 without the guidance provided therein. You are given only the set of objectives to complete.

Lab 1-3: Troubleshooting a Small Network (1.3.3)

In this lab, you are given a completed configuration for a small routed network. The configuration contains design and configuration errors that conflict with stated requirements and prevent end-to-end communication. You examine the given design and identify and correct any design errors. You then cable the network, configure the hosts, and load configurations onto the router. Finally, you wil troubleshoot the connectivity problems to determine where the errors are occurring and correct them using the appropriate commands. When all errors have been corrected, each host should be able to communicate with all other configured network elements and with the other host.

Many of the hands-on labs include Packet Tracer Companion Activities, where you can use Packet Tracer to complete a simulation of the lab. Look for this icon in *LAN Switching and Wireless, CCNA Exploration Labs and Study Guide* (ISBN 1-58713-202-8) for hands-on labs that have a Packet Tracer Companion.

Check Your Understanding

Complete all the review questions listed here to test your understanding of the topics and concepts in this chapter. Answers are listed in the appendix, "Check Your Understanding and Challenge Questions Answer Key."

1. Which three options correctly associate a layer of the hierarchical design model with its function? (Choose three.)

   A. Core—interface for end devices

   B. Distribution—traffic control and security policies

   C. Access—interface for end devices

   D. Distribution—high-speed backbone

   E. Core—high-speed backbone

   F. Access—implementation of security policies

2. With respect to network design, what is convergence?

   A. Implementation of standard equipment sets for LAN design

   B. Implementation of a core-distribution-access design model for all sites in an enterprise

   C. A point in the network where all traffic "converges" before transmission to the destination, normally the core switch

   D. Combining conventional data with voice and video on a common network

3. Which three options are potential benefits of a converged network? (Choose three.)

   A. Simplified data network configuration

   B. Combines voice and data network staffs

   C. Combines voice, video, and applications in one computer

   D. Simpler maintenance than hierarchical networks

   E. Simplified network changes

   F. Lower quality of service configuration requirements

4. Which four options describe data store and data server analysis actions? (Choose four.)

   A. Workstation ports required for a department

   B. Amount of server-to-server traffic

   C. Intensity of use of a department application server

   D. Amount of traffic for a SAN

   E. Anticipated department port growth

   F. Data backed up to tape

   G. Network attached storage

5. What factor may complicate user community analysis?

   A. Application changes may radically affect predicted data growth.

   B. Server-to-server traffic may skew user port usage data.

   C. Application usage is not always bound by department or physical location.

   D. Different organization applications may share data stores.

6. Which two of the following pairings are accurate? (Choose two.)

   A. Port density—capability to use multiple switch ports concurrently for higher throughput data communication

   B. Forwarding rates—processing capabilities of a switch by quantifying performance of the switch by how much data it can process per second

   C. Link aggregation—number of ports available on a single switch

   D. Wire speed—data rate that each port on the switch is capable of attaining

7. What would be the port capacity of a single port on a 48-port Gigabit Ethernet switch?

   A. 48 Gbps

   B. 10 Mbps

   C. 1000 Mbps

   D. 100 Mbps

8. A switch that uses MAC addresses to forward frames operates at which layer of the OSI model?

   A. Layer 1

   B. Layer 2

   C. Layer 3

   D. Layer 4

9. What is a feature offered by all stackable switches?

   A. Predetermined number of ports

   B. Fully redundant backplane

   C. Support for Gigabit connectivity

   D. Low bandwidth for interswitch communications

   E. PoE capability

10. What function is performed by a Cisco Catalyst access layer switch?

    A. Inter-VLAN support

    B. Routing

    C. Providing PoE

    D. Link aggregation

11. Which three features are associated with the core layer of the hierarchical design model? (Choose three.)

    A. Port security

    B. Layer 3 support

    C. Redundant components

    D. VLANs

    E. 10 Gigabit Ethernet

    F. PoE

12. Which two characteristics describe the core layer of the hierarchical network model? (Choose two.)

    A. Redundant paths

    B. High-level policy enforcement

    C. PoE

    D. Controls access of end devices to network

    E. Rapid forwarding of traffic

Challenge Questions and Activities

These questions require a deeper application of the concepts covered in this chapter. You can find the answers in the appendix, "Check Your Understanding and Challenge Questions Answer Key."

1. List and describe the three layers of the hierarchical network model.

2. Match the terms with the correct descriptions.

__Fixed Configuration Switch

__Forwarding Rate

__Quality of Service

__Power over Ethernet

__Modular Switch

__Link Aggregation

__Port Density

__Stackable Switch

__Redundancy

A. Ratio of number of ports to number of switches.

B. Ratio of quantity of data to time.

C. Capable of interconnection via a special backplane cable.

D. Ports cannot be added to the device.

E. Binding together of distinct links for enhanced throughput.

F. Allows for the installation of line cards or modules.

G. Capability of a device to power another device using Ethernet.

H. Capability to recover connectivity after a network failure.

I. Prioritization of network traffic.

Packet Tracer
☐ Challenge

Look for this icon in *LAN Switching and Wireless, CCNA Exploration Labs and Study Guide* (ISBN 1-58713-202-8) for instructions on how to perform the Packet Tracer Skills Integration Challenge for this chapter.

CHAPTER 2

Basic Switch Concepts and Configuration

Objectives

Upon completion of this chapter, you will be able to answer the following questions:

- What are the principal Ethernet operations pertinent to a 100/1000/10000 Mbps LAN in the IEEE 802.3 standard?

- What are the functions that enable a switch to forward Ethernet frames in a LAN?

- How do you configure a switch for operation in a network designed to support voice, video, and data communication?

- How do you configure basic security on a switch that operates within a network designed to support voice, video, and data communication?

Key Terms

This chapter uses the following key terms. You can find the definitions in the Glossary.

In this chapter, you build upon the skills learned in *CCNA Exploration 4.0: Network Fundamentals*, reviewing and reinforcing these skills. You also learn about some key malicious threats to switches and learn to enable a switch with a secure initial configuration.

Introduction to Ethernet/802.3 LANs

In this section, you learn about key components of the Ethernet standard that play a significant role in the design and implementation of switched networks. You explore how Ethernet communications function and how switches play a role in the communication process.

Key Elements of Ethernet/802.3 Networks

Ethernet/802.3 networks rely on carrier sense multiple access/collision detect (CSMA/CD), unicast transmission, broadcast transmission, multicast transmission, duplex settings, switch port settings, and MAC address table management. We next review each of these concepts from *CCNA Exploration 4.0: Networking Fundamentals*.

CSMA/CD

Ethernet signals are transmitted to every host connected to the LAN using a special set of rules to determine which station can access the network. The set of rules that Ethernet uses is based on the IEEE carrier sense multiple access/collision detect (CSMA/CD) technology. Recall that CSMA/CD is used only with half-duplex communication typically found with hubs. Full-duplex ports do not use CSMA/CD.

In the CSMA/CD access method, all network devices that have messages to send must listen before transmitting. If a device detects a signal from another device, it waits for a specified amount of time before attempting to transmit. When there is no traffic detected, a device transmits its message. While this transmission is occurring, the device continues to listen for traffic or collisions on the LAN. After the message is sent, the device returns to its default listening mode.

If the distance between devices is such that the latency of the signals of one device means that signals are not detected by a second device, the second device may also start to transmit. The media now has two devices transmitting signals at the same time. The messages propagate across the media until they encounter each other. At that point, the signals mix and the messages are destroyed, a collision. Although the messages are corrupted, the jumble of remaining signals continues to propagate across the media.

When a device is in listening mode, it can detect when a collision occurs on the shared media because all devices can detect an increase in the amplitude of the signal above the normal level. When a collision occurs, the other devices in listening mode, as well as all the transmitting devices, detect the increase in the signal amplitude. Every device that is transmitting continues to transmit to ensure that all devices on the network detect the collision.

content addressable Memory (CAM)

When a collision is detected, the transmitting devices send out a jamming signal. The jamming signal notifies the other devices of a collision so that they invoke a backoff algorithm. This backoff algorithm causes all devices to stop transmitting for a random amount of time, which allows the collision signals to subside.

After the delay has expired on a device, the device goes back into the "listening before transmit" mode. A random backoff period ensures that the devices that were involved in the collision do not try to send traffic again at the same time, which would cause the whole process to repeat. However, during the backoff period, a third device may transmit before either of the two involved in the collision have a chance to retransmit.

Ethernet Communications

Reference Figure 2-1 for the Ethernet communications discussion that follows. Communications in a switched LAN occur in three ways: unicast, broadcast, and multicast.

Figure 2-1   Ethernet Communications

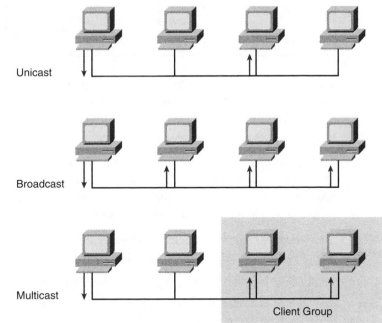

With unicast communication, a frame is sent from one host and addressed to one specific destination. In unicast transmission, there is just one sender and one receiver. Unicast transmission is the predominant form of transmission on LANs and within the Internet. Examples of unicast transmissions include HTTP, SMTP, FTP, and Telnet.

With broadcast communication, a frame is sent from one address to all other addresses. In this case, there is just one sender, but the information is sent to all connected receivers. Broadcast transmission is essential when sending the same message to all devices on the LAN. An example of a broadcast transmission is the address resolution query that the address resolution protocol (ARP) sends to all computers on a LAN.

With multicast communication, a frame is sent to a specific group of devices or clients. Multicast transmission clients must be members of a logical multicast group to receive the information. An example of multicast transmission is the video and voice transmissions associated with a network-based, collaborative business meeting.

To briefly review the Ethernet frame structure, recall that the Ethernet frame adds headers and trailers around the Layer 3 PDU to encapsulate the message being sent. Both the Ethernet header and trailer have several sections (or fields) of information that are used by the Ethernet protocol. Figure 2-2 shows the structure of the current Ethernet frame standard, the revised IEEE 802.3 (Ethernet).

Figure 2-2   Ethernet Frame

IEEE 802.3						
7	1	6	6	2	46 to 1500	4
Preamble	Start of Frame Delimiter	Destination Address	Source Address	Length/ Type	802.2 Header and Data	Frame Check Sequence

The Preamble (7 bytes) and Start Frame Delimiter (SFD) (1 byte) fields are used for synchronization between the sending and receiving devices. These first 8 bytes of the frame are used to get the attention of the receiving nodes. Essentially, the first few bytes tell the receivers to get ready to receive a new frame.

The Destination MAC Address field (6 bytes) is the identifier for the intended recipient. This address is used by Layer 2 to assist a device in determining whether a frame is addressed to it. The address in the frame is compared to the MAC address in the device. If there is a match, the device accepts the frame.

The Source MAC Address field (6 bytes) identifies the frame's originating NIC or interface. Switches use this address to add to their lookup tables.

The Length/Type field (2 bytes) defines the exact length of the frame's data field. This field is used later as part of the Frame Check Sequence (FCS) to ensure that the message was received properly. Only a frame length or a frame type can be entered here. If the purpose of the field is to designate a type, the Type field describes which protocol is implemented. When a node receives a frame and the Length/Type field designates a type, the node determines which higher layer protocol is present. If the two-octet value is equal to or greater than 0x0600 hexadecimal or 1536 decimal, the contents of the Data Field are decoded according to the protocol indicated; if the two-byte value is less than 0x0600, the value represents the length of the data in the frame.

The Data and Pad fields (46 to 1500 bytes) contain the encapsulated data from a higher layer, which is a generic Layer 3 PDU, or more commonly, an IPv4 packet. All frames must be at least 64 bytes long (minimum length aides the detection of collisions). If a small packet is encapsulated, the Pad field is used to increase the size of the frame to the minimum size.

The FCS field (4 bytes) detects errors in a frame. It uses a cyclic redundancy check (CRC). The sending device includes the results of a CRC in the FCS field of the frame. The receiving device receives the frame and generates a CRC to look for errors. If the calculations match, no error has occurred. If the calculations do not match, the frame is dropped.

An Ethernet MAC address is a two-part 48-bit binary value expressed as 12 hexadecimal digits. The address formats might be similar to 00-05-9A-3C-78-00, 00:05:9A:3C:78:00, or 0005.9A3C.7800. All devices connected to an Ethernet LAN have MAC-addressed interfaces. The NIC uses the MAC address to determine whether a message should be passed to the upper layers for processing. The MAC address is permanently encoded into a *read-only memory (ROM)* chip on a NIC. This type of MAC address is referred to as a burned-in address (BIA). Some vendors allow local modification of the MAC address. The MAC address is made up of the *organizational unique identifier (OUI)* and the vendor assignment number. The OUI is the first part of a MAC address. It is 24 bits long and identifies the manufacturer of the NIC card. The IEEE regulates the assignment of OUI numbers. Within the OUI are 2 bits that have meaning only when used in the destination address, the broadcast or multicast bit and the locally administered address bit, shown in Figure 2-3.

Figure 2-3   OUI Composition

The broadcast or multicast bit in a MAC address indicates to the receiving interface that the frame is destined for all or a group of end stations on the LAN segment.

The locally administered address bit indicates whether the vendor-assigned MAC address can be modified locally.

The vendor-assigned part of the MAC address is 24 bits long and uniquely identifies the Ethernet hardware. It can be a BIA or it can be modified by software indicated by the local bit.

Duplex Settings

There are two types of duplex settings used for communications on an Ethernet network: *half duplex* and *full duplex.*

Half-duplex communication relies on unidirectional data flow where sending and receiving data are not performed at the same time. This is similar to how walkie-talkies or two-way radios function in that only one person can talk at any one time. If someone talks while someone else is already speaking, a collision occurs. As a result, half-duplex communication implements CSMA/CD to help reduce the potential for collisions and detect them when they do happen. Half-duplex communications have performance issues due to the constant waiting, because data can flow in only one direction at a time. Half-duplex connections are typically found in older hardware, such as hubs. Nodes that are attached to hubs that share their connection to a switch port must operate in half-duplex mode because the end computers must be able to detect collisions. Nodes can operate in a half-duplex mode if the NIC card cannot be configured for full-duplex operations. In this case, the port on the switch defaults to a half-duplex mode as well. Because of these limitations, full-duplex communication has replaced half-duplex in more current hardware.

In full-duplex communication, data flow is bidirectional, so data can be sent and received at the same time. The bidirectional support enhances performance by reducing the wait time between transmissions. Most Ethernet, Fast Ethernet, and Gigabit Ethernet NICs sold today offer full-duplex capability. In full-duplex mode, the collision-detect circuit is disabled. Frames sent by the two connected end nodes cannot collide because the end nodes use two separate circuits in the network cable. Each full-duplex connection uses only one port. Full-duplex connections require a switch that supports full duplex or a direct connection between two nodes that each support full duplex. Nodes that are directly attached to a dedicated switch port with NICs that support full duplex should be connected to switch ports that are configured to operate in full-duplex mode.

Standard, shared hub-based Ethernet configuration efficiency is typically rated at 50 to 60 percent of the 10 Mbps bandwidth. Full-duplex Fast Ethernet, compared to 10 Mbps bandwidth, offers 100 percent efficiency in both directions (100 Mbps transmit and 100 Mbps receive).

Switch Port Settings

A port on a switch needs to be configured with duplex settings that match the media type. Later in this chapter, you will configure duplex settings. The Cisco Catalyst switches have three settings:

- The **auto** option sets autonegotiation of duplex mode. With autonegotiation enabled, the two ports communicate to decide the best mode of operation.

- The **full** option sets full-duplex mode.

- The **half** option sets half-duplex mode.

For Fast Ethernet and 10/100/1000 ports, the default is auto. For 100BASE-FX ports, the default is full. The 10/100/1000 ports operate in either half- or full-duplex mode when they are set to 10 or 100 Mbps, but when set to 1,000 Mbps, they operate only in full-duplex mode.

Note

Autonegotiation can produce unpredictable results. By default, when autonegotiation fails, the Catalyst switch sets the corresponding switch port to half-duplex mode. This type of failure happens when an attached device does not support autonegotiation. If the device is manually configured to operate in half-duplex mode, it matches the default mode of the switch. However, autonegotiation errors can happen if the device is manually configured to operate in full-duplex mode. Having half-duplex on one end and full-duplex on the other causes late collision errors at the half-duplex end. To avoid this situation, manually set the duplex parameters of the switch to match the attached device. If the switch port is in full-duplex mode and the attached device is in half-duplex mode, check for FCS errors on the switch full-duplex port.

Additionally, you used to be required to use certain cable types (crossover, straight-through) when connecting between specific devices, switch-to-switch or switch-to-router. Instead, you can now use the **mdix auto** interface configuration command in the CLI to enable the automatic medium-dependent interface crossover *auto-MDIX* feature.

When the auto-MDIX feature is enabled, the switch detects the required cable type for copper Ethernet connections and configures the interfaces accordingly. Therefore, you can use either a crossover or a straight-through cable for connections to a copper 10/100/1000 port on the switch, regardless of the type of device on the other end of the connection.

The auto-MDIX feature is enabled by default on switches running Cisco IOS Release 12.2(18)SE or later. For releases between Cisco IOS Release 12.1(14)EA1 and 12.2(18)SE, the auto-MDIX feature is disabled by default. It is enabled by default on Catalyst 2960 and 3560 switches, but is not available as an option on Catalyst 2950 and 3550 switches.

Switch MAC Address Table

Switches use MAC addresses to direct network communications through their switch fabric to the appropriate port toward the destination node. The switch fabric is the integrated circuits and the accompanying machine programming that allows the data paths through the switch to be controlled. For a switch to know which port to use to transmit a unicast frame, it must first learn which nodes exist on each of its ports.

A switch determines how to handle incoming data frames by using its MAC address table. A switch builds its MAC address table by recording the MAC addresses of the nodes connected to each of its ports. After a MAC address for a specific node on a specific port is recorded in the address table, the switch then knows to send traffic destined for that specific node out the port mapped to that node for subsequent transmissions.

When an incoming data frame is received by a switch and the destination MAC address is not in the table, the switch forwards the frame out all ports, except for the port on which it was received. When the destination node responds, the switch records the node's MAC address in the address table from the frame's source address field. In networks with multiple interconnected switches, the MAC address tables record multiple MAC addresses for the ports connecting the switches that reflect the nodes beyond. Typically, switch ports used to interconnect two switches have multiple MAC addresses recorded in the MAC address table.

The following six steps describe the process used to populate the MAC address table on a switch:

1. The switch receives a broadcast frame from PC1 on Port 1, as seen in Figure 2-4.

2. The switch enters the source MAC address and the switch port that received the frame into the address table.

3. Because the destination address is a broadcast, the switch *floods* the frame to all ports, except the port on which it received the frame.

Figure 2-4   MAC Address Table Population

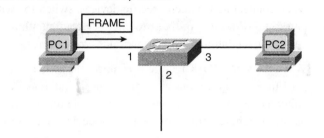

4. The destination device replies to the broadcast with a unicast frame addressed to PC1.

5. The switch enters the source MAC address of PC2 and the port number of the switch port that received the frame into the address table. The destination address of the frame and its associated port are found in the MAC address table.

6. The switch can now forward frames between source and destination devices without flooding, because it has entries in the address table that identify the associated ports.

Design Considerations for Ethernet/802.3 Networks

In this section, you learn about Ethernet design guidelines for hierarchical networks in small and medium-sized businesses. This section focuses on broadcast and collision domains and how they affect LAN designs.

Bandwidth and Throughput

A major disadvantage of Ethernet 802.3 networks is collisions. Collisions occur when two hosts transmit frames simultaneously. When a collision occurs, the transmitted frames are corrupted or destroyed. The sending hosts stop sending further transmissions for a random period, based on the Ethernet 802.3 rules of CSMA/CD.

Because Ethernet has no way of controlling which node will be transmitting at any time, we know that collisions will occur when more than one node attempts to gain access to the network. Ethernet's resolution for collisions does not occur instantaneously. Also, a node involved in a collision cannot start transmitting until the matter is resolved. As more devices are added to the shared media, the likelihood of collisions increases. Because of this, it is important to understand that when stating that the bandwidth of the Ethernet network is 10 Mbps, full bandwidth for transmission is available only after any collisions have been resolved. The net throughput of the port (the average data that is effectively transmitted) will be considerably reduced as a function of how many other nodes want to use the network. A hub offers no mechanisms to either eliminate or reduce these collisions, and the available bandwidth that any one node has to transmit is correspondingly reduced. As a result, the number of nodes sharing the Ethernet network will have an effect on the throughput or productivity of the network.

Collision Domains

When expanding an Ethernet LAN to accommodate more users with more bandwidth requirements, the potential for collisions increases. To reduce the number of nodes on a given network segment, you can create separate physical network segments, called collision domains, as shown in Figure 2-5.

Figure 2-5   Collision Domains

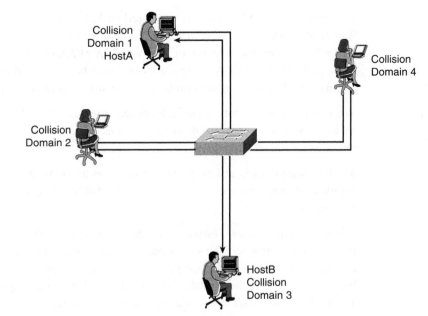

The network area where frames originate and collide is called the collision domain. All shared media environments, such as those created by using hubs, are collision domains. When a host is connected to a switch port, the switch creates a dedicated connection. This connection is considered an individual collision domain because traffic is kept separate from all other traffic, thereby eliminating the potential for a collision. The figure shows unique collision domains in a switched environment. For example, if a 12-port switch has a device connected to each port, 12 collision domains are created.

As you now know, a switch builds a MAC address table by learning the MAC addresses of the hosts that are connected to each switch port. When two connected hosts want to communicate with each other, the switch uses the switching table to establish a connection between the ports. The circuit is maintained until the session is terminated. In Figure 2-5, HostA and HostB want to communicate with each other. The switch creates the connection that is referred to as a microsegment. The microsegment behaves as if the network has only two hosts, one host sending and one receiving, providing maximum utilization of the available bandwidth.

Switches reduce collisions and improve bandwidth use on network segments because they provide dedicated bandwidth to each network segment.

Broadcast Domains

Although switches filter most frames based on MAC addresses, they do not filter broadcast frames. A collection of interconnected switches forms a single broadcast domain. Only a Layer 3 entity, such as a router, or a *virtual LAN (VLAN)*, can bound a Layer 2 broadcast domain. Routers and VLANs are used to segment both collision and broadcast domains. The use of VLANs to segment broadcast domains is discussed in the next chapter.

When a device sends out a Layer 2 broadcast, the destination MAC address in the frame is set to all ones. By setting the destination to this value, all the devices accept and process the broadcasted frame.

The broadcast domain at Layer 2 is referred to as the MAC broadcast domain. The MAC broadcast domain consists of all devices on the LAN that receive frame broadcasts by a host on the LAN.

When a switch receives a broadcast frame, it forwards the frame to each of its ports, except the incoming port where the switch received the broadcast frame. Each attached device recognizes the broadcast frame and processes it. This leads to reduced network efficiency because a portion of the available bandwidth is utilized in propagating the broadcast traffic. When two switches are connected, the broadcast domain is increased.

Network Latency

Latency is the time that a frame or a packet takes to travel from the source to the destination. Users of network-based applications experience latency when they have to wait many minutes to access data stored in a data center or when a website takes many minutes to load in a browser. Latency has at least three sources.

First is the time it takes the source NIC to place voltage pulses on the wire and the time it takes the destination NIC to interpret these pulses. This is sometimes called NIC delay.

Second is the actual *propagation delay* as the signal takes time to travel through the cable. Typically, this is about 0.556 microseconds per 100 m for Cat 5 UTP. Longer cable and slower nominal velocity of propagation (NVP) result in more propagation delay.

Third, latency is added based on network devices that are in the path between two devices. These are either Layer 1, Layer 2, or Layer 3 devices.

Latency does not depend solely on distance and number of devices. For example, if three properly configured switches separate two computers, the computers may experience less latency than if two properly configured routers separated them. This is because routers conduct more complex and time-intensive operations. For example, a router must analyze Layer 3 data, whereas switches just analyze the Layer 2 data. Because Layer 2 data is present earlier in the frame structure than the Layer 3 data, switches can process the frame more quickly. Switches also support the high transmission rates of voice, video, and data networks by employing application-specific integrated circuits (ASIC) to provide hardware support for many networking tasks. Additional switch features such as port-based memory buffering, port level QoS, and congestion management, also help to reduce network latency.

Switch-based latency may also be due to an oversubscribed switch fabric. Many entry level switches do not have enough internal throughput to manage full bandwidth capabilities on all ports simultaneously. The switch needs to be able to manage the amount of peak data expected on the network. As the switching technology improves, the latency through the switch is no longer the issue. The predominant cause of network latency in a switched LAN is more a function of the media, the routing protocols used, and the types of applications running on the network.

Network Congestion

The primary reason for segmenting a LAN into smaller parts is to isolate traffic and to achieve better use of bandwidth per user. Without segmentation, a LAN quickly becomes clogged with traffic and collisions. The most common causes of network congestion are the following:

- **Increasingly powerful computer and network technologies:** Today, CPUs, buses, and peripherals are much faster and more powerful than those used in early LANs; therefore, they can send more data at higher rates through the network, and they can process more data at higher rates.

- **Increasing volume of network traffic:** Network traffic is now more common because remote resources are necessary to carry out basic work. Additionally, broadcast messages, such as address resolution queries sent out by ARP, can adversely affect end-station and network performance.

- **High-bandwidth applications:** Software applications are becoming richer in their functionality and are requiring more and more bandwidth. Desktop publishing, engineering design, video on demand (VoD), electronic learning (e-learning), and streaming video all require considerable processing power and speed.

LAN Segmentation

LANs are segmented into a number of smaller collision and broadcast domains using routers and switches. Previously, bridges were used, but this type of network equipment is rarely seen in a modern switched LAN. Figure 2-6 shows a switch segmenting a LAN into four collision domains.

Figure 2-6   Legacy LAN Segmentation

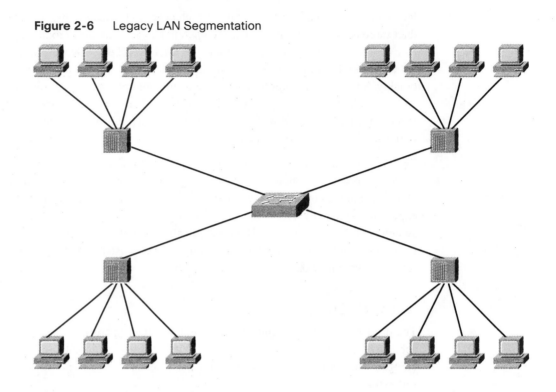

The broadcast domain in Figure 2-6 spans the entire network.

Although bridges and switches share many attributes, several distinctions differentiate these technologies. Bridges are generally used to segment a LAN into a couple of smaller segments. Switches are generally used to segment a large LAN into many smaller segments. Bridges have only a few ports for LAN connectivity, whereas switches have many.

Even though the LAN switch reduces the size of collision domains, all hosts connected to the switch are still in the same broadcast domain. Because routers do not forward broadcast traffic by default, they can be used to create broadcast domains. Creating additional, smaller broadcast domains with a router, as in Figure 2-7, reduces broadcast traffic and provides more available bandwidth for unicast communications. Each router interface connects to a separate network containing broadcast traffic within the LAN segment in which it originated.

LAN Design Considerations

There are two primary considerations when designing a LAN: controlling network latency and removing bottlenecks.

When designing a network to reduce latency, you need to consider the latency caused by each device on the network. Switches can introduce latency on a network when oversubscribed on a busy network. For example, if a core level switch has to support 48 ports, each one capable of running at 1000 Mbps full duplex, the switch should support around 96

Gbps internal throughput if it is to maintain full wire speed across all ports simultaneously. In this example, the throughput requirements stated are typical of core-level switches, not of access-level switches.

Figure 2-7   Modern LAN Segmentation

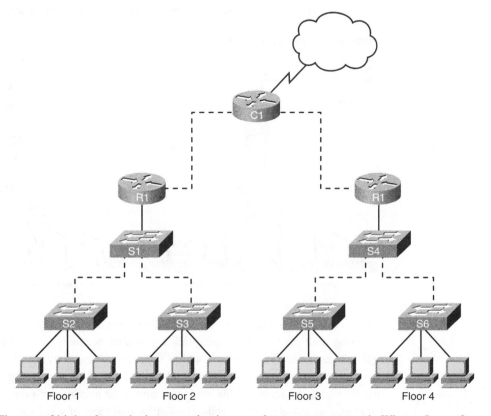

The use of higher layer devices can also increase latency on a network. When a Layer 3 device, such as a router, needs to examine the Layer 3 addressing information contained within the frame, it must read further into the frame than a Layer 2 device, which creates a longer processing time. Limiting the use of higher layer devices can help reduce network latency. However, appropriate use of Layer 3 devices helps prevent contention from broadcast traffic in a large broadcast domain or the high collision rate in a large collision domain.

The second LAN design consideration is bottlenecks in a network. Bottlenecks are places where high network congestion results in slow performance.

Figure 2-8 shows six computers connected to a switch; a single server is also connected to the same switch. Each workstation and the server are all connected using a 1000 Mbps NIC. What happens when all six computers try to access the server at the same time? Does each workstation get 1000 Mbps dedicated access to the server? No, all the computers have to share the 1000 Mbps connection that the server has to the switch. Cumulatively, the computers are capable of 6000 Mbps to the switch. If each connection was used at full capacity, each computer would be able to use only 167 Mbps, one-sixth of the 1000 Mbps bandwidth. To reduce the bottleneck to the server, additional network cards can be installed, which increases the total bandwidth the server is capable of receiving. Figure 2-8 shows five NIC cards in the server and approximately five times the bandwidth. The same logic applies to network topologies. When switches with multiple nodes are interconnected by a single 1000 Mbps connection, a bottleneck is created at this single interconnect.

Figure 2-8   Network Bottlenecks

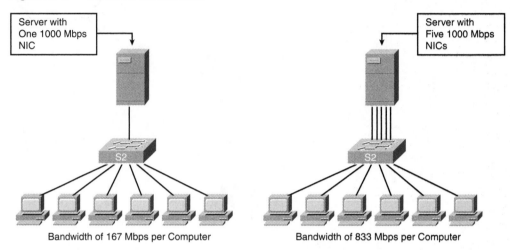

Bandwidth of 167 Mbps per Computer   Bandwidth of 833 Mbps per Computer

Higher capacity links (for example, upgrading from 100 Mbps to 1000 Mbps connections) and using multiple links leveraging link aggregation technologies (for example, combining two links as if they were one to double a connection's capacity) can help to reduce the bottlenecks created by interswitch links and router links. Although configuring link aggregation is outside the scope of this book, it is important to consider a device's capabilities when assessing a network's needs. How many ports and of what speed is the device capable? What is the internal throughput of the device? Can it handle the anticipated traffic loads considering its placement in the network?

Forwarding Frames Using a Switch

In this section, you learn methods that switches use to forward Ethernet frames on a network, what asymmetric switching is, how switches utilize memory buffering, and what Layer 3 switching means. Switches can operate in different modes that can have both positive or negative effects. Modern switches use asymmetric switching. Switches can use port-based or shared memory buffering. Distribution and core layer switches are capable of Layer 3 (and higher) switching.

Switch Forwarding Methods

In the past, switches used one of the following forwarding methods for switching data between network ports: *store-and-forward* or *cut-through switching*. However, store-and-forward is the sole forwarding method used on current models of Cisco Catalyst switches.

In store-and-forward switching, when the switch receives the frame, it stores the data in buffers until the complete frame has been received. During the storage process, the switch analyzes the frame for information about its destination. In this process, the switch also performs an error check using the cyclic redundancy check trailer portion of the Ethernet frame.

CRC uses a mathematical formula, based on the number of 1 bits in the frame, to determine whether the received frame has an error. After confirming the integrity of the frame, the frame is forwarded out the appropriate port toward its destination. When an error is detected in a frame, the switch discards the frame. Discarding frames with errors reduces the amount of bandwidth consumed by corrupt data. Store-and-forward switching is required for quality of service (QoS) analysis on converged networks where frame classification for traffic prioritization is necessary. For example, voice-over-IP data streams need to have priority over web-browsing traffic.

In cut-through switching, the switch acts upon the data as soon as it is received, even if the transmission is not complete. The switch buffers just enough of the frame to read the destination MAC address so that it can determine which port to forward the data to. The destination MAC address is located in the first 6 bytes of the frame following the preamble. The switch looks up the destination MAC address in its switching table, determines the outgoing interface port, and forwards the frame onto its destination through the designated switch port. The switch does not perform any error checking on the frame. Because the switch does not have to wait for the entire frame to be completely buffered, and because the switch does not perform any error checking, cut-through switching is faster than store-and-forward switching. However, because the switch does not perform any error checking, it forwards corrupt frames through the network. The corrupt frames consume bandwidth while they are being forwarded. The destination NIC eventually discards the corrupt frames.

There are two variants of cut-through switching:

- **Fast-forward switching:** Fast-forward switching offers the lowest level of latency. Fast-forward switching immediately forwards a packet after reading the destination address. Because fast-forward switching starts forwarding before the entire packet has been received, there may be times when packets are relayed with errors. This occurs infrequently, and the destination network adapter discards the faulty packet upon receipt. In fast-forward mode, latency is measured from the first bit received to the first bit transmitted. Fast-forward switching is the typical cut-through method of switching.

- **Fragment-free switching:** In fragment-free switching, the switch stores the first 64 bytes of the frame before forwarding. Fragment-free switching can be viewed as a compromise between store-and-forward switching and cut-through switching. The reason fragment-free switching stores only the first 64 bytes of the frame is that most network errors and collisions occur during the first 64 bytes. Fragment-free switching tries to enhance cut-through switching by performing a small error check on the first 64 bytes of the frame to ensure that a collision has not occurred before forwarding the frame. Fragment-free switching is a compromise between the high latency and high integrity of store-and-forward switching and the low latency and reduced integrity of cut-through switching.

Some switches are configured to perform cut-through switching on a per-port basis until a user-defined error threshold is reached, and then they automatically change to store-and-forward. When the error rate falls below the threshold, the port automatically changes back to cut-through switching.

Symmetric and Asymmetric Switching

LAN switching may be classified as symmetric or asymmetric based on the way in which bandwidth is allocated to the switch ports.

Symmetric switching provides switched connections between ports with the same bandwidth, such as all 100 Mbps ports or all 1 Gbps ports. An asymmetric LAN switch provides switched connections between ports of unlike bandwidth, such as a combination of 100 Mbps and 1 Gbps ports. Figure 2-9 contrasts symmetric and asymmetric switching.

Asymmetric switching enables more bandwidth to be dedicated to a server switch port to prevent a bottleneck. This allows smoother traffic flows where multiple clients are communicating with a server at the same time. Memory buffering is required on an asymmetric switch. For the switch to match the different data rates on different ports, entire frames are kept in the memory buffer and are moved to the port one after the other as required.

On a symmetric switch, all ports are of the same bandwidth. Symmetric switching is optimized for a reasonably distributed traffic load, such as in a peer-to-peer desktop environment.

A network manager must evaluate the needed amount of bandwidth for connections between devices to accommodate the data flow of network-based applications. Almost all recent Cisco Catalyst switches are asymmetric switches.

Memory Buffering

A switch analyzes some or all of a packet before it forwards it to the destination host based on the forwarding method. The switch stores the packet for the brief time in a memory buffer. In this section, you learn how two types of memory buffers are used during switch forwarding.

Figure 2-9 Symmetric Versus Asymmetric Switching

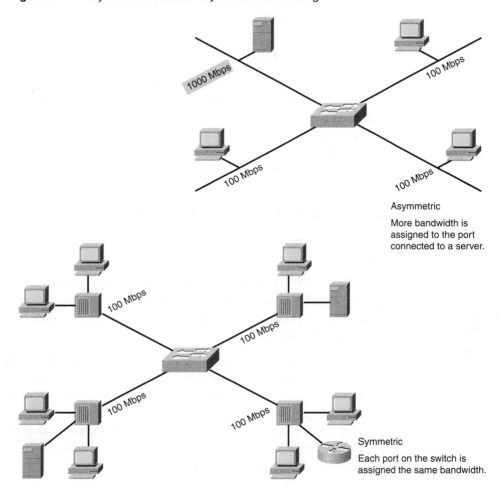

Asymmetric

More bandwidth is assigned to the port connected to a server.

Symmetric

Each port on the switch is assigned the same bandwidth.

An Ethernet switch may use a buffering technique to store frames before forwarding them. Buffering may also be used when the destination port is busy due to congestion and the switch stores the frame until it can be transmitted. The use of memory to store the data is called memory buffering. Memory buffering is built in to the hardware of the switch and, other than increasing the amount of memory available, is not configurable.

There are two methods of memory buffering: port-based and shared memory.

In port-based memory buffering, frames are stored in queues that are linked to specific incoming ports. A frame is transmitted to the outgoing port only when all the frames ahead of it in the queue have been successfully transmitted. It is possible for a single frame to delay the transmission of all the frames in memory because of a busy destination port. This delay occurs even if the other frames could be transmitted to open destination ports.

Shared memory buffering deposits all frames into a common memory buffer that all the ports on the switch share. The amount of buffer memory required by a port is dynamically allocated. The frames in the buffer are linked dynamically to the destination port. This allows the packet to be received on one port and then transmitted on another port, without moving it to a different queue.

The switch keeps a map of frame-to-port links showing where a packet needs to be transmitted. The map link is cleared after the frame has been successfully transmitted. The number of frames stored in the buffer is restricted by the size of the entire memory buffer and is not limited to a single port buffer. This permits larger frames to be transmitted with fewer dropped frames. This is important to asymmetric switching, where frames are being exchanged between different rate ports.

Layer 2 and Layer 3 Switching

In this section, you review the concept of Layer 2 switching and learn about Layer 3 switching.

A Layer 2 LAN switch performs switching and filtering based only on the OSI data link layer (Layer 2) MAC address. A Layer 2 switch is completely transparent to network protocols and user applications. Recall that a Layer 2 switch builds a MAC address table that it uses to make forwarding decisions.

A Layer 3 switch, such as a Catalyst 3560 with an IP Services image, functions similarly to a Layer 2 switch, such as a Catalyst 2960, but instead of using only the Layer 2 MAC address information for forwarding decisions, a Layer 3 switch can also use IP address information. Figure 2-10 illustrates the icons reserved for Layer 2 and Layer 3 switches. Instead of learning only which MAC addresses are associated with each of its ports, a Layer 3 switch can also learn which IP addresses are associated with its interfaces. This allows the Layer 3 switch to direct traffic throughout the network based on IP address information.

Layer 3 switches are also capable of performing Layer 3 routing functions, reducing the need for dedicated routers on a LAN. Because Layer 3 switches have specialized switching hardware, they can typically route data as quickly as they can switch data.

It should be emphasized that Layer 3 switches do not completely replace the need for routers on a network. Routers perform additional Layer 3 services that Layer 3 switches are not capable of performing. Routers are also capable of performing packet-forwarding tasks not found on Layer 3 switches, such as establishing remote access connections to remote networks and devices. Dedicated routers are more flexible in their support of WAN interface cards (WIC), making them the preferred, and sometimes only, choice for connecting to a WAN. Layer 3 switches can provide basic routing functions in a LAN and reduce the need for dedicated routers.

Figure 2-10   Layer 2 and Layer 3 Switching

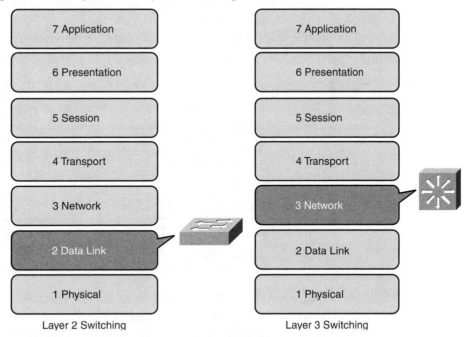

Layer 2 Switching   Layer 3 Switching

Switch Management Configuration

In this section, you review what you learned in *CCNA Exploration: Network Fundamentals* about how to navigate the various command-line interface modes. Despite the steady migration toward web-based graphical user interfaces as a means of device configuration, Cisco routers and switches are still primarily configured by entering commands in the command-line interface. Catalyst switch administration commonly includes management interface and default gateway configuration, speed and duplex configuration, HTTP access, MAC address table management, and configuration file management.

Navigating Command-Line Interface Modes

As a security feature, Cisco IOS Software separated the EXEC sessions into two access levels:

- **User EXEC:** Allows a person to access only a limited number of basic monitoring commands. User EXEC mode is the default mode you enter after logging in to a Cisco switch from the CLI. User EXEC mode is identified by the > prompt.

- **Privileged EXEC:** Allows a person to access all device commands, such as those used for configuration and management, and can be password-protected to allow only authorized users to access the device. Privileged EXEC mode is identified by the # prompt.

To change from user EXEC mode to privileged EXEC mode, enter the **enable** command. To change from privileged EXEC mode to user EXEC mode, enter the **disable** command. On a production network, the switch prompts for the password. Enter the correct password. By default, the password is not configured. Table 2-1 shows the Cisco IOS commands used to navigate from user EXEC mode to privileged EXEC mode and back again.

Table 2-1   Navigating Between User EXEC Mode and Privileged EXEC Mode

Description	CLI
Switch from user EXEC to privileged EXEC mode.	`switch>` **`enable`**
If a password has been set for privileged EXEC mode, you are prompted to enter it now.	`Password:<password>`
The # prompt signifies privileged EXEC mode.	`switch#`
Switch from privileged EXEC to user EXEC mode.	`switch#` **`disable`**
The > prompt signifies user EXEC mode.	`switch>`

After you have entered privileged EXEC mode on the Cisco switch, you can access other configuration modes. Cisco IOS Software uses a hierarchy of commands in its command-mode structure. Each command mode supports specific Cisco IOS commands related to a type of operation on the device.

There are many configuration modes. For now, you will explore how to navigate two common configuration modes: global configuration mode and interface configuration mode.

The example in Table 2-2 starts with the switch in privileged EXEC mode. To configure global switch parameters such as the switch hostname or the switch IP address used for switch management purposes, use global configuration mode. To access global configuration mode, enter the **configure terminal** command in privileged EXEC mode. The prompt changes to (config)#.

Table 2-2   Navigating to and from Global Configuration Mode and Interface Configuration Mode

Description	CLI
Switch from privileged EXEC mode to global configuration mode.	`switch#` **`configure terminal`**
The (config)# prompt signifies that the switch is in global configuration mode.	`switch(config)#`
Switch from global configuration mode to interface configuration mode for Fast Ethernet interface 0/1.	`switch(config)#` **`interface fastethernet 0/1`**

Table 2-2   Navigating to and from Global Configuration Mode and Interface
Configuration Mode   *continued*

Description	CLI
The (config-if)# prompt signifies that the switch is in the interface configuration mode.	`switch(config-if)#`
Switch from interface configuration mode to global configuration mode.	`switch(config-if)#` **exit**
The (config)# prompt signifies that the switch is in global configuration mode.	`switch(config)#`
Switch from global configuration mode to privileged EXEC mode.	`switch(config)#` **exit**
The # prompt signifies that the switch is in privileged EXEC mode.	`switch#`

Configuring interface-specific parameters is a common task. To access interface configuration mode from global configuration mode, enter the **interface** *interface-name* command. The prompt changes to (config-if)#. To exit interface configuration mode, use the **exit** command. The prompt switches back to (config)#, letting you know that you are in global configuration mode. To exit global configuration mode, enter the **exit** command again. The prompt switches to #, signifying privileged EXEC mode.

GUI-Based Alternatives to the CLI

Now we look at some graphical management alternatives for managing a Cisco switch. Using a *GUI* offers simplified switch management and configuration without in-depth knowledge of the Cisco CLI.

Cisco Network Assistant, shown in Figure 2-11, is a PC-based GUI network management application optimized for small- and medium-sized LANs. You can configure and manage groups of switches or standalone switches. The figure shows the management interface for Network Assistant. Cisco Network Assistant is available at no cost and can be downloaded from Cisco (CCO username/password required) at www.cisco.com/go/networkassistant.

The CiscoView device-management application displays a physical view of the switch that you can use to set configuration parameters and to view switch status and performance information. The CiscoView application, purchased separately, can be a standalone application or part of a *Simple Network Management Protocol (SNMP)* platform. Figure 2-12 shows the management interface for the CiscoView Device Manager. Learn more about CiscoView Device Manager at www.cisco.com/en/US/products/sw/cscowork/ps4565/prod_bulletin0900aecd802948b0.html.

Figure 2-11   Cisco Network Assistant

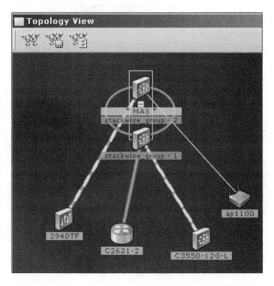

Figure 2-12   CiscoView

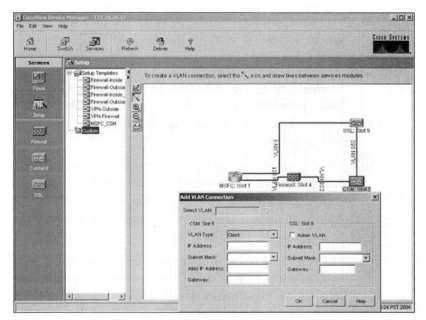

Cisco Device Manager, shown in Figure 2-13, is web-based software that is stored in the switch memory. You can use Device Manager to configure and manage switches. You can access Device Manager from anywhere in your network through a web browser. The figure shows the management interface.

Figure 2-13   Cisco Device Manager

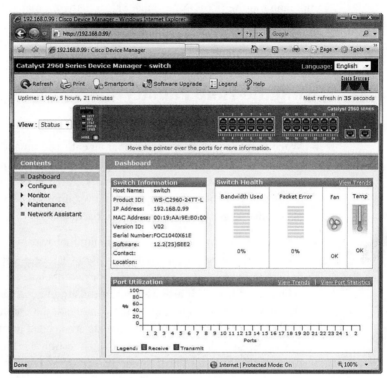

You can manage switches from an SNMP-compatible management station, such as HP OpenView, shown in Figure 2-14.

Figure 2-14   HP OpenView

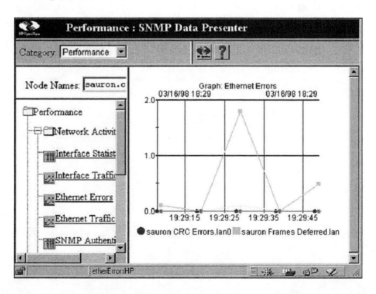

The switch is able to provide comprehensive management information and provide four remote monitoring (RMON) groups. SNMP network management is more common in large enterprise networks.

Learn more about HP OpenView at h20229.www2.hp.com/news/about/index.html.

Using the Help Facility

The Cisco IOS CLI offers two types of help:

- **Word help:** If you do not remember an entire command but do remember the first few characters, enter the character sequence followed by a question mark (**?**). Do not include a space before the question mark. A list of commands that start with the characters that you entered is displayed. For example, entering **sh?** returns a list of all commands that begin with the **sh** character sequence.

- **Command syntax help:** If you are unfamiliar with which commands are available in your current context within the Cisco IOS CLI, or if you do not know the parameters required or available to complete a given command, enter the **?** command. When only **?** is entered, a list of all available commands in the current context is displayed. If the **?** command is entered after a specific command, the command arguments are displayed. If <cr> is displayed, no other arguments are needed to make the command function. Make sure to include a space before the question mark to prevent the Cisco IOS CLI from performing word help rather than command syntax help. For example, enter **show ?** to get a list of the command options supported by the **show** command.

Table 2-3 shows examples of Cisco help functions.

Table 2-3   Context-Sensitive Help

Context	CLI
Example of command prompting. In this example, the help function provides a list of commands available in the current mode that start with **cl**.	switch# **cl?** clear clock
Example of incomplete command.	Switch# **clock** % Incomplete command.
Example of symbolic translation.	switch# **clock** % Unknown command or computer name, or unable to find computer address

Context	CLI
Example of command prompting. Notice the space. In this example, the help function provides a list of subcommands associated with the **clock** command.	`Switch# clock ?` `set Set the time and date`
In this example, the help function provides a list of command arguments required with the **clock set** command.	`switch# clock set ?` `  hh:mm:ss  Current Time`

Using the example of setting the device clock, let's see how CLI help works. If the device clock needs to be set but the **clock** command syntax is not known, the context-sensitive help provides a means to check the syntax.

Context-sensitive help supplies the whole command even if you enter just the first part of the command, such as **cl?**.

If you enter the command **clock** followed by the Enter key, an error message indicates that the command is incomplete. To view the required parameters for the **clock** command, enter **?**, preceded by a space. In the **clock ?** example, the help output shows that the keyword **set** is required after **clock**.

If you now enter the command **clock set**, another error message appears, indicating that the command is still incomplete. Now add a space and enter the **?** command to display a list of command arguments that are available at that point for the given command.

The additional arguments needed to set the clock on the device are displayed: the current time using hours, minutes, and seconds. For an excellent resource on how to use the Cisco IOS CLI, visit **www.cisco.com/univercd/cc/td/doc/product/software/ios124/124cg/hcf_c/ch10/index.htm**.

Console error messages help identify problems when an incorrect command has been entered. Table 2-4 provides an example of error messages, what they mean, and how to get help when they are displayed.

Table 2-4   Console Error Messages

Example Error Message	Meaning	How to Get Help
`switch# cl` `% Ambiguous command:   "cl"`	You did not enter enough characters for your device to recognize the command.	Reenter the command followed by a question mark (**?**), without a space between the command and the question mark. The possible keywords that you can enter with the command are displayed.

continues

Table 2-4   Console Error Messages   *(continued)*

Example Error Message	Meaning	How to Get Help
switch# **clock** % Incomplete command.	You did not enter all the keywords or values required by this command.	Reenter the command followed by a question mark (?), with a space between the command and the question mark.
switch# **clock set aa:12:23** ^ % Invalid input detected at '^' marker.		Enter a question mark (?) to display all the available commands or parameters.

Accessing the Command History

When you are configuring many interfaces on a switch, you can save time retyping commands by using the Cisco IOS command history buffer. In this section, you learn how to configure the command history buffer to support your configuration efforts.

The Cisco CLI provides a history or record of commands that have been entered. This feature, called command history, is particularly useful in helping recall long or complex commands or entries.

With the command history feature, you can complete the following tasks:

- Display the contents of the command buffer.

- Set the command history buffer size.

- Recall previously entered commands stored in the history buffer. There is a buffer for each configuration mode.

By default, command history is enabled, and the system records the last 10 command lines in its history buffer. You can use the **show history** command to view recently entered EXEC commands, as shown in Example 2-1.

Example 2-1 The **show history** Command

```
switch# show history
  enable
  show history
  enable
  config
  t
  confi
  t
  show history
switch#
```

The command history can be disabled for the current terminal session only by using the **terminal no history** command in user or privileged EXEC mode. When command history is disabled, the device no longer retains any previously entered command lines.

To revert the terminal history size back to its default value of 10 lines, enter the **terminal no history size** command in privileged EXEC mode. Table 2-5 provides an explanation and example of these Cisco IOS commands.

Table 2-5   Command History Buffer

Description	Command
Enables terminal history. This command can be run from either user or privileged EXEC mode.	switch# **terminal history**
Configures the terminal history size. The terminal history can maintain 0 to 256 command lines.	switch# **terminal history size 50**
Resets the terminal history size to the default value of 10 command lines.	switch# **terminal no history size**
Disables terminal history.	switch# **terminal no history**

Switch Boot Sequence

In this section, you learn the sequence of Cisco IOS commands that a switch executes from the off state to displaying the login prompt. After a Cisco switch is turned on, it goes through the following boot sequence:

The switch loads the boot loader software. The boot loader is a small program stored in *non-volatile RAM (NVRAM)* and is run when the switch is first turned on.

The boot loader does the following:

- Performs low-level CPU initialization. It initializes the CPU registers, which control where physical memory is mapped, the quantity of memory, and its speed.

- Performs power-on self-test (POST) for the CPU subsystem. It tests the CPU DRAM and the portion of the flash device that makes up the flash file system.

- Initializes the flash file system on the system board.

- Loads a default operating system software image into memory and boots the switch. The boot loader finds the Cisco IOS image on the switch by first looking in a directory that has the same name as the image file (excluding the .bin extension). If it does not find it there, the boot loader software searches each subdirectory before continuing the search in the original directory.

The operating system then initializes the interfaces using the Cisco IOS commands found in the operating system configuration file, config.text, stored in the switch flash memory.

The boot loader also provides access into the switch if the operating system cannot be used. The boot loader has a command-line facility that provides access to the files stored on flash memory before the operating system is loaded. From the boot loader command line, you can enter commands to format the flash file system, reinstall the operating system software image, or recover from a lost or forgotten password.

Prepare to Configure the Switch

The initial startup of a Catalyst switch requires the completion of the following steps:

Step 1.   Before starting the switch, verify the following:

- All network cable connections are secure.

- Your PC or terminal is connected to the console port.

- Your terminal emulator application, such as HyperTerminal, is running and configured correctly.

Step 2.   Attach the power cable plug to the switch power supply socket. The switch starts. Some Catalyst switches, including the Cisco Catalyst 2960 series, do not have power buttons.

Step 3.   Observe the boot sequence: When the switch is turned on, the POST begins. During POST, the LEDs blink while a series of tests determine that the switch is functioning properly. When the POST has completed, the SYST LED rapidly blinks green. If the switch fails POST, the SYST LED turns amber.

Observe the Cisco IOS software output text on the console.

During the initial startup of the switch, if POST failures are detected, they are reported to the console and the switch does not start. If POST completes successfully, and the switch has not been configured before, you are prompted to configure the switch.

Basic Switch Configuration

A few key configuration sequences are typically carried out in the process of implementing a Layer 2 switch in a LAN. These include configuring the switch management interface, the default gateway, the duplex and speed of active interfaces, the support for HTTP access, and the management of the MAC address table.

Management Interface

An access layer switch is much like a PC in that you need to configure an IP address, a subnet mask, and a default gateway. To manage a switch remotely using TCP/IP, you need to assign the switch an IP address. In Figure 2-15, you want to manage S1 from PC1, a computer used for managing the network. To do this, you need to assign switch S1 an IP address. This IP address is assigned to a virtual interface called a virtual LAN (VLAN), and then it is necessary to ensure that the VLAN is assigned to a specific port or ports on the switch.

Figure 2-15   Switch Management Interface

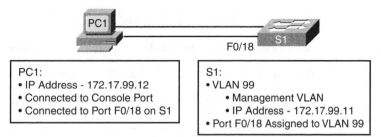

PC1:
• IP Address - 172.17.99.12
• Connected to Console Port
• Connected to Port F0/18 on S1

S1:
• VLAN 99
    • Management VLAN
    • IP Address - 172.17.99.11
• Port F0/18 Assigned to VLAN 99

The default configuration on the switch is to have the management of the switch controlled through VLAN 1. However, a best practice for basic switch configuration is to change the management VLAN to a VLAN other than VLAN 1. The implications and reasoning behind this action are explained in the next chapter. Figure 2-15 illustrates the use of VLAN 99 as the management VLAN; however, it is important to consider that an interface other than VLAN 99 can be used for the management interface.

Note

You will learn more about VLANs in the next chapter. Here the focus is on providing management access to the switch using an alternative VLAN. Some of the commands introduced here are explained more thoroughly in the next chapter. For now, VLAN 99 is created and assigned an IP address. Then the appropriate port on switch S1 is assigned to VLAN 99. Figure 2-15 also shows this configuration information.

To configure an IP address and subnet mask on the management VLAN of the switch, you must be in VLAN interface configuration mode. Use the command **interface vlan 99** and enter the IP address configuration command. You must use the **no shutdown** interface configuration command to make this Layer 3 interface operational. When you see "interface VLAN x", that refers to the Layer 3 interface associated with VLAN x. Only the management VLAN has an interface VLAN associated with it. Table 2-6 illustrates the configuration of the management interface on a Catalyst 2960 switch.

Table 2-6   Management Interface Configuration

Description	Command
Enters global configuration mode.	S1# **configure terminal**
Enters the interface configuration mode for the VLAN 99 interface.	S1(config)# **interface vlan 99**
Configures the interface IP address.	S1(config-if)# **ip address 172.17.99.11 255.255.255.0**
Enables the interface.	S1(config-if)# **no shutdown**
Returns to global configuration mode.	S1(config-if)# **end**
Enters global configuration mode.	S1# **configure terminal**
Enters the interface to assign the VLAN.	S1(config)# **interface fastethernet 0/18**
Defines the VLAN membership mode for the port.	S1(config-if)# **switchport mode access**
Assigns the port to a VLAN.	S1(config-if)# **switchport access vlan 99**
Returns to privileged EXEC mode.	S1(config-if)# **end**
Saves the running configuration to the switch startup configuration.	S1# **copy running-config startup-config**

Note that a Layer 2 switch, such as the Cisco Catalyst 2960, permits only a single VLAN interface to be active at a time. This means that the Layer 3 interface, interface VLAN 99, is active, but the Layer 3 interface, interface VLAN 1, is not active.

Default Gateway

You need to configure the switch so that it can forward IP packets to distant networks. The default gateway is the mechanism for doing this. The switch forwards IP packets with destination IP addresses outside the local network to the default gateway. In Figure 2-16, the IP address of interface F0/1 on router R1, 172.17.99.1, is the default gateway for switch S1.

Figure 2-16   Default Gateway

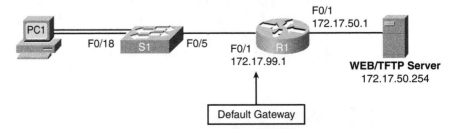

To configure a default gateway for the switch, use the **ip default-gateway** command. Enter the IP address of the next-hop router interface that is directly connected to the switch where a default gateway is being configured. Make sure that you save the configuration running on a switch or router. Use the **copy running-config startup-config** command to back up your configuration.

Example 2-2 displays abbreviated output indicating that interface VLAN 99 has been configured with an IP address and subnet mask, and port F0/18 has been assigned to VLAN 99. You can see more about how to use the **switchport access vlan 99** command in Chapter 3. The **show ip interface brief** command is used to verify port operation and status.

Example 2-2 Verify Basic Switch Configuration

```
S1# show running-config
<output omitted>
!
interface FastEthernet0/18
 switchport access vlan 99
 switchport mode access
<output omitted>
!
interface Vlan99
 ip address 172.17.99.11 255.255.255.0
 no ip route-cache
!
ip default-gateway 172.17.99.1
!
<output omitted>
S1#
S1# show ip interface brief
Interface          IP-Address      OK?    Method      Status
Protocol
<output omitted>
Vlan99             172.17.99.11    YES    manual      up          down
<output omitted>
FastEthernet0/18   unassigned      YES    unset       down        down
FastEthernet0/19   unassigned      YES    unset       down        down
<output omitted>
GigabitEthernet0/2 unassigned      YES    unset       down        down
S1#
```

Duplex and Speed

You can use the **duplex** interface configuration command to specify the duplex mode of operation for switch ports. You can manually set the duplex mode and speed of switch ports to avoid intervendor issues with autonegotiation. Although there can be issues when you configure switch port duplex settings to **auto**, in Figure 2-17, switches S1 and S2 have the same duplex and speed settings resulting from the configuration in Example 2-3.

Figure 2-17   Duplex and Speed

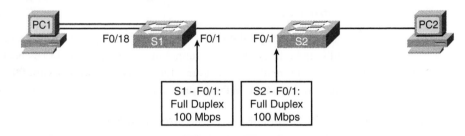

Example 2-3 describes the steps to configure interface F0/1 on switch S1.

Example 2-3 duplex and **speed** Commands

```
S1# configure terminal
S1(config)# interface fastethernet 0/1
S1(config-if)# duplex auto
S1(config-if)# speed auto
S1(config-if)# end
S1# copy running-config startup-config
```

HTTP Access

Modern Cisco switches have a number of web-based configuration tools that require that the switch is configured as an HTTP server. These applications include the Cisco web browser user interface, Cisco router and Security Device Manager (SDM), and IP Phone and Cisco IP telephony service applications. Example 2-4 illustrates a basic configuration on Catalyst 2960 switch enabling HTTP access.

Example 2-4 HTTP Access

```
S1# configure terminal
S1(config)# ip http authentication enable
S1(config)# ip http server
```

To control who can access the HTTP services on the switch, you can optionally configure authentication. Authentication methods can be complex. You may have so many people using the HTTP services that you require a separate server specifically to handle user authentication. AAA and TACACS authentication are examples that use this type of enterprise authentication solutions. AAA and TACACS are authentication protocols that can be used in networks to validate user credentials. It is very possible that you will require a less-complex authentication method, such as creating a local username database on the switch, coupled with the **ip http authentication enable** global configuration mode command, as in Example 2-4.

For more information on TACACS, visit www.cisco.com/en/US/tech/tk583/tk642/ tsd_technology_support_sub-protocol_home.html. For more information on AAA, visit www.cisco.com/en/US/products/ps6350/products_configuration_guide_chapter09186a0080 4ec61e.html.

MAC Address Table Management

Switches use MAC address tables to determine how to forward traffic between ports. These MAC tables include dynamic and static addresses. The MAC address table is displayed with the **show mac-address-table** command; the output includes static and dynamic MAC addresses.

Note

In the past, the MAC address table was referred to as content addressable memory (CAM) or as the CAM table.

Dynamic addresses are source MAC addresses that the switch learns and then ages when they are not in use. You can change the aging time setting for MAC addresses. The default time is 300 seconds. Setting too short an aging time can cause addresses to be prematurely removed from the table. Then, when the switch receives a packet for an unknown destination, it floods the packet to all ports in the same VLAN as the receiving port. This unnecessary flooding can impact performance. Setting too long an aging time can cause the address table to be filled with unused addresses, which prevents new addresses from being learned.

The switch provides dynamic addressing by learning the source MAC address of each frame that it receives on each port and then adding the source MAC address and its associated port number to the MAC address table. As computers are added or removed from the network, the switch updates the MAC address table, adding new entries and aging out those that are not currently in use.

A network administrator can specifically assign static MAC addresses to certain ports. Static addresses are not aged out, and the switch always knows which port to send out traffic destined for that specific MAC address. As a result, there is no need to relearn or refresh which port the MAC address is connected to. One reason to implement static MAC addresses is to provide the network administrator complete control over access to the network. Only those devices that are known to the network administrator can connect to the network.

To create a static mapping in the MAC address table, use the **mac-address-table static** *mac-addr* **vlan** *vlan-id* **interface** *interface-id* command.

To remove a static mapping in the MAC address table, use the **no mac-address-table static** *mac-addr* **vlan** *vlan-id* **interface** *interface-id* command.

The maximum size of the MAC address table varies with different switch platforms. For example, the Catalyst 2960 series switch can store up to 8192 MAC addresses. There are other protocols that may limit the absolute number of MAC address available to a switch.

Verifying Switch Configuration

Now that you have performed the initial switch configuration, you should confirm that the switch has been configured correctly. In this section, you learn how to verify the switch configuration using various **show** commands.

When you need to verify the configuration of your Cisco switch, **show** commands are very useful. **show** commands are executed from privileged EXEC mode. Table 2-7 presents some of the key options for the **show** command that verify many of the configurable switch features. You will learn many additional **show** commands throughout this book.

Table 2-7   **show** Commands

Description	Command
Displays interface status and configuration for a single or all interfaces available on the switch.	`show interface {interface-id ¦ cr}`
Displays contents of startup configuration.	`show startup-config`
Displays current operating configuration.	`show running-config`
Displays information about flash: file system.	`show flash:`
Displays system hardware and software status.	`show version`
Displays the session command history.	`show history`
Displays IP information. The **interface** option displays IP interface status and configuration. The **http** option displays HTTP information about Device Manager running on the switch. The **arp** option displays the IP ARP table.	`show ip {interface	http	arp}`
Displays the MAC forwarding table.	`show mac-address-table`

One of the more valuable **show** commands is the **show running-config** command, as illustrated in Example 2-5.

Example 2-5 show running-config Command

```
S1# show running-config
Building configuration...

Current configuration : 1664 bytes
!
version 12.2
<output omitted>
!
interface FastEthernet0/18
 switchport access vlan 99
 switchport mode access
<output omitted>
!
interface Vlan99
 ip address 172.17.99.11 255.255.255.0
 no ip route-cache
!
ip default-gateway 172.17.99.1
ip http server
!
!
<output omitted>
!
end
S1#
```

The **show running-config** command displays the configuration currently running on the switch. Use this command to verify that you have correctly configured the switch. Example 2-5 has shaded portions of the output of the S1 switch showing the following:

- Fast Ethernet 0/18 interface configured with the management VLAN 99

- VLAN 99 configured with an IP address of 172.17.99.11 255.255.255.0

- Default gateway set to 172.17.99.1

- HTTP server configured

Another commonly used command is the **show interfaces** command, which displays status and statistics information for the interfaces on the switch. The **show interfaces** command is used frequently while configuring and monitoring network devices. Recall that you can type partial commands at the command prompt and, as long as no other command option is the same, the Cisco IOS software interprets the command correctly. For example, you can use **show int** for this command. Example 2-6 shows output from the **show interfaces FastEthernet 0/1** command.

Example 2-6 show interfaces fastethernet 0/1 Command

```
S1# show interfaces fastEthernet 0/1
FastEthernet0/1 is up, line protocol is up
  Hardware is Fast Ethernet, address is 0019.aa9e.b001 (bia 0019.aa9e.b001)
  MTU 1500 bytes, BW 10000 Kbit, DLY 1000 usec,
      reliability 255/255, txload 1/255, rxload 1/255
  Encapsulation ARPA, loopback not set
  Keepalive set (10 sec)
  Auto-duplex, Auto-speed, media type is 10/100BaseTX
  input flow-control is off, output flow-control is unsupported
  ARP type: ARPA, ARP Timeout 04:00:00
  Last input never, output never, output hang never
  Last clearing of "show interface" counters never
  Input queue: 0/75/0/0 (size/max/drops/flushes); Total output drops: 0
  Queueing strategy: fifo
  Output queue: 0/40 (size/max)
  5 minute input rate 0 bits/sec, 0 packets/sec
  5 minute output rate 0 bits/sec, 0 packets/sec
     0 packets input, 0 bytes, 0 no buffer
     Received 0 broadcasts (0 multicast)
     0 runts, 0 giants, 0 throttles
     0 input errors, 0 CRC, 0 frame, 0 overrun, 0 ignored
     0 watchdog, 0 multicast, 0 pause input
     0 input packets with dribble condition detected
     0 packets output, 0 bytes, 0 underruns
<output omitted>
S1#
```

The first shaded line in Example 2-6 indicates that the Fast Ethernet 0/1 interface is up and running. The next shaded line shows that the duplex and speed settings are set to auto.

Basic Switch Management

After a switch is up and running in a LAN, a switch administrator must still maintain the switch. This includes backing up and restoring switch configuration files, clearing configuration information, and deleting configuration files.

Backing Up and Restoring Switch Configuration Files

A typical job for an apprentice network technician is to load a switch with a configuration. In this topic, you learn how to load and store a configuration on the switch flash memory and to a *Trivial File Transfer Protocol (TFTP)* server.

You have already learned how to back up the running configuration of a switch to the startup configuration file. You have used the **copy running-config startup-config** privileged EXEC command to back up the configurations you have made so far. As you may already know, the running configuration is saved in RAM and the startup configuration is stored in the NVRAM portion of flash memory. When you issue the **copy running-config startup-config** command, the Cisco IOS software copies the running configuration to NVRAM so that when the switch boots, the startup-config file with your new configuration is loaded.

You do not always want to save configuration changes you make to the running configuration of a switch. For example, you might want to change the configuration for a short time period rather than permanently when testing out some configurations.

If you want to maintain multiple distinct startup-config files on the device, you can copy the configuration to different filenames, using the **copy startup-config flash:***filename* command. Storing multiple startup-config versions allows you to roll back to a point in time if your configuration has problems. Table 2-8 shows three examples of backing up the configuration to flash memory.

Table 2-8   Backing Up Configuration Files

Example	CLI

Formal version of Cisco IOS copy command. Confirm the destination filename. Press **Enter** to accept or **Crtl+C** to cancel.	`S1# copy system:running-config`
	`flash:startup-config`
	`    Destination filename [startup-config]?`

Informal version of the copy command. The assumptions are that the running-config is running on the system and that the startup-config file will be stored in Flash NVRAM. Press **Enter** key to accept or **Crtl+C** to cancel.	`S1# copy running-config startup-config` `    Destination filename [startup-config]?`

Back up the startup-config to a file stored in Flash NVRAM. Confirm the destination filename. Press **Enter** to accept or **Crtl+C** to cancel.	`S1# copy startup-config`
	`flash:config.bak1`
	`    Destination filename [config.bak1]?`

The first is the formal and complete syntax. The second is the syntax commonly used. Use the first syntax when you are unfamiliar with the network device you are working with, and use the second syntax when you know that the destination is the Flash NVRAM installed on the switch. The third is the syntax used to save a copy of the startup-config file in flash.

Restoring a configuration is a simple process. You just need to copy the saved configuration over the current configuration. For example, if you had a saved configuration called config.bak1, you could restore it over your existing startup-config by entering the Cisco IOS command **copy flash:config.bak1 startup-config**. After the configuration has been restored to the startup-config, you restart the switch with the **reload** command in privileged EXEC mode, as seen in Table 2-9; this reloads the switch with the new startup configuration.

Table 2-9   Restoring Configuration Files

Description	CLI

Copy the config.bak1 file stored in flash to the startup-configuration assumed to be stored in flash. Press Enter to accept or Crtl+C to cancel.	S1# `copy flash:config.bak1`
	`startup-config`
	  `Destination filename [startup-config]?`

Have the Cisco IOS restart the switch. If you have modified the running configuration file, you are asked to save it. Confirm with a "y" or an "n." To confirm the reload, press **Enter** to accept or **Crtl+C** to cancel.	S1# `reload`
	`System configuration has been modified.`
	`Save? [yes/no]: n`
	`Proceed with reload? [confirm]`

The **reload** command halts the system. Use the **reload** command after configuration information is entered into a file and saved to the startup configuration.

Note

You cannot reload from a virtual terminal if the switch is not set up for automatic booting. This restriction prevents the system from dropping to the ROM monitor (ROMMON), thereby taking the system out of the remote user's control.

After issuing the **reload** command, the system prompts you to answer whether to save the configuration. Normally you would indicate "yes," but in this particular case you need to answer "no." If you answered "yes," the file you just restored would be overwritten. In every case you need to consider whether the current running configuration is the one you want to be active after reload.

For more details on the **reload** command, review the Cisco IOS Configuration Fundamentals Command Reference, Release 12.4 found at this website: www.cisco.com/en/US/products/ps6350/products_command_reference_book09186a008042deb0.html.

Note

You also have the option of entering the **copy startup-config running-config** command. Unfortunately, this command does not entirely overwrite the running configuration; it only adds existing commands from the startup configuration to the running configuration. This can cause unintended results, so be careful when you do this.

Using a TFTP Server with Switch Configuration Files

After you have configured your switch with all the options you want to set, it is a good idea to back up the configuration on the network where it can then be archived along with the rest of your network data being backed up nightly. Having the configuration stored safely off the switch protects it in the event that some major problem occurs with your switch.

Some switch configurations take several minutes to get working correctly. If you lost the configuration because of switch hardware failure, you need to configure a new switch. If a backup configuration exists for the failed switch, it can be loaded quickly onto the new switch. If no backup configuration exists, you must configure the new switch from scratch.

You can use TFTP to back up your configuration files over the network. Cisco IOS software comes with a built-in TFTP client that allows you to connect to a TFTP server on your network.

Note

Free TFTP server software packages are available on the Internet; you can use them if you do not already have a TFTP server running. One commonly used TFTP server is obtained from www.solarwinds.com.

To upload a configuration file from a switch to a TFTP server for storage, follow these steps:

How To

Step 1.   Verify that the TFTP server is running on your network.

Step 2.   Log in to the switch through the console port or a Telnet session. Ensure that the switch has connectivity with the TFTP server by using **ping**.

Step 3.   Upload the switch configuration to the TFTP server. Specify the IP address or hostname of the TFTP server and the destination filename. The Cisco IOS command is **copy system:running-config tftp:**[[[*//location*]/*directory*]/*filename*] or **copy nvram:startup-config tftp:**[[[*//location*]/*directory*]/*filename*].

Example 2-7 shows an example of backing up a configuration file to a TFTP server.

Example 2-7 Using TFTP to Backup Switch Configuration Files

```
S1# copy system:running-config tftp://172.16.2.155/tokyo-config
Write file tokyo-config on host 172.16.2.155? [confirm]
Writing tokyo-config!!! [OK]
S1#
```

After the configuration is stored successfully on the TFTP server, it can be copied back to the switch using the following steps:

How To

Step 1.   Copy the configuration file to the appropriate TFTP directory on the TFTP server if it is not already there.

Step 2.   Verify that the TFTP server is running on your network.

Step 3.   Log in to the switch through the console port or a Telnet session. Use **ping** to verify connectivity with the TFTP server.

Step 4.   Download the configuration file from the TFTP server to configure the switch. Specify the IP address or hostname of the TFTP server and the name of the file to download. The Cisco IOS command is **copy tftp**:[[[*//location*]/*directory*]/*filename*] system:running-config or copy tftp:[[[*//location*]/*directory*]/*filename*] **nvram:startup-config**.

If the configuration file is downloaded onto the running-config, the commands are executed as the file is parsed line by line. If the configuration file is downloaded onto the startup-config, the switch must be reloaded for the changes to take effect.

Clearing Switch Configuration Information

You can clear the configuration information from the startup configuration. You might do this to prepare a used switch to be shipped to a customer or a different department and you want to ensure that the switch gets reconfigured. When you erase the startup configuration file and the switch reboots, it enters the setup program.

To clear the contents of your startup configuration, use the **erase nvram:** or the **erase startup-config** privileged EXEC command. Example 2-8 illustrates erasing the configuration files stored in NVRAM.

Example 2-8 Erasing Configuration Files in NVRAM

```
S1# erase nvram:
Erasing the nvram filesystem will remove all configuration files!
Continue? [confirm]
[OK]
Erase of nvram: complete
S1#
```

Caution

You cannot restore the startup configuration file after it has been erased, so make sure that you have a backup of the configuration in case you need to restore it at a later point.

You may have been working on a complex configuration task and stored many backup copies of your files in flash. To delete a file from flash memory, use the **delete flash:***filename* privileged EXEC command. Depending on the setting of the **file prompt** global configuration command, you might be prompted for confirmation before you delete a file. By default, the switch prompts for confirmation when deleting a file.

After the configuration has been erased or deleted, you can reload the switch to initiate a new configuration for the switch.

Configuring Basic Switch Management (2.3.8)

Use the Packet Tracer Activity to practice navigating command-line interface modes, using help functions, accessing the command history, configuring boot sequence parameters, setting speed and duplex settings, as well as managing the MAC address table and switch configuration file. Use file e3-2384.pka on the CD-ROM that accompanies this book to perform this activity using Packet Tracer.

Configuring Switch Security

Data is valuable and must be zealously guarded. The U.S. Federal Bureau of Investigation (FBI) estimates that businesses lose $67.2 billion annually because of computer-related crime. Personal customer data, in particular, sells for very high prices. The following are some current prices for stolen data:

- Automatic teller machine (ATM) or debit card with personal identification number (PIN): $500

- Driver's license number: $150

- Social Security number: $100

- Credit card number with expiration date: $15 to $20

In modern networks, security is integral to implementing any device, protocol, or technology. In this section you learn to help secure your LAN by configuring password options, login banners, Telnet and SSH, and port security. You learn common security attacks and tools for mitigating these attacks.

Configuring Password Options

Securing your switches starts with protecting them from unauthorized access. Next you will explore configuring passwords for the console line, virtual terminal lines, and access to privileged EXEC mode. You also learn how to encrypt and recover passwords on a switch.

Securing Console Access

You can perform all configuration options directly from the console. To access the console, you need to have local physical access to the device. If you do not secure the console port properly, a malicious user could compromise the switch configuration.

To secure the console port from unauthorized access, set a password on the console port using the **password** *password* line configuration mode command. Use the **line console 0** command to switch from global configuration mode to line configuration mode for console 0, which is the console port on Cisco switches. The prompt changes to (config-line)#, indicating that the switch is now in line configuration mode. From line configuration mode, you can set the password for the console by entering the **password** *password* command. To ensure that a user on the console port is required to enter the password, use the **login** command. Even when a password is defined, it is not required to be entered until the **login** command has been issued.

Table 2-10 shows the commands used to configure and require the password for console access. Recall that you can use the **show running-config** command to verify your configuration. Before you complete the switch configuration, remember to save the running configuration file to the startup configuration.

Table 2-10   Securing Console Access

Description	Command
Switches from privileged EXEC mode to global configuration mode.	S1# **configure terminal**
Switches from global configuration mode to line configuration mode for console 0.	S1(config)# **line console 0**
Sets **cisco** as the password for the console 0 line on the switch.	S1(config-line)# **password cisco**
Sets the console line to require the password to be entered before access is granted.	S1(config-line)# **login**
Exits from line configuration mode and returns to privileged EXEC mode.	S1(config-line)# **end**

If you need to remove the password and remove the requirement to enter the password at login, use the following steps:

How To

Step 1.   Switch from privileged EXEC mode to global configuration mode. Enter the **configure terminal** command.

Step 2.   Switch from global configuration mode to line configuration mode for console 0. The command prompt (config-line)# indicates that you are in line configuration mode. Enter the command **line console 0**.

Step 3.   Remove the password from the console line using the **no password** command.

Caution

If no password is defined and login is still enabled, there is no access to the console.

Step 4.   Remove the requirement to enter the password at login to the console line using the **no login** command.

Step 5.   Exit line configuration mode and return to privileged EXEC mode using the **end** command.

Securing Virtual Terminal Access

The vty lines on a Cisco switch allow you to access the device remotely. You can perform all configuration options using the vty lines. You do not need physical access to the switch to access the vty lines, so it is very important to secure the vty lines. Any user with network access to the switch can establish a vty remote terminal. If the vty lines are not properly secured, a malicious user could compromise the switch configuration.

To secure the vty lines from unauthorized access, you can set a vty password that is required before access is granted. To set the password on the vty lines, you must be in line configuration mode.

Many vty lines are available on a Cisco switch. Multiple ports permit more than one administrator to connect to and manage the switch. To secure all vty lines, make sure that a password is set and that login is enforced on all lines. Leaving some lines unsecured compromises security and allows unauthorized users to access the switch.

Use the **line vty 0 4** command to switch from global configuration mode to line configuration mode for vty lines 0 through 4.

Note

If the switch has more vty lines available, adjust the range to secure them all. For example, a Catalyst 2960 has lines 0 through 15 available.

Table 2-11 shows the commands used to configure and require the password for vty access. You can use the **show running-config** command to verify your configuration and the **copy running-config startup config** command to save your work.

Table 2-11   Securing Virtual Terminal Access

Description	Command
Switches from privileged EXEC mode to global configuration mode.	S1# **configure terminal**
Switches from global configuration mode to line configuration mode for vty terminals 0 through 15.	S1(config)# **line vty 0 15**
Sets **cisco** as the password for the vty lines on the switch.	S1(config-line)# **password cisco**
Sets the vty line to require the password to be entered before access is granted.	S1(config-line)# **login**
Exits from line configuration mode and returns to privileged EXEC mode.	S1(config-line)# **end**

If you need to remove the password and the requirement to enter the password at login, use the following steps:

How To

Step 1. Switch from privileged EXEC mode to global configuration mode. Enter the **configure terminal** command.

Step 2. Switch from global configuration mode to line configuration mode for vty lines 0 through 15. The command prompt (config-line)# indicates that you are in line configuration mode. Enter the command **line vty 0 15**.

Step 3. Remove the password from the console line using the **no password** command. Caution: If no password is defined and login is still enabled, there is no access to the console.

Step 4. Remove the requirement to enter the password at login to the console line using the **no login** command.

Step 5. Exit line configuration mode and return to privileged EXEC mode using the **end** command.

Securing Privileged EXEC Access

Privileged EXEC mode allows any user accessing that mode on a Cisco switch to configure any option available on the switch. You can also view all the currently configured settings on the switch, including some of the unencrypted passwords! For these reasons, it is important to secure access to privileged EXEC mode.

The **enable password** global configuration command allows you to specify a password to restrict access to privileged EXEC mode. However, one problem with the **enable password** command is that it stores the password in readable text in the startup-config and running-config files. If someone were to gain access to a stored startup-config file, or temporary access to a Telnet or console session that is logged in to privileged EXEC mode, that person could see the password. As a result, Cisco introduced a new password option to control access to privileged EXEC mode that stores the password in an encrypted format.

You can assign an encrypted form of the enable password, called the enable secret password, by entering the **enable secret** command with the desired password at the global configuration mode prompt. If the enable secret password is configured, it is used instead of the enable password, not in addition to it. There is also a safeguard built in to the Cisco IOS software that prevents you from setting the enable secret password to the same password that is used for the enable password.

Table 2-12 shows the commands used to configure privileged EXEC mode passwords. You can use the **show running-config** command to verify your configuration and the **copy running-config startup config** command to save your work.

Table 2-12   Securing Privileged EXEC Access

Description	Command
Switches from privileged EXEC mode to global configuration mode.	S1# **configure terminal**
Configures the enable secret password to enter privileged EXEC mode.	S1(config)# **enable secret** *password*
Exits from line configuration mode and returns to privileged EXEC mode.	S1(config)# **end**

If you need to remove the password requirement to access privileged EXEC mode, you can use the **no enable password** and **no enable secret** commands from global configuration mode.

Encrypting Switch Passwords

When configuring passwords in the Cisco IOS CLI, by default all passwords, except for the enable secret password, are stored in clear-text format within the startup-config and running-config files. Example 2-9 shows an abbreviated screen output from the **show running-config** command on the S1 switch. The clear-text passwords are shaded. It is universally accepted that passwords should be encrypted and not stored in clear-text format. The Cisco IOS command **service password-encryption** encrypts the passwords in the configuration file.

Example 2-9 Encrypting Passwords in the **running-config** File

```
<output omitted>
!
line con 0
 password cisco
 login
line vty 0 4
 password cisco
 no login
line vty 5 15
 password cisco
 no login
!
end

S1# configure terminal
S1(config)# service password-encryption
S1(config)# end
```

```
S1# show running-config
<output omitted>
!
line con 0
 password 7 030752180500
 login
line vty 0 4
 password 7 1511021F0725
 no login
line vty 5 15
 password 7 1511021F0725
 no login
!
end
```

When the **service password-encryption** command is entered from global configuration mode, all system passwords are stored in an encrypted form. As soon as the command is entered, all the currently set passwords are converted to encrypted passwords. At the bottom of Example 2-9, the encrypted passwords are shaded.

If you want to remove the requirement to store all system passwords in an encrypted format, enter the **no service password-encryption** command from global configuration mode. Removing password *encryption* does not convert currently encrypted passwords back into readable text. However, all newly set passwords are stored in clear-text format.

Note

The encryption standard used by the **service password-encryption** command is referred to as type 7. This encryption standard is very weak, and easily accessible tools exist on the Internet for decrypting passwords encrypted with this standard. Type 5 is more secure but must be invoked manually for each password configured.

Password Recovery

After you set passwords to control access to the Cisco IOS CLI, you need to make sure that you remember them. In case you have lost or forgotten access passwords, Cisco has a password recovery mechanism that allows administrators to gain access to their Cisco devices. The password recovery process requires physical access to the device.

You may not be able to actually recover the passwords on the Cisco device, especially if password encryption has been enabled, but you are able to reset them to a new value.

To recover the password on a Catalyst 2960 switch, use the following steps:

Step 1.   Connect a terminal or PC with terminal-emulation software to the switch console port.

Step 2.   Set the line speed on the emulation software to 9600 baud.

Step 3.   Power off the switch. Reconnect the power cord to the switch and within 15 seconds, press the Mode button while the System LED is still flashing green. Continue pressing the Mode button until the System LED turns briefly amber and then solid green. Then release the Mode button.

Step 4.   Initialize the flash file system using the **flash_init** command.

Step 5.   Load any helper files using the **load_helper** command.

Step 6.   Display the contents of flash memory using the **dir flash:** command:

```
Directory of flash:
13 drwx 192 Mar 01 1993 22:30:48 c2960-lanbase-mz.122-25.FX
11 -rwx 5825 Mar 01 1993 22:31:59 config.text
18 -rwx 720 Mar 01 1993 02:21:30 vlan.dat
16128000 bytes total (10003456 bytes free)
```

Step 7.   Rename the configuration file to config.text.old, which contains the password definition, using the **rename flash:config.text flash:config.text.old** command.

Step 8.   Boot the system with the **boot** command.

Step 9.   You are prompted to start the setup program. Enter **N** at the prompt and then, when the system prompts whether to continue with the configuration dialog, enter **N**.

Step 10. At the switch prompt, enter privileged EXEC mode using the **enable** command.

Step 11. Rename the configuration file to its original name using the **rename flash:config.text.old flash:config.text** command.

Step 12. Copy the configuration file into memory using the **copy flash:config.text system:running-config** command. After this command has been entered, the following is displayed on the console:

```
Source filename [config.text]?


Destination filename [running-config]?
```

Press **Return** in response to the confirmation prompts. The configuration file is now reloaded, and you can change the password.

Step 13. Enter global configuration mode using the **configure terminal** command.

Step 14. Change the password using the **enable secret** *password* command.

Step 15. Return to privileged EXEC mode using the **exit** command.

Step 16. Copy the running configuration to the startup configuration file using the **copy running-config startup-config** command.

Step 17. Reload the switch using the **reload** command.

Note

The password recovery procedure can be different depending on the Cisco switch series, so you should refer to the product documentation before you attempt a password recovery. See www.cisco.com/en/US/products/sw/iosswrel/ps1831/products_tech_note09186a00801746e6.shtml for password recovery procedures for each Cisco product.

Login Banners

The Cisco IOS command set includes a feature that allows you to configure messages that anyone logging on to the switch sees. These messages are called login banners and message of the day (MOTD) banners. In this topic, you learn how to configure them.

You can define a customized banner to be displayed before the username and password login prompts by using the **banner login** command in global configuration mode. Enclose the banner text in quotations or using a delimiter unique relative to any other character appearing in the banner string.

Table 2-13 shows the S1 switch being configured with a login banner "Authorized Personnel Only!"

Table 2-13   Securing Privileged EXEC Access

Description	Command
Switches from privileged EXEC mode to global configuration mode.	S1# `configure terminal`
Configures a login banner.	S1(config)# `banner login "Authorized Personnel Only!"`

To remove the login banner, enter the **no** form of this command in global configuration mode; for example, S1(config)# **no banner login**.

The MOTD banner displays on all connected terminals at login and is useful for sending messages that affect all network users (such as impending system shutdowns). The MOTD banner displays before the login banner if it is also configured.

Define the MOTD banner by using the **banner motd** command in global configuration mode. Enclose the banner text in quotations or with a delimiter that is unique relative to all the text enclosed by it.

Table 2-14 shows the S1 switch being configured with a MOTD banner to display "Device maintenance will be occurring on Friday!"

Table 2-14   Securing Privileged EXEC Access

Description	Command
Switches from privileged EXEC mode to global configuration mode.	S1# **configure terminal**
Configures a MOTD login banner.	S1(config)# **banner motd "Device maintenance will be occurring on Friday!"**

To remove the MOTD banner, enter the **no** format of this command in global configuration mode; for example S1(config)# **no banner motd**.

Configure Telnet and SSH

Older switches may not support secure communication with Secure Shell (SSH). This topic will help you choose between the Telnet and SSH methods of remotely accessing a vty on a Catalyst switch.

Telnet is the original method that was supported on early Cisco switch models. Telnet is a popular protocol used for terminal access because most current operating systems come with a Telnet client built in. However, Telnet is an insecure way of accessing a network device, because it sends all communications across the network in clear-text. Using network monitoring software, an attacker can read every keystroke that is sent between the Telnet client and the Telnet service running on the Cisco switch. Because of the security concerns of the Telnet protocol, SSH has become the preferred protocol for remotely accessing virtual terminal lines on a Cisco device.

SSH gives the same type of access as Telnet with the added benefit of security. Communication between the SSH client and SSH server is encrypted. SSH has gone through a few versions, with Cisco devices currently supporting both SSHv1 and SSHv2. It is recommended that you implement SSHv2 when possible, because it uses a more enhanced security encryption algorithm than SSHv1.

Configuring Telnet

Telnet is the default vty-supported protocol on a Cisco switch. When a management IP address is assigned to the Cisco switch, you can connect to it using a Telnet client. Initially, the vty lines are unsecured, allowing access by any user attempting to connect to them.

You have already learned how to secure access to the switch over the vty lines by requiring password authentication. This makes running the Telnet service a little more secure.

Because Telnet is the default transport for the vty lines, you do not need to specify it after the initial configuration of the switch has been performed. However, if you have switched the transport protocol on the vty lines to permit only SSH, you need to enable the Telnet protocol to permit Telnet access manually.

If you need to reenable the Telnet protocol on a Cisco 2960 switch, use the following command from vty line configuration mode: **transport input telnet** or **transport input all**. By permitting all transport protocols, you still permit SSH access to the switch as well as Telnet access.

Configuring SSH

SSH is a cryptographic security feature that is subject to export restrictions. To use this feature, a cryptographic image must be installed on your switch.

The SSH feature has an SSH server and an SSH integrated client, which are applications that run on the switch. You can use any SSH client running on a PC or the Cisco SSH client running on the switch to connect to a switch running the SSH server.

The switch supports SSHv1 or SSHv2 for the server component. The switch supports only SSHv1 for the client component.

SSH supports the Data Encryption Standard (DES) algorithm, the Triple DES (3DES) algorithm, and password-based user authentication. DES offers 56-bit encryption, and 3DES offers 168-bit encryption. Encryption takes time, but DES takes less time to encrypt text than 3DES. Typically, encryption standards are specified by the client, so if you have to configure SSH, ask which one to use. (A discussion of data encryption methods is beyond the scope of this book.)

To implement SSH, you need to generate RSA keys. RSA involves a public key, kept on a public RSA server, and a private key, kept only by the sender and receiver. The public key can be known to everyone and is used for encrypting messages. Messages encrypted with the public key can be decrypted only using the private key. This is known as asymmetric encryption and is discussed in greater detail in the *Accessing the WAN, CCNA Exploration Companion Guide*.

To configure a Catalyst 2960 switch as an SSH server, beginning in privileged EXEC mode, follow these steps:

How To

Step 1. Enter global configuration mode using the **configure terminal** command.

Step 2. Configure a hostname for your switch using the **hostname** *hostname* command.

Step 3. Configure a host domain for your switch using the **ip domain-name** *domain-name* command.

Step 4. Enable the SSH server for local and remote authentication on the switch and generate an encrypted RSA key pair using the **crypto key generate rsa** command.

When you generate RSA keys, you are prompted to enter a modulus length. Cisco recommends using a modulus size of 1024 bits. A longer modulus length might be more secure, but it takes longer to generate and to use. This step completes a rudimentary configuration of an SSH server. The remaining steps describe several options available to fine-tune the SSH configuration.

Step 5.   Return to privileged EXEC mode using the **end** command.

Step 6.   Show the status of the SSH server on the switch using the **show ip ssh** or **show ssh** command.

Step 7.   Enter global configuration mode using the **configure terminal** command.

Step 8.   (Optional) Configure the switch to run SSHv1 or SSHv2 using the **ip ssh version [1 | 2]** command.

If you do not enter this command or do not specify keyword options **1** or **2.**, the SSH server selects the latest SSH version supported by the SSH client. For example, if the SSH client supports SSHv1 and SSHv2, the SSH server selects SSHv2.

Step 9.   Configure the SSH control parameters:

Specify the timeout value in seconds; the default is 120 seconds. The range is 0 to 120 seconds. For an SSH connection to be established, a number of phases must be completed, such as connection, protocol negotiation, and parameter negation. The timeout value applies to the amount of time the switch allows for a connection to be established.

By default, up to five simultaneous encrypted SSH connections for multiple CLI-based sessions over the network are available (session 0 to session 4). After the execution shell starts, the CLI-based session timeout value returns to the default of 10 minutes.

Specify the number of times that a client can reauthenticate to the server. The default is 3; the range is 0 to 5. For example, a user can allow the SSH session to sit for more than 10 minutes three times before the SSH session is terminated.

Repeat this step when configuring both parameters. To configure both parameters, use the **ip ssh {timeout** *seconds* **| authentication-retries** *number*} command.

Step 10.   Return to privileged EXEC mode using the **end** command.

Step 11.   Display the status of the SSH server connections on the switch using the **show ip ssh** or the **show ssh** command.

Step 12.   (Optional) Save your entries in the configuration file using the **copy running-config startup-config** command.

To delete the RSA key pair, use the **crypto key zeroize rsa** global configuration command. After the RSA key pair is deleted, the SSH server is automatically disabled.

If you want to prevent non-SSH connections, add the **transport input ssh** command in line configuration mode to limit the switch to SSH connections only. Straight (non-SSH) Telnet connections are refused.

Example 2-10 demonstrates a set of commands to enable SSH on a Catalyst 2960 switch. The default version for SSH would be version 2, but we configure it anyway. This configuration prevents Telnet access on the vty lines. It is assumed that there are entries in the local username database and that a vty password has been configured. Step 3 and 4 in the preceding list provide an absolute minimum set of commands to enable SSH.

Example 2-10   Enabling the SSH Server on the Catalyst 2960

```
S1(config)# ip domain-name mydomain.com
S1(config)# crypto key generate rsa
S1(config)# ip ssh version 2
S1(config)# line vty 0 15
S1(config-line)# transport input ssh
```

For a detailed discussion on SSH, visit: www.cisco.com/en/US/tech/tk583/tk617/tsd_technology_support_protocol_home.html.

For an overview of RSA technology, visit en.wikipedia.org/wiki/Public-key_cryptography.

For a detailed discussion on RSA technology, visit: www.rsa.com/rsalabs/node.asp?id=2152.

Common Security Attacks

Unfortunately, basic switch security does not stop malicious attacks from occurring. In this section, you learn about a few common security attacks and how dangerous they are. This topic provides introductory-level information about security attacks. The details of how some of these common attacks work are beyond the scope of this book. If you would like to delve deeper into network security, refer to the *Accessing the WAN, CCNA Exploration Companion Guide*.

We proceed to explore some of the more common Layer 2 security attacks.

MAC Address Flooding

The MAC address table in a switch contains the MAC addresses available on a given physical port of a switch and the associated VLAN parameters for each. When a Layer 2 switch receives a frame, the switch looks in the MAC address table for the destination MAC address. All Catalyst switch models use a MAC address table for Layer 2 switching. As frames arrive on switch ports, the source MAC addresses are learned and recorded in the MAC address table. If an entry exists for the MAC address, the switch forwards the frame to the MAC address port designated in the MAC address table. If the MAC address does not exist, the switch forwards the frame out every other port on the switch. MAC address table overflow attacks are sometimes referred to as MAC flooding attacks. To understand the mechanism of a MAC address table overflow attack, we recall the basic operation of a switch.

In Figure 2-18, Host A sends traffic to Host B. The switch receives the frames and looks up the destination MAC address in its MAC address table. If the switch cannot find the destination MAC in the MAC address table, the switch then copies the frame and sends it out every other switch port.

Figure 2-18   Switch Receives Unicast Frame

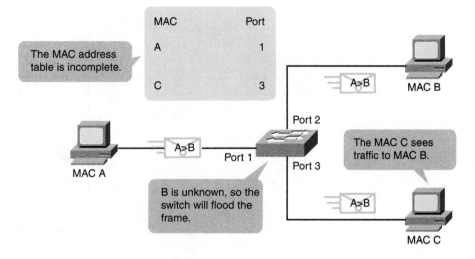

In Figure 2-19, Host B receives the frame and sends a reply to Host A. The switch then learns that the MAC address for Host B is located on port 2 and writes that information into the MAC address table.

Figure 2-19   Host B Receives Unicast Frame

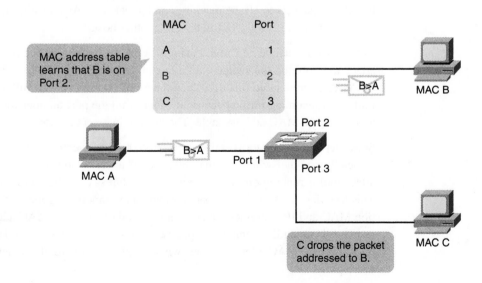

You see that Host C also receives the frame from Host A to Host B, but because the destination MAC address of that frame is Host B, Host C drops that frame.

In Figure 2-20, any frame sent now by Host A (or any other host) to Host B is forwarded to port 2 of the switch and not sent out every port.

Figure 2-20   Switch Forwards Frame Out Single Port

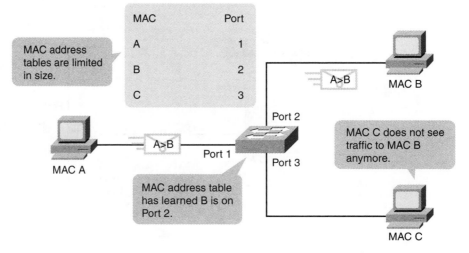

The key to understanding how MAC address table overflow attacks work is to know that MAC address tables are limited in size. MAC flooding makes use of this limitation to bombard the switch with fake source MAC addresses until the switch MAC address table is full. The switch then enters into what is known as a fail-open mode, starts acting as a hub, and broadcasts packets to all the machines on the network. As a result, the attacker can see all of the frames sent from a victim host to another host.

MAC flooding can be performed using a network attack tool. The network intruder uses the attack tool to flood the switch with a large number of invalid source MAC addresses until the MAC address table fills up. When the MAC address table is full, the switch floods all ports with incoming traffic because it cannot find the port number for a particular MAC address in the MAC address table. The switch, in essence, acts like a hub.

Some network attack tools can generate 155,000 MAC entries on a switch per minute. Depending on the switch, the maximum MAC address table size varies. In Figure 2-21, the attack tool is running on the host with MAC address C in the bottom right of the screen. This tool floods a switch with packets containing randomly generated source and destination MAC and IP addresses. Over a short period of time, the MAC address table in the switch fills up until it cannot accept new entries. When the MAC address table fills up with invalid source MAC addresses, the switch begins to forward all frames that it receives to every port.

Figure 2-21   Host C Sends Frames with Bogus Sources

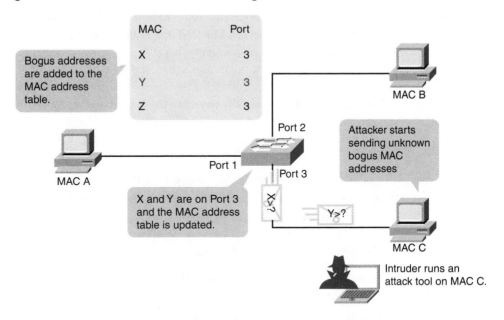

As long as the network attack tool is left running, the MAC address table on the switch remains full. When this happens, the switch begins to send all received frames out every port so that frames sent from Host A to Host B are also sent out of port 3 on the switch, as shown in Figure 2-22.

Figure 2-22   Host C Sees All Frames Sent from Host A to Host B

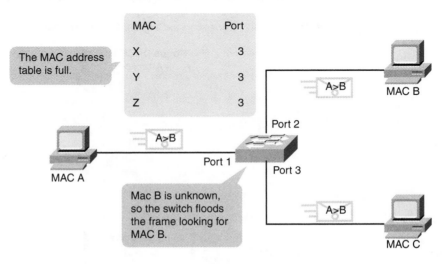

Spoofing Attacks

One way an attacker can gain access to network traffic is to *spoof* responses that would be sent by a valid DHCP server. The DHCP spoofing device replies to client DHCP requests. The legitimate server may also reply, but if the spoofing device is on the same segment as the client, its reply to the client may arrive first. The intruder DHCP reply offers an IP address and supporting information that designates the intruder as the default gateway or Domain Name System (DNS) server. In the case of a gateway, the clients then forward packets to the attacking device, which in turn, sends them to the desired destination. This is referred to as a man-in-the-middle attack, and it may go entirely undetected as the intruder intercepts the data flow through the network.

You should be aware of another type of DHCP attack called a DHCP starvation attack. The attacker PC continually requests IP addresses from a real DHCP server by changing the source MAC addresses of the requests. If successful, this kind of DHCP attack causes all the leases on the real DHCP server to be allocated, thus preventing the real users (DHCP clients) from obtaining an IP address.

To prevent DHCP attacks, use the DHCP snooping and port security features on the Cisco Catalyst switches.

DHCP snooping is a Cisco Catalyst feature that determines which switch ports can respond to DHCP requests. Ports are identified as trusted and untrusted, as illustrated in Figure 2-23. Trusted ports can source all DHCP messages; untrusted ports can source requests only. Trusted ports host a DHCP server or can be an uplink toward the DHCP server. If a rogue device on an untrusted port attempts to send a DHCP response packet into the network, the port is shut down. This feature can be coupled with DHCP options in which switch information, such as the port ID of the DHCP request, can be inserted into the DHCP request packet.

Figure 2-23   DHCP Snooping to Prevent DHCP Attacks

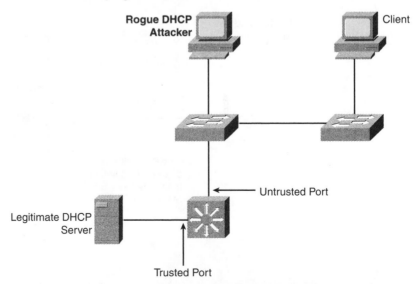

Untrusted ports are those not explicitly configured as trusted. A DHCP binding table is built for untrusted ports. Each entry contains a client MAC address, IP address, lease time, binding type, VLAN number, and port ID recorded as clients make DHCP requests. The table is then used to filter subsequent DHCP traffic. From a DHCP snooping perspective, untrusted access ports should not send any DHCP server responses.

These steps illustrate how to configure DHCP snooping on a Cisco IOS switch:

How To

Step 1. Enable DHCP snooping using the **ip dhcp snooping** global configuration command.

Step 2. Enable DHCP snooping for specific VLANs using the **ip dhcp snooping vlan number** [*number*] command.

Step 3. Define ports as trusted or untrusted at the interface level by defining the trusted ports using the **ip dhcp snooping trust** command.

Step 4. (Optional) Limit the rate at which an attacker can continually send bogus DHCP requests through untrusted ports to the DHCP server using the **ip dhcp snooping limit rate** *rate* command.

CDP Attacks

The ***Cisco Discovery Protocol (CDP)*** is a proprietary protocol that all Cisco devices can be configured to use. CDP discovers other Cisco devices that are directly connected, which allows the devices to autoconfigure their connection in some cases, simplifying configuration and connectivity. CDP messages are not encrypted.

By default, most Cisco devices have CDP enabled. CDP information is sent in periodic broadcasts that are updated locally in each device's CDP database. Because CDP is a Layer 2 protocol, it is not propagated by routers.

CDP contains information about the device, such as the IP address, software version, platform, capabilities, and the native VLAN. When this information is available to an attacker, they can use it to find exploits to attack your network, typically in the form of a Denial of Service (DoS) attack.

Figure 2-24 is a portion of a packet capture showing the inside of a CDP packet. The Cisco IOS Software version discovered via CDP, in particular, would allow the attacker to research and determine whether there were any security vulnerabilities specific to that particular version of code. Also, because CDP is unauthenticated, an attacker could craft bogus CDP packets and have them received by the attacker's directly connected Cisco device.

To address this vulnerability, it is recommended that you disable the use of CDP on devices that do not need to use it.

Figure 2-24 CDP Packet Capture

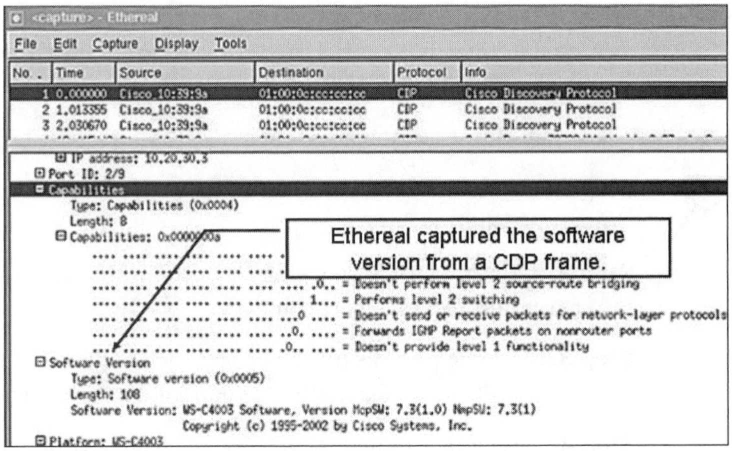

Telnet Attacks

The Telnet protocol can be used by an attacker to gain remote access to a Cisco switch. You have configured a login password for vty lines and set the lines to require password authentication to gain access. This ensures an essential and basic level of security to help protect the switch from unauthorized access. However, it is not a secure method of securing access to the vty lines. There are tools available that allow an attacker to launch a brute-force password-cracking attack against the vty lines on the switch.

The first phase of a brute-force password attack starts with the attacker using a list of common passwords and a program designed to try to establish a Telnet session using each word on the dictionary list. Because your passwords do not resemble any dictionary words, you are safe for now. In the second phase of a brute-force attack, the attacker uses a program that creates sequential character combinations in an attempt to "guess" the password. Given enough time, a brute force password attack can crack almost any passwords used.

The simplest thing that you can do to limit the vulnerability to brute-force password attacks is to change your passwords frequently and use strong passwords, randomly mixing upper and lowercase letters with other alphanumeric characters. More advanced configurations allow you to limit who can communicate with the vty lines by using access lists, but that is beyond the scope of this book.

Another type of Telnet attack is the DoS attack. In a DoS attack, the attacker exploits a flaw in the Telnet server software running on the switch that renders the Telnet service unavailable. This sort of attack is mostly a nuisance because it prevents an administrator from performing switch management functions.

Vulnerabilities in the Telnet service that permit DoS attacks to occur are usually addressed in security patches that are included in newer Cisco IOS revisions. If you are experiencing a

DoS attack against the Telnet service, or any other service on a Cisco device, check to see if a newer Cisco IOS revision is available.

Last, if an attacker uses a MAC flooding attack, for example, by using any packet capture software, the attacker may then capture the Telnet password as you type it.

Security Tools

After you have configured switch security, you need to verify that you have not left any weakness for an attacker to exploit. Network security is a complex and evolving set of technologies. In this section, you are introduced to how network security tools are used to protect a network from malicious attacks.

Network security tools help you to test your network for various weaknesses. They are tools that allow you to play the role of both a hacker and a network security analyst. Using these tools, you can launch an attack and audit the results to determine how to adjust your security policies to prevent specific attacks.

The features used within network security tools are many and varied. For example, network security tools formerly focused only on the services of listening on the network and examined these services for flaws. Today, viruses and worms are able to propagate because of flaws in mail clients and web browsers. Modern network security tools not only detect the remote flaws of the hosts on the network, but also determine whether application-level flaws exist, such as missing patches on client computers. Network security extends beyond network devices, all the way to the desktop of users. Security auditing and penetration testing are two basic functions that network security tools perform.

Network security tools allow you to perform a security audit of your network. A security audit reveals what sort of information an attacker can gather simply by monitoring network traffic. Network security-auditing tools allow you to flood the MAC table with bogus MAC addresses. Then you can audit the switch ports as the switch starts flooding traffic out all ports as the legitimate MAC address mappings are aged out and replaced with more bogus MAC address mappings. In this way, you can determine which ports are compromised and have not been correctly configured to prevent this type of attack.

Timing is an important factor in performing a successful audit. Different switches support varying numbers of MAC addresses in their MAC address tables. It can be tricky to determine the ideal amount of spoofed MAC addresses to throw out on the network. You also have to contend with the age-out period of the MAC table. If the spoofed MAC addresses start to age out while you are performing your network audit, valid MAC addresses start to populate the MAC table, limiting the data that you can monitor with a network-auditing tool.

Network security tools can also be used for penetration testing against your network. This allows you to identify weaknesses within the configuration of your networking devices. There are numerous attacks that you can perform, and most tool suites come with extensive documentation detailing the syntax needed to execute the desired attack. Because these types of tests can have adverse effects on the network, they are carried out under very controlled conditions, following documented procedures detailed in a comprehensive network security policy. Of course, if you have a lab-based network, you can arrange to try your own network penetration tests.

In the next section, you learn how to implement port security on your Cisco switches so that you can ensure these network security tests do not reveal any flaws in your security configuration.

A secure network really is a process, not a product. You cannot just enable a switch with a secure configuration and declare the job to be done. To say you have a secure network, you need to have a comprehensive network security plan defining how to regularly verify that your network can withstand the latest malicious network attacks. The changing landscape of security risks means that you need auditing and penetration tools that can be updated to look for the latest security risks. Common features of a modern network security tool include the following:

- **Service identification:** Tools that are used to target hosts using the Internet Assigned Numbers Authority (IANA) port numbers. These tools should also be able to discover an FTP server running on a nonstandard port or a web server running on port 8080. The tool should also be able to test all the services running on a host.

- **Support of SSL services:** Testing services that use SSL level security, including HTTPS, SMTPS, IMAPS, and security certificates.

- **Nondestructive and destructive testing:** Performing nondestructive security audits on a routine basis that do not compromise or only moderately compromise network performance. The tools should also let you perform destructive audits that significantly degrade network performance. Destructive auditing allows you to see how well your network withstands attacks from intruders.

- **Database of vulnerabilities:** Vulnerabilities change with time.

Network security tools need to be designed so that they can plug into a module of code and then run a test for a specific vulnerability. In this way, a large database of vulnerabilities can be maintained and uploaded to the tool to ensure that the most recent vulnerabilities are being tested.

You can use network security tools to

- Capture chat messages

- Capture files from NFS traffic

- Capture HTTP requests in Common Log Format

- Capture mail messages in Berkeley mbox format

- Capture passwords

- Display captured URLs in browser in real-time

- Flood a switched LAN with random MAC addresses

- Forge replies to DNS address or pointer queries

- Intercept packets on a switched LAN

Configuring Port Security

A switch that does not provide port security allows an attacker to attach a system to an unused, enabled port and to perform information gathering or to launch attacks. A switch can be configured to act like a hub, which means that every system connected to the switch can potentially view all network traffic passing through the switch to all systems connected to the switch. Thus, an attacker could collect traffic that contains usernames, passwords, or configuration information about the systems on the network.

All switch ports or interfaces should be secured before the switch is deployed. Port security limits the number of valid MAC addresses allowed on a port. When you assign secure MAC addresses to a secure port, the port does not forward packets with source addresses outside the group of defined addresses.

If you limit the number of secure MAC addresses to one and assign a single secure MAC address to that port, the workstation attached to that port is assured the full bandwidth of the port, and only that workstation with that particular secure MAC address can successfully communicate through that switch port.

If a port is configured as a secure port and the maximum number of secure MAC addresses is reached, a security violation occurs when the MAC address of a workstation attempting to access the port is different from any of the identified secure MAC addresses. Summarizing, you should implement security on all switch ports to

- Specify a group of valid MAC addresses allowed on a port.

- Allow only one MAC address to access the port at a time.

- Specify that the port automatically shuts down if unauthorized MAC addresses are detected.

There are a number of ways to configure port security. The following describes the ways you can configure port security on a Cisco switch:

- **Static secure MAC addresses:** MAC addresses are manually configured by using the **switchport port-security mac-address** *mac-address* interface configuration command. MAC addresses configured in this way are stored in the address table and are added to the running configuration on the switch.

- **Dynamic secure MAC addresses:** MAC addresses are dynamically learned and stored only in the address table. MAC addresses configured in this way are removed when the switch restarts.

- **Sticky secure MAC addresses:** You can configure a port to dynamically learn MAC addresses and then save these MAC addresses to the running configuration.

Sticky secure MAC addresses have the following characteristics:

- When you enable sticky learning on an interface by using the **switchport port-security mac-address sticky** interface configuration command, the interface converts all the dynamic secure MAC addresses, including those that were dynamically learned before sticky learning was enabled, to sticky secure MAC addresses and adds all sticky secure MAC addresses to the running configuration.

- If you disable sticky learning by using the **no switchport port-security mac-address sticky** interface configuration command, the sticky secure MAC addresses remain part of the running configuration but are removed from the address table. The addresses that were removed can be dynamically reconfigured and added to the address table as dynamic addresses.

- When you configure sticky secure MAC addresses by using the **switchport port-security mac-address sticky** *mac-address* interface configuration command, these addresses are added to the address table and the running configuration. If port security is disabled, the sticky secure MAC addresses remain in the running configuration.

- If you save the sticky secure MAC addresses in the configuration file, when the switch restarts or the interface shuts down, the interface does not need to relearn these addresses. If you do not save the sticky secure addresses, they are lost. If sticky learning is disabled, the sticky secure MAC addresses are converted to dynamic secure addresses and are removed from the running configuration.

- If you disable sticky learning and enter the **switchport port-security mac-address sticky** *mac-address* interface configuration command, an error message appears, and the sticky secure MAC address is not added to the running configuration.

It is a security violation when either of these situations occurs:

- The maximum number of secure MAC addresses have been added to the address table, and a station whose MAC address is not in the address table attempts to access the interface.

- An address learned or configured on one secure interface is seen on another secure interface in the same VLAN.

You can configure the interface for one of three violation modes, based on the action to be taken if a violation occurs.

- **protect:** When the number of secure MAC addresses reaches the limit allowed on the port, packets with unknown source addresses are dropped until you remove a sufficient number of secure MAC addresses or increase the number of maximum allowable addresses. You are not notified that a security violation has occurred.

■ **restrict:** When the number of secure MAC addresses reaches the limit allowed on the port, packets with unknown source addresses are dropped until you remove a sufficient number of secure MAC addresses or increase the number of maximum allowable addresses. In this mode, you are notified that a security violation has occurred. Specifically, an SNMP trap is sent, a syslog message is logged, and the violation counter increments.

■ **shutdown:** In this mode, a port security violation causes the interface to immediately become error-disabled and turns off the port LED. It also sends an SNMP trap, logs a syslog message, and increments the violation counter. When a secure port is in the error-disabled state, you can bring it out of this state by entering the **shutdown** followed by the **no shutdown** interface configuration commands. This is the default mode.

The effect of each mode is summarized in Table 2-15.

Table 2-15   Port Security Violation Modes

Violation Mode	Forwards Traffic	Sends SNMP Trap	Sends Syslog Message	Displays Error Message	Increases Violation Counter	Shuts Down Port
Protect	No	No	No	No	No	No
Restrict	No	Yes	Yes	No	Yes	No
Shutdown	No	Yes	Yes	No	Yes	Yes

The ports on a Catalyst switch are preconfigured with defaults. Table 2-16 summarizes the default port security configuration.

Table 2-16   Port Security Default Settings

Feature	Default Setting
Port security	Disabled on a port.
Maximum number of secure MAC addresses	1
Violation mode	Shutdown. The port shuts down when the maximum number of secure MAC addresses is exceeded, and an SNMP trap notification is sent.
Sticky address learning	Disabled.

Table 2-17 shows the Cisco IOS CLI commands needed to configure port security on the interface F0/18 of switch S1. Notice that the example does not specify a violation mode. In this example, the violation mode defaults to **shutdown**.

Table 2-17   Port Security Command Syntax

Description	Command
Enters global configuration mode.	S1# `configure terminal`
Specifies the type and number of the physical interface to configure—for example, fastEthernet 0/18—and enters interface configuration mode.	S1(config)# `interface fastEthernet 0/18`
Sets the interface mode as access. An interface in the dynamic desirable default mode cannot be configured as a secure port.	S1(config-if)# `switchport mode access`
Enables port security on the interface.	S1(config-if)# `switchport port-security`
Returns to privileged EXEC mode.	S1# `end`

Table 2-18 shows how to enable sticky port security on interface F0/18 of switch S1. Recall that you can configure the maximum number of secure MAC addresses. In this example, you see the Cisco IOS command syntax used to set the maximum number of MAC addresses to 50. The violation mode is again set to **shutdown** by default.

Table 2-18   Port Security Command Syntax with Sticky Addresses

Description	Command
Enters global configuration mode.	S1# `configure terminal`
Specifies the type and number of the physical interface to configure.	S1(config)# `interface fastEthernet 0/18`
Sets the interface mode as access.	S1(config-if)# `switchport mode access`
Enables port security on the interface.	S1(config-if)# `switchport port-security`
Sets the maximum number of secure addresses to 50.	S1(config-if)# `switchport port-security maximum 50`
Enables sticky learning.	S1(config-if)# `switchport port-security mac-address sticky`
Returns to privileged EXEC mode.	S1# `end`

Other port security settings exist that you may find useful. For a complete listing of port security configuration options, visit: cisco.com/en/US/docs/switches/lan/catalyst2950/software/release/12.1_19_ea1/configuration/guide/swtrafc.html#wp1038501.

After you have configured port security for your switch, you should verify that it has been configured correctly. You need to check each interface to verify that you have set the port security correctly. You also have to check to make sure that you have configured any static MAC addresses correctly.

To display port security settings for the switch or for the specified interface, use the **show port-security** [**interface** *interface-id*] command, as illustrated in Example 2-11.

Example 2-11   Verifying Port Security

```
S1# show port-security interface fastEthernet 0/18
Port Security                 :Enabled
Port Status                   :Secure-down
Violation Mode                :Shutdown
Aging Time                    :0 mins
Aging Type                    :Absolute
SecureStatic Address Aging    :Disabled
Maximum MAC Addresses         :1
Total MAC Addresses           :1
Configured MAC Addresses      :0
Sticky MAC Addresses          :0
Last Source Address:Vlan      :0000.0000.0000:0
Security Violation Count      :0
```

The output displays the following:

- Maximum allowed number of secure MAC addresses for each interface

- Number of secure MAC addresses on the interface

- Number of security violations that have occurred

- Violation mode

To display all secure MAC addresses configured on all switch interfaces or on a specified interface with aging information for each, use the **show port-security** [**interface** *interface-id*] **address** command, as illustrated in Example 2-12.

Example 2-12   Verifying Secure MAC Addresses

```
S1# show port-security address
       Secure Mac Address Table
-----------------------------------------------------------------------
Vlan     Mac Address       Type            Ports     Remaining Age (mins)
99       0050.BAA6.06CE    SecureConfigured  Fa0/18    -
-----------------------------------------------------------------------
Total Addresses in System (excluding one mac per port)     : 0
Max Addresses limit in System (excluding one mac per port) : 8320
```

Securing Unused Ports

Securing unused switch ports is a security best practice for switch configuration. Here you learn a simple Cisco IOS command to secure unused switch ports. A method many administrators use to help secure their networks from unauthorized access is to disable all unused ports on a network switch. For example, imagine that a Cisco 2960 switch has 24 ports. If three Fast Ethernet connections are in use, good security practice demands that you disable the 21 unused ports. Example 2-13 shows partial output for this configuration.

Example 2-13   Shutdown Unused Ports

```
interface FastEthernet0/4
 shutdown
!
interface FastEthernet0/5
 shutdown
!
interface FastEthernet0/6
 shutdown
!
<output omitted>
!
interface FastEthernet0/18
 switchport mode access
 switchport port-security
```

It is simple to disable multiple ports on a switch. Navigate to each unused port and issue this Cisco IOS **shutdown** command. A better way to shut down multiple ports is to use the **interface range** command. If a port needs to be activated, you can manually enter the **no shutdown** command on that interface.

The process of enabling and disabling ports can become a tedious task, but the value in terms of enhancing security on your network is well worth the effort. In the next chapter you will also see that it is a security best practice to configure all unused switch ports to be members of a "black hole" VLAN, which is a dummy VLAN that is not used anywhere in the switched LAN.

Packet Tracer
☐ **Activity**

Configure Switch Security (2.4.7)

Use the Packet Tracer Activity to configure basic switch commands and then configure and test port security. Use File e3-2472.pka on the CD-ROM that accompanies this book to perform this activity using Packet Tracer.

Summary

In this chapter, we discussed IEEE 802.3 Ethernet communication using unicast, broadcast, and multicast traffic. Early implementations of Ethernet networks needed to use CSMA/CD to help prevent and detect collisions between frames on the network. Duplex settings and LAN segmentation improve performance and reduce the need for CSMA/CD.

LAN design is a process; the intended result of LAN design is a determination of how a LAN is to be implemented. LAN design considerations include collision domains, broadcast domains, network latency, and LAN segmentation.

We discussed how switch forwarding methods influence LAN performance and latency. Memory buffering plays a role in switch forwarding, symmetric and asymmetric switching, and multilayer switching.

An introduction to navigating the Cisco IOS CLI on a Cisco Catalyst 2960 switch was presented. Built-in help functions are used to identify commands and command options. The Cisco IOS CLI maintains a command history that allows you to more quickly configure repetitive switch functions.

We discussed the initial switch configuration and how to verify the switch configuration. Backing up a switch configuration and restoring a switch configuration are key skills for anyone administering a switch.

We learned how to secure access to the switch: implementing passwords to protect console and virtual terminal lines, implementing passwords to limit access to privileged EXEC mode, configuring password encryption, and enabling SSH. There are a number of security risks common to Cisco Catalyst switches, many of which are mitigated by using port security.

Labs

The labs available in the companion *LAN Switching and Wireless, CCNA Exploration Labs and Study Guide* (ISBN 1-58713-202-8) provide hands-on practice with the following topics introduced in this chapter:

Lab 2-1: Basic Switch Configuration (2.5.1)

In this lab, you examine and configure a standalone LAN switch. Although a switch performs basic functions in its default out-of-the-box condition, a network administrator should modify a number of parameters to ensure a secure and optimized LAN. This activity introduces you to the basics of switch configuration.

Lab 2-2: Managing Switch Operating System and Configuration Files (2.5.2)

In this lab, you create and save a basic switch configuration, set up a TFTP server, back up the switch Cisco IOS Software to the TFTP server and restore it, back up and restore a switch configuration to the TFTP server, upgrade the Cisco IOS Software from a TFTP server, and recover the password for a 2960 switch.

Lab 2-3: Managing Switch Operating System and Configuration Files—Challenge (2.5.3)

In this lab, you explore file management and password recovery procedures on a Cisco Catalyst switch.

Many of the hands-on labs include Packet Tracer Companion Activities, where you can use Packet Tracer to complete a simulation of the lab. Look for this icon in *LAN Switching and Wireless, CCNA Exploration Labs and Study Guide* (ISBN 1-58713-202-8) for hands-on labs that have a Packet Tracer Companion.

Check Your Understanding

Complete all the review questions listed here to test your understanding of the topics and concepts in this chapter. Answers are listed in the Appendix, "Check Your Understanding and Challenge Questions Answer Key."

1. What does the following error message signify?

   ```
   R2# clock set 19:56:00 04 8
                           ^
   % Invalid input detected at '^' marker
   ```

   A. A parameter is missing.

   B. The command was entered in the wrong CLI mode.

   C. The data of one of the parameters is incorrect.

   D. The command is ambiguous.

2. What is the effect of entering the **banner login #Authorized Personnel Only!#** command?

   A. **#Authorized Personnel Only!** appears after the user logs in.

   B. **Authorized Personnel Only!** appears only when the user makes a Telnet connection.

   C. **#Authorized Personnel Only!#** appears only when the user enters global configuration mode.

   D. **Authorized Personnel Only!** appears before the username and password login prompts for any connection.

3. Which three options correctly associate the command with the paired behavior? (Choose three.)

   A. **switchport port-security violation protect**: Frames with unknown source addresses are dropped and a notification is sent.

   B. **switchport port-security violation restrict:** Frames with unknown source addresses are dropped and no notification is sent.

   C. **switchport port-security violation shutdown:** Frames with unknown source addresses result in the port becoming error-disabled and a notification is sent.

   D. **switchport port-security mac-address sticky:** Allows dynamically learned MAC addresses to be stored in the running-configuration.

   E. **switchport port-security maximum:** Defines the number of MAC addresses associated with a port.

4. Refer to Figure 2-25. An Ethernet switch has built the MAC address table shown. What action will the switch take when it receives the frame shown at the bottom of the exhibit?

Figure 2-25 MAC Address Table

Station	Interface1	Interface2	Interface3	Interface4
00-00-3D-1F-11-01			X	
00-00-3D-1F-11-02				X
00-00-3D-1F-11-03	X			

Destination	Source	Data	CRC
00-00-3D-1F-11-03	00-00-3D-1F-11-01		

   A. Forward the frame out all interfaces.

   B. Forward the frame out all interfaces except Interface3.

   C. Discard the frame.

   D. Forward the frame out Interface1.

   E. Forward the frame out Interface2.

   F. Forward the frame out Interface3.

5. What can be determined from the following command output?

```
Switch# show version
<output omitted>
Compiled Wed 18-May-07 22:31
<output omitted>
Running Standard Image
```

```
24 FastEthernet/IEEE 802.3 interface(s)
2 Gigabit Ethernet/IEEE 802.3 interface(s)

32K bytes of flash-simulated non-volatile configuration memory.
<output omitted>
```

A. The system has 32 KB of NVRAM.

B. The switch has 24 physical ports

C. The system was last restarted on May 18, 2005.

D. The Cisco IOS is a nonstandard image.

6. What advantage does SSH offer over Telnet when remotely connecting to a device?

A. Encryption

B. More connection lines

C. Connection-oriented services

D. Username and password authentication

7. Refer to Figure 2-26. How many collision and broadcast domains are displayed in the network?

Figure 2-26 Collision and Broadcast Domains

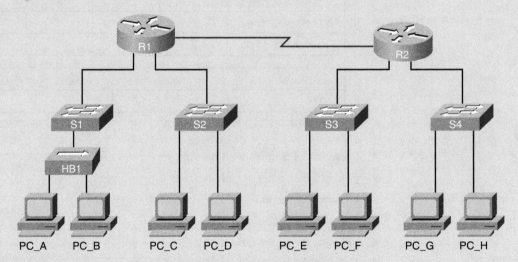

A. 8 collision, 2 broadcast

B. 8 collision, 3 broadcast

C. 11 collision, 4 broadcast

D. 13 collision, 2 broadcast

8. Which option correctly associates the Layer 2 security attack with the description?

   A. **MAC address flooding:** Broadcast requests for IP addresses with spoofed MAC addresses.

   B. **DHCP starvation**: Using proprietary Cisco protocols to gain information about a switch.

   C. **CDP attack:** The attacker fills the switch MAC address table with invalid MAC addresses.

   D. **Telnet attack**: Using brute force password attacks to gain access to a switch.

9. Which three statements are true about the CSMA/CD access method? (Choose three.)

   A. In an Ethernet LAN, each station continuously listens for traffic on the medium to determine when gaps between frame transmissions occur and then sends the frame.

   B. In an Ethernet LAN, stations may begin transmitting anytime they detect that the network is quiet (there is no traffic).

   C. In the CSMA/CD process, priorities are assigned to particular stations, and the station with the highest priority transmits frames on the medium.

   D. If a collision occurs in an Ethernet LAN, transmitting stations stop transmitting and wait a random length of time before attempting to retransmit the frame.

   E. If a collision occurs in an Ethernet LAN, only the station with the highest priority continues to transmit, and the rest of the stations wait a random length of time before attempting to retransmit the frame.

   F. In an Ethernet LAN, all stations execute a backoff algorithm based on their assigned priorities before they transmit frames on the medium.

10. How does the Ethernet switch process the incoming traffic using port-based memory buffering?

    A. The frames are stored in queues that are linked to specific incoming ports.

    B. The frames are stored in queues that are linked to specific outgoing ports.

    C. The frames are transmitted to the outgoing port immediately.

    D. The frames are stored in queues that are linked to the common memory area.

11. What are two key features of an Ethernet switch with Layer 2 capabilities? (Choose two.)

    A. Full-duplex operation

    B. Broadcast and multicast traffic management

    C. Security through access lists

    D. Layer 3 routing functions

    E. Filtering based on MAC address

    F. Network address translation (NAT)

12. The network administrator wants to configure an IP address on a Cisco switch. How does the network administrator assign the IP address?

A. In privileged EXEC mode

B. On the switch interface FastEthernet0/0

C. On the management VLAN

D. On the physical interface connected to the router or next-hop device

13. Why should a default gateway be assigned to a switch?

A. So that there can be remote connectivity to the switch via such programs as Telnet and ping

B. So that frames can be sent through the switch to the router

C. So that frames generated from workstations and destined for remote networks can pass to a higher level

D. So that other networks can be accessed from the command prompt of the switch

14. Which two tasks does autonegotiation in an Ethernet network accomplish? (Choose two.)

A. Sets the link speed

B. Sets the IP address

C. Sets the link duplex mode

D. Sets MAC address assignments on switch port

E. Sets the ring speed

15. What is the effect of entering the SW1(config-if)# **duplex full** command on a Fast Ethernet switch port?

A. The connected device communicates in two directions, but only one direction at a time.

B. The switch port returns to its default configuration.

C. If the connected device is also set for full duplex, it participates in collision-free communication.

D. The efficiency of this configuration is typically rated at 50 to 60 percent.

E. The connected device should be configured as half duplex.

16. Which term describes the time delay between a frame being sent from a source device and received on a destination device?

A. Bandwidth

B. Latency

C. Attenuation

D. Time-to-live

E. Frame check sequence

17. Which option correctly associates the command with the description?

    A. **copy startup-config running-config:** Copy the current running configuration to a TFTP server.

    B. **copy running-config tftp:** Save the current running configuration as the startup configuration.

    C. **copy tftp startup-config:** Restore a configuration from a TFTP server to the running configuration.

    D. **copy tftp running-config:** Restore the startup configuration to the running system.

    E. **copy startup-config tftp:** Restore the configuration from a TFTP server to the startup configuration.

    F. **copy running-config startup config:** Save the current running configuration to the startup configuration

18. Which three options correctly associate the command with the description? (Choose three.)

    A. **enable:** Enter the global configuration mode.

    B. **configure terminal:** Enter configuration mode for the console line.

    C. **line vty 0 15:** Set a password.

    D. **line console 0:** Enter configuration mode for the console line.

    E. **password cisco:** Set a password.

    F. **username admin password cisco:** Enable AAA.

    G. **login:** Permit login.

Challenge Questions and Activities

Complete all the review questions listed here to test your understanding of the topics and concepts in this chapter. Answers are listed in the Appendix, "Check Your Understanding and Challenge Questions Answer Key."

1. Refer to Figure 2-27. There are six steps in the process of a switch learning a MAC address for the purposes of forwarding Ethernet frames. Put the following six steps in order by placing the appropriate number in the blank.

Figure 2-27 Learning MAC Addresses

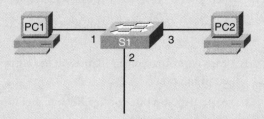

_____The intended destination device replies to the broadcast with a unicast frame addressed to PC 1.

_____The switch enters the source MAC address and the switch port that received the frame into the address table.

_____The switch enters the source MAC address of PC 2 and the port number of the switch port that received the frame into the address table. The destination address of the frame and its associated port is found in the MAC address table.

_____The switch can now forward frames between source and destination devices without flooding, because it has entries in the address table that identify the associated ports.

_____Because the destination address is a broadcast, the switch floods the frame to all ports, except the port on which it received the frame.

_____The switch receives an ARP broadcast frame from PC 1 on Port 1.

2. List the two principal switch forwarding methods and the two primary methods of memory buffering in switches.

_____

_____

3. From the following output, what is the likely reason for interface VLAN 99 displaying "up/down" as its status?

```
S1# show running-config
<output omitted>
!
interface FastEthernet0/18
 switchport access vlan 99
 switchport mode access
<output omitted>
!
interface Vlan99
 ip address 172.17.99.11 255.255.255.0
 no ip route-cache
```

```
!
<output omitted>
S1# show ip interface brief
Interface              IP-Address       OK? Method Status        Protocol
<output omitted>
Vlan99                 172.17.99.11     YES NVRAM  up            up
<output omitted>
FastEthernet0/18       unassigned       YES unset  down          down
FastEthernet0/19       unassigned       YES unset  down          down
<output omitted>
GigabitEthernet0/2     unassigned       YES unset  down          down
```

_____

_____

4. From the following configuration, which two commands are unnecessary for a basic SSH configuration providing remote access for SSH clients? (Choose two.)

```
Switch(config)# ip domain-name mydomain.com
Switch(config)# crypto key generate rsa
Switch(config)# ip ssh version 2
Switch(config)# line vty 0 15
Switch(config-if)# transport input ssh
```

_____

_____

5. List and describe the three port security violation modes.

_____

_____

_____

_____

_____

_____

_____

_____

Packet Tracer
☐ Challenge

Look for this icon in *LAN Switching and Wireless, CCNA Exploration Labs and Study Guide* (ISBN 1-58713-202-8) for instructions on how to perform the Packet Tracer Skills Integration Challenge for this chapter.

CHAPTER 3

VLANs

Objectives

Upon completion of this chapter, you will be able to answer the following questions:

- What is the role of a VLAN in a switched LAN?

- What is the role of a VLAN trunk in a switched LAN?

- How do you configured VLANs on switches in a switched LAN?

- How do you troubleshoot common software and hardware configuration problems associated with VLANs in a switched LAN?

Key Terms

This chapter uses the following key terms. You can find the definitions in the Glossary.

Network performance can be a factor in an organization's productivity and its reputation for delivering as promised. One of the technologies contributing to excellent network performance is the separation of large broadcast domains into smaller ones with VLANs. Smaller broadcast domains limit the number of devices participating in broadcasts and allow devices to be separated into functional groups, such as database services for an accounting department and high-speed data transfer for an engineering department. In this chapter, you learn how to configure, manage, and troubleshoot VLANs and Ethernet trunk links.

Introducing VLANs

Switches and VLANs go together—you cannot have one without the other. Although it is possible to configure a modern switch to have only one VLAN, normally a switch will have two or more VLANs. VLANs give network administrators flexibility in LAN design. VLANs extend the traditional router-bounded broadcast domain to a VLAN-bounded broadcast domain; VLANs make it possible to sculpt a broadcast domain into any shape that can be defined and bounded by the switches within the network. In this section, you learn what the different types of VLANs are and how to configure them and extend them using Ethernet trunks. First you explore the historical implementation of VLANs versus the modern implementation.

Defining VLANs

To appreciate why VLANs are being widely used today, consider a small university with student dorms and faculty offices all in one building. Figure 3-1 shows the student computers in one LAN and the faculty computers in another LAN. This works fine because each department is physically together, so it is easy to provide them with their network resources.

Figure 3-1   Before VLANs—One Building

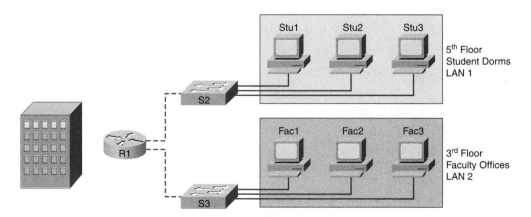

A year later, the university has grown and now has three buildings. In Figure 3-2, the original network is the same, but student and faculty computers are spread out across three buildings. The student dorms remain on the fifth floor and the faculty offices remain on the third floor. However, now the IT department wants to ensure that student computers all share the same security features and bandwidth controls. How can the network accommodate the shared needs of the geographically separated departments? Do you create a large LAN and wire each department together? How easy would it be to make changes to that network? It would be nice to be able to group the people with the resources they use regardless of their geographic location, and it would make it easier to manage their specific security and bandwidth requirements.

Figure 3-2   Before VLANs—Three Buildings

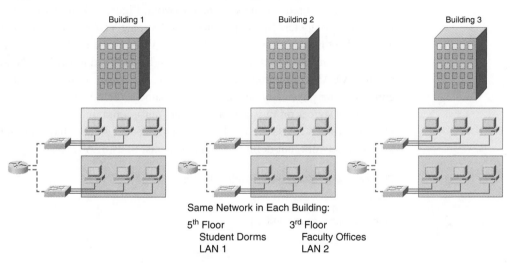

The solution for the university is to use a networking technology called a virtual LAN (VLAN). A VLAN allows a network administrator to create groups of logically networked devices that act as if they are on their own independent network, even if they share a common infrastructure with other VLANs. When you configure a VLAN, you can name it to describe the primary role of the users for that VLAN. As another example, all the student computers in a university can be configured in the "Student" VLAN. Using VLANs, you can logically segment switched networks based on functions, departments, or project teams. You can also use a VLAN to geographically structure your network to support the growing reliance of companies on home-based workers. In Figure 3-3, one VLAN is created for students and another for faculty. These VLANs allow the network administrator to implement access and security policies to particular groups of users. For example, the faculty, but not the students, can be allowed access to e-learning management servers for developing online course materials.

Figure 3-3   After VLANs—Three Buildings

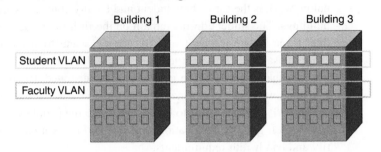

A VLAN is a logically separate IP subnetwork. VLANs allow multiple IP networks and subnets to exist on the same switched network. Figure 3-4 shows a network with three computers. For computers to communicate on the same VLAN, each must have an IP address and a subnet mask that is consistent for that VLAN. The switch has to be configured with the VLAN, and each port in the VLAN must be assigned to the VLAN. A switch port with a singular VLAN configured on it is called an access port. Remember that just because two computers are physically connected to the same switch does not mean that they can communicate. Devices on two separate subnets must communicate via a router (Layer 3), whether or not VLANs are used. You do not need VLANs to have multiple subnets on a switched network, but definite advantages exist to using VLANs.

Figure 3-4   Switches Define VLANs

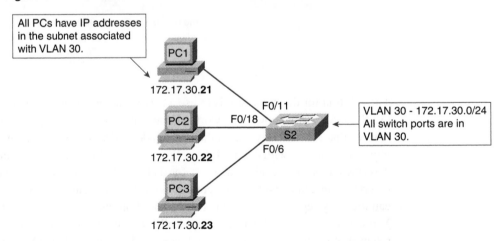

Benefits of VLANs

User productivity and network adaptability are key drivers for business growth and success. Implementing VLAN technology enables a network to more flexibly support business goals. The primary benefits of using VLANs are the following:

- **Security:** Groups that have sensitive data are separated from the rest of the network, decreasing the chances of confidential information breaches. Faculty computers are on VLAN 10 and completely separated from student and guest data traffic.

- **Cost reduction:** Cost savings result from less need for expensive network upgrades and more efficient use of existing bandwidth and uplinks.

- **Higher performance:** Dividing flat Layer 2 networks into multiple logical workgroups (broadcast domains) reduces unnecessary traffic on the network and boosts performance.

- **Broadcast storm mitigation:** Dividing a network into VLANs reduces the number of devices that may participate in a broadcast storm. LAN segmentation prevents a broadcast storm from propagating throughout the entire network. In Figure 3-5, you can see three broadcast domains: Faculty, Student, and Guest.

- **Improved IT staff efficiency:** VLANs make it easier to manage the network because users with similar network requirements share the same VLAN. When you provision a new switch, all the policies and procedures already configured for the particular VLAN are implemented when the ports are assigned. It is also easy for the IT staff to identify the function of a VLAN by giving it an appropriate name. In Figure 3-5, for easy identification VLAN 10 is Faculty, VLAN 20 is Student, and VLAN 30 is Guest.

Figure 3-5 Naming VLANs

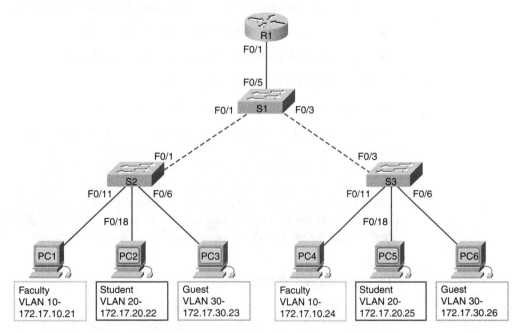

- **Simpler project or application management:** VLANs aggregate users and network devices to support business or geographic requirements. Having separate functions makes managing a project or working with a specialized application easier—for example, e-learning development software for faculty. VLANs also ease the determination of the effects of upgrading network services.

VLAN ID Ranges

VLANs are divided numerically into a normal range and an extended range. Normal range VLANs are characterized as follows:

- Used in small- and medium-sized business and enterprise networks.

- Identified by a VLAN ID between 1 and 1005.

- IDs 1002 through 1005 are reserved for Token Ring and FDDI VLANs.

- IDs 1 and 1002 to 1005 are automatically created and cannot be removed. You learn more about VLAN 1 later in this chapter.

- Configurations are stored within a VLAN database file, called *vlan.dat*. The vlan.dat file is located in the *Flash* memory of the switch.

- The *VLAN trunking protocol (VTP)*, which helps manage VLAN configurations between switches, can learn only normal range VLANs and stores them in the VLAN database file.

Extended range VLANs are characterized as follows:

- Enable service providers to extend their infrastructure to a greater number of customers. Some global enterprises could be large enough to need extended-range VLAN IDs.

- Are identified by a VLAN ID between 1006 and 4094.

- Support fewer VLAN features than normal range VLANs.

- Are saved in the running configuration file.

- VTP does not learn extended range VLANs.

One Cisco Catalyst 2960 switch can support up to a combination of 255 VLANs among the collection of both normal and extended range VLANs. The number of VLANs configured affects the performance of the switch hardware. Because an enterprise network may need a switch with a lot of ports, Cisco has developed enterprise-level switches that can be clustered or stacked together to create a single switching unit. For example, nine switches with 48 ports can be clustered to operate as a single switching unit with 432 ports. In this case, the 255 VLAN limit per single switch may be a constraint for some enterprise customers.

Types of VLANs

Today there is essentially one way of implementing VLANs: port-based VLANs. With a port-based VLAN, a VLAN is associated with a set of switch ports in the broadcast domain. The ports that are associated with a port-based VLAN are called access ports. In a sense, a VLAN is defined by the access ports assigned to it.

Among the (port-based) VLANs are a number of types of VLANs. Some VLAN types are defined by the type of traffic they support; others are defined by the specific functions they perform. The principal VLAN types are data VLANs, the default VLAN, the black hole VLAN, native VLANs, management VLANs, and voice VLANs.

Because switches will be carrying traffic associated with several VLANs, ports connecting to other switches are used to carry traffic for more than one VLAN; these are called trunk ports. Figure 3-6 shows trunk links between switches. A detailed discussion of trunks is developed in the next section.

A *data VLAN* is a VLAN that is configured to carry only user-generated traffic. Typically, multiple data VLANs populate a switched infrastructure. A VLAN could carry voice-based traffic or traffic used to manage the switch, but this traffic would not be part of a data VLAN. It is common practice to separate voice and management traffic from data traffic. The importance of separating user data from switch management traffic and voice traffic is highlighted by the use of a special term used to identify VLANs that carry only user data— a data VLAN. A data VLAN is sometimes called a user VLAN. Figure 3-6 illustrates the portion of a network covered by user VLANs.

Figure 3-6   Data VLANs

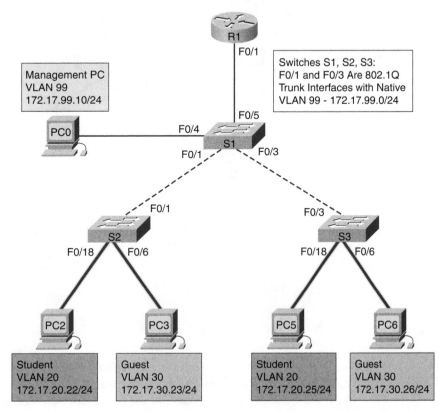

The *default VLAN* is the VLAN that all the ports on a switch are members of when a switch is reset to factory defaults. All switch ports are members of the default VLAN after the initial boot of the switch. If all the switch ports are members of the default VLAN, they are all part of the same broadcast domain; this allows any device connected to any switch port to communicate with any device on any other switch port. The default VLAN for Cisco switches is VLAN 1. VLAN 1 has all the features of any VLAN, except that you cannot rename it and you cannot delete it. Layer 2 control traffic, such as CDP and Spanning Tree Protocol traffic, will always be associated with VLAN 1—this cannot be changed. It is a security best practice to restrict VLAN 1 to serve as a conduit only for Layer 2 control traffic, supporting no other traffic. In Figure 3-7, VLAN 1 traffic is forwarded over the VLAN trunks connecting interfaces F0/1 and F0/3 on the S1, S2, and S3 switches. VLAN trunks support the transmission of traffic from more than one VLAN. Although VLAN trunks are mentioned in this section, they are formally introduced in the next section, "VLAN Trunking."

Figure 3-7   VLAN 1—Default VLAN on Catalyst Switches

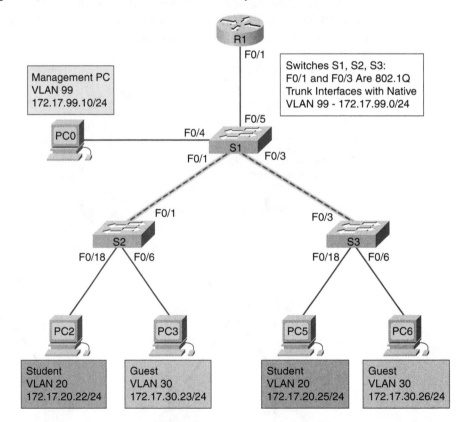

Some network administrators use the term *default VLAN* to mean a VLAN other than VLAN 1 defined by the network administrator as the VLAN that all ports are assigned to when they are not in use. We introduce the term *black hole VLAN* to distinguish this VLAN from the default VLAN. The default VLAN is intrinsic to the switch out-of-the-box; it is

VLAN 1 on Cisco switches. The black hole VLAN is defined by the switch administrator. It is a security best practice to define a black hole VLAN to be a dummy VLAN distinct from *all* other VLANs defined in the switched LAN. All unused switch ports are assigned to the black hole VLAN so that any device connecting to an unused switch port will be assigned to the black hole VLAN. Any traffic associated with the black hole VLAN is not allowed on trunk links, thus preventing any device associated with the black hole VLAN from communicating beyond the switch to which it is connected.

A *native VLAN* is assigned to an 802.1Q trunk port. An *IEEE 802.1Q* trunk port supports traffic coming from many VLANs (tagged traffic) as well as traffic that does not come from a VLAN (untagged traffic). The 802.1Q trunk port places untagged traffic on the native VLAN. In Figure 3-8, the native VLAN is VLAN 99. Untagged traffic is generated by a computer attached to a switch port that is configured with the native VLAN. Native VLANs are set out in the IEEE 802.1Q specification to maintain backward compatibility with untagged traffic common to legacy LAN scenarios. For our purposes, a native VLAN serves as a common identifier on opposing ends of a trunk link. It is a security best practice to define a native VLAN to be a dummy VLAN distinct from all other VLANs defined in the switched LAN. The native VLAN is not used for any traffic in the switched network unless legacy bridging devices happen to be present in the network, or a multiaccess interconnection exists between switches joined by a hub (not likely in a modern network).

Figure 3-8   Native VLAN

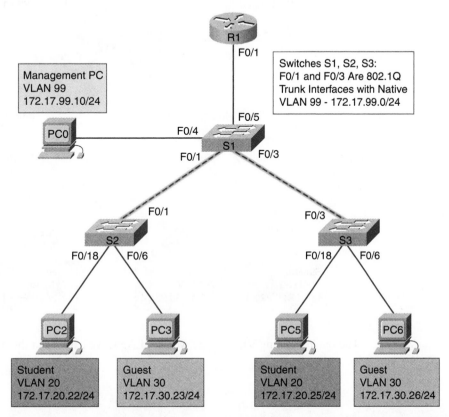

A *management VLAN* is a VLAN defined by the switch administrator as a means to access the management capabilities of a switch. VLAN 1 would serve as the management VLAN if you did not proactively define a unique VLAN to serve as the management VLAN. You assign the management VLAN an IP address and subnet mask. A switch can be managed via HTTP, Telnet, SSH, or SNMP. Because the out-of-the-box configuration of a Catalyst switch has VLAN 1 as the default VLAN, you see that VLAN 1 or the black hole VLAN would be a bad choice as the management VLAN; you wouldn't want an arbitrary user connecting to a switch to default to the management VLAN. It is a security best practice to define the management VLAN to be a VLAN distinct from all other VLANs defined in the switched LAN. For simplicity, because of the 24-port limitation of the Catalyst 2960 switches that we reference in Packet Tracer activities, labs, and illustrative examples, for our purposes in this book we use VLAN 99 for both the management VLAN and the native VLAN. A management VLAN is depicted in Figure 3-9.

Figure 3-9   Management VLAN

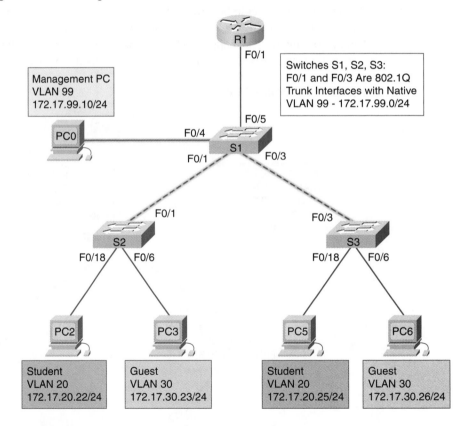

The one remaining VLAN type, voice VLANs, we explore in the next section.

Voice VLANs

It is easy to appreciate why a separate VLAN is needed to support Voice over IP (VoIP). Imagine that you are receiving an emergency call and suddenly the quality of the transmission degrades so much you cannot understand what the caller is saying. VoIP traffic requires the following:

- Assured bandwidth to ensure voice quality

- Transmission priority over other types of network traffic

- Ability to be routed around congested areas on the network

- Delay of less than 150 milliseconds (ms) across the network

To meet these requirements, the entire network has to be designed to support VoIP. The details of how to configure a network to support VoIP are beyond the scope of this book, but it is useful to summarize how a *voice VLAN* works between a Catalyst switch, a Cisco IP phone, and a computer.

In Figure 3-10, VLAN 150 is designed to carry voice traffic. The student computer, PC5, is attached to the Cisco IP phone, and the phone is attached to switch S3. PC5 is in VLAN 20, which is used for student data. The F0/18 port on S3 is configured as an access port with the voice VLAN feature enabled; as such, the switch uses CDP to instruct the phone to tag voice frames with VLAN 150.

Figure 3-10   Voice VLANs

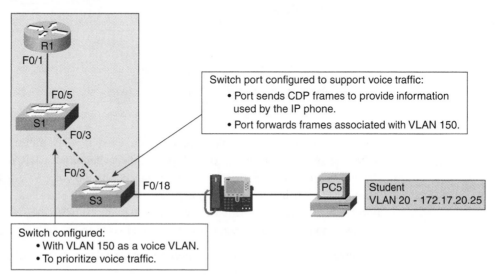

Note

Communication between the switch and IP phone is facilitated by the CDP protocol. This protocol is discussed in greater detail in the *Routing Protocols and Concepts CCNA Exploration Companion Guide.*

Data frames coming through the Cisco IP phone from PC5 are left untagged. Data destined for PC5 coming from port F0/18 is tagged with VLAN 20 on the way to the phone, which strips the VLAN tag before the data is forwarded to PC5. Tagging refers to the addition of VLAN information to a field in the data frame that is used by the switch to identify which VLAN the data frame should be sent to. You learn later about how data frames are tagged.

The Cisco IP phone contains an integrated three-port 10/100 switch, as shown in Figure 3-11. The ports provide dedicated connections to these devices:

- Port 1 connects to the switch or other VoIP device.

- Port 2 is an internal 10/100 interface that carries the IP phone traffic.

- Port 3 (access port) connects to a PC or other device.

Figure 3-11   Cisco IP Phone Integrated Switch

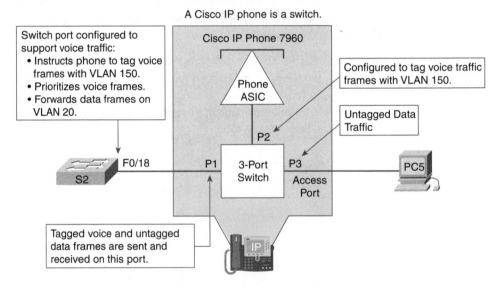

The voice VLAN feature enables switch ports to carry IP voice traffic from an IP phone. When the switch is connected to an IP phone, the switch sends CDP messages that instruct the attached IP phone to send voice traffic tagged with the voice VLAN ID 150. The traffic from the PC attached to the IP phone passes through the IP phone untagged. When the switch port has been configured with a voice VLAN, the link between the switch and the IP phone acts as a modified trunk to carry both the tagged voice traffic and untagged data traffic.

Example 3-1 shows sample switch port output associated with an IP phone-connected port.

Example 3-1 Voice VLAN Output

```
S3# show interfaces f0/18 switchport
Name: Fa0/18
Switchport: Enabled
Administrative Mode: static access
Operational Mode: down
Administrative Trunking Encapsulation: dot1q
Negotiation of Trunking: Off
Access Mode VLAN: 20 (VLAN0020)
Trunking Native Mode VLAN: 1 (default)
Administrative Native VLAN tagging: enabled
Voice VLAN: 150 (VLAN0150)
<output omitted>
Operational private-vlan: none
Trunking VLANs Enabled: ALL
Pruning VLANs Enabled: 2-1001
Capture Mode Disabled
Capture VLANs Allowed: ALL
```

A discussion of the voice-related Cisco IOS commands is beyond the scope of this book, but you can see that the highlighted areas in the sample output show the F0/18 interface configured with a VLAN configured for data (VLAN 20) and a VLAN configured for voice (VLAN 150).

Network Application Traffic Types

In *CCNA Exploration: Network Fundamentals*, you learned about the different kinds of traffic a LAN handles. Because a VLAN has all the characteristics of a LAN, a VLAN must accommodate the same network traffic as a LAN. This includes network management traffic, control traffic, IP telephony traffic, multicast traffic, normal data traffic, and scavenger class traffic.

Many types of network management and control traffic can be present on the network, such as CDP messaging, Simple Network Management Protocol (SNMP) traffic, and Remote Network Monitoring (RMON) traffic. Network management traffic is pictured in Figure 3-12.

IP telephony traffic consists of *signaling traffic* and voice traffic. Signaling traffic is responsible for call setup, progress, and teardown. The other type of telephony traffic consists of the actual voice conversation, illustrated in Figure 3-13. As you just learned, in a network configured with VLANs, it is strongly recommended that you assign a VLAN distinct from all other VLANs as the management VLAN. Data traffic should be associated with a data VLAN (other than VLAN 1), and voice traffic should be associated with a voice VLAN.

Figure 3-12   Network Management Traffic

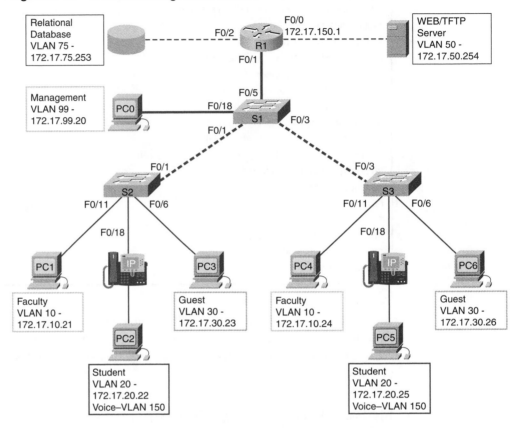

IP multicast traffic is sent from a particular source address to a multicast group that is identified by a single IP address representing a set of receivers configured with that multicast IP address. You learn in multicast theory how multicast MAC addresses are mapped to multicast IP addresses. An example of an application that generates this type of traffic is a Cisco IP/TV broadcast. Multicast traffic can produce a large amount of data streaming across the network. When the network must support multicast traffic, VLANs should be configured to ensure that multicast traffic goes only to those user devices that use the service provided, such as remote video or audio applications. Routers must be configured to ensure that multicast traffic is forwarded strictly to the network areas where it is requested. Figure 3-14 illustrates sample multicast traffic flow.

Normal data traffic is related to file creation and storage, print services, e-mail database access, and other shared network applications that are common to business uses. Figure 3-15 shows sample data traffic flow. VLANs are a natural solution for this type of traffic because you can segment users by their functions or geographic area to more easily manage their specific needs.

Figure 3-13 IP Telephony Traffic

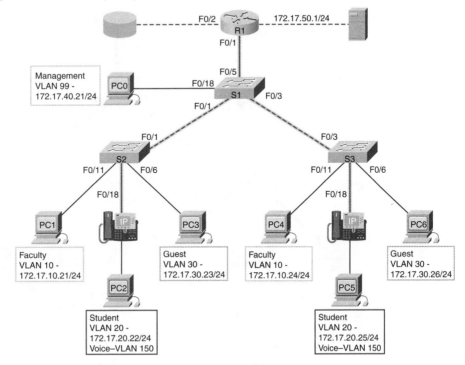

Figure 3-14 IP Multicast Traffic

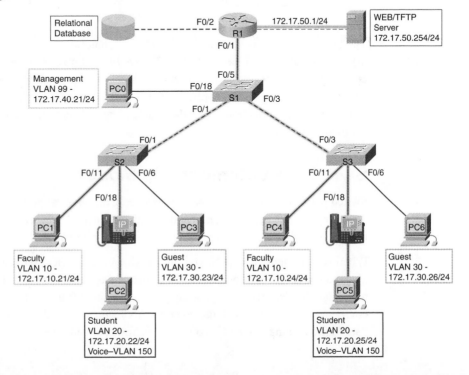

Figure 3-15   Normal Data Traffic

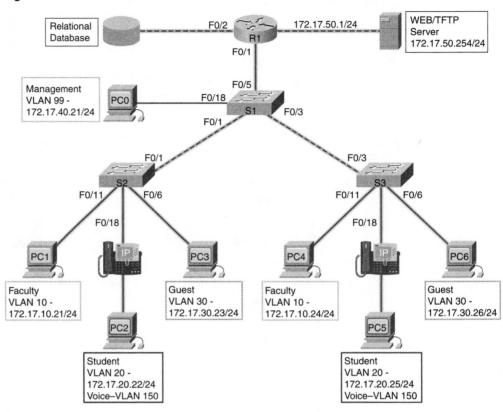

The Scavenger class is intended to provide less-than-best-effort services to certain applications. Applications assigned to this class have little or no contribution to the organizational objectives of the enterprise and are typically entertainment oriented in nature. These include peer-to-peer media-sharing applications (Kazaa, Morpheus, Grokster, Napster, iMesh, and so on), gaming applications (DOOM, Quake, Unreal Tournament, and the like), and any entertainment video applications.

Switch Port Membership Modes

Switch ports are Layer 2 interfaces associated with physical ports. Switch ports are used for managing the physical interfaces and associated Layer 2 protocols. They do not handle routing or bridging. Switch ports belong to one or more VLANs.

When you configure a VLAN, you must assign it a numerical ID, and you can optionally give it a name. The purpose of VLAN implementations is to judiciously associate ports with particular VLANs. You configure the port to forward a frame to a specific VLAN. You can configure a switch port with the voice VLAN feature enabled so as to support both voice and data traffic coming from a Cisco IP phone. You can configure a port to belong to a VLAN by assigning a membership mode that specifies the kind of traffic the port carries and the VLANs to which it belongs. A port can be configured to support these VLAN options:

- *Static VLAN:* Ports on a switch are manually assigned to a VLAN. Static VLANs are configured using the Cisco CLI. This can also be accomplished with GUI management applications, such as the Cisco Network Assistant. However, a convenient feature of the CLI is that if you assign an interface to a VLAN that does not exist, the new VLAN is created for you. Example 3-2 illustrates a sample static VLAN configuration.

Example 3-2 Static VLAN Configuration

```
S3# configure terminal
Enter configuration commands, one per line. End with CNTL/Z.
S3(config)# interface fastEthernet 0/18
S3(config-if)# switchport mode access
S3(config-if)# switchport access vlan 20
S3(config-if)# end
```

- *Dynamic VLAN:* This option is not widely used in production networks and is not explored in this book. However, it is useful to know what a dynamic VLAN is. Dynamic port VLAN membership is configured using a special server called a VLAN Membership Policy Server (VMPS). With VMPS, you assign switch ports to VLANs dynamically, based on the source MAC address of the device connected to the port. The benefit comes when you move a host from a port on one switch in the network to a port on another switch in the network; the switch dynamically assigns the new port to the proper VLAN for that host. A sample dynamic VLAN implementation is pictured in Figure 3-16.

Figure 3-16   Dynamic VLANs

- **Voice VLAN:** A port is configured with the voice VLAN feature enabled so that it can support an IP phone attached to it. To configure voice support on the port, you need to configure a VLAN for voice and a VLAN for data. In Example 3-3, VLAN 150 is the voice VLAN, and VLAN 20 is the data VLAN. Assume that the network has been configured to ensure that voice traffic can be transmitted with a priority status over the network. When a phone is first plugged into a switch port with voice support enabled, the switch port sends messages to the phone, providing the phone with the appropriate voice VLAN ID and configuration. The IP phone tags the voice frames with the voice VLAN ID and forwards all voice traffic through the voice VLAN.

Example 3-3 Voice VLAN Configuration

```
S3# configure terminal
Enter configuration commands, one per line.  End with CNTL/Z.
S3(config)# interface fastEthernet 0/18
S3(config-if)# mls qos trust cos
S3(config-if)# switchport voice vlan 150
S3(config-if)# switchport mode access
S3(config-if)# switchport access vlan 20
S3(config-if)# end
S3# show interfaces fa0/18 switchport
Name: Fa0/18
Switchport: Enabled
Administrative Mode: static access
Operational Mode: down
Administrative Trunking Encapsulation: dot1q
Negotiation of Trunking: Off
Access Mode VLAN: 20 (VLAN0020)
Trunking Native Mode VLAN: 1 (default)
Administrative Native VLAN tagging: enabled
Voice VLAN: 150 (VLAN0150)
<output omitted>
```

The switch port configuration supporting voice and data has the following characteristics:

- The configuration command **mls qos trust cos** ensures that voice traffic is identified as priority traffic. Remember that the entire network must be set up to prioritize voice traffic. You cannot just configure the port with this command.

- The **switchport voice vlan 150** command identifies VLAN 150 as the voice VLAN. You can see this highlighted in the example: **Voice VLAN: 150 (VLAN0150)**.

- The **switchport access vlan 20** command configures VLAN 20 as the access mode (data) VLAN. You can see this highlighted in the example: **Access Mode VLAN: 20 (VLAN0020)**.

For more details about configuring a voice VLAN, visit this Cisco.com site:

www.cisco.com/en/US/products/ps6406/products_configuration_guide_chapter09186a0080 81d9a6.html#wp1050913.

Controlling Broadcast Domains with VLANs

In normal operation, when a switch receives a broadcast frame on one of its ports, it forwards the frame out all other ports on the switch. In Figure 3-17, the entire network is configured in the same subnet, 172.17.40.0/24. As a result, when the faculty computer, PC1, sends out a broadcast frame, switch S2 sends that broadcast frame out all of its ports. Eventually the entire network receives it; the network is one broadcast domain.

Figure 3-17   Single VLAN

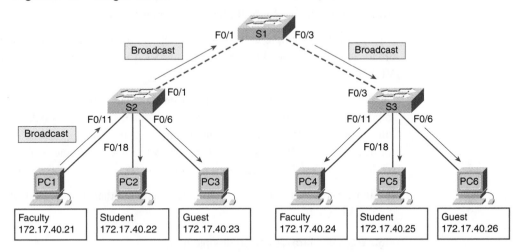

In Figure 3-18, the network has been segmented into two VLANs: Faculty as VLAN 10 and Student as VLAN 20. When the broadcast frame is sent from the faculty computer, PC1, to switch S2, the switch forwards that broadcast frame to only those switch ports configured to support VLAN 10. In the figure, the ports that make up the connection between switches S2 and S1 (ports F0/1) and between S1 and S3 (ports F0/3) have been configured to support all the VLANs in the network. This connection is called a *trunk*. You learn more about trunks later in this chapter.

Figure 3-18   Two VLANs

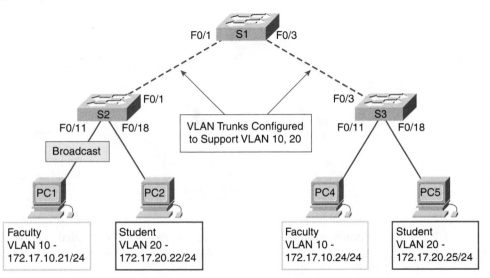

When S1 receives the broadcast frame on port F0/1, S1 forwards that broadcast frame out the only port configured to support VLAN 10, port F0/3. When S3 receives the broadcast frame on port F0/3, it forwards that broadcast frame out the only port configured to support VLAN 10, port F0/11. The broadcast frame arrives at the only other computer in the network configured on VLAN 10, faculty computer PC4.

When VLANs are implemented on a switch, the transmission of unicast, multicast, and broadcast traffic from a host on a particular VLAN is constrained to the devices on the VLAN.

Breaking up a big broadcast domain into several smaller ones reduces broadcast traffic and improves network performance. Breaking up domains into VLANs also allows for better information confidentiality within an organization. Breaking up broadcast domains can be performed either with VLANs (on switches) or with routers. A router is needed anytime devices on different Layer 3 networks need to communicate, regardless of whether VLANs are used.

In Figure 3-19, PC1 wants to communicate with another device, PC4. PC1 and PC4 are both in VLAN 10.

Figure 3-19 Intra-VLAN Communication

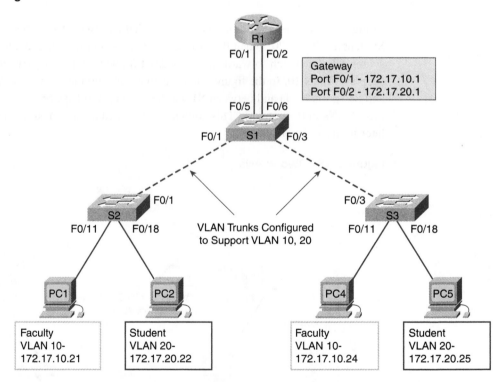

Communicating with a device in the same VLAN is called intra-VLAN communication. The following describes how this process is accomplished:

1. PC1 in VLAN 10 sends an ARP request frame (broadcast) to switch S2. Switch S2 sends the ARP request out port F0/1. Switch S1 sends it out ports F0/5 and F0/3.

Note

There are two connections from switch S1 to the router: one to carry transmissions on VLAN 10 and the other to carry transmissions on VLAN 20 to the router interface.

Switch S3 sends it out port F0/11 to PC4 on VLAN 10.

2. PC4 sends an ARP reply to switch S3, which forwards it out port F0/3 to switch S1 (router R1 does not reply). Switch S1 forwards the reply out port F0/1. Switch S2 forwards the reply out F0/11. PC1 receives the reply that contains the MAC address of PC4.

3. PC1 now has the destination MAC address of PC4 and uses this to create a unicast frame with PC4's MAC address as the destination. Switches S2, S1, and S3 deliver the frame to PC4.

Again, in Figure 3-19, PC1 in VLAN 10 wants to communicate with PC5 in VLAN 20. Communicating with a device in another VLAN is called inter-VLAN communication.

The following describes how this process is accomplished:

1. PC1 in VLAN 10 wants to communicate with PC5 in VLAN 20. PC1 sends an ARP request frame for the MAC address of the default gateway R1.

2. Router R1 replies with an ARP reply frame from its interface configured on VLAN 10. The reply passes through S1 and S2 and reaches PC1.

3. PC1 then creates an Ethernet frame with the MAC address of the default gateway. The frame is sent through switch S2 and S1 to router R1.

4. Router R1 sends an ARP request frame on VLAN 20 to determine the MAC address of PC5. Switches S1, S2, and S3 broadcast the ARP request frame out ports configured for VLAN 20. PC5 on VLAN 20 receives the ARP request frame from router R1.

5. PC5 on VLAN 20 sends an ARP reply through switches S3 and S1 to router R1 with the destination MAC address of interface F0/2 on router R1.

6. Router R1 sends the frame received from PC1 though S1 and S3 to PC5 (on VLAN 20).

We next explore basic Layer 3 switching. Figure 3-20 shows the Catalyst 3750G-24PS switch, one of many Cisco Catalyst switches that supports Layer 3 switching. The icon that represents a Layer 3 switch is shown. A full discussion of Layer 3 switching is beyond the scope of this book, but a brief description of the *switch virtual interface (SVI)* technology that allows a Layer 3 switch to route between VLANs is helpful.

Figure 3-20   Layer 3 Switch

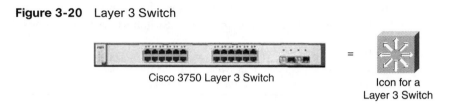

Cisco 3750 Layer 3 Switch

=

Icon for a
Layer 3 Switch

An SVI is a Layer 3 logical interface associated with a specific VLAN. You need to config-ure an SVI for a VLAN if you want to route between VLANs or to provide IP host connec-tivity to the switch. By default, an SVI is created for VLAN 1 on a Catalyst switch.

A Layer 3 switch has the capability to route transmissions between VLANs. The procedure is the same as described for the inter-VLAN communication using a separate router, except that the SVIs act as the router interfaces for routing the data between VLANs. Refer to Figure 3-21 for an explanation of the process of inter-VLAN communication via SVIs.

Figure 3-21   Inter-VLAN Communication with SVIs

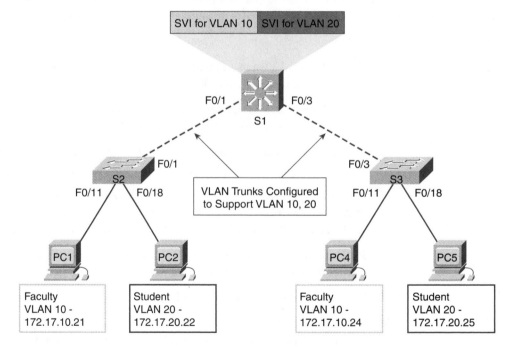

In the figure, PC1 wants to communicate with PC5. The following steps outline the com-munication through the Layer 3 switch S1:

1. PC1 sends an ARP request (broadcast) on VLAN10. S2 forwards the ARP request out all ports configured for VLAN 10.

2. Switch S1 forwards the ARP request out all ports configured for VLAN 10, including the SVI for VLAN 10. Switch S3 forwards the ARP request out all ports configured for VLAN 10.

3. Switch S1 knows the location of VLAN 20 because it is a directly connected Layer 3 network in the manner of SVI 20. The SVI for VLAN 10 in switch S1 sends an ARP reply back to PC1 with its MAC address information.

4. PC1 sends data, destined for PC5, as a unicast frame through switch S2 to the SVI for VLAN 10 in switch S1.

5. The SVI for VLAN 20 sends an ARP request broadcast out all switch ports configured for VLAN 20. Switch S3 sends that ARP request broadcast out all switch ports configured for VLAN 20.

6. PC5 on VLAN 20 sends an ARP reply to the SVI for VLAN 20 on S1.

7. The SVI for VLAN 20 forwards the data, sent from PC1, in a unicast frame to PC5 using the destination address it learned from the ARP reply in step 6.

Investigating a VLAN Implementation (3.1.4)

Packet Tracer
☐ Activity

Use the Packet Tracer Activity to observe how broadcast traffic is forwarded by the switches when VLANs are configured and when VLANs are not configured. Use File e3-3144.pka on the CD-ROM that accompanies this book to perform this activity using Packet Tracer.

VLAN Trunking

VLANs and VLAN trunks are inextricably linked. VLANs in a modern switched LAN would be practically useless without VLAN trunks. We know that VLANs control network broadcasts, and we know that VLAN trunks transmit traffic to different parts of the network within a given VLAN. In Figure 3-22, the links between switches S1 and S2, and S1 and S3, are configured to transmit traffic coming from VLAN 10, 20, 30, and 99. This network simply could not function without VLAN trunks. You will find that most networks that you encounter are configured with VLAN trunks. This section brings together the knowledge you already have on VLAN trunking and delves into the details necessary for a complete conceptual understanding of the role of trunks in a switched LAN.

Figure 3-22   VLAN Trunking

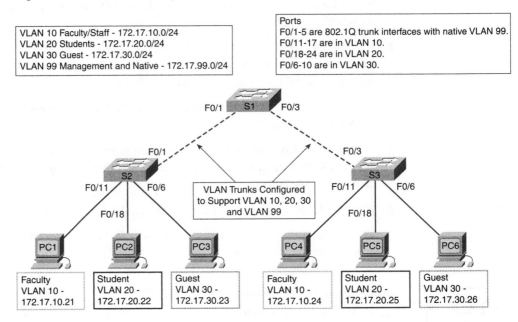

VLAN 10 Faculty/Staff - 172.17.10.0/24
VLAN 20 Students - 172.17.20.0/24
VLAN 30 Guest - 172.17.30.0/24
VLAN 99 Management and Native - 172.17.99.0/24

Ports
F0/1-5 are 802.1Q trunk interfaces with native VLAN 99.
F0/11-17 are in VLAN 10.
F0/18-24 are in VLAN 20.
F0/6-10 are in VLAN 30.

VLAN Trunks Configured
to Support VLAN 10, 20, 30
and VLAN 99

Faculty
VLAN 10 -
172.17.10.21

Student
VLAN 20 -
172.17.20.22

Guest
VLAN 30 -
172.17.30.23

Faculty
VLAN 10 -
172.17.10.24

Student
VLAN 20 -
172.17.20.25

Guest
VLAN 30 -
172.17.30.26

VLAN Trunks

A *VLAN trunk* is an Ethernet point-to-point link between an Ethernet switch interface and an Ethernet interface on another networking device, such as a router or a switch, carrying the traffic of multiple VLANs over the singular link. A VLAN trunk allows you to extend the VLANs across an entire network. Cisco switches support IEEE 802.1Q for trunk formation on Fast Ethernet and Gigabit Ethernet interfaces. You learn about 802.1Q later in this section. A VLAN trunk does not belong to a specific VLAN, but rather it serves as a conduit for VLANs between switches.

In Figure 3-23, you see the standard topology used in this chapter, except that instead of the VLAN trunk you are used to seeing between switches S1 and S2, a separate link exists for each subnet. Four separate links connect switches S1 and S2, leaving three fewer ports to allocate to end-user devices. Each time a new subnetwork is needed, a new link is required for each switch in the network.

In Figure 3-24, the network topology shows a VLAN trunk connecting switches S1 and S2 with a single physical link. This is the way a network should be configured. The four separate links in Figure 3-23 have been replaced by a single trunk link.

Figure 3-23   Without VLAN Trunks

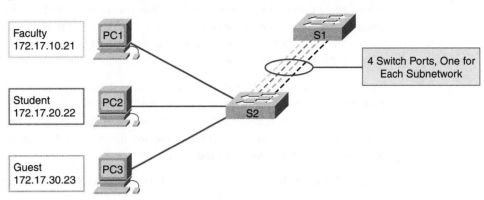

Figure 3-24   With VLAN Trunks

VLAN 1   – Control Traffic - 172.17.1.0/24
VLAN 10 – Faculty/Staff - 172.17.10.0/24
VLAN 20 – Students - 172.17.20.0/24
VLAN 30 – Guest (Default) - 172.17.30.0/24
VLAN 99 – Management and Native - 172.17.99.0/24

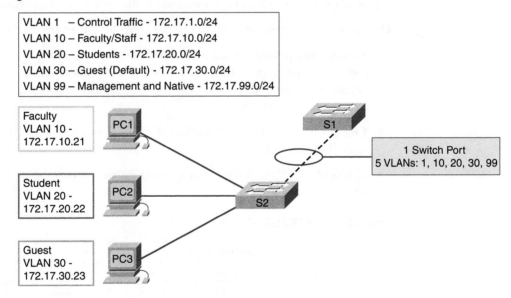

IEEE 802.1Q Frame Tagging

Access layer switches are Layer 2 devices. They use only the Ethernet frame header information to forward frames. When an Ethernet frame arrives on an access port from a connected device, the frame header does not contain information about which VLAN the frame belongs to. Subsequently, when Ethernet frames are placed on a trunk, they need additional information about the VLANs they belong to. This is accomplished by using 802.1Q frame tagging. This header adds a tag to the original Ethernet frame specifying the VLAN to which the frame belongs.

We briefly discussed frame tagging earlier in the context of voice-enabled switch ports, where voice frames are tagged to differentiate them from data frames destined for the computer attached to the IP phone, which is directly connected to the access port. You also learned that VLAN IDs can be in a normal range, 1–1005, or an extended range, 1006–4094. But how do VLAN IDs get inserted into an Ethernet frame?

Before exploring the details of 802.1Q tag fields, it is helpful to understand what a switch does when it forwards a frame out a trunk link. Roughly, when a switch receives a frame on a port configured in access mode (static VLAN) and destined for a remote device via a trunk link, the switch takes apart the frame and inserts a VLAN tag, recalculates the FCS, and sends the tagged frame out the trunk port.

The VLAN tag field consists of an EtherType field and a tag control information field.

The EtherType field is set to the hexadecimal value of 0x8100. This value is called the tag protocol ID (TPID) value. With the EtherType field set to the TPID value, the switch receiving the frame knows to look for information in the tag control information field.

The tag control information field, shown in Figure 3-25, contains the following:

- **3 bits of user priority:** Used by the *IEEE 802.1p* standard, which specifies how to provide expedited transmission of Layer 2 frames. A description of the IEEE 802.1p is beyond the scope of this book; however, you learned a little about it earlier in the discussion on voice VLANs.

- **1 bit of** *Canonical Format Identifier (CFI)*: Enables Token Ring frames to be carried across Ethernet links easily.

- **12 bits of** *VLAN ID (VID)*: VLAN identification numbers; supports up to 4096 VLAN IDs.

Figure 3-25   IEEE 802.1Q VLAN Tag Fields

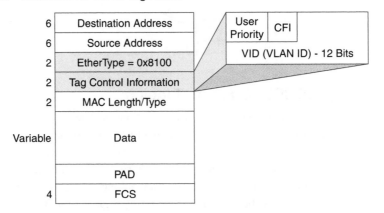

After the switch inserts the EtherType and tag control information fields, it recalculates the FCS values and inserts it into the frame.

Native VLANs

Now that you know more about how a switch tags a frame with the appropriate VLAN, it is time to explore how the native VLAN supports the switch in handling tagged and *untagged frames* that arrive or are sent on an 802.1Q trunk port.

Some devices that support trunking tag native VLAN traffic as a default behavior. If an 802.1Q trunk port receives a tagged frame on the native VLAN, it drops the frame. Consequently, when configuring a switch port on a Cisco Catalyst switch, you need to identify these devices and configure them so that they do not send tagged frames on the native VLAN. Devices from other vendors that support tagged frames on the native VLAN include IP phones, servers, routers, and non-Cisco switches.

When a Cisco switch trunk port receives untagged frames, it forwards those frames to the native VLAN. As you may recall, the default native VLAN is VLAN 1. When you configure an 802.1Q trunk port, a Port VLAN ID (PVID) is assigned to the port according to the value of the native VLAN ID. All untagged traffic coming in or out of the 802.1Q port is forwarded based on the PVID value. For example, if VLAN 99 is configured as the native VLAN, the PVID is 99, and all untagged traffic is forwarded to VLAN 99. If the native VLAN has not been reconfigured, the PVID value is set to VLAN 1.

In Table 3-1, VLAN 99 is configured as the native VLAN on port F0/1 of switch S1, changing it from the default value of 1.

Table 3-1   Native VLAN Trunk Configuration

Description	CLI
Enter global configuration mode on switch S1.	S1# **configure terminal**
Enter interface configuration mode.	S1(config)# **interface f0/1**
Configure the VLAN 99 to send and receive untagged traffic on the trunk port F0/1. The range for vlan-id is 1 to 4094.	S1(config-if)# **switchport trunk native vlan 99**
Return to privileged EXEC mode.	S1(config-if)# **end**

Using the **show interfaces** *interface-id* **switchport** command, you can quickly verify that you have correctly reconfigured the native VLAN from VLAN 1 to VLAN 99. In Example 3-4, the highlighted output indicates that the configuration was successful.

Example 3-4 Voice VLAN Configuration

```
S1# show interfaces F0/1 switchport
Name: Fa0/1
Switchport: Enabled
Administrative Mode: dynamic auto
```

```
Operational Mode: down
Administrative Trunking Encapsulation: dot1q
Negotiation of Trunking: On
Access Mode VLAN: 50
Trunking Native Mode VLAN: 99 (VLAN0099)
Administrative Native VLAN tagging: enabled
<output omitted>
Administrative private-vlan trunk Native VLAN tagging: enabled
Administrative private-vlan trunk encapsulation: dot1q
<output omitted>
Trunking VLANs Enabled: ALL
```

Trunking Operation

You have learned how a switch handles untagged traffic on a trunk link: Frames traversing a
trunk link are tagged with the VLAN ID of the access port the frame arrived on, or they remain
untagged if associated with the native VLAN. In Figure 3-26, PC1 on VLAN 10 and PC3 on
VLAN 30 send broadcast frames to switch S2. Switch S2 tags these frames with the appropriate VLAN ID and then forwards the frames over the trunk to switch S1. Switch S1 reads the
VLAN ID on the frames and broadcasts them to each port configured to support VLAN 10 and
VLAN 30, respectively. Switch S3 receives these frames, strips off the VLAN IDs, and forwards the untagged frames to PC4 on VLAN 10 and PC6 on VLAN 30.

Figure 3-26   Trunking Operation

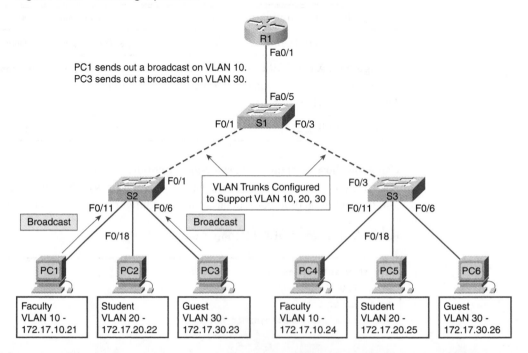

Trunking Modes

You have learned how 802.1Q trunking works on Cisco Catalyst switch ports. Now it is time to examine the 802.1Q trunk port mode configuration options. First we need to discuss a Cisco legacy trunking protocol called *inter-switch link (ISL)*, because you will see this option in the switch software configuration guides, and it is supported by all current Cisco Catalyst switches other than the Catalyst 29xx series switches.

Although most Cisco Catalyst switches can be configured to support two types of trunk ports, IEEE 802.1Q and ISL, today only 802.1Q is used in practice. However, legacy networks may still use ISL, and it is useful to be aware of each trunk encapsulation option:

- An IEEE 802.1Q trunk port simultaneously supports both tagged and untagged traffic. An 802.1Q trunk port is assigned a default PVID, which is associated with all untagged traffic on the port. All traffic with a null VLAN ID is assumed to belong to the port default PVID. A packet with a VLAN ID equal to the outgoing port default PVID is sent untagged. All other traffic is sent with a VLAN tag.

- With ISL trunk ports, all received packets are expected to be encapsulated with an ISL header, and all transmitted packets are sent with an ISL header. Native (nontagged) frames received from an ISL trunk port are dropped. ISL is no longer a recommended trunk port mode, and it is not supported on a number of Cisco Catalyst switches.

Dynamic Trunking Protocol (DTP) is a Cisco proprietary protocol that negotiates both the status of trunk ports as well as the trunk encapsulation of trunk ports. Switches from other vendors do not support DTP. DTP is automatically enabled on a switch port when certain *trunking modes* are configured on the switch port. DTP manages trunk negotiation only if the port on the other switch is configured in a trunk mode that supports DTP. DTP supports both ISL and 802.1Q trunks. This book focuses on the 802.1Q implementation of DTP; a detailed discussion on DTP is beyond the scope of this book. Switches do not need DTP to enable trunks, and some Cisco switches and routers do not support DTP.

A switch port on a Cisco Catalyst switch supports a number of trunking modes. The trunking mode defines how the port negotiates using DTP to set up a trunk link with its peer port. The following provides a brief description of the available trunking modes and how DTP is implemented in each.

- The switch port periodically sends DTP frames, called advertisements, to the remote port. The command used is **switchport mode trunk** and is the default configuration. The local switch port advertises to the remote port that it is dynamically changing to a trunking state. The local port then, regardless of what DTP information the remote port sends as a response to the advertisement, changes to a trunking state. The local port is considered to be in an unconditional (always on) trunking state.

- The switch port periodically sends DTP frames to the remote port. The command used is **switchport mode dynamic auto**. The local switch port advertises to the remote switch port that it is able to trunk but does not request to go to the trunking state. After a DTP negotiation, the local port ends up in trunking state only if the remote port trunk mode has been configured to be **on** or **desirable**. If both ports on the switches are set to **auto,** they do not negotiate to be in a trunking state. They negotiate to be in the access (nontrunk) mode state.

■ DTP frames are sent periodically to the remote port. The command used is **switchport mode dynamic desirable**. The local switch port advertises to the remote switch port that it is able to trunk and asks the remote switch port to go to the trunking state. If the local port detects that the remote has been configured in **on**, **desirable**, or **auto** mode, the local port ends up in trunking state. If the remote switch port is in the *nonegotiate* mode, the local switch port remains as a nontrunking port.

■ You can turn off DTP for the trunk so that the local port does not send out DTP frames to the remote port. Use the command **switchport nonegotiate**. The local port is then considered to be in an unconditional trunking state. Use this feature when you need to configure a trunk with a switch from another switch vendor.

To learn about DTP support on Cisco switches, visit www.cisco.com/en/US/tech/tk389/tk689/technologies_tech_note09186a008017f86a.shtml.

As an example, refer to Figure 3-27 with three Catalyst 2960 switches represented. The F0/1 ports on switches S1 and S2 are configured with trunk mode **on** (**switchport mode trunk**). The F0/3 ports on switches S1 and S3 are configured as *dynamic auto* (**switchport mode dynamic auto**). When the switch configurations are complete and the switches are fully configured, which links will be active trunks?

Figure 3-27   Dynamic Trunking Protocol

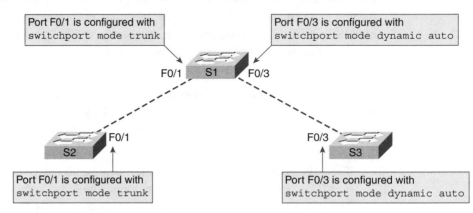

The link between switches S1 and S2 becomes an active trunk because the F0/1 ports on switches S1 and S2 are configured to ignore all DTP advertisements. The F0/3 ports on switches S1 and S3 are set to **auto**; in this case, the result is an inactive trunk link because the ports negotiate to be in the access (nontrunk) mode state.

Note

The default switchport mode for an interface on a Catalyst 2950 switch is *dynamic desirable*, but the default switchport mode for an interface on a Catalyst 2960 switch is dynamic auto. If S1 and S3 were Catalyst 2950 switches with interface F0/3 in default switchport mode, the link between S1 and S3 would become an active trunk.

As a very useful reference giving the results of trunk status based on the various DTP configuration options on Catalyst 2960 switches, see Table 3-2.

Table 3-2   Trunk Negotiation Combinations

	Dynamic Auto	Dynamic Desirable	Trunk	Access
Dynamic Auto	Access	Trunk	Trunk	Access
Dynamic Desirable	Trunk	Trunk	Trunk	Access
Trunk	Trunk	Trunk	Trunk	Not Recommended
Access	Access	Access	Not Recommended	Access

Use the **show dtp interface** privileged EXEC command, introduced in IOS Release 12.2(37)EY on Catalyst 2960 switches, to determine the current settings.

For information on which Cisco switches support 802.1Q, ISL, and DTP, visit www.cisco.com/en/US/tech/tk389/tk689/technologies_tech_note09186a008017f86a.shtml#topic1.

For information on how to support ISL on legacy networks, visit www.cisco.com/en/US/tech/tk389/tk689/tsd_technology_support_troubleshooting_technotes_list.html.

Packet Tracer
☐ Activity

Investigating VLAN Trunks (3.2.3)

Use this Packet Tracer Activity to practice working with VLAN trunks. Trunks carry the traffic of multiple VLANs through a single link, making them a vital part of communicating between switches with VLANs. This activity focuses on viewing switch configuration, trunk configuration, and VLAN tagging information. Use file e3-3232.pka on the CD-ROM that accompanies this book to perform this activity using Packet Tracer.

Configure VLANs and Trunks

In this chapter, you have already seen some examples of the commands used to configure VLANs and VLAN trunks. In this section, you learn the key Cisco IOS commands needed to create, delete, and verify VLANs and VLAN trunks. Often these commands have many optional parameters that extend the capabilities of the VLAN and VLAN trunk technology.

Some specialized optional commands are not presented; however, references are provided if you want to research these options. The focus of this section is to provide you with the ability to confidently configure VLANs and VLAN trunks with their key features.

Configure a VLAN

In this section we discuss the configuration of static VLANs on Cisco Catalyst switches. Two different modes exist for configuring VLANs on a Cisco Catalyst switch: database configuration mode and global configuration mode. Although the Cisco documentation mentions VLAN database configuration mode, it is being deprecated in favor of VLAN global configuration mode. It is evident that the database configuration mode will eventually go away; the intent of the change is to migrate the switch operating system toward a more Cisco-routerlike operating system. Over the years, the line between Cisco routers and Catalyst switches is becoming increasingly blurred.

You will configure VLANs with IDs in the normal range. Recall that there are two ranges of VLAN IDs. The normal range includes IDs 1 to 1001, and extended range consists of IDs 1006 to 4094. VLAN 1 and 1002 to 1005 are reserved ID numbers. When you configure normal range VLANs, the configuration details are stored automatically in Flash memory on the switch in a file called vlan.dat. Because you often configure other aspects of a Catalyst switch at the same time, it is good practice to save running-config file changes to the startup-config file.

Table 3-3 reviews the Cisco IOS commands used to add a VLAN to a switch.

Table 3-3   Adding a VLAN

Description	CLI
Enter global configuration mode.	S1# **configure terminal**
Create a VLAN. vlan-id is the VLAN number that is to be created. The CLI switches to VLAN configuration mode for VLAN vlan-id.	S1(config)# **vlan** *vlan-id*
(Optional) Specify a unique VLAN name to identify the VLAN. If no name is entered, the VLAN number, with padded zeros, is appended to the word "VLAN"; for example, VLAN0020.	S1(config-vlan)# **name** *vlan-name*
Return to privileged EXEC mode. You must end your configuration session for the configuration to be saved in the vlan.dat file and for configuration to take effect.	S1(config-vlan)# **end**

Figure 3-28 shows a basic topology with the student VLAN, VLAN 20, being configured on switch S1.

Figure 3-28   Switch Topology for Basic VLAN Configuration

Example 3-5 displays commands for adding VLAN 20.

Example 3-5 Adding a VLAN

```
S1# configure terminal
S1(config)# vlan 20
S1(config-vlan)# name student
S1(config-vlan)# end
```

Example 3-6 demonstrates the use of the **show vlan brief** command to display the contents of the vlan.dat file. The student VLAN, VLAN 20, is highlighted. The default VLAN IDs of 1 and 1002 to 1005 can be seen in the output. Notice that no ports are configured yet for VLAN 20.

Example 3-6 show vlan brief

```
S1# show vlan brief

VLAN Name                             Status    Ports
-------------------------------------------------------------------------------
1    default                          active    Fa0/1, Fa0/2, Fa0/3, Fa0/4
                                                Fa0/5, Fa0/6, Fa0/7, Fa0/8
                                                Fa0/9, Fa0/10, Fa0/11, Fa0/12
                                                Fa0/13, Fa0/14, Fa0/15, Fa0/16
                                                Fa0/17, Fa0/18, Fa0/19, Fa0/20
                                                Fa0/21, Fa0/22, Fa0/23, Fa0/24
                                                Gi0/1, Gi0/2
20   student                          active
1002 fddi-default                     act/unsup
1003 token-ring-default               act/unsup
1004 fddinet-default                  act/unsup
1005 trnet-default                    act/unsup
```

Interface F0/18 is connected to the student computer, PC2, and must be added to VLAN 20. Example 3-7 demonstrates the configuration commands. A static access port can belong to only one VLAN at a time. When VLAN 20 is configured on other switches, the switch administrator configures the other student computers to be in the same subnet as PC2: 172.17.20.0/24.

Example 3-7 Static VLAN Interface Configuration

```
S1# configure terminal
S1(config)# interface f0/18
S1(config-if)# switchport mode access
S1(config-if)# switchport access vlan 20
S1(config-if)# end
```

After adding interface F0/18 to VLAN 20, the **show vlan brief** output changes, as seen in Example 3-8.

Example 3-8 show vlan brief Updated

```
S1# show vlan brief

VLAN Name                             Status    Ports
- - - - - - - - - - - - - - - - - - - - - - - - - - - - - - - - - - - - - - - - - - - - - - - - - - - - - -
1    default                          active    Fa0/1, Fa0/2, Fa0/3, Fa0/4
                                                Fa0/5, Fa0/6, Fa0/7, Fa0/8
                                                Fa0/9, Fa0/10, Fa0/11, Fa0/12
                                                Fa0/13, Fa0/14, Fa0/15, Fa0/16
                                                Fa0/17, Fa0/19, Fa0/20, Fa0/21
                                                Fa0/22, Fa0/23, Fa0/24, Gi0/1
                                                Gi0/2
20   student                          active       Fa0/18
1002 fddi-default                     act/unsup
1003 token-ring-default               act/unsup
1004 fddinet-default                  act/unsup
1005 trnet-default                    act/unsup
```

Note

In addition to entering a single VLAN ID, you can enter a series of VLAN IDs separated by commas, or a range of VLAN IDs separated by hyphens using the **vlan** *vlan-id* command; for example: switch(config)# **vlan 100,102,105-107**.

Managing VLANs

After you configure a VLAN, you can validate the VLAN configurations using Cisco IOS show commands. The command syntax for the **show vlan** command is

```
show vlan [brief ¦ id vlan-id ¦ name vlan-name ¦ summary]
```

The syntax is explained in Table 3-4.

Table 3-4   **show vlan** Command Syntax

Explanation	Syntax
Display one line for each VLAN with the VLAN name, status, and its ports.	**brief**
Display information about a single VLAN identified by VLAN ID number. For *vlan-id*, the range is 1 to 4094.	**id** *vlan-id*
Display information about a single VLAN identified by VLAN name. The VLAN name is an ASCII string from 1 to 32 characters.	**name** *vlan-name*
Display VLAN summary information.	**summary**

The command syntax for the **show interfaces switchport** command is the following:

```
show interfaces [interface-id ¦ vlan vlan-id] ¦ switchport
```

The syntax is explained in Table 3-5.

Table 3-5   **show interfaces switchport** Command Syntax

Explanation	Syntax
Valid interfaces include physical ports (including type, module, and port number) and port channels. The port-channel range is 1 to 6.	*interface-id*
VLAN identification. The range is 1 to 4094.	**vlan** *vlan-id*
Display the administrative and operational status of a switching port, including port blocking and port protection settings.	**switchport**

In Example 3-9, you can see that the **show vlan name student** command does not produce clearly discernible output. The preference here is to use the **show vlan brief** command, as in Example 3-8.

Example 3-9 show vlan name Output

```
S1# show vlan name student

VLAN Name                             Status    Ports
--------------------------------------------------------------------------------
20    student                         active    Fa0/18

VLAN Type  SAID        MTU  Parent RingNo BridgeNo Stp BrdgMode Trans1 Trans2
--------------------------------------------------------------------------------
20    enet 100020      1500 -      -      -        -   -        0      0

Remote SPAN VLAN
----------------
Disabled

Primary Secondary Type              Ports
--------------------------------------------------------------------------------
```

The **show vlan summary** command output, shown in Example 3-10, displays the count of all configured VLANs. The output shows six VLANs: 1, 1002–1005, and the student VLAN, VLAN 20.

Example 3-10   show vlan summary Output

```
S1# show vlan summary
Number of existing VLANs          : 6
Number of existing VTP VLANs      : 6
Number of existing extended VLANs : 0
```

The **show interfaces vlan 20** command displays detail that is beyond the scope of this chapter. The key information appears on the second line of the output in Example 3-11, indicating that VLAN 20 is up.

Example 3-11   show interfaces Output

```
S1# show interfaces vlan 20
Vlan20 is up, line protocol is up
  Hardware is EtherSVI, address is 001c.57ec.0641 (bia 001c.573c.0641)
  MTU 1500 bytes, BW 1000000 Kbit, DLY 1000 usec,
     reliability 255/255, txload 1/255, rxload 1/255
  Encapsulation ARPA, loopback not set
  ARP type: ARPA, ARP Timeout 04:00:00
  Last input never, output never, output hang never
```

```
Last clearing of "show interface" counters never
Input queue: 0/75/0/0 (size/max/drops/flushes); Total output drops: 0
Queueing strategy: fifo
Output queue :0/40 (size/max)
5 minute input rate 0 bits/sec, 0 packets/sec
5 minute output rate 0 bits/sec, 0 packets/sec
   0 packets input, 0 bytes, 0 no buffer
   Received 0 broadcasts (0 IP multicast)
   0 runts, 0 giants, 0 throttles
   0 input errors, 0 CRC, 0 frame, 0 overrun, 0 ignored
   0 packets output, 0 bytes, 0 underruns
   0 output errors, 0 interface resets
   0 output buffer failures, 0 output buffers swapped out
```

The **show interfaces switchport** command is one of the most useful commands on a
Catalyst switch. It displays pertinent information about the referenced interface(s). In
Example 3-12, you can see that the F0/18 is assigned to VLAN 20 and that the native
VLAN is VLAN 1. We used this command once before in the context of voice VLANs.

Example 3-12   show interfaces switchport Output

```
S1# show interfaces f0/18 switchport
Name: Fa0/18
Switchport: Enabled
Administrative Mode: static access
Operational Mode: static access
Administrative Trunking Encapsulation: dot1q
Negotiation of Trunking: Off
Access Mode VLAN: 20 (student)
Trunking Native Mode VLAN: 1 (default)
Administrative Native VLAN tagging: enabled
Voice VLAN: none
Administrative private-vlan host-association:10 (VLAN0010) 502 (VLAN0502)
Administrative private-vlan mapping: none
Administrative private-vlan trunk native VLAN: none
Administrative private-vlan trunk native VLAN tagging: enabled
Administrative private-vlan trunk encapsulation: dot1q
Administrative private-vlan trunk normal VLANs: none
Administrative private-vlan trunk private VLANs: none
Operational private-vlan: none
Trunking VLANs Enabled: ALL
Pruning VLANs Enabled: 2-1001
Capture Mode Disabled
Capture VLANs Allowed: ALL
```

```
Protected: false
Unknown unicast blocked: disabled
Unknown multicast blocked: disabled
Appliance trust: none
```

For more details on the **show vlan** and **show interfaces** command output fields, visit www.cisco.com/en/US/products/ps6406/products_command_reference_chapter09186a0080 81874b.html#wp7730585.

Managing VLAN Memberships

You can manage VLANs and VLAN port memberships in a number of ways. Table 3-6 explains the commands for removing VLAN membership.

Table 3-6   Managing VLAN Membership

Description	CLI
Enter global configuration mode.	S1# **configure terminal**
Enter the interface configuration mode for the interface to be configured.	S1(config)# **interface interface-id**
Remove the VLAN assignment on that switch port interface and revert to the default VLAN membership of VLAN 1.	S1(config-if)# **no switchport access vlan**
Return to privileged EXEC mode.	S1(config-if)# **end**

To reassign a port to VLAN 1, you can use the **no switchport access vlan** command in interface configuration mode. After entering this command, examine the output of the **show vlan brief** command in Example 3-13. Notice how VLAN 20 is still active. Interface F0/18 has been removed from VLAN 20. The **show interfaces f0/18 switchport** command shows that the access VLAN for interface F0/18 has been reset to VLAN 1.

Example 3-13   Reassign Port to VLAN 1

```
S1(config)# interface f0/18
S1(config-if)# no switchport access vlan
S1(config-if)# end
S1# show vlan brief

VLAN Name                             Status    Ports
- - - - - - - - - - - - - - - - - - - - - - - - - - - - - - - - - - - - - - - - - - - - - - -
1    default                          active    Fa0/1, Fa0/2, Fa0/3, Fa0/4
```

```
                                          Fa0/5, Fa0/6, Fa0/7, Fa0/8
                                          Fa0/9, Fa0/10, Fa0/11, Fa0/12
                                          Fa0/13, Fa0/14, Fa0/15, Fa0/16
                                          Fa0/17, Fa0/18, Fa0/19, Fa0/20
                                          Fa0/21, Fa0/22, Fa0/23, Fa0/24
                                          Gi0/1, Gi0/2
20   student                    active
1002 fddi-default               act/unsup
1003 token-ring-default         act/unsup
1004 fddinet-default            act/unsup
1005 trnet-default              act/unsup
S1# show interfaces f0/18 switchport
Name: Fa0/18
Switchport: Enabled
Administrative Mode: static access
Operational Mode: down
Administrative Trunking Encapsulation: dot1q
Negotiation of Trunking: Off
Access Mode VLAN: 1 (default)
<output omitted>
```

A static access port can have only one VLAN. With Cisco IOS software, you do not need to first remove a port from a VLAN to change its VLAN membership. When you reassign a static access port to an existing VLAN, the port is automatically removed from the previous VLAN. In Example 3-14, port F0/11 has been reassigned to VLAN 20.

Example 3-14 Reassign Port to VLAN 20

```
S1# show vlan brief

VLAN Name                       Status    Ports
-------------------------------------------------------------------------
1    default                    active    Fa0/1, Fa0/2, Fa0/3, Fa0/4
                                          Fa0/5, Fa0/6, Fa0/7, Fa0/8
                                          Fa0/9, Fa0/10, Fa0/12, Fa0/13
                                          Fa0/14, Fa0/15, Fa0/16, Fa0/17
                                          Fa0/18, Fa0/19, Fa0/20, Fa0/21
                                          Fa0/22, Fa0/23, Fa0/24, Gi0/1
                                          Gi0/2
20   student                    active    Fa0/11
1002 fddi-default               act/unsup
1003 token-ring-default         act/unsup
1004 fddinet-default            act/unsup
1005 trnet-default              act/unsup
```

Example 3-15 demonstrates the deletion of a VLAN with the global configuration command **no vlan** *vlan-id*. The **show vlan brief** command verifies that VLAN 20 is no longer in the vlan.dat file.

Example 3-15   Deleting a VLAN

```
S1# no vlan 20
S1# show vlan brief

VLAN Name                             Status    Ports
---------------------------------------------------------------------------
1    default                          active    Fa0/1, Fa0/2, Fa0/3, Fa0/4
                                                Fa0/5, Fa0/6, Fa0/7, Fa0/8
                                                Fa0/9, Fa0/10, Fa0/12, Fa0/13
                                                Fa0/14, Fa0/15, Fa0/16, Fa0/17
                                                Fa0/18, Fa0/19, Fa0/20, Fa0/21
                                                Fa0/22, Fa0/23, Fa0/24, Gi0/1
                                                Gi0/2
1002 fddi-default                     act/unsup
1003 token-ring-default               act/unsup
1004 fddinet-default                  act/unsup
1005 trnet-default                    act/unsup
```

Alternatively, the entire vlan.dat file can be deleted using the command **delete flash:vlan.dat** in privileged EXEC mode. After the switch is reloaded, the previously configured VLANs will no longer be present. This effectively places the switch into "factory default" condition with its VLAN configuration.

Note

Before deleting a VLAN, be sure to first reassign all member ports to a different VLAN. Any ports that are not moved to an active VLAN remain members of the deleted inactive VLAN and are unable to communicate with other systems after you delete the VLAN.

Configure a Trunk

To configure a trunk on a switch port, use the **switchport mode trunk** command. When you enter this command on a switch port, the interface changes to permanent trunking mode, and the port enters into a DTP negotiation to convert the link into a trunk, even if the opposing interface does not agree to the change. In this book, you configure a trunk using the **switchport mode trunk** command. The Cisco IOS command syntax to specify a native VLAN other than VLAN 1 is also shown in Table 3-7.

Table 3-7   IEEE 802.1Q Trunk Configuration

Description	CLI
Enter global configuration mode.	S1# **configure terminal**
Enter the interface configuration mode for the defined interface.	S1(config)# **interface** *interface-id*
Force the link connecting the switches to be a trunk link.	S1(config-if)# **switchport mode trunk**
Specify another VLAN as the native VLAN for untagged frames for IEEE 802.1Q trunks.	S1(config-if)# **switchport trunk native vlan** *vlan-id*
Add the VLANs allowed on this trunk.	S1(config-if)# **switchport trunk allowed vlan add vlan-list**
Return to privileged EXEC mode.	S1(config-if)# **end**

Refer to Figure 3-29. VLANs 10, 20, and 30 support the Faculty, Student, and Guest computers: PC1, PC2, and PC3. The F0/1 port on switch S1 will be configured as a trunk port to allow only VLANs 1, 10, 20, and 30 (recall that VLAN 1 is unconditionally supported on a trunk link, as all control traffic is associated with VLAN 1). VLAN 99 will be configured as the native VLAN.

Figure 3-29   Enabling a Trunk Link

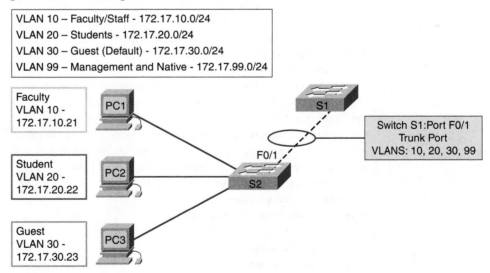

VLAN 10 – Faculty/Staff - 172.17.10.0/24
VLAN 20 – Students - 172.17.20.0/24
VLAN 30 – Guest (Default) - 172.17.30.0/24
VLAN 99 – Management and Native - 172.17.99.0/24

Faculty
VLAN 10 -
172.17.10.21

Student
VLAN 20 -
172.17.20.22

Guest
VLAN 30 -
172.17.30.23

Switch S1:Port F0/1
Trunk Port
VLANS: 10, 20, 30, 99

Example 3-16 demonstrates the configuration of switch S1. Port F0/1 is configured as the trunk port. The native VLAN is reconfigured from VLAN 1 to VLAN 99, with VLANs 10, 20, and 30 on port F0/1.

Example 3-16   Enabling a Restricted Trunk Link

```
S1# configure terminal
Enter configuration commands, one per line.  End with CNTL/Z.
S1(config)# interface f0/1
S1(config-if)# switchport mode trunk
S1(config-if)# switchport trunk native vlan 99
S1(config-if)# switchport trunk allowed vlan add 10,20,30
S1(config-if)# end
```

For more detail on all the parameters associated with the **switchport mode** interface command, visit www.cisco.com/en/US/docs/switches/lan/catalyst2960/software/release/ 12.2_37_se/command/reference/cli3.html#wp1948171.

Example 3-17 displays the administrative and operational status of switch port F0/1 on switch S1. The command used is the **show interfaces** *interface-ID* **switchport** command.

Example 3-17   Verify Trunk Configuration

```
S1#show interfaces f0/1 switchport
Name: Fa0/1
Switchport: Enabled
Administrative Mode: trunk
Operational Mode: down
Administrative Trunking Encapsulation: dot1q
Negotiation of Trunking: On
Access Mode VLAN: 1 (default)
Trunking Native Mode VLAN: 99 (management)
Administrative Native VLAN tagging: enabled
Voice VLAN: none
Administrative private-vlan host-association: none
Administrative private-vlan mapping: none
Administrative private-vlan trunk native VLAN: none
Administrative private-vlan trunk Native VLAN tagging: enabled
Administrative private-vlan trunk encapsulation: dot1q
Administrative private-vlan trunk normal VLANs: none
Administrative private-vlan trunk private VLANs: none
Operational private-vlan: none
Trunking VLANs Enabled: 10,20,30
Pruning VLANs Enabled: 2-1001
Capture Mode Disabled
Capture VLANs Allowed: ALL
<output omitted>
```

The first highlighted area shows that port F0/1 has its administrative mode set to trunk; the port is set to form a trunk regardless of the configuration of the opposing interface. The next highlighted area verifies that the native VLAN is VLAN 99. The last highlighted area shows that the enabled trunking VLANs are VLANs 10, 20, and 30.

Table 3-8 displays the commands to reset the *allowed VLANs* and the native VLAN of the trunk to the default state. The command to reset the switch port to an access port and remove the trunk is also shown.

Table 3-8   IEEE 802.1Q Trunk Modification

Description	CLI
Use this command in the interface configuration mode to reset all the VLANs configured on the trunk interface.	S1(config-if)# **no switchport trunk allowed vlan**
Use this command in the interface configuration mode to reset the native VLAN back to VLAN 1.	S1(config-if)# **no switchport trunk native vlan**
Use this command in the interface configuration mode to reset the trunk port back to a static access mode port.	S1(config-if)# **switchport mode access**

Example 3-18 shows the commands used to reset all trunking characteristics of a trunking interface to the default settings. The **show interfaces f0/1 switchport** command reveals that the trunk has been reconfigured to a default state.

Example 3-18   Resetting a Trunk

```
S1# configure terminal
Enter configuration commands, one per line.  End with CNTL/Z.
S1(config)# interface f0/1
S1(config-if)# no switchport trunk allowed vlan
S1(config-if)# no switchport trunk native vlan
S1(config-if)# end
S1# show interfaces f0/1 switchport
Name: Fa0/1
Switchport: Enabled
Administrative Mode: trunk
Operational Mode: down
Administrative Trunking Encapsulation: dot1q
Negotiation of Trunking: On
Access Mode VLAN: 1 (default)
Trunking Native Mode VLAN: 1 (default)
Administrative Native VLAN tagging: enabled
Voice VLAN: none
<output omitted>
Trunking VLANs Enabled: ALL
```

Last, in Example 3-19, the output demonstrates the commands used to remove the trunk from the F0/1 switch port on switch S1. The **show interfaces f0/1 switchport** command reveals that the F0/1 interface is in static access mode.

Example 3-19   Removing a Trunk

```
S1(config)# interface f0/1
S1(config-if)# switchport mode access
S1(config-if)# end
S1# show interfaces f0/1 switchport
Name: Fa0/1
Switchport: Enabled
Administrative Mode: static access
Operatioss Mode VLAN: 1 (default)
Trunking Native Mode VLAN: 1 (default)
Administrative Native VLAN tagging: enabled
Voice VLAN: none
Administrative private-vlan host-association: none
<output omitted>
Trunking VLANs Enabled: ALL
Pruning VLANs Enabled: 2-1001
Capture Mode Disabled
Capture VLANs Allowed: ALL
```

Packet Tracer
☐ Activity

Configuring VLANs and Trunks (3.3.4)

Use this Packet Tracer Activity to enhance your skills with VLAN and VLAN trunk configuration. VLANs are helpful in the administration of logical groups, allowing members of a group to be easily moved, changed, or added. This activity focuses on creating and naming VLANs, assigning access ports to specific VLANs, changing the native VLAN, and configuring trunk links. Use File e3-3344.pka on the CD-ROM that accompanies this book to perform this activity using Packet Tracer.

Troubleshooting VLANs and Trunks

Common VLAN and trunking issues are usually associated with incorrect configurations. When you configure VLANs and trunks on a switched infrastructure, these configuration errors occur in decreasing frequency as follows:

- **Native VLAN mismatches:** Trunk ports are configured with different native VLANs—for example, if one port has defined VLAN 99 as the native VLAN and the other trunk port has defined VLAN 100 as the native VLAN. This configuration error generates console notifications, causes control and management traffic to be misdirected, and poses a security risk.

- **Trunk mode mismatches:** One trunk port is configured with trunk mode "off" and the other with trunk mode "on". This configuration error causes the trunk link to stop working.

- **VLANs and IP subnets:** User computers, for example, may have been configured with the incorrect IP addresses or subnet masks or default gateways. The result is loss of connectivity.

- **Allowed VLANs on trunks:** The list of allowed VLANs on a trunk has not been updated with the current VLAN trunking requirements. In this situation, unexpected traffic or no traffic is being sent over the trunk.

If you have discovered an issue with a VLAN or trunk and do not know what the problem is, start your troubleshooting by examining the trunks for a native VLAN mismatch and then work down the list. The rest of this topic examines how to fix the common problems with trunks.

Common Problems with Trunks

Refer to Figure 3-30. You are a network administrator and you get a call that the person using computer PC4 cannot connect to the internal web server, the web/TFTP Server. You learn that a new technician was recently configuring switch S3. The topology diagram seems correct, so why does a problem exist? You decide to check the configuration on S3.

Figure 3-30 Native VLAN Issues

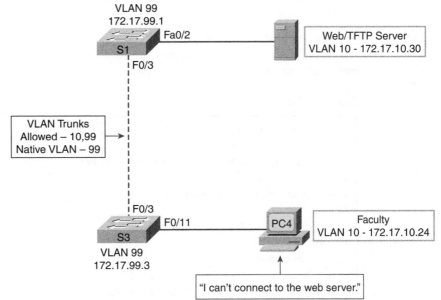

As soon as you connect to switch S3, the error message shown in the top highlighted area in Example 3-20 appears in your console window. You take a look at the interface using the **show interfaces f0/3 switchport** command. You notice that the native VLAN, the second highlighted area in the example, has been set to VLAN 100 and is inactive. As you scan further down the output, you see that the allowed VLANs are 10 and 99, shown in the bottom highlighted area.

Example 3-20   Native VLAN Mismatch

```
S3#
%CDP-4-NATIVE_VLAN_MISMATCH: Native VLAN mismatch discovered on FastEthernet0/3
  (100), with S1 FastEthernet0/1 (99).
S3# show interfaces f0/3 switchport
Name: Fa0/3
Switchport: Enabled
Administrative Mode: trunk
Operational Mode: trunk
Administrative Trunking Encapsulation: dot1q
Operational Trunking Encapsulation: dot1q
Negotiation of Trunking: On
Access Mode VLAN: 1 (default)
Trunking Native Mode VLAN: 100 (Inactive)
<output omitted>
Trunking VLANs Enabled: 10,99
<output omitted>
```

You need to reconfigure the native VLAN on trunk port F0/3 to VLAN 99. In Example 3-21, the top highlighted area shows the command to configure the native VLAN as VLAN 99. The next two highlighted areas confirm that the trunk port F0/3 has the native VLAN reset to VLAN 99.

Example 3-21   Native VLAN Fix

```
S3# configure terminal
S3(config)# interface f0/3
S3(config-if)# switchport trunk native vlan 99
S3(config-if)# end
S3# show interfaces f0/3 switchport
Name: Fa0/3
Switchport: Enabled
Administrative Mode: trunk
<output omitted>
Access Mode VLAN: 1 (default)
Trunking Native Mode VLAN: 99 (management)
<output omitted>
Trunking VLANs Enabled: 10,99
<output omitted>
```

The screen output in Example 3-22 for the computer PC4 shows that connectivity has been restored to the Web/TFTP server found at IP address 172.17.10.30.

Example 3-22   Connectivity Test

```
PC4> ping 172.17.10.30
Pinging 172.17.10.30 with 32 bytes of data:
Reply from 172.17.10.30: bytes=32 time=147ms TTL=128
<output omitted>
```

You have configured trunks manually with the **switchport mode trunk** command. You also learned that the trunk ports use DTP advertisements to negotiate the state of the link with the remote port. When a port on a trunk link is configured with a trunk mode that is incompatible with the other trunk port, a trunk link fails to form between the two switches.

For the next trunk troubleshooting scenario, refer to Figure 3-31.

Figure 3-31   Trunk Mode Issues

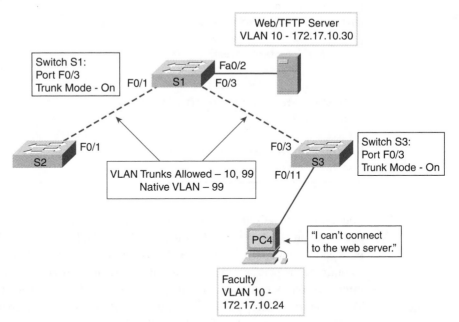

In this scenario, the person using computer PC4 cannot connect to the internal web server. Figure 3-31 show a topology diagram with the current configuration settings. What is the problem?

The first thing you do is check the status of the trunk ports on switch S1 using the **show interfaces trunk** command, as shown in Example 3-23. It reveals that there is not a trunk on interface F0/3 on switch S1. You examine interface F0/3 to learn that the switch port is in dynamic auto mode, the first highlighted area in the top figure. An examination of the trunks on switch S3 reveals that are no active trunk ports. Further checking reveals that the F0/3 interface is also in dynamic auto mode, as seen in the first highlighted area in the bottom of Example 3-23. The trunk is down because both ends are in dynamic auto mode.

Example 3-23   show interfaces trunk and **show interfaces switchport**

```
S1# show interfaces trunk
Port      Mode      Encapsulation     Status      Native vlan
Fa0/1     on        802.1q            trunking    99
Port    Vlans allowed on trunk
Fa0/1   10,99
Port    Vlans allowed and active in management domain
Fa0/1   10,99
Port    Vlans in spanning tree forwarding state and not pruned
Fa0/1   10,99
S1# show interface f0/3 switchport
Name: Fa0/3
Switchport: Enabled
Administrative Mode: dynamic auto

S3# show interfaces trunk

S3#
S3# show interface f0/3 switchport
Name: Fa0/3
Switchport: Enabled
Administrative Mode: dynamic auto
<output omitted>
```

You need to reconfigure the trunk mode of the F0/3 ports on switches S1 and S3 (or at least one of the ports). In the top of Example 3-24, the highlighted area shows that the switch S1 F0/3 port is now in trunking mode. The output for switch S3 shows the commands used to reconfigure the port as well as the results of the **show interfaces switchport** and **show interfaces trunk** command, revealing that interface F0/3 has been reconfigured as a trunk. The output from computer PC4 indicates that PC4 has regained connectivity to the web/TFTP server found at IP address 172.17.10.30.

Example 3-24   show interfaces trunk

```
S1# configure terminal
S1(config)# interface f0/3
S1(config-if)# switchport mode trunk
```

```
S1(config-if)# end
S1# show interfaces f0/3 switchport
Name: Fa0/3
Switchport: Enabled
Administrative Mode: trunk
<output omitted>
S1#


S3# configure terminal
S3(config)# interface f0/3
S3(config-if)# switchport mode trunk
S3(config-if)# end
S3# show interfaces f0/3 switchport
Name: Fa0/3
Switchport: Enabled
Administrative Mode: trunk
<output omitted>
S3# show interfaces trunk
Port     Mode      Encapsulation    Status       Native vlan
Fa0/3    on        802.1q           trunking     99
Port    Vlans allowed on trunk
Fa0/3   10,99
Port    Vlans allowed and active in management domain
Fa0/3   10,99
Port    Vlans in spanning tree forwarding state and not pruned
Fa0/3   10,99
S3#


PC4> ping 172.17.10.30
Pinging 172.17.10.30 with 32 bytes of data:
Reply from 172.17.10.30: bytes=32 time=147ms TTL=128
<output omitted>
```

For the final trunk troubleshooting scenario, refer to Figure 3-32. You have learned that for traffic from a VLAN to be transmitted across a trunk, it has to be allowed on the trunk. The command used to do this is the **switchport trunk allowed vlan** *vlan-list* command. In Figure 3-32, VLAN 20 (Student) and computer PC5 have been added to the network. The documentation has been updated to show that the VLANs allowed on the trunk are 10, 20, and 99.

In this scenario, the person using computer PC5 cannot connect to the student e-mail server shown in Figure 3-32.

Figure 3-32   Allowed VLAN List Issues

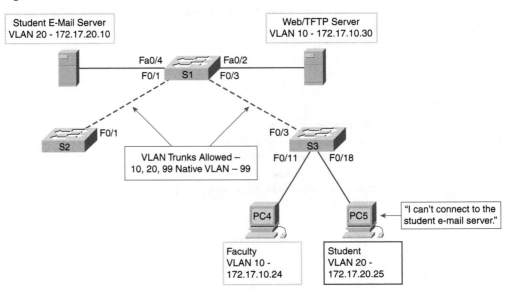

You check the trunk ports on switch S1 using the **show interfaces trunk** command, as illustrated in Example 3-25. The command reveals that interface F0/3 on switch S3 is correctly configured to allow VLANs 10, 20, and 99. An examination of interface F0/3 on switch S1 reveals that interfaces F0/1 and F0/3 allow only VLANs 10 and 99. It seems someone updated the documentation but forgot to reconfigure the ports on the S1 switch.

Example 3-25   Allowed VLANs in **show interfaces trunk**

```
S3# show interfaces trunk
Port     Mode      Encapsulation    Status     Native vlan
Fa0/3    on        802.1q           trunking   99
Port    Vlans allowed on trunk
Fa0/3   10,20,99
Port    Vlans allowed and active in management domain
Fa0/3   10,20,99
Port    Vlans in spanning tree forwarding state and not pruned
Fa0/3   10,20,99


S1# show interfaces trunk
Port     Mode      Encapsulation   Status      Native vlan
Fa0/1    on        802.1q          trunking    99
Fa0/3    on        802.1q          trunking    99
Port     Vlans allowed on trunk
Fa0/1          10,99
Fa0/3          10,99
<output omitted>
S1#
```

You need to reconfigure the F0/1 and the F0/3 ports on switch S1 using the **switchport trunk allowed vlan 10,20,99** command. Example 3-26 output shows that VLANs 10, 20, and 99 are now added to the F0/1 and F0/3 ports on switch S1. The **show interfaces trunk** command is an excellent tool for revealing common trunking problems. Last, Example 3-26 shows that PC5 has regained connectivity to the student e-mail server at 172.17.20.10.

Example 3-26   switchport trunk allowed vlan *vlan-list*

```
S1# configure terminal
S1(config)# interface f0/3
S1(config-if)# switchport trunk allowed vlan 10,20,99
S1(config-if)# end
S1# show interfaces trunk
Port         Mode         Encapsulation  Status        Native vlan
Fa0/1        on           802.1q         trunking      99
Fa0/3        on           802.1q         trunking      99
Port         Vlans allowed on trunk
Fa0/1        10,20,99
Fa0/3        10,20,99

PC5> ping 172.17.20.10
Pinging 172.17.20.10 with 32 bytes of data:
Reply from 172.17.20.10: bytes=32 time=147ms TTL=128
<output omitted>
```

A Common Problem with VLAN Configurations

In modern switched LANs, each VLAN corresponds to a unique IP subnet. If two devices in the same VLAN have different subnet IP addresses, they cannot communicate. This type of incorrect configuration is not uncommon, and it is easy to solve by identifying the offending device and changing the subnet IP addresses to the correct ones.

In the scenario pictured in Figure 3-33, the person using PC1 cannot connect to the faculty web server.

In Example 3-27, a check of the IP configuration settings of PC1 reveals the most common error in configuring VLANs: an incorrectly configured IP address. The PC1 computer is configured with an IP address of 172.172.10.21, but it should have been configured with 172.17.10.21; the mistake results in PC1 being on the wrong subnet.

Figure 3-33   VLAN Configuration Issues

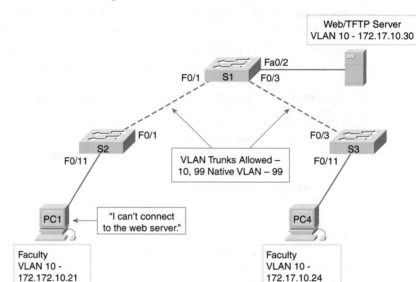

Example 3-27   IP Addressing on LAN Workstation

```
PC1> ipconfig

IP Address......................: 172.172.10.21
Subnet Mask.....................: 255.255.255.0
Default Gateway.................: 0.0.0.0

PC1>
```

After changing the IP address of PC1 to 172.17.10.21, Example 3-28 reveals that PC1 has regained connectivity to the web/TFTP server found at IP address 172.17.10.30.

Example 3-28   Connectivity Test After IP Address Adjustment

```
PC1> ping 172.17.10.30
Pinging 172.17.10.30 with 32 bytes of data:
Reply from 172.17.10.30: bytes=32 time=147ms TTL=128
<output omitted>
```

Packet Tracer
☐ Activity

Troubleshooting a VLAN Implementation (3.4.2)

Use this Packet Tracer Activity to troubleshoot connectivity problems between PCs on the same VLAN. Use File e3-3422.pka on the CD-ROM that accompanies this book to perform this activity using Packet Tracer.

Summary

In this chapter, we introduced VLANs. VLANs are used to segment broadcast domains in a switched LAN. This improves the performance and manageability of LANs. VLANs provide network administrators flexible control over traffic associated with devices in the LAN.

The principal type of VLANs are data VLANs, the default VLAN, the black hole VLAN, native VLANs, management VLANs, and voice VLANs.

VLAN trunks facilitate interswitch communication with multiple VLANs. IEEE 802.1Q frame tagging enables differentiation between Ethernet frames associated with distinct VLANs as they traverse common trunk links.

We discussed the configuration, verification, and troubleshooting of VLANs and VLAN trunks using the Cisco IOS CLI.

Labs

The labs available in the companion *LAN Switching and Wireless, CCNA Exploration Labs and Study Guide* (ISBN 1-58713-202-8) provide hands-on practice with the following topics introduced in this chapter:

Lab 3-1: Basic VLAN Configuration (3.5.1)

In this lab, you are guided to limit the effects of network broadcasts. One way to do this is to break up a large physical network into a number of smaller logical or virtual networks. This is one of the goals of VLANs. This lab teaches you the basics of configuring VLANs.

Lab 3-2: Challenge VLAN Configuration (3.5.2)

In this lab, with minimal guidance you limit the effects of network broadcasts. One way to do this is to break up a large physical network into a number of smaller logical or virtual networks. This is one of the goals of VLANs. This lab teaches you the basics of configuring VLANs.

Lab 3-3: Troubleshooting VLAN Configurations (3.5.3)

In this lab, you troubleshoot a misconfigured VLAN environment. You or your instructor loads the provided configurations into your lab equipment. Your objective is to locate and correct any and all errors in the configurations and establish end-to-end connectivity. Your final configuration should match the provided topology diagram and addressing table.

Many of the hands-on labs include Packet Tracer Companion Activities, where you can use Packet Tracer to complete a simulation of the lab. Look for this icon in *LAN Switching and Wireless, CCNA Exploration Labs and Study Guide* (ISBN 1-58713-202-8) for hands-on labs that have a Packet Tracer Companion.

Check Your Understanding

Complete all the review questions listed here to test your understanding of the topics and concepts in this chapter. Answers are listed in the Appendix, "Check Your Understanding and Challenge Questions Answer Key."

1. Switch S1 and Switch S2 are both configured with ports in the Marketing, Sales, Production, and Admin VLANs. Each VLAN contains 12 users. How many subnets are needed to address the VLANs?

   A. 1

   B. 2

   C. 4

   D. 8

   E. 12

   F. 24

2. What mechanism is used to achieve the separation between different VLANs as they cross a trunk link?

   A. VLAN tagging using 802.1Q protocol

   B. VLAN tagging using 802.1p protocol

   C. VLAN multiplexing

   D. VLAN set as a native VLAN

3. What are two options to consider when configuring a trunk link between two switches? (Choose two.)

   A. The **switchport nonegotiate** command must be configured for trunks that use DTP.

   B. Port security cannot be configured on the trunk interfaces.

   C. The native VLAN must be the same on both ends of the trunk.

   D. Different encapsulation types can be configured on both ends of the trunk link.

   E. Trunk ports can be configured only on Gigabit Ethernet interfaces.

4. A 12-port switch has been configured to support three VLANs named Sales, Marketing, and Finance. Each VLAN spans four ports on the switch. The network administrator has deleted the Marketing VLAN from the switch. What two statements describe the status of the ports associated with this VLAN? (Choose two.)

   A. The ports are inactive.

   B. The ports are administratively disabled.

   C. The ports will become trunks to carry data from all remaining VLANs.

   D. The ports will remain part of the Marketing VLAN until reassigned to another VLAN.

   E. The ports were released from the Marketing VLAN and automatically reassigned to VLAN 1.

5. Which three statements are true about hosts configured in the same VLAN? (Choose three.)

   A. Hosts in the same VLAN must be on the same IP subnet.

   B. Hosts in different VLANs can communicate with the aid of only the Layer 2 switch.

   C. Hosts in the same VLAN share the same broadcast domain.

   D. Hosts in the same VLAN share the same collision domain.

   E. Hosts in the same VLAN comply with the same security policy.

   F. Hosts in the same VLAN must be on the same physical segment.

6. Refer to Figure 3-34. Host C is unable to transfer data because it does not have the MAC address of the destination host. If Host C sends out an ARP request, which of the other hosts will see the message?

Figure 3-34   LAN Connectivity

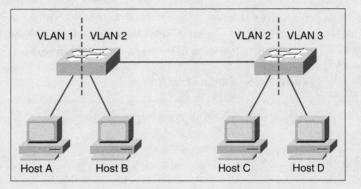

   A. Host A

   B. Host B

   C. Hosts A and B

   D. Hosts A and D

   E. Hosts B and D

   F. Hosts A, B, and D

7. With each listed VLAN characteristic on the right, indicate in the blank on the left whether it is a static VLAN characteristic or a dynamic VLAN characteristic. Use S for static and D for dynamic.

   _____   Each port associated with specific VLAN.

   _____   Manual configuration of port assignment required.

   _____   Ports work out their own configuration.

   _____   Less administrative overhead when users moved.

   _____   Requires administrator interaction when users moved.

   _____   Configured based on database.

8. With each listed characteristic on the right, indicate in the blank on the left whether it reflects a normal range VLAN, an extended range VLAN, or VLAN 1. Use N for normal range VLAN, E for extended range VLAN, and 1 for VLAN 1.

_____   1–1001

_____   1006–4094

_____   Not learned by VTP

_____   Stored in vlan.dat

_____   Default management VLAN

_____   Default native VLAN

_____   All ports are a member of by default

9. Refer to Figure 3-35. Brand new switches with empty MAC address tables are interconnected via a trunk link. All hosts on both switches are configured with the VLAN memberships shown. How is a frame sent from Host A forwarded to Host B?

Figure 3-35   Frame Flow

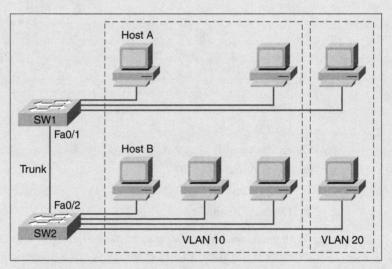

A. Switch SW1 floods the message from Host A to all hosts attached to SW1 that are members of VLAN 10.

B. Switch SW1 floods the message from Host A to all hosts attached to SW1.

C. Switch SW1 floods the message from Host A to all hosts attached to both switches.

D. Switch SW1 tags the frame with VLAN ID 10, and the frame is then flooded to all hosts on switch SW2 that are members of VLAN 10.

E. Switch SW1 tags the frame with VLAN ID 10, and the frame is then flooded to all hosts on switch SW2.

10. Refer to Example 3-29. Host 1 is connected to interface F0/4 with IP address 192.168.1.22/28. Host 2 is connected to interface F0/5 with IP address 192.168.1.33/28. Host 3 is connected to interface F0/6 with IP address 192.168.1.30/28. Select the three statements that describe the success of pinging from one host to another. (Choose three.)

Example 3-29   Connectivity After VLAN Configuration

```
Switch# configure terminal
Switch(config)# vlan 10
Switch(config-vlan)# name Accounting
Switch(config-vlan)# vlan 20
Switch(config-vlan)# name Marketing
Switch(config-vlan)# interface range f0/4 , f0/6
Switch(config-if-range)# switchport mode access
Switch(config-if-range)# switchport access vlan 10
Switch(config-if-range)# interface f0/5
Switch(config-if)# switchport mode access
Switch(config-if)# switchport access vlan 20
```

A. Host 1 can ping Host 2.

B. Host 1 cannot ping Host 2.

C. Host 1 can ping Host 3.

D. Host 1 cannot ping Host 3.

E. Host 2 can ping Host 3.

F. Host 2 cannot ping Host 3.

11. Which three options accurately associate the Catalyst switch command with the result? (Choose three.)

A. **show vlan id** *vlan-id*: displays information about a specific VLAN.

B. **show vlan**: displays detailed information about all VLANs on the switch.

C. **show vlan brief**: displays detailed information about all VLANs on the switch.

D. **show interface f0/1 switchport**: displays information about a specific port.

E. **show interface f0/1**: displays VLAN information about a specific port.

12. Match the commands with the correct descriptions.

_____   **switchport mode trunk**

_____   **switchport mode dynamic desirable**

_____   **switchport nonegotiate**

_____   **switchport mode access**

A. Configures the port to negotiate a trunk

B. Configures the trunk to not send DTP packets

C. Configures the port as a permanent 802.1Q trunk

D. Disables trunk mode

13. Match the problem definition with the correct problem description.

_____   Native VLAN mismatch

_____   Trunk mode mismatch

_____   Incorrect VLAN list

_____   VLAN subnet conflict

A. Both switches are configured to dynamic auto and will not negotiate a link.

B. Not all the VLANs needed are allowed to traverse a trunk.

C. Two VLANs are sharing the same address space.

D. The VLAN configured for untagged frames is not the same on two switches connected by a trunk.

14. Which three options accurately associate the static, dynamic, or voice VLAN membership with the port membership statement? (Choose three.)

A. Static VLAN port membership: port on a switch that can change the manually assigned VLAN configuration dynamically

B. Static VLAN port membership: port on a switch that maintains its assigned VLAN configuration until it is changed manually

C. Dynamic VLAN port membership: port on a switch using VMPS and associating a port to a VLAN based on the destination MAC address

D. Dynamic VLAN port membership: port on a switch using VMPS and associating a port to a VLAN based on the source MAC address

E. Voice VLAN port membership: access port attached to a PC, configured to use one VLAN for voice traffic and another VLAN for data traffic

F. Voice VLAN port membership: access port attached to an IP phone, configured to use one VLAN for voice traffic and another VLAN for data traffic

Challenge Questions and Activities

These questions require a deeper application of the concepts covered in this chapter. You can find the answers in the Appendix.

1. Which of the following best describes the mapping between VLANs and IP subnets in a modern switched network?

A. One IP subnet to many VLANs

B. One VLAN to many IP subnets

C. Two IP subnets to one VLAN

D. Two VLANs to one IP subnet

E. One IP subnet to one VLAN

F. Varies with the model of Cisco Catalyst switch

2. Refer to Figure 3-36. The dashed line indicates a trunk link. S1 and S2 are members of VLAN 99. Which two of the following are true? (Choose two.)

Figure 3-36   LAN Connectivity

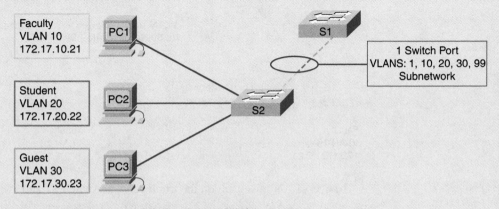

A. All PCs can successfully ping each other.

B. No PC can successfully ping another PC.

C. Switch S1 can successfully ping switch S2.

D. All the PCs can successfully ping switch S1.

E. All the PCs can successfully ping switch S2.

3. Which of the following is normally performed at the `Switch(config-vlan)#` prompt?

A. Addition of VLANs

B. Deletion of VLANs

C. Assignment of ports to VLANs

D. Naming of VLANs

E. Assignment of the native VLAN

4. Refer to Figure 3-37. What are some of the possible causes of the lack of connectivity?

Figure 3-37   Lack of Connectivity

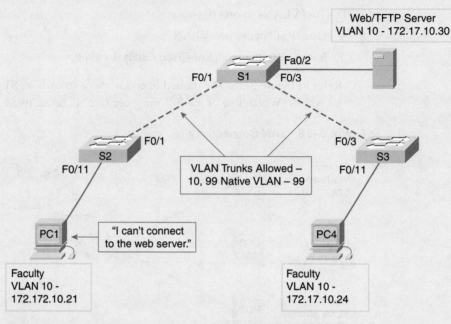

A. Native VLAN mismatch on the trunk between switch S1 and switch S2.

B. Trunk mode mismatch between switch S1 and switch S2.

C. Misconfigured set of allowed VLANs on trunk between switch S1 and switch S2.

D. Misconfigured IP addresses associated with VLAN 10.

E. A link is down along the path between PC1 and the web/TFTP server.

Look for this icon in *LAN Switching and Wireless, CCNA Exploration Labs and Study Guide*, (ISBN 1-58713-202-8) for instructions on how to perform the Packet Tracer Skills Integration Challenge for this chapter.

Objectives

Upon completion of this chapter, you will be able to answer the following questions:

- What is the role of VTP in a converged switched LAN?

- How does VTP operate using VTP domains, VTP modes, VTP advertisements, and VTP pruning?

- How do you configure VTP on the switches in a switched LAN?

Key Terms

This chapter uses the following key terms. You can find the definitions in the Glossary.

As the size of the network for a small- or medium-sized business grows, the management involved in maintaining the network grows. In the previous chapter, you learned how to create and manage VLANs and trunks using Cisco IOS commands. The focus was on managing VLAN information on a single switch. But what if you have many switches to manage? How will you manage the VLAN database across many switches? In this chapter, you will explore how you can use the *VLAN Trunking Protocol (VTP)* of Cisco Catalyst switches to simplify management of the VLAN database across multiple switches.

VTP Concepts

As the number of switches increases on a small- or medium-sized business network, the overall administration required to manage VLANs and trunks in a network becomes a challenge. Cisco engineers invented a technology to help network administrators automate some of the tasks related to VLAN creation, deletion, and synchronization.

What Is VTP?

In Figure 4-1, a network manager adds a new VLAN, VLAN 30, the guest VLAN, on S1. S2 and S3 do not know about this addition unless VLAN 30 is manually configured on each switch.

Figure 4-1   Adding VLAN 30

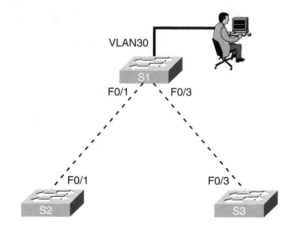

When you consider the larger network in Figure 4-2, the VLAN management challenge becomes clearer. After you have manually updated this network a few times, you may want to know if there is a way for the switches to learn what the VLANs are so that you do not have to manually configure them on each switch. You are ready to learn about VTP, which solves the problem of automated VLAN additions and changes based on a singular configuration.

Figure 4-2   Large Number of Switches Multiplies Configuration

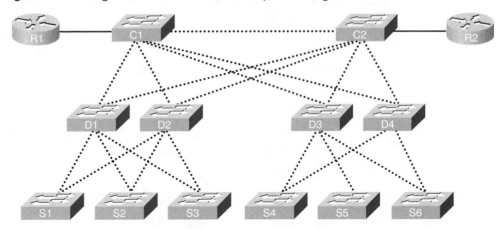

VTP allows a network manager to configure a switch so that it will propagate VLAN configurations to other switches in the network, as illustrated in Figure 4-3. The switch can be configured in the role of a VTP server or a VTP client or in the VTP transparent mode. VTP only learns about normal-range VLANs (VLAN IDs 1 to 1005). Extended-range VLANs (IDs greater than 1005) are not supported by VTP.

Figure 4-3   VLAN Propagation from VTP Server

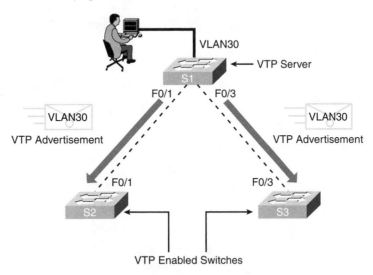

VTP allows a network manager to make changes on a switch that is configured as a VTP server. Basically, the VTP server distributes and synchronizes VLAN information to VTP-enabled switches throughout the switched network. VTP reduces maintenance overhead and configuration errors involved with making VLAN changes on multiple switches. VTP stores VLAN configurations in the VLAN database file: vlan.dat.

After a trunk is established between a VTP server and a VTP client, VTP advertisements are exchanged between the switches. Both the server and client leverage advertisements from one another to ensure that each has an accurate record of VLAN information. VTP advertisements will not be exchanged if the trunk between the switches is inactive. The details of how VTP works constitute the remainder of this chapter.

Benefits of VTP

VTP maintains VLAN configuration consistency by managing the addition, deletion, and renaming of VLANs across multiple Catalyst switches in a network. VTP offers a number of benefits for network managers:

- VLAN configuration consistency across the network

- Accurate tracking and monitoring of VLANs

- Dynamic reporting of added VLANs across a network

VTP Components

You need to be familiar with a number of key components when learning about VTP. Here is a brief description of the components, which will be elaborated on throughout the chapter:

- **VTP domain:** Consists of one or more interconnected switches. All switches in a domain, as illustrated in Figure 4-4, share VLAN configuration details using VTP advertisements. A router or Layer 3 switch defines the boundary of each domain.

Figure 4-4 VTP Domains

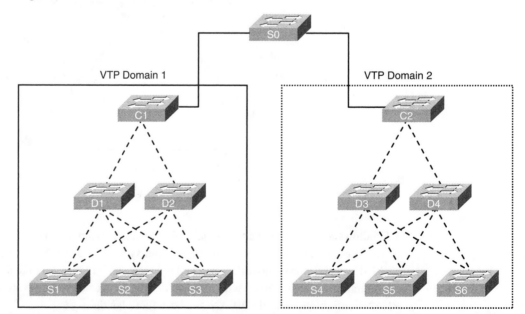

■ *VTP advertisements*: VTP uses a hierarchy of advertisements, as pictured in Figure 4-5, to distribute and synchronize the VLAN configuration across a VTP domain. Switches share information about VLANs using VTP advertisements (messages), as depicted in Figure 4-5. In this chapter, we study three VTP message types: summary advertisements, subset advertisements, and advertisement requests.

Figure 4-5   VTP Advertisements

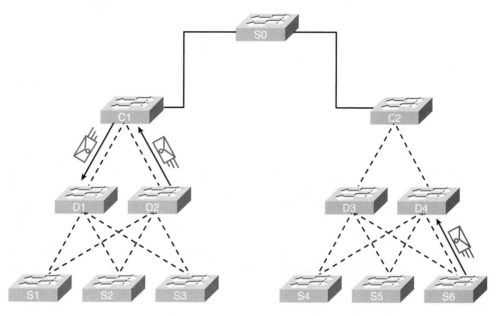

■ *VTP modes*: A switch can be configured in one of three modes: server, client, or transparent, as illustrated in Figure 4-6.

■ *VTP server*: VTP servers advertise the VTP domain VLAN information to other VTP-enabled switches in the same VTP domain. VTP servers store the VLAN information for the entire domain in NVRAM. The server is where VLANs can be created, deleted, or renamed for the domain.

■ *VTP client*: VTP clients function similar to the way VTP servers do, but you cannot create, change, or delete VLANs on a VTP client. A VTP client stores VLAN information for the entire domain only while the switch is on. A switch reset deletes the VLAN information. You must configure a switch to change its VTP mode to client.

■ *VTP transparent*: VTP transparent mode switches forward VTP advertisements to VTP clients and VTP servers, but do not originate or otherwise process VTP advertisements. VLANs that are created, renamed, or deleted on a VTP transparent mode switch are local to that switch only.

■ *VTP pruning*: VTP pruning increases available network bandwidth by restricting flooded traffic to trunk links that the traffic must use to reach the destination devices. Without VTP pruning, a switch floods broadcast, multicast, and unknown unicast traffic across all trunk links within a VLAN in a VTP domain.

Figure 4-6   VTP Modes

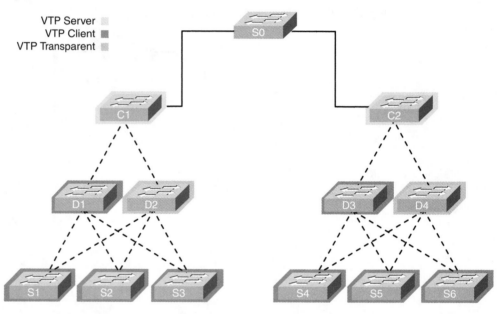

VTP Operation

In this section, we delve into the operation of VTP. We analyze the default VTP configuration, VTP domains, VTP messaging, VTP modes, and VTP pruning. This provides a solid foundation to prepare for VTP configuration.

Default VTP Configuration

A Catalyst switch comes from the factory with default settings. The default VTP settings are as follows:

■ *VTP Version*: 1

■ VTP Domain Name: null

■ VTP Mode: Server

■ Configuration Revision: 0

■ VLANs: 1 (VLAN 1)

VTP automatically distributes VLAN information across a VTP domain. However, the benefit of this automation comes at a cost—when you add a switch, it must be in its default VTP configuration. If you add a VTP-enabled switch that is configured with nondefault VTP settings, it is possible that the settings will supersede the existing network VTP configuration and automatically propagate changes throughout the VTP domain that are difficult to correct. In this chapter, you will learn how to properly add switches to a VTP network.

VTP has three versions: 1, 2, and 3. Version 3 is not currently supported on any Catalyst switches running IOS images. Also, only one VTP version is allowed in a VTP domain at a time. The default is VTP version 1. A Cisco 2960 switch supports VTP version 2, but it is disabled by default. A detailed discussion of VTP versions is beyond the scope of this book.

Example 4-1 shows how to view the VTP settings for a Catalyst 2960 switch, S1. The Cisco IOS command **show vtp status** displays the VTP status. The output shows that switch S1 is in VTP server mode by default and that there is no VTP domain name assigned. The output also shows the VTP version 2 available on the switch, but that VTP version 2 is disabled.

Example 4-1 Default VTP Configuration

```
S1# show vtp status
VTP Version                     : 2
Configuration Revision          : 0
Maximum VLANs supported locally : 255
Number of existing VLANs        : 5
VTP Operating Mode              : Server
VTP Domain Name                 :
VTP Pruning Mode                : Disabled
VTP V2 Mode                     : Disabled
VTP Traps Generation            : Disabled
MD5 digest                      : 0x3F 0x37 0x45 0x9A 0x37 0x53 0xA6 0xDE
Configuration last modified by 0.0.0.0 at 3-1-93 00:14:07
```

You will use the **show vtp status** command frequently as you configure and manage VTP on a network. The following briefly describes the **show vtp status** parameters:

- **VTP Version:** Displays the VTP version the switch is capable of running. By default, the switch implements version 1, but can be set to version 2.

- *VTP Configuration Revision Number:* The current configuration revision number on this switch. You will learn more about revision numbers in this chapter.

- **Maximum VLANs Supported Locally:** The maximum number of VLANs supported locally.

- **Number of Existing VLANs:** The number of existing VLANs.

- **VTP Operating Mode:** Can be server, client, or transparent.

- **VTP Domain Name:** The name that identifies the administrative domain for the switch.

- **VTP Pruning Mode**: Displays whether pruning is enabled or disabled.

- **VTP V2 Mode:** Displays whether VTP version 2 mode is enabled. VTP version 2 is disabled by default.

- **VTP Traps Generation:** Displays whether VTP traps are sent to a network management station.

- *MD5 Digest***:** Hashing is a one-way encryption of data and MD5 digest is a hash algorithm. VTP hashes VTP data and a password to generate a unique 15-byte MD5 digest (or data string). VTP adds the hash to VTP messages and neighbor switches use the hash to validate the message.

- **Configuration Last Modified:** Date and time of the last configuration modification. Displays the IP address of the switch that caused the configuration change to the database.

VTP Domains

VTP allows you to separate your network into smaller management domains to help reduce VLAN management. An additional benefit of configuring VTP domains is that it limits the extent to which configuration changes are propagated in the network if an error occurs.

A VTP domain consists of one switch or several interconnected switches sharing the same VTP domain name. A switch can be a member of only one VTP domain at a time. When you create or modify VLANs on a VTP server, VLAN information propagates throughout the VTP domain.

Figure 4-7 shows a network with two VTP domains: Cisco2 and Cisco3. In this chapter, the three switches, S1, S2, and S3, will be configured for VTP.

Figure 4-7   VTP Domains

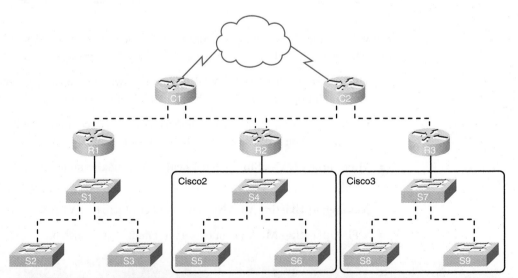

Example 4-2 shows the VTP configuration on switch S4 of VTP domain Cisco2.

Example 4-2 Default VTP Configuration

```
S4# show vtp status
VTP Version                     : 2
Configuration Revision          : 3
Maximum VLANs supported locally : 255
Number of existing VLANs        : 8
VTP Operating Mode              : Server
VTP Domain Name                 : Cisco2
VTP Pruning Mode                : Disabled
VTP V2 Mode                     : Disabled
VTP Traps Generation            : Disabled
MD5 digest                      : 0x3F 0x37 0x45 0x9A 0x37 0x53 0xA6 0xDE
Configuration last modified by 192.168.0.99 at 3-9-93 05:20:38
```

For a VTP server or client switch to participate in a VTP-enabled network, it must be a part of the same VTP domain. When switches are in different VTP domains, they do not exchange VTP messages. A VTP server propagates the VTP domain name to all switches. Domain name propagation uses three VTP components: servers, clients, and advertisements.

In Figure 4-8, three switches, S1, S2, and S3, are in their default VTP configuration; in particular, they are all VTP servers. VTP domain names have not been configured on any of the switches.

Figure 4-8   VTP Domain Name Propagation

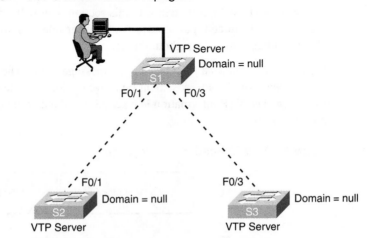

Note

Cisco recommends that access to the domain name configuration functions be protected by a password. The details of password configuration will be presented later.

How does the domain name get placed into a VTP advertisement? What information is exchanged between VTP-enabled switches? In the next topic, you will learn details about VTP advertisements and find answers to these questions.

The network manager configures the VTP domain name as Cisco1 on the VTP server switch S1. The VTP server sends out a VTP advertisement with the new domain name embedded inside. The S2 and S3 VTP server switches update their VTP configuration to the new domain name, as pictured in Figure 4-9.

Figure 4-9   VTP Domain Updates

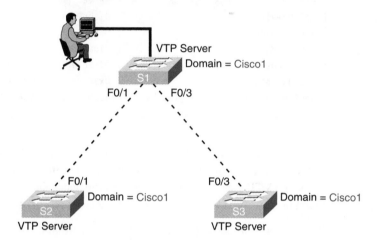

VTP Advertising

VTP advertisements (or messages) distribute VTP domain name and VLAN configuration changes to VTP-enabled switches. In this section, you will learn about the VTP frame structure and how the three types of advertisements enable VTP to distribute and synchronize VLAN configurations throughout the network.

A VTP frame includes a VTP header and message fields. The content of the header and fields depends on the advertisement type. We explore each message type in the forthcoming discussion. The VTP information is inserted into the data field of an Ethernet frame, as seen in Figure 4-10.

Figure 4-10   VTP Header and Message

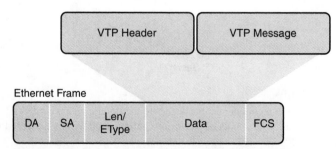

The Ethernet frame is then encapsulated as an 802.1Q frame, as pictured in Figure 4-11. Each switch in the domain sends periodic advertisements out of each trunk port to a reserved multicast address. These advertisements are received by neighboring switches, which update their VTP and VLAN configurations as necessary.

Figure 4-11   VTP Information Within 802.1Q Frame

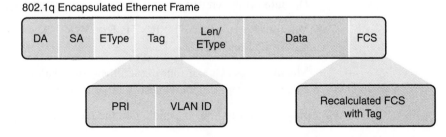

In Figure 4-12, you can see the VTP frame structure in more detail. The VTP advertisement includes a VTP header and message data; the format of the advertisement is determined by the message type. The receiving VTP-enabled switch looks for specific fields and values in the 802.1Q frame to know what to process.

Figure 4-12   VTP Frame Structure

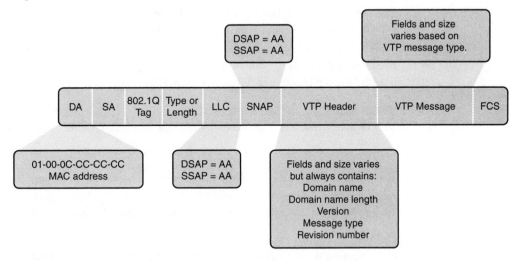

The following key fields are present when a VTP frame is encapsulated as an 802.1Q frame:

- **Destination MAC address:** This address is set to 01-00-0C-CC-CC-CC, which is the reserved multicast address for all VTP messages.

- **LLC field:** The logical link control (LLC) field contains a destination service access point (DSAP) and a source service access point (SSAP) set to the value of AA.

- **SNAP field:** Subnetwork Access Protocol (SNAP) field has an OUI set to AAAA and type set to 2003.

- **VTP header field:** The contents of the VTP header fields vary depending on the VTP message type. In any case, the header information includes the following information:

  - **Domain name:** Identifies the administrative domain for the switch.

  - **Domain name length:** Length of the domain name.

  - **Version:** Set to either VTP 1, VTP 2, or VTP 3. The Cisco 2960 switch supports only VTP 1 and VTP 2.

  - **Message type:** One of four possibilities: summary advertisement, subset advertisement, advertisement request, VTP join message.

- **VTP message field:** Varies depending on the message type.

Note

A VTP frame is encapsulated in an 802.1Q Ethernet frame. The entire 802.1Q Ethernet frame is the VTP advertisement often called a VTP message. Often the terms frame, advertisement, and message are used interchangeably.

VTP Configuration Revision Number

The configuration revision number is a 32-bit number that indicates the level of revision for a VTP frame. The default configuration revision number for a switch is zero. Each time a VLAN is added or removed, the configuration revision number increments. Each VTP summary and subset advertisement has a VTP configuration revision number associated with it, used by the devices to synchronize VLAN information.

Note

A VTP domain name change does not increment the revision number. Instead, it resets the revision number to zero.

The configuration revision number determines whether the configuration information received from another VTP-enabled switch is more recent than the version stored on the switch. Figure 4-13 shows a network manager adding VLANs 10, 20, and 30 to switch S1.

Example 4-3 shows that the revision number on switch S1 is 3 and the number of VLANs is eight because three VLANs have been added to the five default VLANs.

Example 4-3 Modified VTP Configuration

```
S1# show vtp status
VTP Version                     : 2
Configuration Revision          : 3
Maximum VLANs supported locally : 255
```

```
Number of existing VLANs        : 8
VTP Operating Mode              : Server
VTP Domain Name                 : cisco1
VTP Pruning Mode                : Disabled
VTP V2 Mode                     : Disabled
VTP Traps Generation            : Disabled
MD5 digest                      : 0x3F 0x37 0x45 0x9A 0x37 0x53 0xA6 0xDE
Configuration last modified by 192.168.0.99 at 3-9-93 05:20:38
```

Figure 4-13   VTP Revision Number

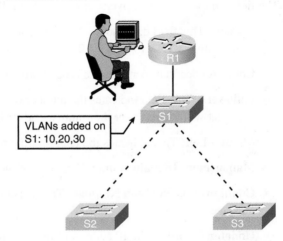

The revision number plays an important and complex role in enabling VTP to distribute and synchronize VTP domain and VLAN configuration information. To fully appreciate the role of the revision number, you first need to learn about the three types of VTP advertisements and more details regarding VTP modes.

VTP Advertisement Types

VTP uses summary, subset, and request advertisements. VTP uses advertisements to distribute and synchronize information about domains and VLAN configurations. Each type of VTP advertisement sends information about several parameters used by VTP.

Summary advertisements constitute the majority of VTP advertisement traffic. A summary advertisement contains the VTP domain name, the current revision number, and some other VTP configuration details. Figure 4-14 shows the fields in a VTP summary advertisement.

Figure 4-14   VTP Summary Advertisement

Summary Advertisement			
Version	Code	Followers	MgmtD Len
Management Domain Name (Zero-Padded to 32 Bytes)			
Configuration Revision Number			
Updater Identity			
Updater Timestamp (12 Bytes)			
MD5 Digest (16 Bytes)			

The fields in the summary advertisement are the following:

- **Version:** This field displays the VTP version used. On Catalyst 2960 switches, the version is either VTP V1 or VTP V2.

- **Code:** A code that identifies the type of advertisement.

- **Followers:** This field indicates the number of subset advertisements (between 0 and 255) that will be sent after the summary advertisement.

- **MgmtD Len:** This indicates the length of the management domain name.

- **Management Domain Name:** The name of the VTP domain.

- **Configuration Revision Number:** The revision number of the VTP server sending the message.

- **Updater Identity:** The IP address of the switch that is the last to have incremented the configuration revision.

- **Update Timestamp:** The date and time of the last increment of the configuration revision.

- **MD5 Digest:** Message Digest 5 (MD5) carries the VTP password if MD5 is configured and is used to authenticate a VTP update.

Summary advertisements are sent

- Every 5 minutes by a VTP server or client to inform neighboring VTP-enabled switches of the current VTP configuration revision number for its VTP domain

- Immediately after a configuration has been made

A *subset advertisement* contains VLAN information. Figure 4-15 displays the fields of a subset advertisement.

Figure 4-15 VTP Subset Advertisement

Subset Advertisements			
Version	Code	Seq-Number	Domain Name Length
Management Domain Name (zero-padded to 32 bytes)			
Configuration Revision Number			
VLAN-info Field 1			
:			
VLAN-info Field N			

The fields in the subset advertisement are the following:

- **Version:** This field displays the VTP version used. On Catalyst 2960 switches, the version is either VTP V1 or VTP V2.

- **Code:** A code that identifies the type of advertisement. 0x02 indicates a subset advertisement.

- **Sequence Number:** This is the sequence of the packet in the stream of packets that follow a summary advertisement. The sequence starts with 1. Up to 255 subset advertisements can follow a summary advertisement. The sequence number is used by VTP to keep track of these subset advertisements.

- **Domain Name Length:** Indicates the length of the management domain name.

- **Management Domain Name:** The name of the VTP domain.

- **Configuration Revision Number:** The revision number configured on the VTP server sending the message.

- **VLAN-Info Field:** The information associated with a particular VLAN, ordered so that lower-valued VLANs occur first.

The contents of the VLAN-info field contain information for each VLAN and its format as displayed in Figure 4-16. Notice that the VLAN name is part of the information propagated.

Figure 4-16 VLAN-Info Field

VLAN-info			
Info Length	Status	VLAN-Type	VLAN-name Len
ISL VLAN-id		MTU Size	
802.10 Index			
VLAN-name (Padded with 0s to Multiples of 4 bytes)			

Changes that trigger the subset advertisement include the following:

- Creating or deleting a VLAN
- Suspending or activating a VLAN
- Changing the name of a VLAN
- Changing the MTU of a VLAN

It may take multiple subset advertisements to fully update the VLAN information.

Request advertisements are sent with a VTP server as the intended recipient of the multicast message. When a request advertisement is sent to a VTP server in the same VTP domain, the VTP server responds by sending a summary advertisement and the necessary number of subset advertisements.

The contents of the request advertisement are displayed in Figure 4-17.

Figure 4-17   VTP Request Advertisement

Advertisement Request			
Version	Code	Rvsd	MgmtD Len
Management Domain Name (zero-padded to 32 bytes)			
Start Value			

The fields in the request advertisement are the following:

- **Version:** This field displays the VTP version used. On Catalyst 2960 switches, the version is either VTP V1 or VTP V2.
- **Code:** The format for this is 0x03 for an advertisement request.
- **Rsvd:** This is a reserved field, always set to zero.
- **MgmtD Len:** This indicates the length of the VTP domain name.
- **Management Domain Name:** This is the name of the VTP domain.
- **Start Value:** This field is used when there are several subset advertisements. If the first *n* subset advertisements have been received and the subsequent one, *n+1*, has not been received, the VTP-enabled switch requests only advertisements beginning with subset advertisement *n+1*.

Request advertisements are sent if

- The VTP domain name has been changed.
- The switch receives a summary advertisement with a higher configuration revision number than its own.
- A subset advertisement message is missed.
- The switch has been reset.

VTP Modes

A Catalyst switch configured with Cisco IOS Software can be configured in either server, client, or transparent mode. These modes differ in how they are used to manage and advertise VTP domains and VLANs.

In VTP server mode, the switch administrator can create, modify, and delete VLANs for the entire VTP domain. VTP server mode is the default mode for a Catalyst switch. VTP servers advertise their VLAN configurations to other switches in the same VTP domain and synchronize their VLAN configurations with other switches based on advertisement exchanges over trunk links. VTP servers keep track of updates through a configuration revision number. Other switches in the same VTP domain compare their configuration revision number with the revision number received from a VTP server to see if they need to synchronize their VLAN database.

If a switch is in client mode, you cannot create, change, or delete VLANs. In addition, the VLAN configuration information that a VTP client switch receives from a VTP server switch is stored in RAM, not NVRAM. When a VTP client is shut down and restarted, VLAN information is lost, and it sends a request advertisement to a VTP server for VLAN configuration information.

Switches configured as VTP clients are more typically found in large networks; in a network consisting of several hundred switches, it is harder to coordinate network upgrades. Often there are many network administrators working at different times of the day. Having only a few switches that are physically able to maintain VLAN configurations makes it easier to control VLAN upgrades and to track which network administrators performed them.

For large networks, having client switches is also more cost-effective. By default, all switches are configured to be VTP servers. This configuration is suitable for small networks in which the amount of VLAN information is small and easily stored in NVRAM on the switches. In a large network, the network administrator must decide if the cost of purchasing switches with enough NVRAM to store the duplicate VLAN information is too much. A cost-conscious network administrator could choose to configure a few well-equipped switches as VTP servers and then use switches with less memory as VTP clients. The number of VTP servers should be chosen to provide the degree of redundancy that is desired in the network.

Switches configured in transparent mode forward VTP advertisements received over trunk links to other switches in the VTP domain. VTP transparent mode switches do not advertise their VLAN configuration and do not synchronize their VLAN configuration with any other switch. Configure a switch in VTP transparent mode when you have VLAN configurations that have local significance and should not be shared with the rest of the network.

In transparent mode, VLAN configurations are saved in NVRAM (but not advertised to other switches), so the configuration is available after reloading the switch. This means that when a VTP transparent mode switch reboots, it does not revert to the default VTP server mode, but remains in VTP transparent mode.

Table 4-1 summarizes the characteristics of the three VTP modes.

Table 4-1   VTP Modes

	VTP Server	VTP Client	VTP Transparent
Description	Manage domain and VLAN configurations	Updates VTP configurations VTP client switches cannot change VLAN configurations	Able to manage local VLAN configurations Local VLAN configurations not shared with VTP network
Respond to VTP advertisements?	Participates fully	Participates fully	Forwards only VTP advertisements
Global VLAN configuration preserved on restart?	Yes, global configurations stored in NVRAM	No, global configurations stored in RAM, not in NVRAM	No, local VLAN configuration only is stored in NVRAM
Update other VTP enabled switches?	Yes	Yes	No

VTP Server-to-Client Behavior

Let us look at the various VTP features used together to distribute and synchronize VTP domain and VLAN configurations in a VTP-enabled network. Three switches, S1, S2, and S3, are configured with their factory default settings in the topology displayed in Figure 4-18.

Figure 4-18   VTP Default Settings

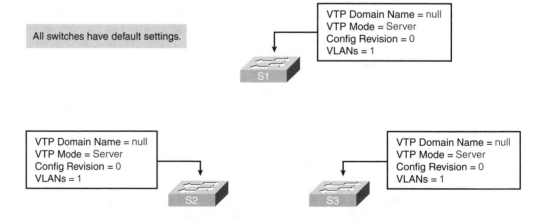

All switches have default settings.

VTP Domain Name = null
VTP Mode = Server
Config Revision = 0
VLANs = 1

VTP Domain Name = null
VTP Mode = Server
Config Revision = 0
VLANs = 1

VTP Domain Name = null
VTP Mode = Server
Config Revision = 0
VLANs = 1

Next, S2 is configured as a client and S3 in transparent mode, as shown in Figure 4-19.

Figure 4-19 Conversion to Client and Transparent

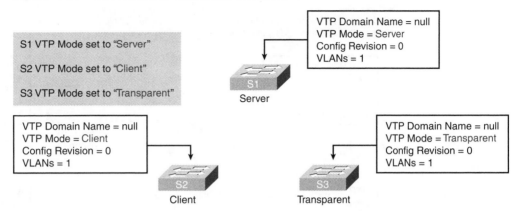

Then, the VTP domain name on S1 is changed to cisco1 and VLAN 2 and VLAN 3 are also added. S1 is trunked to S2 and S3. Summary advertisements are sent to S2 and S3 over the 802.1Q trunks. Switch S2, a VTP client, changes its VTP domain name to cisco1. Switch S3 does not act on the VTP messages from S1. S2 sends a request advertisement to S1 for VLAN information; S1 then sends a summary advertisement and a subset advertisement to S2 with detailed VLAN information. S1 updates its domain name, configuration revision number, and VLAN list, as shown in Figure 4-20, and S3 changes its VTP domain name to cisco1.

Figure 4-20 Updated VLAN Information

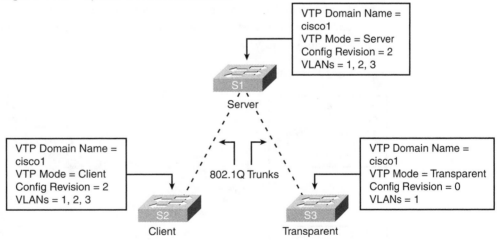

S2's configuration revision number is incremented from 0 to 2 because VLAN 2 and VLAN 3 were added on VTP server S1.

VTP Server-to-Transparent-to-Client Behavior

Let us look at a second example exemplifying the distribution and synchronization of VTP domain and VLAN configurations in a VTP-enabled network. Four switches, S1, S2, S3, and S4, are configured as shown in the topology displayed in Figure 4-21.

Figure 4-21   Initial VTP Settings

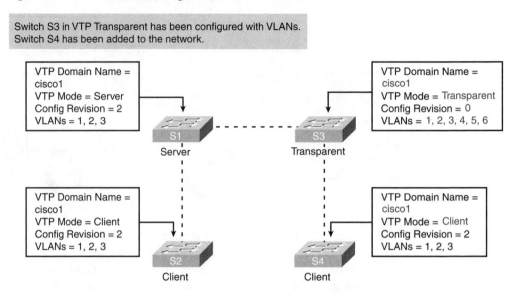

S1 sends out a periodic summary advertisement, which is forwarded by S3 to S4. S4 sends a request advertisement, which is forwarded by S3 to S1. S1 responds with a summary advertisement followed by a subset advertisement containing VLAN information, passing through S3 and arriving at S4; S4 updates its VLAN information to include VLAN 2 and VLAN 3 and an updated configuration revision number of 2. Throughout this process, S3 never updates its VLAN information based on the VTP messages. Figure 4-22 reflects the final VTP settings and VLAN information.

Figure 4-22   Final VTP Settings

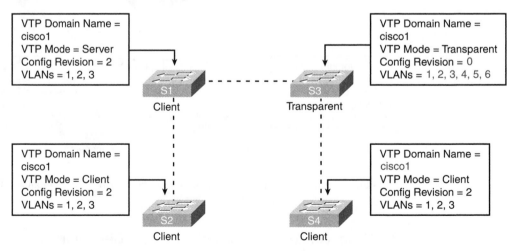

VTP Pruning

Quiz 1.

VTP pruning prevents unnecessary flooding of broadcast information from one VLAN across all trunks in a VTP domain. VTP pruning permits switches to negotiate which VLANs are associated to ports at the opposing end of trunks and, hence, prune the VLANs that are not associated with ports on the remote switch. VTP pruning is disabled by default. VTP pruning is enabled using the **vtp pruning** global configuration command. You need to enable pruning on only one VTP server switch in the domain. In Figure 4-23, you enable VTP pruning on VTP server switch S1. The figure shows a network with VLAN 10 and VLAN 20 configured. Switch S3 has VLAN 20 configured, and switch S2 has VLAN 10 and VLAN 20 configured. Examine the topology in Figure 4-23.

Figure 4-23 VTP Pruning

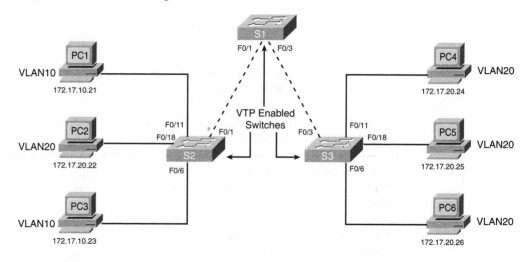

Example 4-4 shows the pertinent configurations of switches S1, S2, and S3.

Example 4-4 VTP Pruning

```
S1# show interfaces trunk
Port            Mode         Encapsulation    Status          Native vlan
Fa0/1           on           802.1q           trunking        1
Fa0/3           on           802.1q           trunking        1


Port            Vlans allowed on trunk
Fa0/1           1-1005
```

```
Fa0/3          1-1005


Port           Vlans allowed and active in management domain
Fa0/1          1,10,20,1002,1003,1004,1005
Fa0/3          1,10,20,1002,1003,1004,1005


Port           Vlans in spanning tree forwarding state and not pruned
Fa0/1          1,10,20,1002,1003,1004,1005
Fa0/3          1,10,20,1002,1003,1004,1005
```

```
S2# show interfaces trunk
Port           Mode       Encapsulation    Status        Native vlan
Fa0/1          on         802.1q           trunking      1


Port           Vlans allowed on trunk
Fa0/1          1-1005


Port           Vlans allowed and active in management domain
Fa0/1          1,10,20,1002,1003,1004,1005


Port           Vlans in spanning tree forwarding state and not pruned
Fa0/1          1,10,20,1002,1003,1004,1005
```

```
S3# show interfaces trunk
Port           Mode       Encapsulation    Status        Native vlan
Fa0/3          on         802.1q           trunking      1


Port           Vlans allowed on trunk
Fa0/3          1-1005


Port           Vlans allowed and active in management domain
Fa0/3          1,10,20,1002,1003,1004,1005


Port           Vlans in spanning tree forwarding state and not pruned
Fa0/3          1,10,20,1002,1003,1004,1005
```

VTP Pruning in Action

Recall that a VLAN creates an isolated broadcast domain. A switch floods broadcast, multi-cast, and unknown unicast traffic across all trunk links within a VTP domain. When a computer or device broadcasts on a VLAN, such as VLAN 10 pictured in Figure 4-23, the broadcast traffic travels across all trunk links throughout the network to all ports on all switches in VLAN 10.

In Figure 4-23, switches S1, S2, and S3 all receive broadcast frames from computer PC1. The broadcast traffic from PC1 consumes bandwidth on the trunk link between S1 and S3 and consumes processor time on S1 and S2. In this closed LAN topology, it is unnecessary for ANY VLAN 10 traffic to traverse either of the trunk links. Broadcast traffic from PC1 is stopped from entering the trunk connecting switches S1 and S2. VTP pruning prevents egress VLAN 10 traffic from port F0/1 on switch S2, as pictured in Figure 4-24.

Figure 4-24   Pruning of VLAN 10

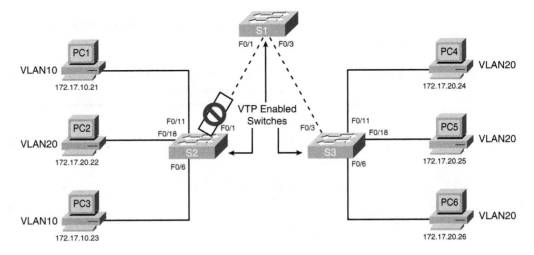

When VTP pruning is enabled on a network, it reconfigures the trunk links based on which ports are configured with which VLANs. Example 4-5 displays the supported VLANs on the trunks of switches S1 and S2.

Example 4-5 show interfaces trunk with VTP Pruning

```
S1# show interfaces trunk
Port          Mode          Encapsulation      Status        Native vlan
Fa0/1         on            802.1q             trunking      1
Fa0/3         on            802.1q             trunking      1


Port          Vlans allowed on trunk
Fa0/1         1-1005
Fa0/3         1-1005


Port          Vlans allowed and active in management domain
Fa0/1             1,10,20,1002,1003,1004,1005
Fa0/3             1,10,20,1002,1003,1004,1005


Port          Vlans in spanning tree forwarding state and not pruned
Fa0/1             1,10,20,1002,1003,1004,1005
```

```
Fa0/3              1,10,20,1002,1003,1004,1005

S2# show interfaces trunk
Port          Mode         Encapsulation        Status         Native vlan
Fa0/1         on           802.1q               trunking       1


Port          Vlans allowed on trunk
Fa0/1         1-1005


Port          Vlans allowed and active in management domain
Fa0/1         1,10,20,1002,1003,1004,1005


Port          Vlans in spanning tree forwarding state and not pruned
Fa0/1         1,20,1002,1003,1004,1005
```

The shaded area shows that the trunk on port F0/1 does not allow VLAN 10 traffic. VLAN 10 is not listed.

For more details on VTP pruning, visit

www.cisco.com/en/US/products/ps6406/products_configuration_guide_chapter09186a0080 81d9ac.html#wp1035139.

Configure VTP

Now that you are familiar with the functioning of VTP, you are ready to learn how to configure a Cisco Catalyst switch to use VTP. It is often the case in computer networking that the underlying concepts and processes of a given protocol are complicated, but the configuration is relatively simple. This is the case for VTP, and we'll see this is even more true with STP, which we explore in Chapter 5.

Configuring VTP

Figure 4-25 shows the reference topology for this chapter. VTP will be configured based on this topology.

Follow these guidelines to ensure that you configure a VTP server successfully:

- Confirm that all the switches you are going to configure have been set to their default settings.

- Always reset the configuration revision number before installing a previously configured switch into a VTP domain. Not resetting the configuration revision number allows for potential disruption in the VLAN configuration across the rest of the switches in the VTP domain.

- Configure at least two VTP server switches in your network. Because only server switches can create, delete, and modify VLANs, you should make sure that you have one backup VTP server in case the primary VTP server becomes disabled. If all the switches in the network are configured in VTP client mode, you cannot create new VLANs on the network.

- Configure a VTP domain on the VTP server. Configuring the VTP domain on the first switch enables VTP to start advertising VLAN information. Other switches connected through trunk links receive the VTP domain information automatically through VTP advertisements.

- If there is an existing VTP domain, make sure that you match the name exactly. VTP domain names are case sensitive.

- If you are configuring a VTP password, ensure that the same password is set on all switches in the domain that need to be able to exchange VTP information. Switches without a password or with the wrong password reject VTP advertisements.

- Ensure that all switches are configured to use the same VTP protocol version. VTP version 1 is not compatible with VTP version 2. By default, Cisco Catalyst 2960 switches run version 1 but are capable of running version 2. When the VTP version is set to version 2, all version 2–capable switches in the domain autoconfigure to use version 2 through the VTP announcement process. Any version 1–only switches cannot participate in the VTP domain after that point.

- Create the VLANs after you have enabled VTP on the VTP server. Always ensure that trunk ports are configured to interconnect switches in a VTP domain. VTP information is exchanged only on trunk ports.

Figure 4-25   VTP Reference Topology

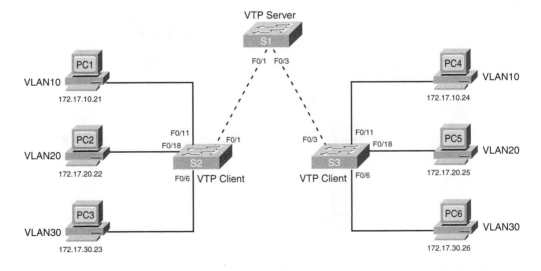

Follow these guidelines to ensure that you configure a VTP client successfully:

- As on the VTP server switch, confirm that the default settings are present.

- Configure VTP client mode. Recall that the switch is not in VTP client mode by default. You have to configure this mode.

- Configure trunks. VTP works over trunk links.

- Connect to a VTP server. When you connect to a VTP server or another VTP-enabled switch, it takes a few moments for the various advertisements to make their way back and forth to the VTP server.

- Verify VTP status. Before you begin configuring the access ports, confirm that the configuration revision number and the VLANs have been updated.

- Configure access ports. When a switch is in VTP client mode, you cannot add new VLANs. You can only assign access ports to existing VLANs.

Steps to Configuring VTP

Three principal steps are required for VTP configuration:

How To

Step 1. Configure the VTP server.

Step 2. Configure the VTP clients.

Step 3. Connect and confirm.

Refer to the topology in Figure 4-26 for this step-by-step configuration example.

Figure 4-26 VTP Topology for Step-by-Step Configuration

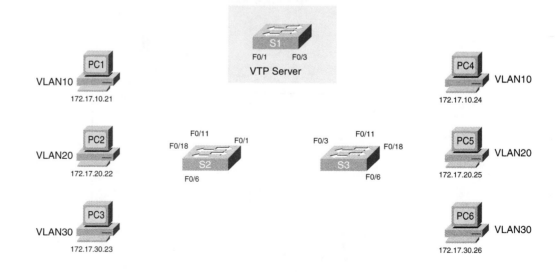

We will configure one VTP server and two VTP clients. The following shows an example of the three steps to VTP configuration.

Step 1: Configure the VTP Server

Initially, none of the devices are connected. The topology highlights switch S1. You will configure this switch to be a VTP server. The commands to configure the trunk ports are provided for interface F0/1 in Example 4-6.

Example 4-6 show vtp status Output

```
S1# configure terminal
S1(config)# interface f0/1
S1(config-if)# switchport mode trunk
S1(config-if)# end
S1# show vtp status
VTP Version                    : 2
Configuration Revision         : 0
Maximum VLANs supported locally  : 64
Number of existing VLANs       : 5
VTP Operating Mode             : Server
VTP Domain Name                :
VTP Pruning Mode               : Disabled
VTP V2 Mode                    : Disabled
VTP Traps Generation           : Disabled
MD5 digest                     : 0x7D 0x5A 0xA6 0x0E 0x9A 0x72 0xA0 0x3A
Configuration last modified by 0.0.0.0 at 0-0-00 00:00:00
```

The output of the **show vtp status** command confirms that the switch is by default a VTP server. Because no VLANs have yet been configured, the revision number is still set to 0 and the switch does not belong to a VTP domain.

If the switch were not already configured as a VTP server, you would configure it using the **vtp mode server** command.

The domain name is configured using the **vtp domain** *domain-name* command. In Example 4-7, switch S1 has been configured with the domain name cisco1.

Example 4-7 show vtp status After Domain Name Added

```
S1# configure terminal
S1(config)# vtp domain cisco1
!Changing VTP domain name from NULL to cisco1
S1(config)# exit
S1# show vtp status
```

```
VTP Version                    : 2
Configuration Revision         : 0
Maximum VLANs supported locally : 64
Number of existing VLANs       : 8
VTP Operating Mode             : Server
VTP Domain Name                : cisco1
<output omitted>
```

For security reasons, a password could be configured using the **vtp password** *password* command.

Most switches can support VTP versions 1 and 2. However, the default setting for Catalyst 2960 switches is version 1. When the **vtp version 1** command is entered on the switch, it informs us that the switch is already configured to be in version 1, as shown in Example 4-8.

Example 4-8 vtp version Command

```
S1(config)# vtp version 1
VTP mode already in V1.
```

VLANs 10, 20, and 30 are added and are assigned names. The output in Example 4-9 displays the result of these changes.

Example 4-9 show vlan brief, show interfaces switchport, show vtp status Output

```
S1# show vlan brief
VLAN    Name            Status          Ports
------------------------------------------------
<output omitted>
10      faculty         active
20      student         active
30      guest           active
<output omitted>
S1# show interfaces 0/1 switchport
Name: Fa0/1
Switchport: Enabled
Administrative Mode: trunk
<output omitted>
S1# show vtp status
VTP Version                    : 2
Configuration Revision         : 6
Maximum VLANs supported locally : 64
Number of existing VLANs       : 8
VTP Operating Mode             : Server
VTP Domain Name                : cisco1
<output omitted>
```

The configuration revision number changed from 0 to 6 because three VLANs were added and three VLANs were named.

Step 2: Configure the VTP Clients

Figure 4-27 highlights switches S2 and S3. You will be shown the VTP client configuration for S2. To configure S3 as a VTP client, you will follow the same procedure.

Figure 4-27   VTP Client Configuration

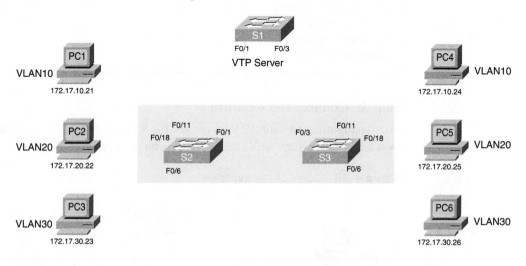

Before configuring a switch as a VTP client, verify its current VTP status, as in Example 4-10.

Example 4-10   VTP Client Default Configuration

```
S2# show vtp status
VTP Version                    : 2
Configuration Revision         : 0
Maximum VLANs supported locally : 64
Number of existing VLANs       : 5
VTP Operating Mode             : Server
VTP Domain Name                :
VTP Pruning Mode               : Disabled
VTP V2 Mode                    : Disabled
VTP Traps Generation           : Disabled
MD5 digest                     : 0x7D 0x5A 0xA6 0x0E 0x9A 0x72 0xA0 0x3A
Configuration last modified by 0.0.0.0 at 0-0-00 00:00:00
```

After you've confirmed status, you will configure the switch to operate in VTP client mode. Configure VTP client mode using the Cisco IOS command **vtp mode client**, as in Example 4-11.

Example 4-11   vtp mode client and Verification

```
S2# configure terminal
S2(config)# vtp mode client
Setting device to VTP CLIENT mode.
S2(config)# exit
S2# show vtp status
VTP Version                    : 2
Configuration Revision         : 0
Maximum VLANs supported locally : 64
Number of existing VLANs       : 5
VTP Operating Mode             : Client
<output omitted>
```

Step 3: Connect and Confirm

After configuring the main VTP server and the VTP clients, you will connect the VTP client switch S2 to the switch S1 VTP server, as pictured in Figure 4-28.

Figure 4-28   Connect the Switches

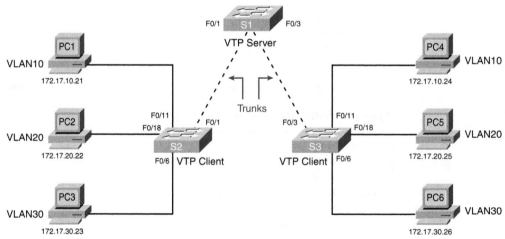

The topology highlights the trunks that will be added to this topology. In the figure, switch S2 is connected to switch S1. Switch S2 is configured to support the computers PC1, PC2, and PC3. The same procedure is applied to switch S3, but the commands for S3 are not shown.

There are two Cisco IOS commands for confirming that VTP domain and VLAN configurations have been transferred to switch S2: **show vtp status** and **show vtp counters**. Confirm the VTP operation on S2, as seen in Example 4-12.

Example 4-12   VTP Status on S2 After Connection

```
S2# show vtp status
VTP Version                    : 2
Configuration Revision         : 6
Maximum VLANs supported locally : 64
Number of existing VLANs       : 8
VTP Operating Mode             : Client
VTP Domain Name                : cisco1
<output omitted>
S2# show vtp counters
VTP statistics:
Summary advertisements received    : 1
Subset advertisements received     : 1
Request advertisements received    : 0
Summary advertisements transmitted : 1
Subset advertisements transmitted  : 1
<output omitted>
```

Example 4-12 verifies that

- The configuration revision number has been incremented to 6.

- There are now three new VLANs, as indicated by the number of existing VLANs displaying 8.

- The domain name is cisco1.

The next task is to configure the access ports in the appropriate VLANs. This is illustrated for S2 in Example 4-13.

Example 4-13   Configuring Access Ports

```
S2# configure terminal
Enter configuration commands, one per line.  End with CNTL/Z.
S2(config)# vlan 10
%VTP VLAN configuration not allowed when device is in CLIENT mode.
S2(config)# interface fastEthernet 0/11
S2(config-if)# switchport access vlan 10
```

The first shaded portion in Example 4-13 confirms that switch S2 is in VTP client mode. The bottom shaded portion shows the Cisco IOS command used to configure port F0/11 on switch S2 to be in VLAN 10.

Troubleshooting VTP Configurations

You have learned how VTP can be used to simplify managing a VLAN database across multiple switches. In this section, you will learn about common VTP configuration problems. This information, combined with your VTP configuration skills, will help you when troubleshooting VTP configuration problems.

The common VTP configuration issues explored are the following:

- Incompatible VTP versions
- VTP password issues
- Incorrect VTP domain name
- All switches set to VTP client mode

Incompatible VTP Versions

VTP versions 1 and 2 are not compatible with each other. Modern Cisco Catalyst switches, such as the 2960, are configured to use VTP version 1 by default. However, older switches may support only VTP version 1. Switches that support only version 1 cannot participate in the VTP domain along with version 2 switches. If your network contains switches that support only version 1, you need to manually configure the version 2 switches to operate in version 1 mode.

Table 4-2 illustrates the command used to change the VTP version.

Table 4-2   Cisco IOS Command Syntax for **vtp version**

Description	IOS Command Syntax
Enters global configuration mode	Switch# **configure terminal**
Configures the VTP version number	Switch(config)# **vtp version** *number*

VTP Password Issues

When using a VTP password to control participation in the VTP domain, ensure that the password is set correctly on all switches in the VTP domain. Forgetting to set a VTP password is a very common problem. If a password is used, it must be configured on each switch in the VTP domain. By default, a Catalyst switch does not have a VTP password. The switch does not automatically set the password parameter, unlike other parameters that are set automatically when a VTP advertisement is received.

Table 4-3 illustrates the command used to change the VTP password.

Table 4-3   Cisco IOS Command Syntax for **vtp password**

Description	IOS Command Syntax
Enters global configuration mode	Switch# **configure terminal**
Configures the VTP password	Switch(config)# **vtp password** *password*

For example, entering **vtp password cisco** in global configuration mode would require all other switches in the domain to do the same.

Incorrect VTP Domain Name

The VTP domain name is a key parameter set on a switch. An improperly configured VTP domain affects VLAN synchronization between switches. As you learned earlier, if a switch receives the wrong VTP advertisement, the switch discards the message. If the discarded message contains legitimate configuration information, the switch does not synchronize its VLAN database as expected.

Figure 4-29 illustrates a VTP domain name mismatch.

Figure 4-29   VTP Domain Name Synchronization

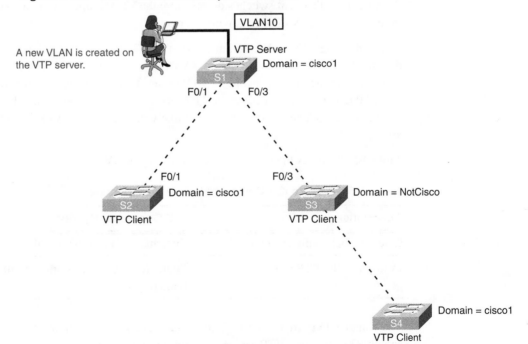

When VTP summary advertisements are sent out, switch S2 accepts the advertisements and synchronizes its VLAN database with S1. However, switch S3 discards the summary advertisements. As a result, switch S4 does not add VLAN 10 to its VLAN database.

The solution is to change the VTP domain name on switch S3 to cisco1. To avoid incorrectly configuring a VTP domain name, set the VTP domain name on only one VTP server switch. All other switches in the same VTP domain will accept and automatically configure their VTP domain name when they receive the first VTP summary advertisement.

Table 4-4 illustrates the command used to change the VTP domain name.

Table 4-4   Cisco IOS Command Syntax for **vtp domain**

Description	IOS Command Syntax
Enters global configuration mode	Switch# **configure terminal**
Configures the VTP domain name	Switch(config)# **vtp domain** *domain-name*

The command **vtp domain cisco1** is the required command in global configuration mode on switch S3.

All Switches Set to VTP Client Mode

It is possible to change the operating mode of all switches to VTP client. By doing so, you lose all ability to create, delete, and manage VLANs within your network environment. Because the VTP client switches do not store the VLAN information in NVRAM, they need to refresh the VLAN information after a reload.

To avoid losing all VLAN configurations in a VTP domain by accidentally reconfiguring the only VTP server in the domain as a VTP client and reloading, you can configure a second switch in the same domain as a VTP server. It is not uncommon for small networks that use VTP to have all the switches in VTP server mode. If the network is being managed by a couple of network administrators, it is unlikely that conflicting VLAN configurations will arise.

Table 4-5 illustrates the command used to change the VTP mode.

Table 4-5   Cisco IOS Command Syntax for **vtp mode**

Description	IOS Command Syntax
Enters global configuration mode	Switch# **configure terminal**
Configures the VTP mode	Switch(config)# **vtp mode** {**client** I **server** I **transparent**}

The command **vtp mode server** is the required command in global configuration mode on switch S3 so that two VTP servers are present in the network.

VTP Troubleshooting Example

Even after you have configured the switches in your VTP domain correctly, other factors can adversely affect the functionality of VTP.

The topology in Figure 4-30 is configured with VTP. There is one VTP server switch, S1, and two VTP client switches, S2 and S3.

Figure 4-30   Incorrect Revision Number

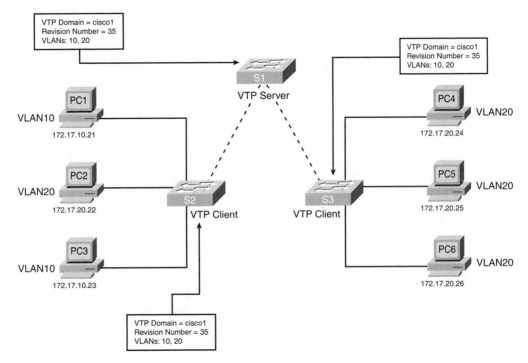

Switch S4 has been previously configured as a VTP client, has a configuration revision number of 35, and is added to the network via a trunk link to switch S3.

Switches S1, S2, and S3 have a revision number of 17. S4 comes preconfigured with two VLANs, 30 and 40, that are not configured in the existing network. The existing network has VLANs 10 and 20.

When switch S4 is connected to switch S3, VTP summary advertisements announce the arrival of a VTP-enabled switch with the highest revision number in the network. Switch S3, switch S1, and, finally, switch S2 all reconfigure themselves to the configuration found in switch S4, as shown in Figure 4-31.

Figure 4-31   Updated VLAN Configuration

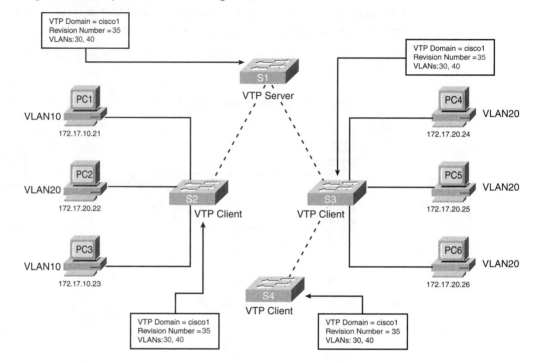

As each switch reconfigures itself with VLANs that were not supported in the original net-work, the ports no longer forward traffic from the computers because they are configured with VLANs that no longer exist on the newly reconfigured switches. The ports connected to PCs 1 to 6 are associated with inactive VLANs.

The solution to the problem is to reset each switch back to an earlier configuration and then reconfigure the correct VLANs, 10 and 20, on switch S1. To prevent this problem in the first place, reset the configuration revision number on previously configured switches being added to a VTP-enabled network. This can be done in various ways, one of which is to change the VTP domain name on the respective switch to a dummy domain name and then to switch it back to the correct VTP domain name for the network. Example 4-14 illustrates this process on switch S4.

Example 4-14   Resetting Configuration Revision Number

```
S4(config)# vtp domain name test
S4(config)# vtp domain name cisco1
S4(config)# exit
S4# show vtp status
VTP Version      : 2
Configuration Revision         : 0
```

```
Maximum VLANs supported locally : 64
Number of existing VLANs        : 5
VTP Operating Mode              : Server
VTP Domain Name                 : cisco1
VTP Pruning Mode                : Disabled
VTP V2 Mode                     : Disabled
VTP Traps Generation            : Disabled
MD5 digest                      : 0x7D 0x5A 0xA6 0x0E 0x9A 0x72 0xA0 0x3A
Configuration last modified by 0.0.0.0 at 0-0-00 00:00:00
```

Managing VLANs on a VTP Server

You have learned about VTP and how it can be used to simplify managing VLANs in a
VTP-enabled network. Consider the topology in Figure 4-32. When a new VLAN, for
example, VLAN 10, is added to the network, the network manager adds the VLAN to the
VTP server; in the figure, switch S1 is the VTP server. As you know, VTP takes care of
propagating the VLAN configuration details to the rest of the network. It does not have any
effect on which ports are configured in VLAN 10 on switches S1, S2, and S3.

Figure 4-32 Managing VLANs

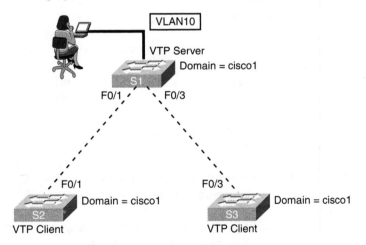

Example 4-15 displays the commands used to configure VLAN 10 and port F0/11 on switch
S1. The commands to configure the correct ports for switches S2 and S3 are not shown.

Example 4-15 VLAN Configuration on Switch S1

```
S1> enable
Password:
S1# configure terminal
```

```
Enter configuration commands, one per line. End with CNTL/Z.
S1(config)# vlan 10
S1(config-vlan)# name faculty
S1(config-vlan)# interface f0/11
S1(config-if)# switchport access vlan 10
```

After you have configured the new VLAN on switch S1 and configured the ports on switches S1, S2, and S3 to support the new VLAN, confirm that VTP updated the VLAN database on switches S2 and S3. Example 4-16 illustrates the updated VLAN information on S2.

Example 4-16   VTP-Updated VLAN Information on Switch S2

```
S2# show vtp status
VTP Version              : 2
Configuration Revision          : 4
Maximum VLANs supported locally : 64
Number of existing VLANs        : 8
VTP Operating Mode             : Client
VTP Domain Name                : cisco1
VTP Pruning Mode               : Disabled
VTP V2 Mode                    : Disabled
VTP Traps Generation           : Disabled
MD5 digest                     : 0x59 0x67 0x4C 0xFD 0x8B 0xD9 0xA7 0x9A
Configuration last modified by 0.0.0.0 at 3-1-93 00:41:42
S2# show interfaces trunk
Port       Mode       Encapsulation       Status       Native vlan
Fa0/1      on         802.1q              trunking     1


Port       Vlans allowed on trunk
Fa0/1      1-1005


Port       Vlans allowed and active in management domain
Fa0/1      1,10,20,30,1002,1003,1004,1005


Port       Vlans in spanning tree forwarding state and not pruned
Fa0/1      1,10,20,30,1002,1003,1004,1005
```

The output confirms that the new VLAN has been added to F0/1 on switch S2 and is now active in the VTP domain.

Configure VTP (4.3.3)

Use the Packet Tracer Activity to practice configuring VTP. Use file e3-4332.pka on the CD-ROM that accompanies this book to perform this activity using Packet Tracer.

Summary

In this chapter, we discussed the VLAN Trunking Protocol. VTP is a Cisco-proprietary protocol used to exchange VLAN information across trunk links, reducing VLAN administration and configuration errors. VTP allows you to create a VLAN once within a VTP domain and have that VLAN propagated to all other switches in the VTP domain.

There are three VTP operating modes: server, client, and transparent. VTP client mode switches are more prevalent in large networks, where their definition reduces the administration of VLAN information. In small networks, network managers can more easily keep track of network changes, so switches are often left in the default VTP server mode.

VTP pruning limits the unnecessary propagation of VLAN traffic across a LAN. VTP determines which trunk ports forward which VLAN traffic. VTP pruning improves overall network performance by restricting the unnecessary flooding of traffic across trunk links. Pruning permits VLAN traffic only for VLANs that are assigned to some switch port of a switch on the other end of a trunk link. By reducing the total amount of flooded traffic on the network, bandwidth is freed up for other network traffic.

We discussed VTP configuration and preventative measures to take to avoid common problems with VTP.

Labs

The labs available in the companion *LAN Switching and Wireless, CCNA Exploration Labs and Study Guide* (ISBN 1-58713-202-8) provide hands-on practice with the following topics introduced in this chapter:

Lab 4-1: Basic VTP Configuration (4.4.1)

In this lab, you will be guided to perform basic switch configurations, configure VTP, trunking, learn about VTP modes, create and distribute VLAN information, and assign ports to VLANs.

Lab 4-2: VTP Configuration Challenge (4.4.2)

In this lab, with minimal guidance you perform basic switch configurations, configure VTP, trunking, learn about VTP modes, create and distribute VLAN information, and assign ports to VLANs.

Lab 4-3: Troubleshooting VTP Configuration (4.4.3)

In this lab, a number of errors exist in the VTP and VLAN configuration, which you must troubleshoot and correct before end-to-end connectivity is restored. You will have successfully resolved all errors when the same VLANs are configured on all three switches, and you can ping between any two hosts in the same VLAN.

Many of the hands-on labs include Packet Tracer Companion activities, where you can use Packet Tracer to complete a simulation of the lab. Look for this icon in *LAN Switching and Wireless, CCNA Exploration Labs and Study Guide* (ISBN 1-58713-202-8) for hands-on labs that have a Packet Tracer Companion.

Check Your Understanding

Complete all the review questions listed here to test your understanding of the topics and concepts in this chapter. Answers are listed in the Appendix, "Check Your Understanding and Challenge Questions Answer Key."

1. How does VTP affect VLAN administration?

   A. All Port VLAN assignments for an entire VTP domain can be done on a single switch.

   B. VLANs are visible only on switches that have ports assigned to them.

   C. VTP propagates VLAN numbers, but not names, to all switches in a VTP domain.

   D. VTP is required to allow VLAN naming across switches.

   E. VTP propagates VLAN names to all switches in a VTP domain.

2. A Catalyst switch must be in which VTP mode to delete or add VLANs to a management domain?

   A. Client

   B. Server

   C. Domain

   D. Transparent

   E. Designated

3. What is the purpose of VTP transparent mode?

   A. It permits VLAN creation on a single "transparent" switch and subsequent propagation to all other VTP switches.

   B. It allows propagation of extended range VLANs.

   C. It makes VTP traffic "transparent" to other devices by allowing VLANs other than VLAN 1 to act as the management VLAN.

   D. It enables VTP advertisements to pass through a nonparticipating switch.

4. Two switches running VTP are connected with an 802.1Q trunk link. One of the switches is not receiving VTP update information. What could cause this problem?

    A. FastEthernet cannot be used for trunking.

    B. The switches are not set to the same VTP mode.

    C. The VTP domain name is not the same on both switches.

    D. The configuration revision number does not match on both switches.

5. A switch in a VTP domain sends an advertisement request. What will be the response?

    A. A configuration status reply will be issued from the closest client switch.

    B. A three-way handshake will establish a configuration session with the VTP server.

    C. Summary and subset advertisements will be sent by the VTP server.

    D. The configuration version number will be set to zero and all switches in the domain will issue advertisements regarding the state of their VLANs.

6. Which function, when enabled on a switched network, prevents broadcast, multicast, and unknown unicast traffic to a VLAN from being flooded to switches that do not have that particular VLAN assigned to them?

    A. Trunking

    B. VTP domain

    C. VTP pruning

    D. VTP transparent mode

7. Which three options are required when adding a new switch to an existing VTP domain? (Choose three.)

    A. All VTP switches must use the same version of VTP.

    B. Token Ring switches must run VTP version 3 or later.

    C. The VTP pruning settings must be identical.

    D. The VTP domain passwords must be unique.

    E. The VTP domain names must be identical.

    F. The connection to the VTP domain must be a trunked link.

8. Fill in the blank with the appropriate VTP term.

    _____ specifies that the switch cannot create or delete VLANs shared in VTP advertisements.

    _____ configures the name used to determine which switches belong to the same management group.

    _____ restricts flooded traffic to trunk links that the traffic must use to reach destination devices.

9. What is the purpose of the VLAN Trunking Protocol?

A. Maintaining consistency in VLAN configuration across the network

B. Routing frames from one VLAN to another

C. Routing the frames along the best path between switches

D. Tagging user data frames with VLAN membership information

E. Distributing BPDUs to maintain loop-free switched paths

10. See Figure 4-33. Switch SW1 and switch SW2 are configured in the same VTP domain but fail to exchange VLAN information. What could be done to fix the problem?

Figure 4-33   VTP Scenario

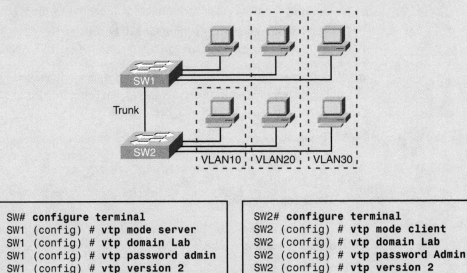

```
SW# configure terminal
SW1 (config) # vtp mode server
SW1 (config) # vtp domain Lab
SW1 (config) # vtp password admin
SW1 (config) # vtp version 2
SW1 (config) # vtp pruning
SW1 (config) # vtp end
```

```
SW2# configure terminal
SW2 (config) # vtp mode client
SW2 (config) # vtp domain Lab
SW2 (config) # vtp password Admin
SW2 (config) # vtp version 2
SW2 (config) # vtp pruning
SW2 (config) # vtp end
```

A. Configure the same VLANs on the VTP client and VTP server.

B. Configure the same VTP mode on the VTP client and VTP server.

C. Configure the same password on the VTP client and VTP server.

D. Configure different VTP domain names on the VTP client and VTP server.

E. Configure the VTP client in VTP transparent mode.

F. Configure the trunk link as an access link.

11. A network engineer is implementing a new VLAN design on an existing structure. The plan is to rename the VTP domain and implement 25 VLANs. The engineer takes an existing production switch to the lab, enters the proposed VLANs, and changes the VTP domain name. All new VLANs are verified present with the **show vlan** command. The network administrator subsequently decides to retain the original domain name, so the name is changed back and the switch reconnected to the production network. The **show vlan** command shows that none of the new VLANs are synchronizing on the other network switches. All switches can ping each other and trunking is correct. What is the likely problem?

   A. No ports are assigned to the new VLANs yet, so VTP pruning is disabling them.

   B. The switch rejoined the network with the revision number set to zero.

   C. The engineer failed to save the new VLAN configuration to NVRAM.

   D. The other switches are all in server mode by default and do not accept VTP updates.

12. Fill in the blank with the appropriate VTP term.

   _____ forwards VTP advertisements that are received out the trunk ports, but cannot advertise and synchronize the VLAN configuration based on received advertisements.

   _____ advertises and synchronizes the VLAN configuration to other switches in the same VTP domain, but cannot create, change, or delete VLANs.

   _____ creates, modifies, and deletes VLANs and specifies other configuration parameters, such as VTP version and VTP pruning for the entire VTP domain.

13. See Figure 4-34. The switches in the exhibit are interconnected by trunk links and are configured for VTP as shown. A new VLAN is added to Switch1. Which three actions will occur? (Choose three.)

Figure 4-34   Mixed Client, Server, Transparent Environment

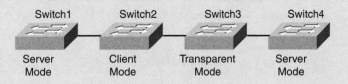

   A. Switch1 will send a VTP update to Switch2.

   B. Switch2 will add the VLAN to its database and pass the update to Switch3.

   C. Switch3 will pass the VTP update to Switch4.

   D. Switch3 will add the VLAN to its database.

   E. Switch4 will not add the VLAN to its database.

   F. Switch4 will not receive the update.

Challenge Questions and Activities

These questions require a deeper application of the concepts covered in this chapter. You can find the answers in the Appendix.

1. Match the terms with the correct descriptions.

    __VTP domain

    __VTP advertisements

    __VTP modes

    __VTP server

    __VTP client

    __VTP transparent

    __VTP pruning

    A. Either server or client or transparent.

    B. Forwards VTP advertisements to VTP clients and VTP servers. Does not participate in VTP.

    C. Controls which ports on a switch can flood traffic, optimizing bandwidth by restricting traffic.

    D. Cannot create, change, or delete VLANs, but stores the VLAN information for the entire domain.

    E. One or more interconnected switches sharing VLAN configuration details.

    F. Used to distribute and synchronize VLAN configurations across the network.

    G. Default for a Catalyst switch, advertising VLAN configurations to other VTP-enabled switches.

2. List the default VTP configuration on a Catalyst switch for VTP version, VTP domain name, VTP mode, configuration revision number, and number of VLANs.

    VTP Version = _____

    VTP Domain Name = _____

    VTP Mode = _____

    Config Revision = _____

    VLANs = _____

3. See Figure 4-35, a converged VTP domain. Switch S4 is trunked to switch S3. At the instant that switch S4 is connected to switch S3, the VTP statistics for switch S4 include a VTP domain name of cisco1, configuration revision number 35, and exclusive support for VLANs 30 and 40. Which conclusions can be made after VTP has reconverged on the addition of switch S4?

Figure 4-35   Converged VTP Topology

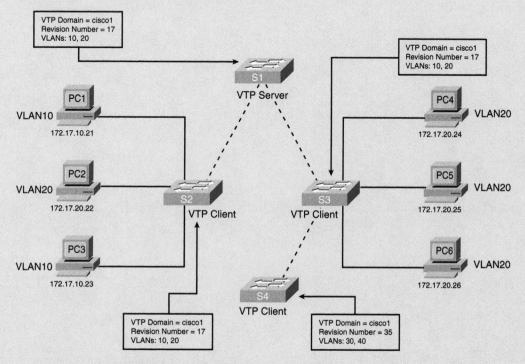

A. PC1 cannot communicate with PC2.

B. PC2 cannot communicate with PC4.

C. PC4 cannot communicate with PC5.

D. All PCs can communicate with other PCs in their respective VLAN.

Packet Tracer
☐ Challenge

Look for this icon in *LAN Switching and Wireless, CCNA Exploration Labs and Study Guide* (ISBN 1-58713-202-8) for instructions on how to perform the Packet Tracer Skills Integration Challenge for this chapter.

CHAPTER 5

STP

Objectives

Upon completion of this chapter, you will be able to answer the following questions:

- What is the role of redundancy in a converged network?

- How does STP work to eliminate Layer 2 loops in a converged network?

- What three steps does STA use to construct a loop-free topology?

- How do you implement rapid PVST+ in a switched LAN to prevent loops between redundantly linked switches?

Key Terms

This chapter uses the following key terms. You can find the definitions in the Glossary.

Computer networks are inextricably linked to productivity in today's small- and medium-sized businesses. Consequently, IT administrators have to implement redundancy in their hierarchical networks. However, adding extra links to switches and routers in the network introduces traffic loops that need to be managed in a dynamic way; when a switch connection is lost, another link needs to quickly take its place without introducing new traffic loops. In this chapter, you learn how Spanning Tree Protocol (STP) logically blocks physical loops in the network and how STP has evolved into a robust protocol that rapidly calculates which ports should be blocked in a VLAN-based network.

Redundant Layer 2 Topologies

The hierarchical design model was introduced in Chapter 1, "LAN Design." The hierarchical design model addresses issues found in "flat" Layer 2 network topologies. One of the issues is redundancy. Layer 2 redundancy improves the availability of the network by implementing alternative network paths using equipment and cabling. Having multiple paths for data to traverse the network allows for a single path to be disrupted without impacting the connectivity of devices on the network.

Redundancy

We begin with a demonstration of how redundancy should work in a switched LAN. Refer to the topology in Figure 5-1.

Figure 5-1   Redundancy

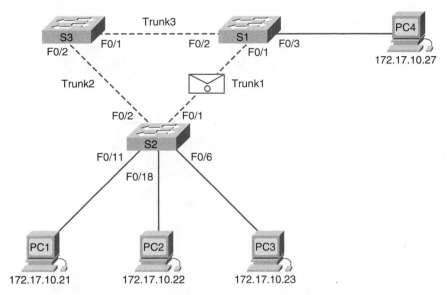

We demonstrate how redundancy works to mitigate a link failure in this topology:

1. PC1 is communicating with PC4 over a redundantly configured network topology.

2. When the network link between switch S1 and switch S2 is disrupted, as shown in Figure 5-2, the path between PC1 and PC4 is automatically adjusted to compensate for the disruption, as shown in Figure 5-3.

Figure 5-2   Blocked Path

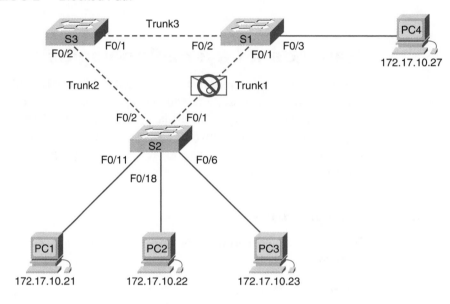

Figure 5-3   Reroute

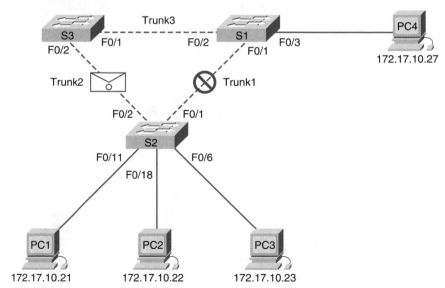

3. When the network connection between S1 and S2 is restored, the path is then readjusted to route traffic directly from S2 through S1 to get to PC4, as in Figure 5-1.

As businesses become increasingly dependent on the network, the availability of the network infrastructure becomes a critical business concern that must be addressed. Redundancy is the solution for achieving the necessary availability.

In a hierarchical design, redundancy is achieved at the distribution and core layers through additional hardware and alternative paths through the additional hardware.

In Figure 5-4, redundant paths are available between the respective access, distribution, and core hierarchical layers. Each access layer switch is connected to two distribution layer switches. Also, each distribution layer switch is connected to both core layer switches. By having multiple paths to get between PC1 and PC4, there is redundancy that can accommodate a single point of failure between the access and distribution layer, and between the distribution and core layer.

Figure 5-4   Redundant Design

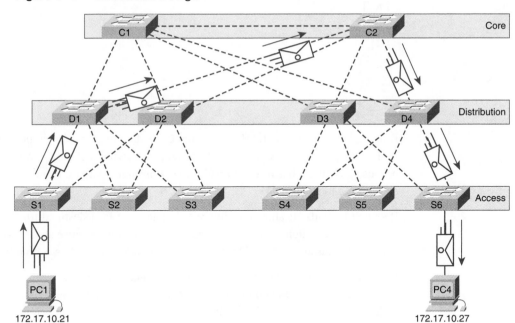

STP, the topic of this chapter, is enabled on all switches. STP has placed some switch ports in forwarding state and other switch ports in blocking state. This is to prevent loops in the Layer 2 network. STP will use a redundant link only if a failure occurs on the primary link. PC1 communicates with PC4 over the identified path.

If the link between switch S1 and switch D1 is disrupted, as shown in Figure 5-5, the data from PC1 destined for PC4 is prevented from reaching switch D1 on its original path.

However, because switch S1 has a second path to PC4 through switch D2, the path is updated and the data is still able to reach PC4.

Figure 5-5  Access-Distribution Path Failure

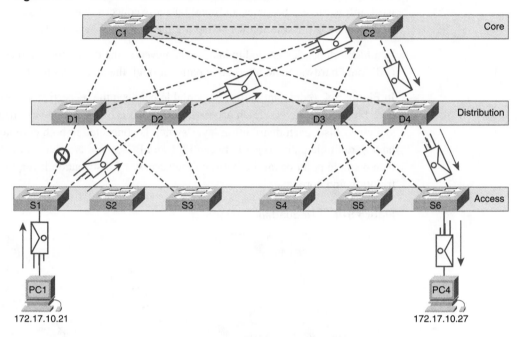

If the link between switch D1 and switch C2 is disrupted, as shown in Figure 5-6, data from PC1 destined for PC4 is prevented from reaching switch C2 on its original path. However, because switch D1 has a second path to PC4 through switch C1, the path is updated and the data is able to reach PC4.

If switch D1 fails, as shown in Figure 5-7, data from PC1 destined for PC4 is prevented from reaching switch C2 on its original path. However, because switch S1 has a second path to PC4 through switch D2, the path is updated and the data is able to reach PC4.

If switch C2 fails, as shown in Figure 5-8, the data from PC1 destined for PC4 is prevented from reaching switch D4 on its original path. However, because switch D1 has a second path to PC4 through switch C1, the path is updated and the data is able to reach PC4.

Redundancy provides flexibility in path selection on a network, allowing data to be transmitted regardless of a single path or device failing in the distribution or core layers. Redundancy does have some complications that need to be addressed before it can be safely deployed on a hierarchical network.

Figure 5-6   Distribution-Core Path Failure

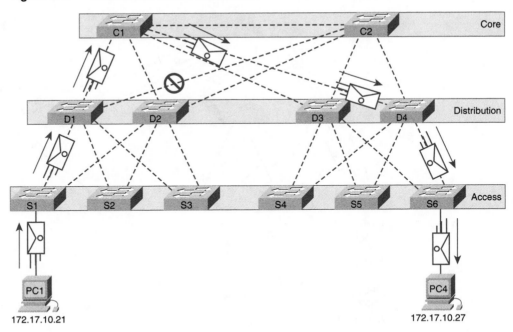

Figure 5-7   Distribution Switch Failure

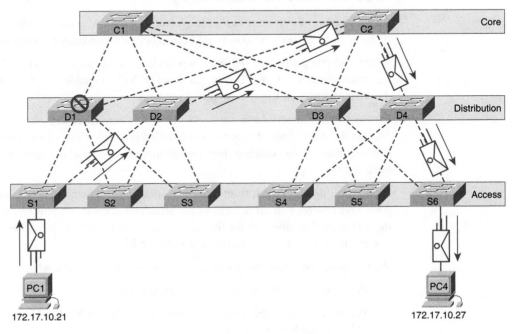

Figure 5-8   Core Switch Failure

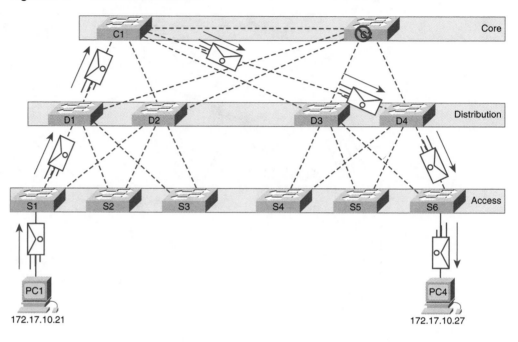

Issues with Redundancy

Redundancy is an important part of hierarchical design. Although it is important for availability, some considerations need to be addressed before redundancy is even possible on a network.

When multiple paths exist between two devices on the network and STP has been disabled on those switches, a Layer 2 loop can occur. If STP is enabled on these switches, which is the default setting, a Layer 2 loop will not occur.

Ethernet frames do not have a *time-to-live (TTL)* parameter associated with them like IP packets do. As a result, if they are not handled properly within a switched network, the Ethernet frames can continue from switch to switch endlessly or until a link is disrupted, breaking the loop.

Also, recall that broadcast frames are forwarded out all switch ports except for the ingress port. This ensures that all devices in the broadcast domain are able to receive the frame. If there is more than one port for the frame to be forwarded out, an endless loop can result. For example, refer to the scenario illustrated in Figure 5-9.

We illustrate how broadcast loops occur in a simple switched LAN:

1. PC1 sends out a broadcast frame to switch S2.

2. When S2 receives the broadcast frame, it updates its MAC address table to record that PC1 is available on port F0/11.

3. Because it is a broadcast frame, S2 forwards the frame out all switch ports, including Trunk1 and Trunk2, as pictured in Figure 5-10.

Figure 5-9   Broadcast Loop

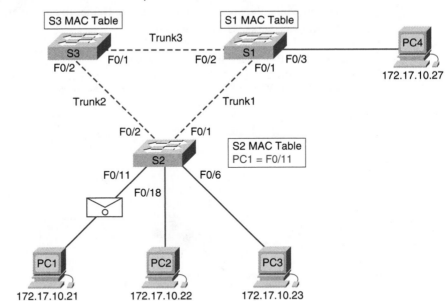

Figure 5-10   Broadcast Frame Egress

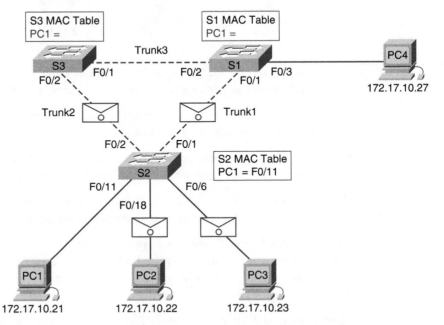

4. When the broadcast frame arrives at switches S3 and S1, they update their MAC address tables to indicate that PC1 is available out port F0/1 on S1 and port F0/2 on S3.

5. Because it is a broadcast frame, S3 and S1 forward it out all switch ports, except the one on which they received the respective frame. In particular, S3 sends the frame to S1 and vice versa, as in Figure 5-11.

Figure 5-11 Broadcast Frame Forwarding

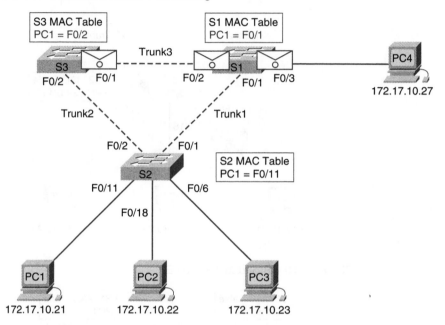

6. S3 and S1 receive the broadcast from each other and update their MAC address tables with the incorrect ports for the PC1s MAC address, as in Figure 5-12.

7. Each switch again forwards the broadcast frame out all its ports, except for the ingress port, resulting in both switches forwarding the frame to S2, as shown in Figure 5-13.

8. When S2 receives the broadcast frames from S3 and S1, the MAC address table is updated again, this time with the last of the two entries received from S3 and S1.

This process repeats over and over until the loop is broken by physically disconnecting the connections causing the loop, or turning the power off on one of the switches in the loop.

Loops result in high CPU load on all switches participating in the loop. Because the same frames are constantly being forwarded back and forth between all switches in the loop, the CPU of the switch ends up having to process a lot of data. This slows down performance on the switch when legitimate traffic arrives.

A host caught in the midst of a network loop is not accessible to other hosts on the network. Because the MAC address table is constantly changing with the updates from the broadcast frames, the switch essentially does not know which port to legitimately forward the unicast frames out to in order to reach the destination MAC address specified in the Ethernet frame.

The unicast frames end up looping around the network as well. As more and more frames end up looping through the network, a broadcast storm occurs, effectively bringing down the network. Layer 2 issues are, in general, much more debilitating to a network than Layer 3 issues.

Figure 5-12   Updated MAC Address Tables

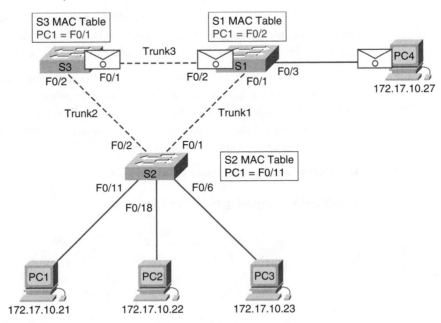

Figure 5-13   Back from Whence They Came

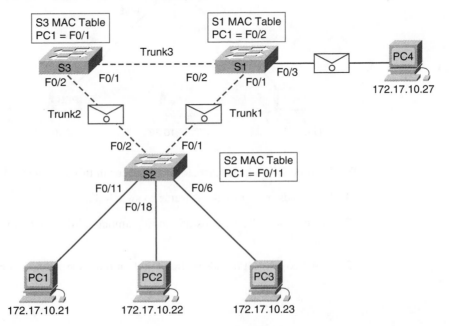

Broadcast Storms

A broadcast storm occurs when so many broadcast frames are caught in a Layer 2 loop that all available bandwidth is consumed. Consequently, no bandwidth is available for legitimate traffic, and the network becomes unavailable for data communication.

A broadcast storm is inevitable in a physically looped network with STP disabled. As more devices send broadcasts out on the network, more and more traffic gets caught in the loop, eventually creating a broadcast storm that causes the network to fail.

Other consequences occur for broadcast storms. Because broadcast traffic is forwarded out every port on a switch, all connected devices have to process all broadcast traffic that is being flooded endlessly around the looped network. This can cause the end device to malfunction because of the high processing requirements to sustain such a high traffic load on the network interface card.

Refer to the scenario illustrated in Figure 5-14.

Figure 5-14   Beginning of a Broadcast Storm

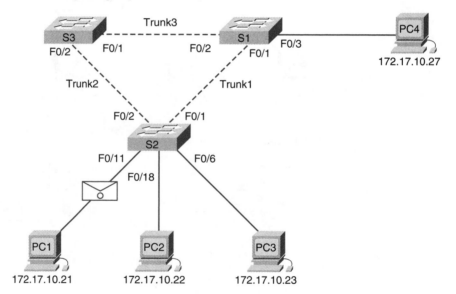

We illustrate how a broadcast storm can occur in this switched LAN:

1. PC1 sends out a broadcast frame to switch S2.

2. The broadcast frame ends up looping among all the interconnected switches on the network.

3. PC4 also sends a broadcast frame out onto the looped network in Figure 5-15.

Figure 5-15   Contribution to a Broadcast Storm

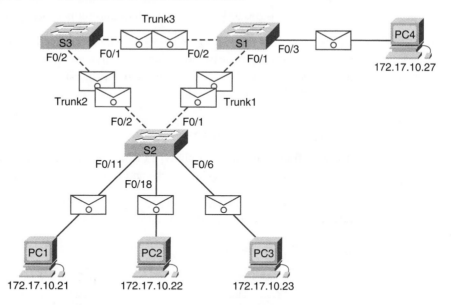

4. The PC4 broadcast frame ends up looping among all the interconnected switches, just like the PC1 broadcast frame.

5. PC3 adds to the mix by sending a broadcast frame out onto the network in Figure 5-16 and adds to the existing traffic on the network, eventually resulting in a broadcast storm.

Figure 5-16   Adding More Toward a Broadcast Storm

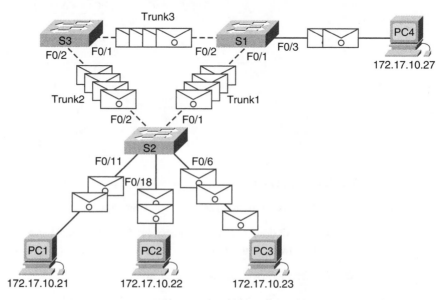

6. When the network is fully saturated with broadcast traffic looping among the switches, new traffic is discarded by the switch because it is unable to process it.

Because devices connected to a network are constantly sending out broadcast frames, such as ARP requests, a broadcast storm can develop in seconds. As a result, when a loop is created, the network quickly becomes disabled. Again, STP is the missing variable required to maintain stability in the network.

Duplicate Unicast Frames

Broadcast frames are not the only type of frames involved with traffic loops. Unicast frames sent onto a physically looped network can result in duplicate frames arriving at the destination device.

Refer to the scenario illustrated in Figure 5-17.

Figure 5-17   Unicast Frame

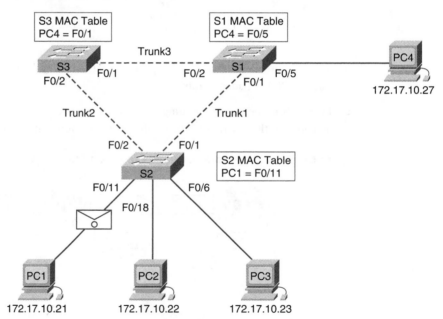

We illustrate the phenomenon of duplicate unicast frames in this switched LAN:

1. PC1 sends a unicast frame destined for PC4.

2. Switch S2 does not have an entry for PC4 in its MAC address table, so it floods the unicast frame out all switch ports in an attempt to find PC4.

3. The frame arrives at switches S1 and S3.

4. S1 does have a MAC address entry for PC4, so it forwards the frame out to PC4.

5. S3 also has an entry in its MAC address table for PC4, so it forwards the unicast frame out Trunk3 to S1.

6. S1 receives the duplicate frame and again forwards the frame out to PC4, as shown in Figure 5-18.

Figure 5-18   Duplicate Unicast Frame

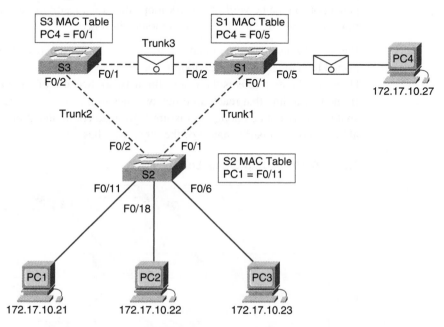

7. PC4 receives the same frame twice.

Most upper-layer protocols are not designed to recognize or cope with duplicate transmissions. In general, protocols that make use of a sequence-numbering mechanism assume that the transmission has failed and that the sequence number has recycled for another communication session. Other protocols attempt to hand the duplicate transmission to the appropriate upper-layer protocol to be processed and possibly discarded.

Fortunately, switches are capable of detecting loops on a network. STP eliminates these loop issues.

Real-World Redundancy Issues

Redundancy is an important component of a highly available hierarchical network topology, but loops can arise as a result of the multiple paths configured on the network. You can prevent loops using STP. However, if STP has not been implemented in preparation for a redundant topology, loops can occur unexpectedly in the wiring closet or in workplace cubicles.

Loops in the Wiring Closet

Network wiring for small- to medium-sized businesses can get very confusing. Network cables between access layer switches, located in the wiring closets, disappear into the walls, floors, and ceilings where they are run back to the distribution layer switches on the network. If the network cables are not properly labeled when they are terminated in the patch panel in the wiring closet, it is difficult to determine where the destination is for the patch panel port on the network. Network loops that are a result of accidental duplicate connections in the wiring closets are a common occurrence.

Figure 5-19 displays a loop that occurs if two connections from the same switch are connected to another switch. The loop is localized to the switches that are interconnected. However, the loop affects the rest of the network because of large increases in broadcast frame forwarding that reach all other switches in the network. The impact on the other switches may not be enough to disrupt legitimate communications, but it could noticeably affect the overall performance of the other switches.

Figure 5-19   Wiring Closet Loop

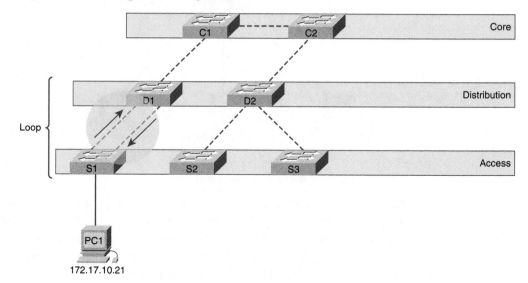

This type of loop is common in the wiring closet. It happens when an administrator mistakenly connects a cable to the same switch it is already connected to. This usually occurs when network cables are not labeled or are mislabeled or when the administrator has not taken the time to verify where the cables are connected.

There is an exception to this problem. An EtherChannel is a grouping of Ethernet ports on a switch that acts as a single logical network connection. Because the switch treats the ports configured for the EtherChannel as a single network link, loops do not occur. Configuring EtherChannels is beyond the scope of this book. If you would like to learn more about EtherChannel, visit

www.cisco.com/en/US/tech/tk389/tk213/technologies_white_paper09186a0080092944.shtml.

Figure 5-20 displays a loop that occurs if a switch is connected to two switches on a network that are both also interconnected. The impact of this type of loop is much greater because it affects more switches directly.

Figure 5-20   Core-Distribution-Access Loop

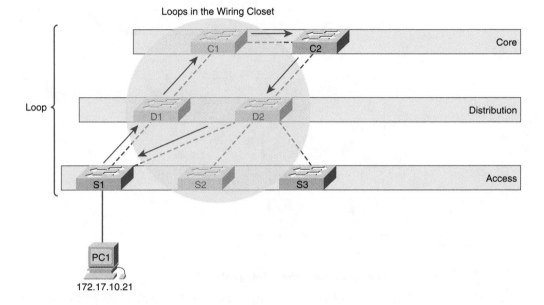

Loops in Cubicles

Because of insufficient network data connections, some end users have a personal switch or hub located in their work environment. Rather than incur the costs of running additional network data connections to the workspace, a simple switch is connected to an existing network data connection, allowing all devices connected to the personal switch to gain access to the network.

Wiring closets are typically secured to prevent unauthorized access, so often the network administrator is the only one who has full control over how and what devices are connected to the network. Unlike the wiring closet, the administrator is not in control of how personal switches are being used or connected, so the end user can accidentally interconnect the switches.

In Figure 5-21, two user hubs are interconnected, resulting in a network loop. The loop disrupts communication between all devices connected to switch S1.

Figure 5-21   Cubicle Loop

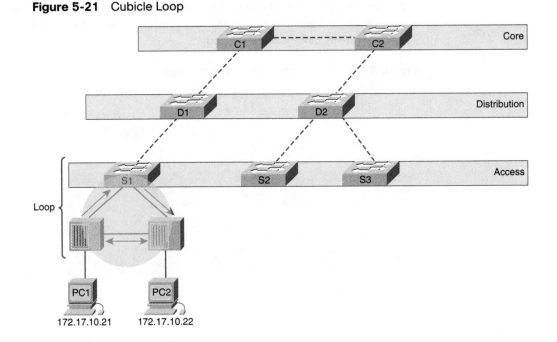

Packet Tracer
☐ Activity

Examining a Redundant Design (5.1.3)

Use the Packet Tracer Activity to examine how STP operates with default configurations. Unconfigured, out-of-the-box Cisco Catalyst switches have been added to the network. Use File e3-5133.pka on the CD-ROM that accompanies this book to perform this activity using Packet Tracer.

Introduction to STP

Redundancy increases the availability of a network topology by protecting the network from a single point of failure, such as a failed network cable or switch. When redundancy is introduced into a Layer 2 design, loops and duplicate frames can occur. Loops and duplicate frames can have severe consequences on a network. The *Spanning Tree Protocol (STP)* was developed by Radia Perlman and published as IEEE Standard 802.1D in 1990 to address these issues.

Spanning-Tree Algorithm (STA)

STP ensures that only one logical path exists between all destinations on the network by intentionally blocking redundant paths that could cause a loop. A switch port is considered blocked when network traffic is prevented from entering or leaving that port. This does not include *bridge protocol data unit (BPDU)* frames that are used by STP to prevent loops. You learn more about STP BPDU frames later in the chapter. Blocking the redundant paths is critical to preventing loops on the network. The physical paths still exist to provide redundancy, but these paths are disabled to prevent the loops from occurring. If the path is ever needed to compensate for a network cable or switch failure, STP recalculates the paths and unblocks the necessary ports to allow the redundant path to become active. The spanning-tree algorithm (STA) is used to carry out these calculations.

STP Topology

In Figure 5-22, all switches have STP enabled. We observe the usual behavior of STP, resulting from the spanning-tree algorithm.

Figure 5-22   STP Topology

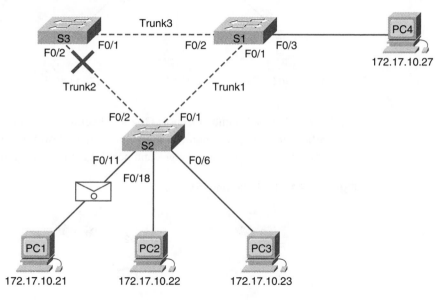

We illustrate basic spanning-tree operation in this switched LAN:

1. PC1 sends a broadcast out onto the network.

2. Switch S3 has set port F0/2 to a blocking state. The blocking state prevents ports from being used to forward switch traffic, thus preventing a loop from occurring. Switch S2 forwards the broadcast frame out ports F0/2, F0/18, F0/6, and F0/1. S3 drops the frame as it arrives over Trunk2 on port F0/2.

3. Switch S1 receives the broadcast frame and forwards it out ports F0/2 and F0/3 toward S3 and PC4, respectively, as pictured in Figure 5-23. S3 does not forward the frame back to S2 over Trunk2 because of the blocked port. The Layer 2 loop is prevented.

Figure 5-23   STP Loop Prevention

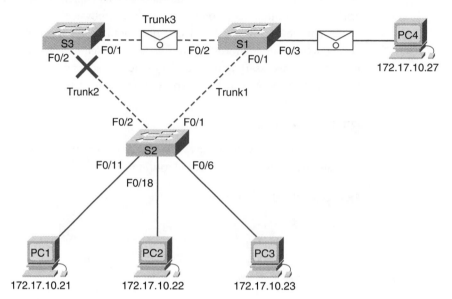

4. If Trunk1 fails, S3 unblocks port F0/2 and begins to forward the previously blocked traffic, permitting communication to continue, as shown in Figure 5-24. If Trunk1 comes back up, STP reconverges and port F0/2 on S3 is again blocked.

Figure 5-24   STP Reconvergence

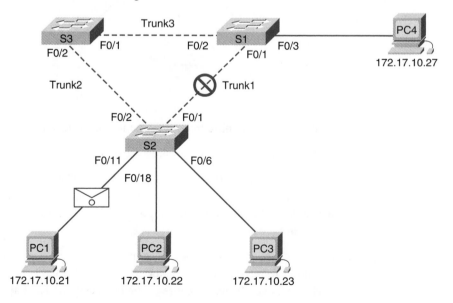

STP prevents loops from occurring by configuring a loop-free environment using strategically placed blocked ports. The switches running STP are able to compensate for failures by dynamically unblocking the previously blocked ports and permitting traffic to traverse the alternative paths. The next topic describes how STP accomplishes this.

Port Types in the Spanning-Tree Algorithm

STP uses the *spanning-tree algorithm (STA)* to determine which switch ports on a network need to be blocked to prevent loops from occurring. The STA designates a single switch as the *root bridge* and uses it as the reference point for all subsequent calculations. In Figure 5-25, the root bridge, switch S1, is chosen through an election process. All switches participating in STP exchange BPDU frames to determine which switch has the lowest *bridge ID (BID)* on the network. The switch with the lowest BID automatically becomes the root bridge for the STA calculations. The root bridge election process is discussed in detail later in this chapter.

Figure 5-25   Spanning-Tree Algorithm

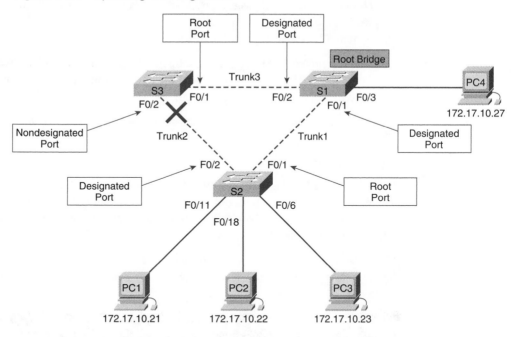

A BPDU is a frame containing STP information exchanged by switches running STP. Each BPDU contains a BID that identifies the switch that sent the BPDU. The BID contains a priority value: the MAC address of the sending switch and an extended system ID. The lowest BID value is determined by the combination of these fields. You will learn more about the root bridge, BPDUs, and BIDs later in the chapter.

After the root bridge has been determined, the STA calculates the shortest path to the root bridge. Each switch uses STA to determine which ports to block. During the time that STA determines the best path to the root bridge for each node in the broadcast domain, all data traffic is prevented from being forwarded through the network. The STA considers both path and port costs when determining which paths to ultimately leave unblocked. The *path costs* are calculated using *port cost* values associated with port speeds for each switch port along a given path. The sum of the egress port cost values determines the overall path cost to the root bridge. If there is more than one path to choose from, STA chooses the path with the lowest path cost. You learn more about path and port costs later in the chapter.

When the STA has determined the "best" paths emanating from the root bridge, it configures the switch ports into distinct port roles. The port roles, as illustrated in Figure 5-25, describe their relation in the network to the root bridge and whether they are allowed to forward traffic:

- *Root ports*: Switch ports closest to the root bridge. In the figure, the root port on switch S2 is F0/1. The root port on switch S3 is F0/1.

- *Designated ports*: All nonroot ports that are still permitted to forward traffic on the network. In the figure, switch ports F0/1 and F0/2 on switch S1 are designated ports. Switch S2 also has its port F0/2 as a designated port.

- *Nondesignated ports*: All ports configured to be in a blocking state to prevent loops. In the figure, STA configures port F0/2 on switch S3 in the nondesignated role. Port F0/2 on switch S3 is in the blocking state.

We discuss port roles and STP port states in detail later in the chapter.

Root Bridge

Every spanning-tree instance in a switched LAN has a switch designated as the root bridge. The root bridge serves as a reference point for all spanning-tree calculations to determine which redundant paths to block. Refer to Figure 5-26. An election process determines which switch becomes the root bridge.

Figure 5-27 shows the fields of the bridge ID. The details of each BID field are discussed later, but it is useful to know now that the BID is made up of a priority value, an extended system ID, and the MAC address of the switch.

All switches in the broadcast domain participate in the election process. After a switch boots, it sends BPDU frames containing the switch BID and the *root ID* every 2 seconds. By default, the root ID matches the local BID for all switches on the network; that is, the root ID identifies the root bridge on the network and, initially, each switch identifies itself as the root bridge after boot.

As the switches forward BPDU frames, adjacent switches in the broadcast domain read the root ID information from the BPDU frame. If the root ID from the BPDU received is lower than the root ID on the receiving switch, the receiving switch updates its cached root ID information to that of the adjacent bridge sending the BPDU.

Figure 5-26   Root Bridge

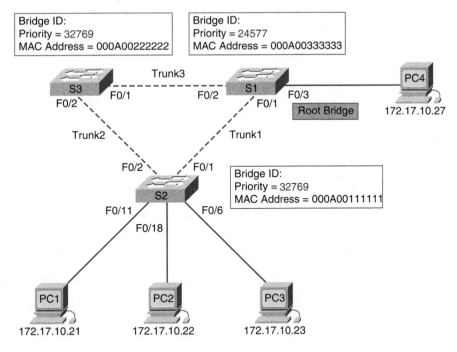

Figure 5-27   Bridge ID

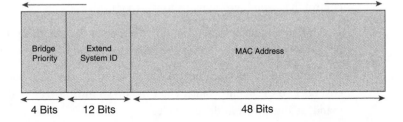

Note

The actual root bridge may not be an adjacent switch, but could be any other switch in the broadcast domain. The switch receiving the BPDU then forwards new BPDU frames with the lower root ID to the other adjacent switches. Eventually, the switch with the lowest BID ends up being identified as the root bridge for the spanning-tree instance.

Best Paths

When the root bridge has been elected for a given spanning-tree instance, the STA starts the process of determining the best paths to the root bridge from all nodes in the broadcast domain. The path information is determined by summing up the individual egress port costs along the path from the respective switch to the root bridge.

The default port costs are defined by the speed at which the port operates. In Table 5-1, you can see that 10 Gbps Ethernet ports have a port cost of 2, 1 Gbps Ethernet ports have a port cost of 4, 100 Mbps Ethernet ports have a port cost of 19, and 10 Mbps Ethernet ports have a port cost of 100.

Table 5-1   Best Paths to Root Bridge

Link Speed	Cost (Revised IEEE Specification)	Cost (Previous IEEE Specification)
10 Gbps	2	1
1 Gbps	4	1
100 Mbps	19	10
10 Mbps	100	100

Note

IEEE defines the port cost values used by STP. As newer, faster Ethernet technologies enter the marketplace, the path cost values may change to accommodate the different speeds available. The nonlinear numbers accommodate some improvements to the Ethernet standard, but be aware that the numbers can be changed by IEEE if necessary. In the table, the values have already been changed to accommodate the newer 10 Gbps Ethernet standard.

Although switch ports have a default port cost associated with them, the port cost is configurable. The ability to configure individual port costs gives the administrator the flexibility to control the spanning-tree paths to the root bridge.

To configure the port cost of an interface, enter the **spanning-tree cost** *value* command in interface configuration mode. The range value can be between 1 and 200,000,000.

In Example 5-1, interface F0/1 has been configured with a port cost of 25. To revert the port cost back to the default value, enter the **no spanning-tree cost** interface configuration command, as illustrated in the example.

Example 5-1 Configuring and Resetting Port Cost

```
S2# configure terminal
Enter configuration commands, one per line.  End with CNTL/Z.
S2(config)# interface f0/1
S2(config-if)# spanning-tree cost 25
S2(config-if)# no spanning-tree cost
```

Path cost is the sum of all the egress port costs along the path to the root bridge. The paths with the lowest path cost become the preferred path, and all other redundant paths are blocked. In Figure 5-28, the path cost from switch S2 to root bridge S1 over Path 1 is 19 (based on the revised IEEE port cost), and the path cost over Path 2 is 38. Because Path 1 has a lower path cost to the root bridge, it is the preferred path. STP then configures the redundant path to be blocked, preventing a loop from occurring.

Figure 5-28 Path Costs

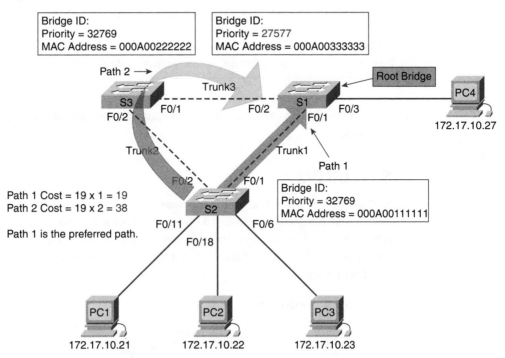

Path 1 Cost = 19 x 1 = 19
Path 2 Cost = 19 x 2 = 38

Path 1 is the preferred path.

To verify the port and path cost to the root bridge, enter the **show spanning-tree** privileged EXEC mode command as shown in Example 5-2. The Cost field in the output is the total path cost to the root bridge. This value changes depending on how many switch ports need to be traversed to get to the root bridge. In the output, each interface is also identified with an individual port cost of 19.

Example 5-2 Verifying Port Cost and Path Cost

```
S2# show spanning-tree

VLAN0001
  Spanning tree enabled protocol ieee
  Root ID    Priority 27589
             Address    000A.0033.3333
             Cost       19
             Port       1
             Hello Time  2 sec  Max Age 20 sec  Forward Delay 15 sec

  Bridge ID  Priority    32769  (priority 32768 sys-id-ext 1)
```

```
        Address      000A.0011.1111
        Hello Time   2 sec  Max Age 20 sec  Forward Delay 15 sec
        Aging Time 300

Interface        Role Sts Cost     Prio.Nbr Type
-------------------------------------------------------------------
F0/1             Root FWD 19       128.1    Edge P2p
F0/2             Desg FWD 19       128.2    Edge P2p
```

Another command to explore is the **show spanning-tree detail** privileged EXEC mode command.

STP BPDU

STP determines a root bridge for the spanning-tree instance by exchanging BPDUs. Here we describe the details of the BPDU frame and how it facilitates the spanning-tree algorithm. The BPDU frame contains 12 distinct fields, shown in Figure 5-29, that are used to convey path and priority information that STP uses to determine the root bridge and paths to the root bridge.

Figure 5-29   BPDU Fields

Bytes	Field
2	Protocol ID
1	Version
1	Message Type
1	Flags
8	Root ID
4	Cost of Path
8	Bridge ID
2	Port ID
2	Message Age
2	Max Age
2	Hello Time
2	Forward Delay

The BPDU can be broken into three main parts:

■ The first four fields identify the protocol, version, message type, and status flags.

■ The next four fields are used to identify the root bridge and the cost of the path to the root bridge.

■ The last four fields are timer fields that determine how frequently BPDU messages are sent and how long the information received through the BPDU process is retained. The role of the timer fields will be covered in more detail later in this book.

Figure 5-30 illustrates BPDU data captured using Wireshark. Here the BPDU frame contains more fields than previously described, because the BPDU message is encapsulated in an Ethernet frame when it is transmitted across the network. The 802.3 header indicates the source and destination addresses of the BPDU frame. This frame has a destination MAC address of 01:80:C2:00:00:00, which is a multicast address for the spanning-tree multicast group. When a frame is addressed with this MAC address, each switch that is configured for spanning tree processes the information from the frame. By using this multicast group address, all other devices on the network that receive this frame disregard its contents. In this capture, the root ID and the BID are the same; this indicates that the frame was sent by a root bridge. The timers are all set to the default values.

Figure 5-30   Wireshark Capture

```
⊞ Frame 1 (60 bytes on wire, 60 bytes captured)
⊟ IEEE 802.3 Ethernet
   ⊞ Destination: Spanning-tree-(for-bridges)_00 (01:80:c2:00:00:00)
   ⊞ Source: Cisco_9e:93:03 (00:19:aa:9e:93:03)
     Length: 38
     Trailer: 0000000000000000
⊞ Logical-Link Control
⊟ Spanning Tree Protocol
     Protocol Identifier: Spanning Tree Protocol (0x0000)
     Protocol Version Identifier: Spanning Tree (0)
     BPDU Type: Configuration (0x00)
   ⊞ BPDU flags: 0x01 (Topology Change)
     Root Identifier: 24577 / 00:19:aa:9e:93:00
     Root Path Cost: 0
     Bridge Identifier: 24577 / 00:19:aa:9e:93:00
     Port Identifier: 0x8003
     Message Age: 0
     Max Age: 20
     Hello Time: 2
     Forward Delay: 15
```

BPDU Process

Each switch in the broadcast domain initially assumes that it is the root bridge for the spanning-tree instance, so the BPDU frames sent contain the BID of the local switch as the root ID. After a switch is booted, BPDU frames are sent every 2 seconds, the default value of the hello timer specified in the BPDU. Each switch maintains local information about its own BID, the root ID, and the path cost to the root.

When adjacent switches receive a BPDU frame, they compare the root ID from the BPDU frame with the local root ID. If the root ID in the BPDU is lower than the local root ID, the switch updates the local root ID and the ID in its BPDU messages. These messages serve to indicate the new root bridge on the network. Also, the path cost is updated to indicate how far away the root bridge is. For example, if the BPDU was received on a Fast Ethernet switch port, the path cost would be increased by 19. If the local root ID is lower than the root ID received in the BPDU frame, the BPDU frame is discarded.

After a root ID has been updated to identify a new root bridge, all subsequent BPDU frames sent from that switch contain the new root ID and updated path cost. That way, all other adjacent switches are able to see the lowest root ID identified at all times. As the BPDU frames pass between other adjacent switches, the path cost is continually updated to indicate the total path cost to the root bridge. Each switch in the spanning tree uses its path costs to identify the best possible path to the root bridge.

The following steps illustrate the BPDU process:

1. Refer to Figure 5-31. Initially, each switch identifies itself as the root bridge. Switch S1 has the lowest priority of all three switches. Because the priority takes precedence in determining the root bridge, S1 becomes the root bridge. If the priorities of all the switches were the same, the MAC addresses would be the deciding factor.

Figure 5-31   BPDU Process 1

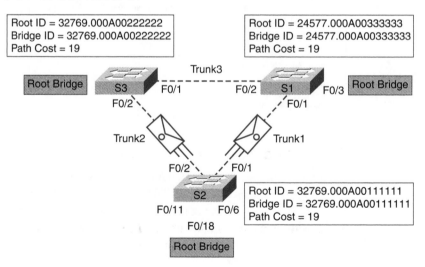

2. When switch S3 receives a BPDU from switch S2, as shown in Figure 5-32, S3 compares its root ID with the BPDU frame it received. The priorities are equal, so the switch examines the MAC address portion to determine which MAC address has a lower value. Because S2 has a lower MAC address value, S3 updates its root ID with the S2 root ID. At this point, S3 considers S2 as the root bridge.

Figure 5-32 BPDU Process 2

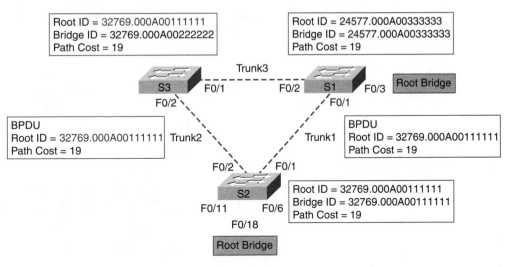

3. When S1 compares its root ID with the one in the received BPDU frame, as in Figure 5-33, it identifies the local root ID as the lower value and discards the BPDU from S2.

Figure 5-33 BPDU Process 3

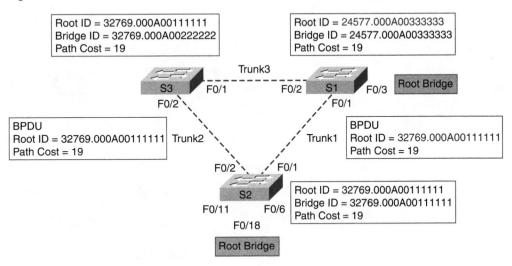

4. When S3 sends out its BPDU frames, as in Figure 5-34, the root ID contained in the BPDU frame is that of S2.

Figure 5-34   BPDU Process 4

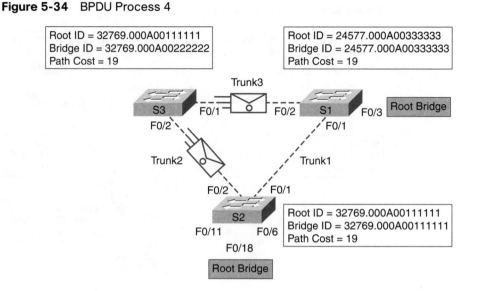

5. When S2 receives the BPDU frame, as in Figure 5-35, it discards it after verifying that the root ID in the BPDU matches its local root ID.

Figure 5-35   BPDU Process 5

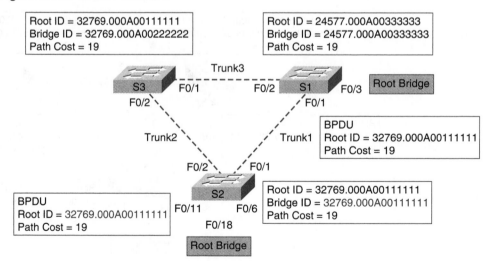

6. Because S1 has a lower priority value in its root ID, as shown in Figure 5-36, it discards the BPDU frame received from S3.

Figure 5-36   BPDU Process 6

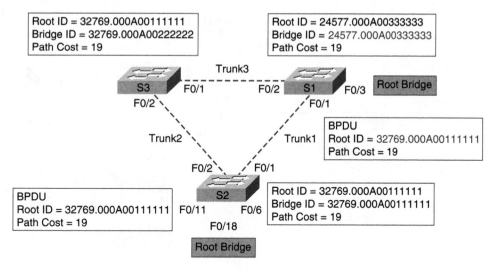

7. S1 sends out its BPDU frames, as in Figure 5-37.

Figure 5-37   BPDU Process 7

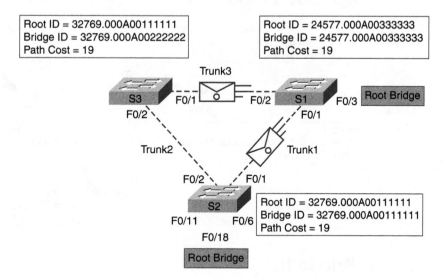

8. S3 identifies the root ID in the BPDU frame as having a lower value and therefore updates its root ID values to indicate that S1 is now the root bridge, as in Figure 5-38.

Figure 5-38   BPDU Process 8

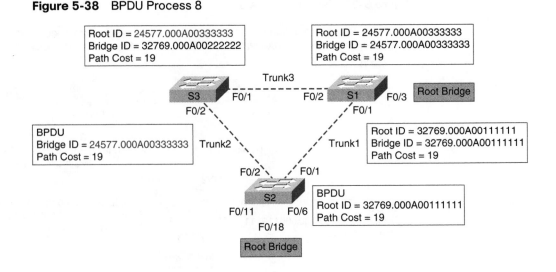

9. S2 identifies the root ID in the BPDU frame as having a lower value and therefore updates its root ID values to indicate that S1 is now the root bridge, as in Figure 5-39.

Figure 5-39   BPDU Process 9

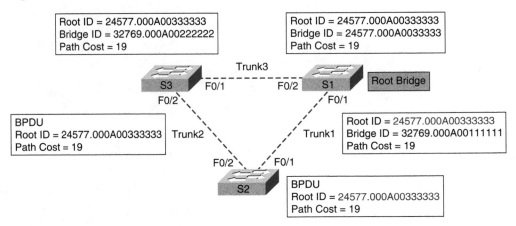

Bridge ID

The bridge ID is used to determine the root bridge on a network. This topic describes what makes up a BID and how to configure the BID on a switch to influence the election process to ensure that specific switches are assigned the role of root bridge on the network.

The BID field of a BPDU frame contains three separate fields, pictured in Figure 5-40: bridge priority, extended system ID, and MAC address. Each field is used during the root bridge election.

Figure 5-40 Bridge ID Fields

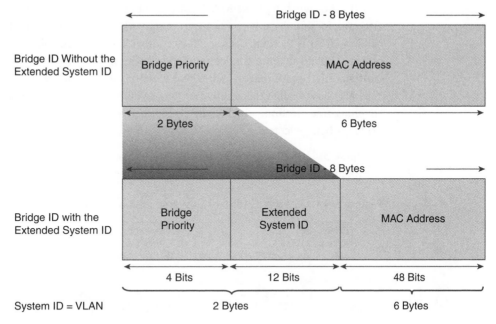

The *bridge priority* is a customizable value that you can use to influence which switch becomes the root bridge. The switch with the lowest priority, whence the lowest BID, becomes the root bridge. For example, to ensure that a specific switch is always the root bridge, you set the priority to a lower value than the rest of the switches in the broadcast domain. The default value for the priority of all Catalyst switches is 32768. The priority range is between 1 and 65536.

As shown in Figure 5-40, the *extended system ID* can be omitted in BPDU frames in certain configurations. The early implementation of STP was designed for networks that did not use VLANs. There was a single common spanning tree across all switches. With its implementation of PVST+, where a single instance of STP is committed to each VLAN, Cisco enhanced its implementation of STP to include support for the extended system ID field, which contains the ID of the VLAN that the BPDU is associated with; it follows that a Catalyst switch must have as many different bridge IDs as VLANs configured on it. Some of the bits previously used for the bridge priority (12 to be exact) are used for the extended system ID (VLAN ID). The result is that fewer bridge priority numbers are reserved for the switch and a larger range of VLAN IDs can be supported, all the while maintaining the uniqueness of the bridge ID.

Because using the extended system ID changes the number of bits available for the bridge priority, the increment for the bridge priority value changes from 1 to 4096. Therefore, bridge priority values can only be multiples of 4096, so there are only 16 possible values it can assume for a given VLAN (previously 1 to 65536). The extended system ID value is added to the bridge priority value in the BID to uniquely identify the priority and VLAN of the BPDU frame.

When two switches are configured with the same priority and have the same extended system ID, the switch with the MAC address with the lowest hexadecimal value has the lower BID. Again, initially all switches are configured with the same default priority value. The MAC address is then the deciding factor on which switch is going to become the root bridge. This results in a nondeterministic choice of the root bridge. It is recommended to configure the appropriate switch with a lower priority to ensure that it is elected root bridge. This also ensures that the addition of new switches to the network does not trigger a new spanning-tree election, which could disrupt network communication while a new root bridge is being elected.

In Figure 5-41, S1 has a lower priority than the other switches; therefore, it is preferred as the root bridge for the particular spanning-tree instance.

Figure 5-41   Lowest Bridge Priority Implies Lowest Bridge ID

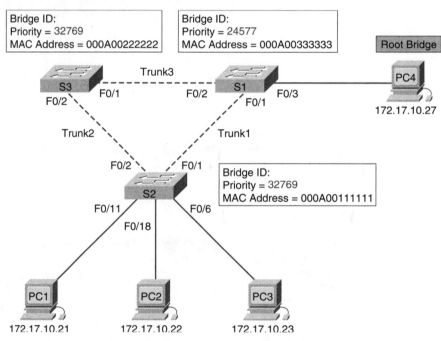

When all switches are configured with the same priority, as is the case with switches in the default configuration (with a priority of 32768), the MAC address becomes the deciding factor for which switch becomes the root bridge. In Figure 5-42, the MAC address determines the root bridge.

Note

In Figure 5-42, the priority of all the switches is 32769. The value is based on the 32768 default priority and the VLAN 1 assignment associated with each switch (1+32768).

Figure 5-42   Default Condition—MAC Address Determines Root

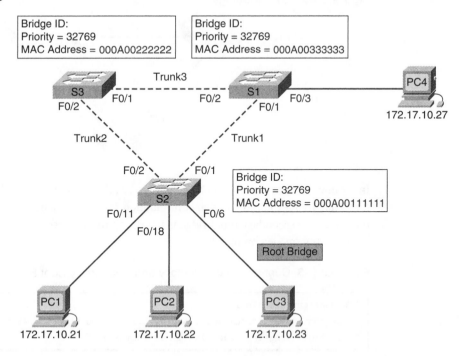

The MAC address with the lowest hexadecimal value is considered to be the preferred root bridge. In Figure 5-42, S2 has the lowest value for its MAC address and is therefore designated as the root bridge for the VLAN 1 spanning-tree instance.

Configure and Verify the BID

If a specific switch is to become the root bridge, the bridge priority value needs to be adjusted to ensure that it is lower than the bridge priority values of all the other switches on the network. You can use two different configuration methods to configure the bridge priority value on a Cisco Catalyst switch. Refer to Figure 5-43.

The first method to ensure that the switch has the lowest bridge priority value is to use the **spanning-tree vlan** *vlan-id* **root primary** command in global configuration mode. The priority for the switch is set to the predefined value of 24576 or to the next 4096 increment value below the lowest bridge priority detected on the network.

If an alternate root bridge is desired, use the **spanning-tree vlan** *vlan-id* **root secondary** global configuration mode command. This command sets the priority for the switch to the predefined value of 28672. This ensures that this switch becomes the root bridge if the primary root bridge fails and a new root bridge election occurs; it assumes that the rest of the switches in the network have the default 32768 priority value defined.

Figure 5-43 STP Topology

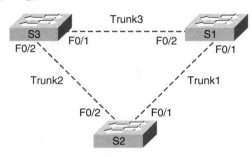

In Example 5-3, switch S1 has been assigned as the primary root bridge using the **spanning-tree vlan 1 root primary** global configuration mode command, and switch S2 has been configured as the secondary root bridge using the **spanning-tree vlan 1 root secondary** global configuration mode command.

Example 5-3 Configuring the Primary and Secondary Root Bridge

```
S1# configure terminal
Enter configuration commands, one per line.  End with CNTL/Z.
S1(config)# spanning-tree vlan 1 root primary

S2# configure terminal
Enter configuration commands, one per line.  End with CNTL/Z.
S2(config)# spanning-tree vlan 1 root secondary
```

The second method for configuring the bridge priority value is using the **spanning-tree vlan *vlan-id* priority *value*** global configuration mode command. This command gives you more granular control over the bridge priority value. The priority value is configured in increments of 4096 between 0 and 65536.

In Example 5-4, switch S3 has been assigned a bridge priority value of 24576 using the **spanning-tree vlan 1 priority 24576** global configuration mode command.

Example 5-4 Configuring the Bridge Priority Directly

```
S3# configure terminal
Enter configuration commands, one per line.  End with CNTL/Z.
S3(config)# spanning-tree vlan 1 priority 24576
```

To verify the bridge priority of a switch, use the **show spanning-tree** privileged EXEC mode command. In Example 5-5, you see that the priority of the switch is 24576. Also notice that the switch is designated as the root bridge for the spanning-tree instance.

Example 5-5 Configuring the Bridge Priority Directly

```
S1# show spanning-tree

VLAN0001
  Spanning tree enabled protocol ieee
  Root ID    Priority    24577
             Address     000A.0033.3333
             This bridge is the root
             Hello Time   2 sec  Max Age 20 sec  Forward Delay 15 sec

  Bridge ID  Priority    24577  (priority 24576 sys-id-ext 1)
             Address     0019.aa9e.b000
             Hello Time   2 sec  Max Age 20 sec  Forward Delay 15 sec
             Aging Time 300

Interface         Role Sts Cost     Prio.Nbr Type
-------------------------------------------------------------------------
Fa0/1             Desg FWD 4        128.1    Shr
Fa0/2             Desg FWD 4        128.2    Shr
```

Port Roles

The root bridge is elected for the spanning-tree instance. The location of the root bridge in the network topology determines how port roles are calculated. This topic describes how the switch ports are configured for specific roles to prevent the possibility of loops on the network. Refer to Figure 5-44.

During the spanning-tree process, switch ports are automatically configured for four distinct port roles.

The root port exists on nonroot bridges and is the switch port with the best path to the root bridge. Root ports forward traffic toward the root bridge. The source MAC address of frames received on the root port are capable of populating the MAC address table. Only one root port is allowed per switch (at this point we are assuming that we are working within a single broadcast domain).

In Figure 5-44, switch S1 is the root bridge, and switches S2 and S3 have root ports defined on the trunk links connecting back to S1.

The designated port exists on root and nonroot bridges. For root bridges, all switch ports are designated ports. For nonroot bridges, a designated port is the switch port that receives and forwards frames toward the root bridge as needed. Only one designated port is allowed per segment. It is a key point that designated ports are a function of LAN segments—there is exactly one designated port per LAN segment. The switch at the end of the segment with the designated port is the *designated bridge* (also called the designated switch). If multiple switches exist on the same segment (an extremely rare scenario in modern switched LANs), an election process determines the designated switch, and the corresponding switch port begins forwarding frames for that segment. Designated ports are capable of populating the MAC address table.

Figure 5-44   STP Port Roles

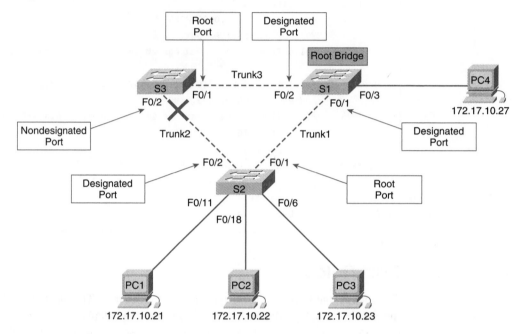

In Figure 5-44, switch S1 has both sets of ports for its two trunk links configured as designated ports. Switch S2 also has a designated port configured on the trunk link going toward switch S3.

A nondesignated port is a switch port that is blocked, so it is not forwarding data frames and not populating the MAC address table with source addresses. A nondesignated port is not a root port or a designated port.

In Figure 5-44, switch S3 has the only nondesignated port in the topology. Nondesignated ports logically block physical loops.

A *disabled port* is a switch port that is administratively shut down. A disabled port does not function in the spanning-tree process. There are no disabled ports in Figure 5-44.

To further explore port roles, refer to Figure 5-45.

The STA determines which port role is assigned to each switch port. When determining the root port on a switch, the switch compares the path costs on all switch ports participating in the spanning tree. The switch port with the lowest overall path cost to the root is automatically assigned the root port role because it is closest to the root bridge. In a network topology, all switches running spanning tree, except for the root bridge, have a single root port defined.

Figure 5-45   STP Port Roles Revisited

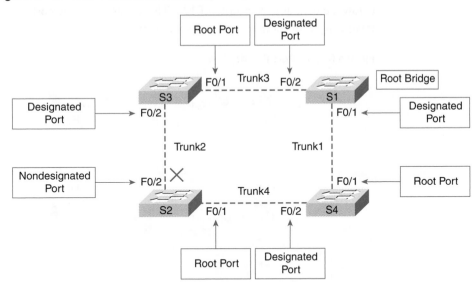

When two switch ports have the same path cost to the root bridge, the switch needs to determine which switch port is the root port. The switch uses the configurable port priority value, or the lowest port number if both port priority values are the same. The default port priority value for a switch port is 128.

Like the bridge ID is composed of the bridge priority and MAC address of the switch (for a particular VLAN), the *port ID* consists of the *port priority* coupled with the *port number* associated with the Layer 2 interface (switch port). For example, Figure 5-45 shows four switches. Port F0/1 and F0/2 on switch S2 have the same path cost value back to the root bridge. However, port F0/1 on switch S2 is the preferred port because it has a lower port number: 1.

The port number is appended to the port priority to form the port ID. For example, switch port F0/1 has a default port ID of 128.1, where 128 is the configurable port priority value, and 1 is the port number.

Configure Port Priority

First, it should be emphasized that configuring port priority will rarely be a requirement with modern switched LAN design, where broadcast domains are geographically contained. Figure 5-46 provides a scenario where it may make sense to tweak the port priority, but this topology does not follow the recommended Cisco switched LAN design.

You can configure the port priority value using the **spanning-tree port-priority** *value* interface configuration mode command. The port priority values range from 0–240, in increments of 16. The default port priority value is 128. As with bridge priority, lower port priority values have precedence.

In Figure 5-46, the port priority for port F0/1 on switch S2 has been set to 112, which is below the default port priority of 128. This ensures that the port is the preferred port when competing with another port for a specific port role.

Figure 5-46   Port Priority Tie

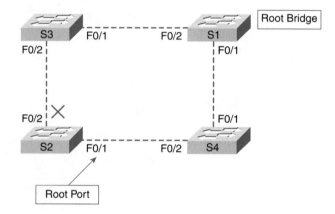

When the switch decides to use one port over another for the root port, the other is configured as a nondesignated port to prevent a loop from occurring. The configuration of F0/1 on S2 is provided in Example 5-6.

Example 5-6 Configuring Port Priority

```
S2# configure terminal
Enter configuration commands, one per line.  End with CNTL/Z.
S2(config)# interface f0/1
S2(config-if)# spanning-tree port-priority 112
```

Port Role Decisions

In Figure 5-47, switch S1 is the root bridge. Switches S2 and S3 have root ports configured for the ports connecting back to S1.

After a switch has determined which of its ports is configured in the root port role, it needs to decide which ports have the designated and nondesignated roles.

The root bridge automatically configures all its switch ports in the designated role. Other switches in the topology configure their nonroot ports as designated or nondesignated ports.

Designated ports are configured for all LAN segments. When two switches are connected to the same LAN segment, and root ports have already been defined, the two switches have to decide which port is to be configured as a designated port and which one is left as the nondesignated port.

Figure 5-47   Port Role Scenario

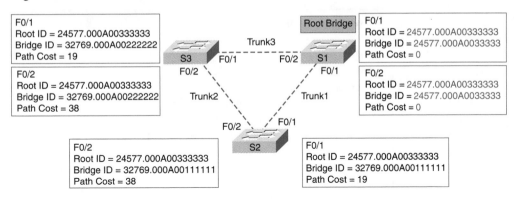

The switches on the LAN segment in question exchange BPDU frames, which contain the respective switch BIDs. Generally, the switch with the lower BID has its port configured as a designated port, whereas the switch with the higher BID has its port configured as a non-designated port. However, keep in mind that the sender BID is used to determine the designated port only if the path costs to the root bridge are equal.

As a result, each switch determines which port roles are assigned to each of its ports to create the loop-free spanning tree, as illustrated in Figure 5-48.

Figure 5-48   Port Role Decisions

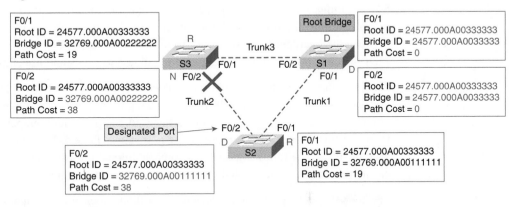

Now that spanning tree has determined the logical loop-free network topology, you may want to confirm which port roles and port priorities are configured for the various switch ports in the network. To verify the port roles and port priorities for the switch ports, use the **show spanning-tree** privileged EXEC mode command.

The **show spanning-tree** output in Example 5-7 displays all switch ports for switch S2 and their defined roles. Switch port F0/1 is a root port and port F0/2 is a designated port. The output also displays the port priority of each switch port. Switch port F0/1 has a port ID of 128.1.

Example 5-7 Verifying the Port Priority

```
S2# show spanning-tree


VLAN0001
  Spanning tree enabled protocol ieee
  Root ID    Priority    24577
             Address     0019.aa9e.b000
             This bridge is the root
             Hello Time    2 sec  Max Age 20 sec   Forward Delay 15 sec

  Bridge ID  Priority    24577   (priority 24576 sys-id-ext 1)
             Address     0019.aa9e.b000
             Hello Time    2 sec  Max Age 20 sec   Forward Delay 15 sec
             Aging Time 300


Interface        Role Sts Cost      Prio.Nbr Type
-------------------------------------------------------------------
Fa0/1            Root FWD 19        128.1    P2p
Fa0/2            Desg FWD 19        128.2    P2p
```

STP Port States and BPDU Timers

STP determines the logical loop-free path throughout the broadcast domain. The spanning tree is determined through the information learned by the exchange of the BPDU frames between the interconnected switches. To facilitate the learning of the logical spanning tree, each switch port transitions through five possible port states and uses three BPDU timers.

The spanning tree is determined immediately after a switch is finished booting. If a switch port were to transition directly from the blocking to the forwarding state and the switch was not aware of all topology information at the time, the port could temporarily create a data loop. For this reason, STP introduces five port states. Table 5-2 summarizes what each port state involves. The following provides some additional information on how the port states ensure that no loops are created during the creation of the logical spanning tree.

- *Blocking*: The port is a nondesignated port and does not participate in frame forwarding. The port continues to process received BPDU frames to determine the location and root ID of the root bridge and what port role the switch port should assume in the final active STP topology.

- *Listening*: STP has determined that the port can be selected as a root port or designated port based upon the information in the BPDU frames it has received so far. At this point, the switch port is not only receiving BPDU frames, it is also transmitting its own BPDU frames and informing adjacent switches that the switch port is preparing to participate in the active topology. The port returns to blocking state if it is determined that the port does not provide the lowest-cost path to the root bridge.

■ *Learning*: The port prepares to participate in frame forwarding and begins to populate the MAC address table.

■ *Forwarding*: The port is considered part of the active topology and forwards frames and also sends and receives BPDU frames.

■ *Disabled*: The Layer 2 port does not participate in spanning tree and does not forward or process frames. The disabled state is set when the switch port is administratively disabled.

Table 5-2   IEEE 802.1D Port States

Port State	Action
Blocking	Discards data frames received on the interface Discards frames switched from another interface for forwarding Does not learn addresses Receives/processes BPDUs
Listening	Discards data frames received on the interface Discards frames switched from another interface for forwarding Does not learn addresses Receives/processes and transmits BPDUs
Learning	Discards data frames received on the interface Discards frames switched from another interface for forwarding Learns addresses Receives/processes and transmits BPDUs
Forwarding	Receives and forwards frames received on the interface Forwards frames switched from another interface Learns addresses Receives/processes and transmits BPDUs
Disabled	Discards frames received on the interface Discards frames switched from another interface for forwarding Does not learn addresses Does not receive/process BPDUs

The amount of time that a port stays in the various port states depends on the BPDU timers. Only a switch in the role of root bridge can send information through the tree to adjust the timers. The following timers determine STP performance and state changes:

■ *Hello time*: The hello time is the time between each BPDU frame sent on a port. The default is 2 seconds but can be tuned between 1 and 10 seconds.

■ *Forward delay*: The forward delay is the time spent in the listening and learning states. The default is 15 seconds but can be tuned between 4 and 30 seconds.

- *Maximum age*: The max age timer controls the maximum length of time a switch port saves configuration BPDU information. The default is 20 seconds but can be tuned between 6 and 40 seconds.

When STP is enabled, every switch port in the network goes through the blocking state and the transitory states of listening and learning as the switches power up. The ports then stabilize to the forwarding or blocking state, as illustrated in Figure 5-49. During a topology change, a port temporarily implements the listening and learning states for a specified period called the forward delay interval.

Figure 5-49   BPDU Timers

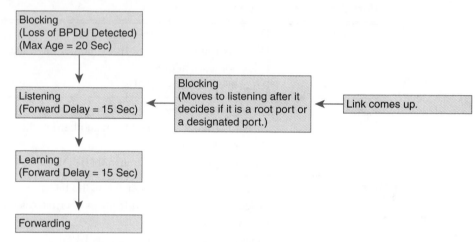

These values allow adequate time for convergence in a network with a switch diameter of seven or less. The *switch diameter* (or network diameter) is the number of switches a frame has to traverse to travel between the two farthest points within the broadcast domain. A seven-switch diameter is the largest diameter that STP permits based on the default STP timers. Convergence in relation to spanning tree is the time it takes to recalculate the spanning tree if a switch or a link fails. You learn how convergence works in the next section.

The BPDU timers should not be adjusted directly because the values have been optimized for the seven-switch diameter, which functions well for a broadcast domain in a modern switched LAN. Adjusting the spanning-tree diameter value on the root bridge to a lower value automatically adjusts the forward delay and maximum age timers proportionally for the new diameter. Typically, you do not adjust the BPDU timers nor reconfigure the network diameter. However, if after research, a network administrator determines that the convergence time of the network could be optimized, the administrator would do so by reconfiguring the network diameter, not the BPDU timers.

To configure a different network diameter for STP, use the **spanning-tree vlan *vlan-id* root primary diameter *value*** global configuration mode command on the root bridge. The *value* parameter can take on any value between 2 and 7.

In Example 5-8, the **spanning-tree vlan 1 root primary diameter 5** global configuration mode command is entered to adjust the spanning tree diameter to five switches.

Example 5-8 Configuring the Network Diameter

```
S1# configure terminal
Enter configuration commands, one per line.  End with CNTL/Z.
S1(config)# spanning-tree vlan 1 root primary diameter 5
```

Cisco PortFast

PortFast is a Cisco technology. When a switch port configured as an access port is configured with PortFast, the port transitions from blocking to forwarding state immediately, bypassing the usual STP listening and learning states. You can use PortFast on access ports that are connected to an end device, such as a workstation, a server, or a printer, to allow the device to connect to the network immediately rather than waiting for spanning tree to converge. If an interface configured with PortFast receives a BPDU frame, spanning tree can put the port into the blocking state using a feature called BPDU guard. Configuring BPDU guard is beyond the scope of this book. For more information on configuring BPDU guard, see www.cisco.com/en/US/tech/tk389/tk621/technologies_tech_note09186a008009482f.shtml.

Because the purpose of PortFast is to minimize the time that access ports must wait for spanning tree to converge, it should be used only on access ports. If you enable PortFast on a port connecting to another switch, you risk creating a spanning-tree loop.

> **Note**
>
> Cisco PortFast technology can be used to support DHCP. Without PortFast, a PC can send a DHCP request before the port is in forwarding state, denying the host from getting a usable IP address and other information. Because PortFast immediately changes the state to forwarding, the PC always gets a usable IP address.

Refer to Figure 5-50. Ports F0/11, F0/18, and F0/6 are ideal candidates for PortFast.

To configure PortFast on a switch port, enter the **spanning-tree portfast** interface configuration mode command on each interface that PortFast is to be enabled. Example 5-9 illustrates the configuration of PortFast on port F0/11 of switch S2.

Example 5-9 Configure PortFast

```
S2# configure terminal
Enter configuration commands, one per line.  End with CNTL/Z.
S2(config)# interface f0/11
S2(config-if)# spanning-tree portfast
```

Figure 5-50   Cisco PortFast

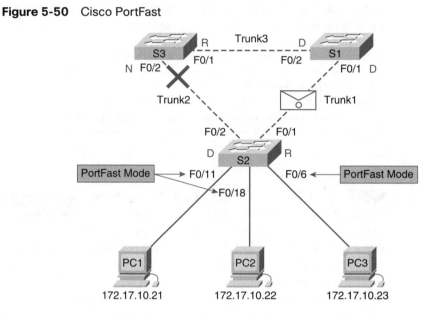

To disable PortFast, enter the **no spanning-tree portfast** interface configuration mode command on each interface for which PortFast is to be disabled.

To verify that PortFast has been enabled for a switch port, use the **show running-config** privileged EXEC mode command, as shown in Example 5-10. The absence of the **spanning-tree portfast** command in the running configuration for an interface indicates that PortFast has been disabled for that interface. PortFast is disabled on all interfaces by default.

Example 5-10   Verify PortFast

```
S2# show running-config
<output omitted>
!
interface FastEthernet0/11
 switchport mode access
 spanning-tree portfast
!
<output omitted>
```

Packet Tracer
☐ **Activity**

Configuring STP (5.2.5)

Use the Packet Tracer Activity to practice configuring STP. Switches are in the out-of-the-box condition, without any configuration. You will manipulate the root bridge election so that the core switches are chosen before the distribution or access layer switches. Use File e3-5254.pka on the CD-ROM that accompanies this book to perform this activity using Packet Tracer.

STP Convergence

The discussion so far in this chapter explored the components that enable STP to create the logical loop-free network topology. In this section, you examine the whole STP process from start to finish.

Convergence is an important aspect of the spanning-tree process. Convergence is the time it takes for the network to determine which switch is going to assume the role of the root bridge, go through all the different port states, and set all switch ports to their final spanning-tree port roles, thus eliminating all potential loops. The convergence process takes time to complete because of the different timers used to coordinate the process.

To understand the convergence process more thoroughly, it is broken down into three distinct steps:

1. Elect a root bridge

2. Elect root ports

3. Elect designated and nondesignated ports

The remainder of this section explores each step in the convergence process.

Step 1. Elect a Root Bridge

The first step of the spanning-tree convergence process is to elect a root bridge. The root bridge is the basis for all spanning-tree path cost calculations and ultimately leads to the assignment of the different port roles used to prevent loops from occurring.

A root bridge election is triggered after a switch has finished booting, or when a path failure has been detected on a network. Initially, all switch ports are configured for the blocking state, which by default lasts 20 seconds. This is done to prevent a loop from occurring before STP has had time to calculate the best root paths and configure all switch ports to their specific roles. While the switch ports are in blocking state, they are still able to receive and process BPDU frames so that the spanning-tree root election can proceed. Spanning tree supports a maximum network diameter of seven switches between end stations. This allows the entire root bridge election process to occur within 14 seconds, which is less than the time the switch ports spend in the blocking state.

Immediately after the switches have finished booting, they start sending BPDU frames advertising their BID in an attempt to become the root bridge. Initially, all switches in the network assume that they are the root bridge for the broadcast domain. The flood of BPDU frames on the network have the root ID field matching the BID field, indicating that each switch considers itself the root bridge. These BPDU frames are sent every 2 seconds based on the default hello timer value.

As each switch receives the BPDU frames from its neighbor switches, they compare the root ID from the received BPDU frame with the root ID cached locally. If the root ID from the received BPDU frame is lower than the root ID it has cached, the root ID field is updated, indicating the new best candidate for the root bridge role.

After the root ID field is updated on a switch, the switch then incorporates the new root ID in all future BPDU frame transmissions. This ensures that the lowest root ID is always conveyed to all other adjacent switches in the network. The root bridge election ends when the lowest bridge ID populates the root ID field of all switches in the broadcast domain.

Even after the root bridge election process has completed, the switches continue to forward their BPDU frames advertising the root ID of the root bridge every 2 seconds. Each switch is configured with a max age timer that determines how long a switch retains the current BPDU configuration in the event it stops receiving updates from its neighbor switches. By default, the max age timer is set to 20 seconds. Therefore, if a switch fails to receive 10 consecutive BPDU frames from one of its neighbors, the switch assumes that a logical path in the spanning tree has failed and that the BPDU information is no longer valid. This triggers another spanning-tree root bridge election.

The root bridge election process occurs with all switches sending and receiving BPDU frames simultaneously. Performing the election process simultaneously allows the switches to determine which switch is going to become the root bridge much faster than if it were carried out serially.

Verify Root Bridge Election

When the root bridge election is complete, you can verify the identity of the root bridge using the **show spanning-tree** privileged EXEC mode command. Refer to the reference topology in Figure 5-51.

Figure 5-51   Topology for Root Bridge Election

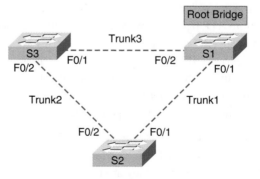

In the figure, switch S1 has the lowest priority value of the three switches, and so becomes the root bridge. The spanning-tree information for switch S1 is displayed in Example 5-11.

Example 5-11   show spanning-tree on S1

```
S1# show spanning-tree

VLAN0001
  Spanning tree enabled protocol ieee
  Root ID    Priority    24577
             Address        000A.0033.3333
             This bridge is the root
             Hello Time    2 sec  Max Age 20 sec  Forward Delay 15 sec
  Bridge ID  Priority    24577  (priority 24576 sys-id-ext 1)
             Address        000A.0033.3333
             Aging Time 300


Interface        Role Sts Cost       Prio.Nbr Type
---------------------------------------------------------------------------

Fa0/1            Desg FWD 19          128.1    Shr
Fa0/2            Desg FWD 19          128.2    Shr
```

The **show spanning-tree** output for switch S1 reveals that it is the root bridge. You can see that the BID matches the root ID, confirming that S1 is the root bridge.

Example 5-12 displays the **show spanning-tree** output for switch S2. The output shows that the root ID matches the expected root ID of switch S1, indicating that S2 considers S1 the root bridge.

Example 5-12   show spanning-tree on S2

```
S2# show spanning-tree

VLAN0001
  Spanning tree enabled protocol ieee
  Root ID    Priority    24577
             Address        000A.0033.3333
             Hello Time    2 sec  Max Age 20 sec  Forward Delay 15 sec
  Bridge ID  Priority    32769  (priority 32768 sys-id-ext 1)
             Address        000A.0011.1111
             Aging Time 300


Interface        Role Sts Cost       Prio.Nbr Type
---------------------------------------------------------------------------

Fa0/1            Root FWD 19          128.1    Shr
Fa0/2            Desg FWD 19          128.2    Shr
```

Example 5-13 displays the **show spanning-tree** output for switch S3. It shows that the root ID matches the expected root ID of switch S1, indicating that S3 considers S1 the root bridge.

Example 5-13   show spanning-tree on S3

```
S3# show spanning-tree

VLAN0001
  Spanning tree enabled protocol ieee
  Root ID    Priority    24577
             Address        000A.0033.3333
             Hello Time   2 sec  Max Age 20 sec  Forward Delay 15 sec
  Bridge ID  Priority    32769  (priority 32768 sys-id-ext 1)
             Address        000A.0022.2222
             Aging Time 300


Interface        Role Sts Cost     Prio.Nbr Type
------------------------------------------------------------------------
Fa0/1            Root FWD 19       128.1    Shr
Fa0/2            Altn  BLK 19       128.2    Shr
```

Step 2. Elect Root Ports

Now that the root bridge has been determined, the switches start configuring the port roles for each of their switch ports. The first port role that needs to be determined is the root port role.

Every switch in a spanning-tree topology, except for the root bridge, has a single root port defined. The root port is the switch port with the lowest path cost to the root bridge. Normally, path cost alone determines which switch port becomes the root port. However, additional port characteristics determine the root port when two or more ports on the same switch have the same path cost to the root. This can happen, for example, when redundant links are used to uplink one switch to another switch without EtherChannel; recall that Cisco EtherChannel technology allows you to configure multiple physical Ethernet type links as one logical link.

Switch ports with equivalent path costs to the root use the sender bridge ID to break the tie. If, as in the case of parallel uplinks, the sender bridge ID is also a match, the configurable port priority value is used to break the tie. If the port priorities are the same, the port number is used to break the tie. In the case of parallel uplinks, when a switch chooses one equal path cost port as a root port over another, the losing port is configured as a nondesignated port to avoid a loop.

The process of determining which port becomes a root port happens during the root bridge election BPDU exchange. Path costs are updated immediately when BPDU frames arrive indicating a new root ID or redundant path. At the time the path cost is updated, the switch enters decision mode to determine whether port configurations need to be updated. The port role decisions do not wait until all switches settle on which switch is going to be the final root bridge. As a result, the port role for a given switch port may change multiple times during convergence, until it finally settles on its final port role after the root ID changes for the last time.

In Figure 5-51, switch S1 has been elected the root bridge. The switches now begin to determine the root ports.

Switch S2 compares the path costs for each of its switch ports in Figure 5-52. S2 elects F0/1 as a root port based on path costs learned from the BPDUs.

Figure 5-52   Switch S2 Chooses Root Port

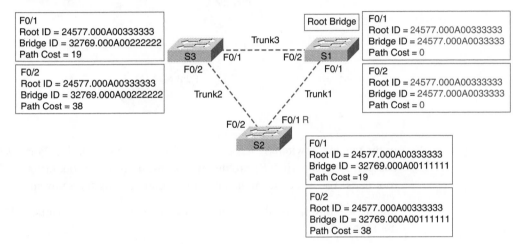

Switch S3 compares the path costs for each of its switch ports in Figure 5-53. S3 elects F0/1 as a root port based on path costs learned from the BPDUs.

Figure 5-53   Switch S3 Chooses Root Port

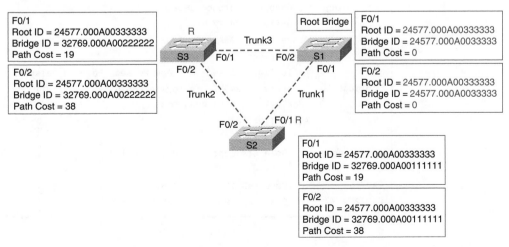

Verify Root Port Election

When the root port election has completed for the topology in Figure 5-54, you can verify the configuration of the root ports using the **show spanning-tree** privileged EXEC mode command.

Figure 5-54   Topology to Verify Root Port Election

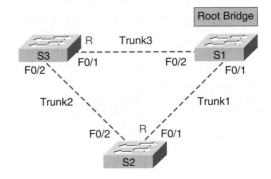

In the topology, switch S1 has been identified as the root bridge. Port F0/1 on switch S2 and port F0/1 on switch S3 are the two closest ports to the root bridge and, therefore, are as root ports. You can confirm the port configuration using the **show spanning-tree** command.

Example 5-14 displays the output for switch S1. You can see that ports F0/1 and F0/2 are not root ports.

Example 5-14   show spanning-tree on S1

```
S1# show spanning-tree


VLAN0001
  Spanning tree enabled protocol ieee
  Root ID    Priority    24577
             Address     000A.0033.3333
             This bridge is the root
             Hello Time   2 sec  Max Age 20 sec  Forward Delay 15 sec
  Bridge ID  Priority    24577   (priority 24576 sys-id-ext 1)
             Address     000A.0033.3333
             Aging Time 300


Interface        Role Sts Cost     Prio.Nbr Type
---------------------------------------------------------------------------
Fa0/1            Desg FWD 19       128.1    Shr
Fa0/2            Desg FWD 19       128.2    Shr
```

Example 5-15 displays the output for switch S2. You see that port F0/1 is a root port.

Example 5-15   show spanning-tree on S2

```
S2# show spanning-tree

VLAN0001
  Spanning tree enabled protocol ieee
  Root ID    Priority    24577
             Address     000A.0033.3333
             Hello Time   2 sec  Max Age 20 sec  Forward Delay 15 sec
  Bridge ID  Priority    32769  (priority 32768 sys-id-ext 1)
             Address     000A.0011.1111
             Aging Time 300


Interface         Role Sts Cost      Prio.Nbr Type
---------------------------------------------------------------------
Fa0/1             Root FWD 19          128.1    Shr
Fa0/2             Desg FWD 19          128.2    Shr
```

Example 5-16 displays the output for switch S3. You see that port F0/1 is a root port.

Example 5-16   show spanning-tree on S3

```
S3# show spanning-tree

VLAN0001
  Spanning tree enabled protocol ieee
  Root ID    Priority    24577
             Address     000A.0033.3333
             Hello Time   2 sec  Max Age 20 sec  Forward Delay 15 sec
  Bridge ID  Priority    32769  (priority 32768 sys-id-ext 1)
             Address     000A.0022.2222
             Aging Time 300


Interface         Role Sts Cost      Prio.Nbr Type
---------------------------------------------------------------------
Fa0/1             Root FWD 19          128.1    Shr
Fa0/2             Altn BLK 19          128.2    Shr
```

Step 3. Elect Designated and Nondesignated Ports

After a switch determines which of its ports is the root port, the remaining ports must be configured as either a designated port (DP) or a nondesignated port (ND) to finish creating the logical loop-free spanning tree.

Each segment in a switched network can have only one designated port. On each LAN segment connecting two switches, a competition for port roles occurs. The two switches exchange BPDU frames to sort out which switch port is designated (the other one will be either a root port or a nondesignated port.

The root path cost is used to determine whether a port on a segment is the designated port. If a tie occurs, the sender BID is used to break the tie. The switch with the lower BID wins the competition, and its port is configured in the designated role. The losing switch configures its switch port to be nondesignated (if it is not a root port) and, therefore, in the blocking state to prevent a loop from occurring.

The process of determining the port roles happens concurrently with the root bridge election and root port election. As a result, the designated and nondesignated roles may change multiple times during the convergence process until the final root bridge has been determined. The entire process of electing the root bridge, determining the root ports, and determining the designated and nondesignated ports happens within the 20-second blocking state. This 20-second upper bound for convergence time, called the max age delay, is based on the 2-second hello timer for BPDU frame transmission and the seven-switch diameter supported by STP.

In Figure 5-55, switch S1 has been elected the root bridge, so ports F0/2 and F0/1 are designated ports on S1. The switches now begin to determine the remaining designated ports in the topology.

Figure 5-55   Topology for Designated Port Election

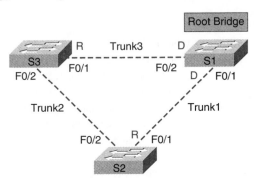

Switch S3 sends out a BPDU to switch S2, as shown in Figure 5-56.

Switch S2 compares the BID values and determines that it has the lower value, as shown in Figure 5-57.

Switch S2 configures port F0/2 in the designated role, as shown in Figure 5-58.

Switch S2 sends a BPDU to switch S3, as shown in Figure 5-59.

Figure 5-56 BPDU from S3 to S2

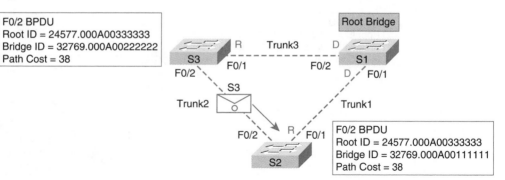

```
F0/2 BPDU
Root ID = 24577.000A00333333
Bridge ID = 32769.000A00222222
Path Cost = 38
```

```
F0/2 BPDU
Root ID = 24577.000A00333333
Bridge ID = 32769.000A00111111
Path Cost = 38
```

Figure 5-57 S2 Compares BIDs

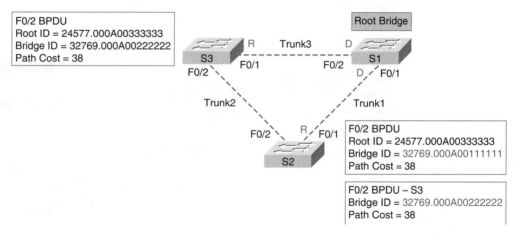

```
F0/2 BPDU
Root ID = 24577.000A00333333
Bridge ID = 32769.000A00222222
Path Cost = 38
```

```
F0/2 BPDU
Root ID = 24577.000A00333333
Bridge ID = 32769.000A00111111
Path Cost = 38
```

```
F0/2 BPDU – S3
Bridge ID = 32769.000A00222222
Path Cost = 38
```

Figure 5-58 Port F0/2 on S2 Is Designated

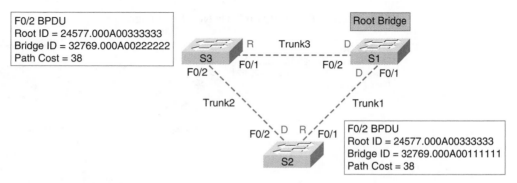

```
F0/2 BPDU
Root ID = 24577.000A00333333
Bridge ID = 32769.000A00222222
Path Cost = 38
```

```
F0/2 BPDU
Root ID = 24577.000A00333333
Bridge ID = 32769.000A00111111
Path Cost = 38
```

Figure 5-59   BPDU from S2 to S3

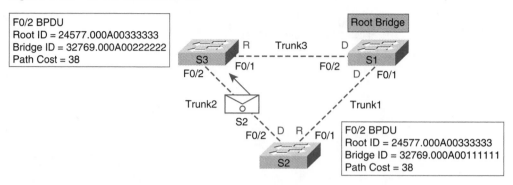

Switch S3 compares the BID values and determines that it has the higher value, as shown in Figure 5-60.

Figure 5-60   S3 Compares BIDs

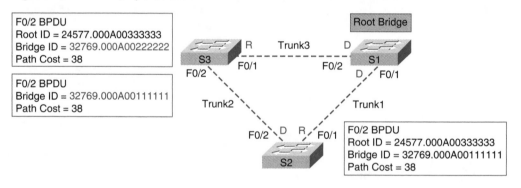

Switch S3 configures port F0/2 in the nondesignated role, as shown in Figure 5-61.

Figure 5-61   Port F0/2 on S3 Is Nondesignated

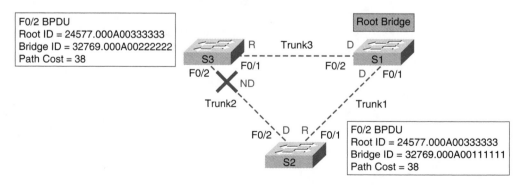

All ports in the spanning-tree topology have now been assigned to their appropriate role, thus creating a loop-free topology.

Verify Designated and Nondesignated Port Election

After the root ports have been assigned, the switches determine which remaining ports are configured as designated and nondesignated ports. You can verify the configuration of the designated and nondesignated ports using the **show spanning-tree** privileged EXEC mode command.

In Figure 5-62, a converged spanning-tree topology is displayed. To verify the designated port election on switch S1, see the **show spanning-tree** output in Example 5-17. You see that ports F0/1 and F0/2 are designated ports.

Figure 5-62   Converged Spanning-Tree Topology

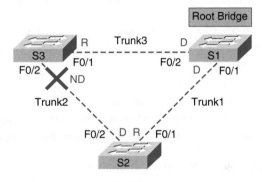

Example 5-17   show spanning-tree on S1

```
S1# show spanning-tree


VLAN0001
  Spanning tree enabled protocol ieee
  Root ID    Priority    24577
             Address     000A.0033.3333
             This bridge is the root
             Hello Time   2 sec  Max Age 20 sec  Forward Delay 15 sec
  Bridge ID  Priority    24577  (priority 24576 sys-id-ext 1)
             Address     000A.0033.3333
             Aging Time 300


Interface        Role Sts Cost      Prio.Nbr Type
---------------------------------------------------------------------------
Fa0/1            Desg FWD 19        128.1    Shr
Fa0/2            Desg FWD 19        128.2    Shr
```

Example 5-18 displays the output for switch S2. You see that port F0/2 is a designated port.

Example 5-18   show spanning-tree on S2

```
S2# show spanning-tree

VLAN0001
  Spanning tree enabled protocol ieee
  Root ID    Priority    24577
             Address     000A.0033.3333
             Hello Time   2 sec  Max Age 20 sec  Forward Delay 15 sec
  Bridge ID  Priority    32769  (priority 32768 sys-id-ext 1)
             Address     000A.0011.1111
             Aging Time 300


Interface        Role Sts Cost       Prio.Nbr Type
------------------------------------------------------------------------
Fa0/1            Root FWD 19          128.1    Shr
Fa0/2            Desg FWD 19          128.2    Shr
```

Example 5-19 displays the output for switch S3. You see that port F0/2 is neither a root port nor a designated port, whence a nondesignated port. The alternate port designation is discussed in the section on rapid spanning-tree protocol (RSTP).

Example 5-19   show spanning-tree on S3

```
S3# show spanning-tree

VLAN0001
  Spanning tree enabled protocol ieee
  Root ID    Priority    24577
             Address     000A.0033.3333
             Hello Time   2 sec  Max Age 20 sec  Forward Delay 15 sec
  Bridge ID  Priority    32769  (priority 32768 sys-id-ext 1)
             Address     000A.0022.2222
             Aging Time 300


Interface        Role Sts Cost       Prio.Nbr Type
------------------------------------------------------------------------
Fa0/1            Root FWD 19          128.1    Shr
Fa0/2            Altn BLK 19          128.2    Shr
```

STP Topology Change

A switch detects a topology change when a port that was forwarding goes down or when a port transitions to forwarding. When a change is detected, the switch notifies the root bridge. The root bridge then broadcasts the information to the whole broadcast domain.

In normal STP operation, a switch keeps receiving *configuration BPDU* frames from the root bridge on its root port. However, it never sends a configuration BPDU toward the root bridge. To achieve that, a special BPDU called a *topology change notification (TCN)* BPDU is used. When a switch needs to signal a topology change, it starts to send TCNs on its root port. The TCN is a very simple BPDU that contains no information and is sent out at the hello time interval. The receiving switch is called the designated bridge, and it acknowledges the TCN by immediately sending back a normal (configuration) BPDU with the *topology change acknowledgement (TCA)* bit set. This exchange continues until the root bridge responds.

For example, in Figure 5-63, switch S2 experiences a topology change. It sends a TCN to its designated bridge, which in this case is switch D1. Switch D1 receives the TCN and acknowledges it back to switch S2 with a TCA. Switch D1 generates a TCN and forwards it to its designated bridge, which in this case is the root bridge.

Figure 5-63   STP Topology Notification and Acknowledgement

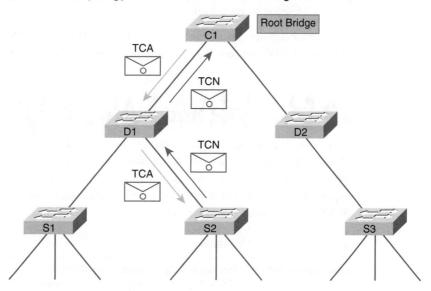

After the root bridge is aware that a topology change event occurred in the network, it starts to send out its configuration BPDUs with the *topology change (TC) bit* set, as illustrated in Figure 5-64. These BPDUs are relayed by every switch in the network with this bit set. As a result, all switches become aware of the topology change and can reduce their aging time to the forward delay interval. Switches receive topology change BPDUs on both forwarding and blocking ports.

Figure 5-64   Configuration BPDUs with TC Bit Set

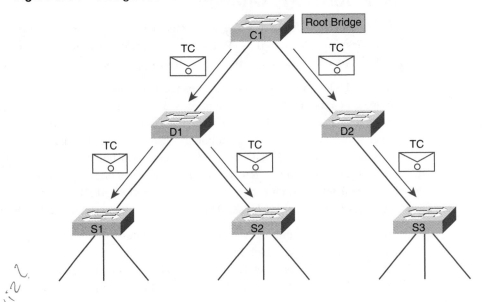

The TC bit is set by the root for a period of max age plus forward-delay seconds, which is 20+15=35 seconds, by default.

This completes our discussion of the IEEE 802.1D version of STP. Next, we look at newer versions of STP and how they fit into the historical scheme of STP variants.

PVST+, RSTP, and Rapid PVST+

Like many networking standards, the evolution of STP has been driven by the need to create industrywide specifications when proprietary protocols become de facto standards. When a proprietary protocol becomes so prevalent that all competitors in the market need to support it, agencies such as the IEEE step in and create a public specification. The evolution of STP has followed this same path, as shown in Table 5-3.

Table 5-3   STP Variants

Cisco Proprietary	**Per-VLAN Spanning Tree (PVST)** -Uses the Cisco proprietary ISL trunking protocol. -Each VLAN has an instance of spanning tree. -Ability to load balance traffic at Layer 2. -Includes extensions BackboneFast, UplinkFast, and, PortFast.
	Per-VLAN Spanning Tree Plus (PVST+) -Supports ISL and IEEE 802.1Q trunking. -Supports Cisco proprietary STP extensions. -Adds BPDU guard and root guard enhancements.

	Rapid PVST+ -Based on IEEE 802.1w standard. -Has faster convergence than 802.1D.
IEEE Standard	**Rapid Spanning Tree Protocol (RSTP)** -Introduced in 1982 and provides faster convergence than 802.1D. -Implements generic versions of the Cisco-proprietary STP extensions. -IEEE has incorporated RSTP into 802.1D, identifying the specification as IEEE 802.1D-2004.
	Multiple Spanning Tree Protocol (MSTP) -Multiple VLANs can be mapped to the same spanning-tree instance. -Inspired by the Cisco Multiple Instances Spanning Tree Protocol (MISTP). -IEEE 802.1Q (2003) now includes MSTP.

Cisco and IEEE STP Variants

When you read about STP on the Cisco.com site, you notice that many types or variants of STP exist. Some of these variants are Cisco proprietary and others are IEEE standards. You will learn more details about some of these STP variants, but to get started you need to have a general knowledge of what the key STP variants are. Table 5-3 summarizes the following descriptions of the key Cisco and IEEE STP variants.

Per-VLAN Spanning-Tree (PVST) Overview

Per-VLAN Spanning Tree (PVST) protocol maintains a spanning-tree instance for each VLAN configured in the network. It uses the Cisco proprietary ISL trunking protocol that allows a VLAN trunk to be forwarding for some VLANs while blocking for other VLANs. Because PVST treats each VLAN as a separate network, it can *load balance* traffic at Layer 2 by forwarding some VLANs on one trunk and other VLANs on another trunk without causing a loop. For PVST, Cisco developed a number of proprietary extensions to the original IEEE 802.1D STP, such as BackboneFast, UplinkFast, and PortFast. The BackboneFast and UplinkFast Cisco STP extensions are not covered in this book. To learn more about these extensions, visit

www.cisco.com/en/US/docs/switches/lan/catalyst4000/7.4/configuration/guide/stp_enha.html.

Per-VLAN Spanning-Tree Plus (PVST+) Overview

Cisco developed *Per-VLAN Spanning Tree Plus (PVST+)* to provide support for IEEE 802.1Q trunking. PVST+ provides the same functionality as PVST, including the Cisco proprietary STP extensions. PVST+ is not supported on non-Cisco devices. PVST+ includes the PortFast BPDU guard enhancement, as well as root guard. To learn more about BPDU guard, visit
www.cisco.com/en/US/tech/tk389/tk621/technologies_tech_note09186a008009482f.shtml.

To learn more about root guard, visit
www.cisco.com/en/US/tech/tk389/tk621/technologies_tech_note09186a00800ae96b.shtml.

Rapid Spanning-Tree Protocol (RSTP) Overview

Rapid Spanning Tree Protocol (RSTP) was first introduced in 1982 as an evolution of the IEEE 802.1D standard. It provides faster spanning-tree convergence after a topology change. RSTP incorporates a vendor-neutral implementation of the Cisco-proprietary STP extensions, BackboneFast, UplinkFast, and PortFast, into the public standard. As of 2004, the IEEE has incorporated RSTP into 802.1D, identifying the specification as IEEE 802.1D-2004. You learn more about RSTP later in this chapter.

Multiple Spanning-Tree Protocol (MSTP) Overview

Multiple Spanning Tree Protocol (MSTP) enables multiple VLANs to be mapped to the same spanning-tree instance, reducing the number of instances needed to support a large number of VLANs. MSTP was inspired by the Cisco-proprietary *Multiple Instance STP (MISTP)* and is an evolution of STP and RSTP. It was introduced in IEEE 802.1s as an amendment to the 1998 edition of IEEE 802.1Q. Standard IEEE 802.1Q-2003 now includes MSTP. MSTP provides for multiple forwarding paths for data traffic and enables load balancing. A discussion of MSTP is beyond the scope of this book. To learn more about MSTP, visit
www.cisco.com/en/US/docs/switches/lan/catalyst2950/software/release/12.1_19_ea1/configuration/guide/swmstp.html.

PVST+

Cisco developed PVST+ so that a network can run an STP instance for each VLAN in the network. With PVST+, trunks can selectively block traffic on a per-VLAN basis, depending on the spanning tree built for each VLAN. PVST+ also enables the implementation of load sharing. However, implementing PVST+ means that all switches in the network are engaged in converging the network, and the switch ports have to accommodate the additional bandwidth used for each spanning-tree instance (one per VLAN) to send its own BPDUs.

In a Cisco PVST+ environment, you can tune the spanning-tree parameters so that half of the VLANs forward on each uplink trunk. In Figure 5-65, port F0/3 on switch S2 is the forwarding port for VLAN 20, and F0/2 on switch S2 is the forwarding port for VLAN 10. This is accomplished by configuring one switch to be elected the root bridge for half of the total number of VLANs in the network, and a second switch to be elected the root bridge for the other half of the VLANs. In the figure, switch S3 is the root bridge for VLAN 20, and switch S1 is the root bridge for VLAN 10. Creating different STP root switches per VLAN creates a more redundant network.

Figure 5-65   PVST+

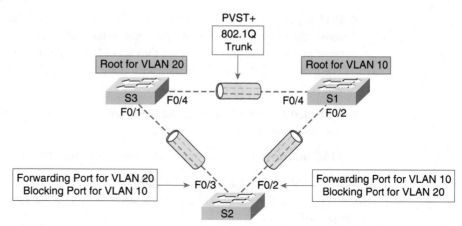

As you recall, in the original 802.1D standard, an 8-byte BID is composed of a 2-byte bridge priority and a 6-byte MAC address of the switch. There was no need to identify a VLAN because there was only one spanning tree in a network. PVST+ requires that a separate instance of spanning tree run for each VLAN. To support PVST+, the 8-byte BID field is modified to carry a VLAN ID (VID). In Figure 5-66, the bridge priority field is reduced to 4 bits, and a new 12-bit field, the extended system ID field, contains the VID. The 6-byte MAC address remains unchanged.

Figure 5-66   Extended System ID

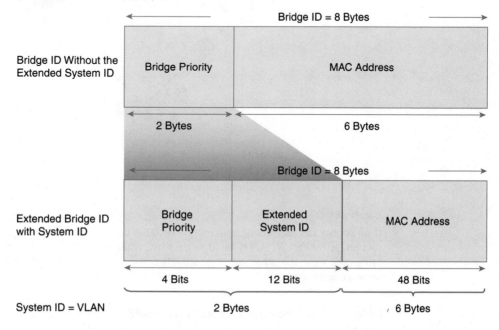

The following provides more details on the PVST+ fields:

- **Bridge priority:** This 4-bit field carries the bridge priority. Because of the limited bit count, the priority is conveyed in discrete values in increments of 4096 rather than discrete values in increments of 1, as they would be if the full 16-bit field was available. The default priority, in accordance with IEEE 802.1D, is 32768, which is the midrange value.

- **Extended system ID:** This 12-bit field carries the VID for PVST+. There are 4096 possible combinations.

- **MAC address:** This is a 6-byte field with the MAC address of a single switch.

The MAC address is what makes a BID unique. When the priority and extended system ID are prepended to the switch MAC address, each VLAN on the switch can be represented by a unique BID.

In Figure 5-67, the values for priority, VLAN, and MAC address for switch S1 are shown. They are combined to form the BID.

Figure 5-67   PVST+ BIDs

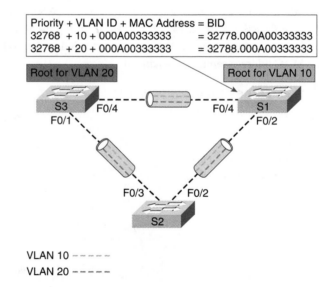

Priority + VLAN ID + MAC Address = BID
32768 + 10 + 000A00333333   = 32778.000A00333333
32768 + 20 + 000A00333333   = 32788.000A00333333

Root for VLAN 20

Root for VLAN 10

S3   F0/4

F0/4   S1

F0/1

F0/2

F0/3

F0/2

S2

VLAN 10 ‒ ‒ ‒ ‒ ‒
VLAN 20 ‒ ‒ ‒ ‒ ‒

Caution

If no priority has been configured, every switch has the same default priority, and the election of the root bridge for each VLAN is based on the MAC address. Therefore, to ensure that you get the root bridge you want, it is advisable to proactively assign a lower priority value to the switch that should serve as the root bridge.

Table 5-4 shows the default spanning-tree configuration for a Cisco Catalyst 2960 series switch. Notice that the default spanning-tree mode is PVST+.

Table 5-4   Default Switch Configuration

Feature	Default Setting
Enable state	Enabled on VLAN 1
Spanning-tree mode	PVST+ (Rapid PVST+ and MSTP are disabled.)
Switch priority	32768
Spanning-tree port priority (configurable on a per-interface basis)	128
Spanning-tree port cost (configurable on a per-interface basis)	1000 Mbps: 4, 100 Mbps: 19, 10 Mbps: 100
Spanning-tree VLAN port priority (configurable on a per-VLAN basis)	128
Spanning-tree VLAN port cost (configurable on a per-VLAN basis)	1000 Mbps: 4, 100 Mbps: 19, 10 Mbps: 100
Spanning-tree timers	Hello time: 2 seconds Forward-delay time: 15 seconds Maximum-aging time: 20 seconds Transmit hold count: 6 BPDUs

Configure PVST+

The topology in Figure 5-68 shows three switches with 802.1Q trunks connecting them. There are two VLANs, 10 and 20, which are being trunked across these links. This network has not been configured for spanning tree.

Figure 5-68   Configure PVST+

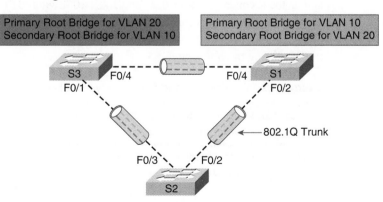

The goal is to configure S3 as the root bridge for VLAN 20 and S1 as the root bridge for VLAN 10, so that port F0/3 on S2 is the forwarding port for VLAN 20 and the blocking port for VLAN 10, and port F0/2 on S2 is the forwarding port for VLAN 10 and the blocking port for VLAN 20. The steps to configure PVST+ on this example topology are as follows:

How To Q

Step 1.   Select the switches you want for the primary and secondary root bridges for each VLAN.

Step 2.   Configure a switch to be the primary bridge for one VLAN; for example, switch S3 is the primary bridge for VLAN 20.

Step 3.   Configure a switch to be the secondary bridge for the other VLAN; for example, switch S3 is the secondary bridge for VLAN 10.

Optionally, set the spanning-tree priority to be low enough on the respective switch so that it is selected as the primary bridge.

We configure switch S3 as the primary root bridge for VLAN 20 and configure switch S1 as the primary root bridge for VLAN 10. To configure a switch to become the root bridge for a specified VLAN, use the **spanning-tree vlan** *vlan-ID* **root primary** global configuration mode command. Recall that you are starting with a network that has not been configured with spanning tree, so assume that all the switches are in their default configuration. In this example, switch S1, which has VLAN 10 and 20 enabled, retains its default STP priority.

A secondary root is a switch that may become the root bridge for a VLAN if the primary root bridge fails. To configure a switch as the secondary root bridge, use the **spanning-tree vlan** *vlan-ID* **root secondary** global configuration mode command. Assuming that the other bridges in the VLAN retain their default STP priority, this switch becomes the root bridge if the primary root bridge fails. This command can be executed on more than one switch to configure multiple backup root bridges.

The required configurations for switches S3 and S1 are given in Example 5-20. You see the Cisco IOS command syntax to specify switch S3 as the primary root bridge for VLAN 20 and as the secondary root bridge for VLAN 10. Switch S1 becomes the primary root bridge for VLAN 10 and the secondary root bridge for VLAN 20. This configuration permits spanning-tree load balancing, with VLAN 10 traffic passing through switch S1 and VLAN 20 traffic passing through switch S3.

Example 5-20   Primary and Secondary Root Bridges

```
S3(config)# spanning-tree vlan 20 root primary
S3(config)# spanning-tree vlan 10 root secondary

S1(config)# spanning-tree vlan 10 root primary
S1(config)# spanning-tree vlan 20 root secondary
```

Another option to accomplish the requirements is to configure the PVST+ switch priority. Earlier in this chapter you learned that the default settings used to configure spanning tree are adequate for most networks. This is true for Cisco PVST+ as well. There are a number of ways to tune PVST+. A discussion on how to tune a PVST+ implementation is beyond the scope of this book. However, you can set the switch priority for the specified spanning-tree instance. This setting affects the likelihood that the switch is selected as the root switch. A lower value increases the probability that the switch is selected. The range is 0 to 61440 in increments of 4096. For example, a valid priority value is $4096 \times 2 = 8192$. All other values are rejected.

Example 5-21 shows the Cisco IOS command syntax. The first command, on switch S3, sets the priority for S3 to be the lowest possible, resulting in S3 becoming the primary root for VLAN 20. The second command, on switch S1, sets the priority for S1 to be the lowest possible, resulting in S1 becoming the primary root for VLAN 10.

Example 5-21   Bridge Priority for Primary and Secondary Root Bridges

```
S3(config)# spanning-tree vlan 20 priority 4096

S1(config)# spanning-tree vlan 10 priority 4096
```

To verify that the configuration has worked as intended, you can use the privileged EXEC command **show spanning-tree active**; this command output shows spanning-tree configuration details for the active interfaces only. The output in Example 5-22 is for switch S1 configured with PVST+.

Example 5-22   Verify PVST+

```
S1# show spanning-tree active
<output omitted>
VLAN0010
  Spanning tree enabled protocol ieee
  Root ID    Priority    4106
             Address     0019.aa9e.b000
             This bridge is the root
             Hello Time   2 sec  Max Age 20 sec  Forward Delay 15 sec
  Bridge ID  Priority    4106   (priority 4096 sys-id-ext 10)
             Address     0019.aa9e.b000
             Hello Time   2 sec  Max Age 20 sec  Forward Delay 15 sec
             Aging Time 300
Interface         Role Sts Cost       Prio.Nbr Type
---------------- ---- --- ---------- -------- --------------------------------
Fa0/2             Desg FWD 19         128.2    P2p
Fa0/4             Desg FWD 19         128.2    P2p
<output omitted>
```

A number of Cisco IOS command parameters are associated with the **show spanning-tree** command. For a complete description, visit www.cisco.com/en/US/docs/switches/lan/catalyst2960/software/release/12.2_37_se/command/reference/cli2.html#wpxref47293.

Last, use the **show run** command to verify the spanning-tree commands entered on the switch. You can see in Example 5-23 that the priority for VLAN 10 is 4096, the lowest of the three VLAN priorities. This priority setting ensures that this switch is the primary root bridge for VLAN 10.

Example 5-23   show run to Verify PVST+

```
S1# show run
Building configuration...


Current configuration : 1595 bytes
!
version 12.2
<output omitted>
!
spanning-tree mode pvst
spanning-tree extend system-id
spanning-tree vlan 1 priority 24576
spanning-tree vlan 10 priority 4096
spanning-tree vlan 20 priority 28672
!
<output omitted>
```

RSTP

RSTP is specified in IEEE 802.1w. RSTP is an evolution of the 802.1D standard. The 802.1w STP terminology remains primarily the same as the IEEE 802.1D STP terminology. Most parameters have been left unchanged, so users familiar with 802.1D STP can rapidly learn to configure the new protocol.

In Figure 5-69, a network is implemented with RSTP. Switch S1 is the root bridge with two designated ports in forwarding state. RSTP supports a new port type; port F0/3 on switch S2 is an alternate port in discarding state (DIS). Notice that no blocking ports exist. RSTP does not have a blocking port state. RSTP defines port states as discarding, learning, or forwarding. You will learn more about port types and states later in the chapter.

RSTP speeds the recalculation of the spanning tree when the Layer 2 network topology changes. RSTP can achieve much faster convergence in a properly configured network, sometimes in as little as a few hundred milliseconds. RSTP redefines the type of ports and their state. If a port is configured to be an alternate or a backup port, it can immediately change to forwarding state without waiting for the network to converge.

Figure 5-69   What Is RSTP?

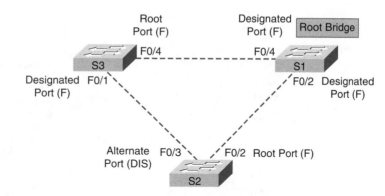

RSTP is the preferred protocol for preventing Layer 2 loops in a switched network environment. Many of the differences between RSTP and 802.1D came from the Cisco-proprietary enhancements to 802.1D. These enhancements, such as BPDUs carrying and sending information about port roles only to neighboring switches, require no additional configuration and generally perform better than the earlier Cisco-proprietary versions. They are now transparent and integrated in the RSTP operation. Cisco-proprietary enhancements to 802.1D, such as UplinkFast and BackboneFast, are not compatible with RSTP.

802.1w supersedes 802.1D while retaining backward compatibility. Much of the STP terminology remains and most parameters are unchanged. In addition, 802.1w is capable of reverting back to 802.1D to interoperate with legacy switches on a per-port basis. For example, the RSTP spanning-tree algorithm elects a root bridge in the same way as 802.1D.

RSTP keeps the same BPDU format as IEEE 802.1D, except that the version field is set to 2 to indicate RSTP, and the flags field uses all 8 bits. The RSTP BPDU is discussed later.

RSTP is able to actively confirm that a port can safely transition to the forwarding state without having to rely on any timer configuration.

RSTP BPDU

RSTP (802.1w) uses type 2, version 2 BPDUs, so an RSTP bridge can communicate 802.1D on any shared link or with any switch running 802.1D. Refer to Figure 5-70.

RSTP sends BPDUs and populates the flag byte in a slightly different manner than in 802.1D:

- Protocol information can be immediately aged on a port if hellos are not received for three consecutive hello times, 6 seconds by default, or if the max age timer expires.

- Because BPDUs are used as a keepalive mechanism, three consecutively missed BPDUs indicate lost connectivity between a bridge and its neighboring root or designated bridge. The fast aging of the information allows failures to be detected quickly.

Figure 5-70   RSTP BPDU

RSTP Version 2 BPDU

Field	Byte Length
Protocol ID = 0x0000	2
Protocol Version ID = 0x02	1
BPDU Type = 0x02	1
Flags	1
Root ID	8
Root Path Cost	4
Bridge ID	8
Port ID	2
Message Age	2
Max Age	2
Hello Time	2
Forward Delay	2

Flag Field

Field	Bits
Topology Change	7
Proposal	6
Port Role Unknown Port Alternate or Backup Port Root Port Designated Port	4-5 00 01 10 11
Learning	3
Forwarding	2
Agreement	1
Topology Change Acknowledgment	0

Note

Like STP, an RSTP bridge sends a BPDU with its current information every hello time period (2 seconds by default), even if the RSTP bridge does not receive any BPDUs from the root bridge.

RSTP uses the flag byte of version 2 BPDU as shown in Figure 5-70:

- Bits 0 and 7 are used for topology change notification and acknowledgment as they are in 802.1D.

- Bits 1 and 6 are used for the Proposal Agreement process (used for rapid convergence).

- Bits 2-5 encode the role and state of the port originating the BPDU.

- Bits 4 and 5 are used to encode the port role using a 2-bit code.

Edge Ports

An RSTP *edge port* is a switch port that is never intended to be connected to another switch device. It immediately transitions to the forwarding state when enabled.

The edge port concept is well-known to Cisco spanning-tree users because it corresponds to the PortFast feature in which ports directly connected to end stations assume that no switch device is connected to them. The PortFast ports immediately transition to the STP forwarding state, thereby skipping the time-consuming listening and learning stages. Neither edge ports nor PortFast-enabled ports generate topology changes when the port transitions to a disabled or enabled status.

Unlike PortFast, an RSTP edge port that receives a BPDU loses its edge port status immediately and becomes a normal spanning-tree port. Figure 5-71 illustrates three edge ports on switch S2 and one edge port on switch S4.

Figure 5-71   Edge Ports

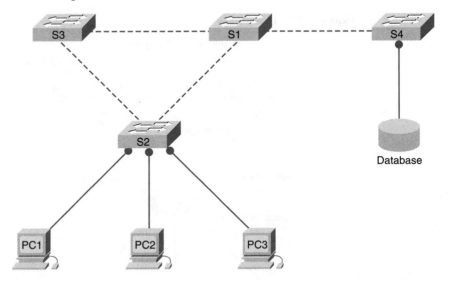

The Cisco RSTP implementation maintains the **portfast** keyword using the **spanning-tree portfast** command for edge port configuration, making an overall network transition to RSTP more seamless. Configuring an edge port to be attached to another switch can have negative implications for RSTP when it is in sync state because a temporary loop can result, possibly delaying the convergence of RSTP because of BPDU contention with loop traffic.

Link Types

The link type provides a categorization for each port participating in RSTP. The link type can predetermine the active role that the port plays as it stands by for immediate transition to forwarding state if certain conditions are met. These conditions are different for edge ports and non-edge ports. Non-edge ports are categorized into two link types: *point-to-point* and *shared*. The link type is automatically determined, but can be overwritten with an explicit port configuration. In Figure 5-72, all links are point-to-point link type except for the shared link connecting switch S1 to device S4, whose ports are configured for half-duplex.

Edge ports, the equivalent of PortFast-enabled ports, and point-to-point links are candidates for rapid transition to forwarding state. However, before the link type parameter is considered, RSTP must determine the port role. You learn about port roles next, but for now know that

- Root ports do not use the link type parameter. Root ports are able to make a rapid transition to the forwarding state as soon as the port is in sync.

■ Alternate and backup ports do not use the link type parameter in most cases.

■ Designated ports make the most use of the link type parameter. Rapid transition to the forwarding state for the designated port occurs only if the link type parameter indicates a point-to-point link.

Figure 5-72 Link Types

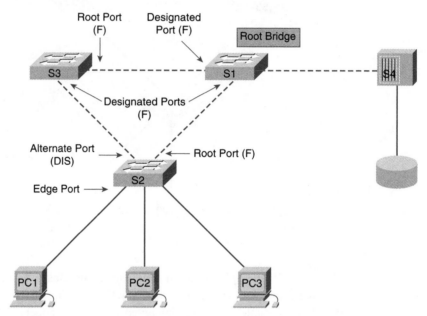

RSTP Port States and Port Roles

RSTP provides rapid convergence following a failure or during reestablishment of a switch, switch port, or link. An RSTP topology change causes a transition in the appropriate switch ports to the forwarding state through either explicit handshakes or a proposal and agreement process and synchronization. You will learn more about the proposal and agreement process shortly.

With RSTP, the role of a port is separated from the state of a port. For example, a designated port could be in the discarding state temporarily, even though its final state is to be forwarding. Figure 5-73 shows the three possible RSTP port states: discarding, learning, and forwarding.

Figure 5-73   RSTP Port States

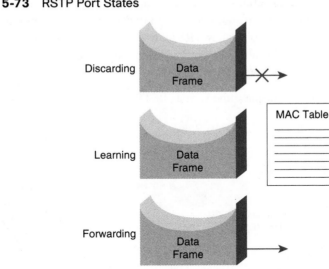

The RSTP port states are further described as follows:

- *Discarding*: This state is seen in both a stable active topology and during topology synchronization changes. The discarding state prevents the forwarding of data frames, thus breaking the continuity of a Layer 2 loop.

- *Learning*: This state is seen in both a stable active topology and during topology synchronization changes. The learning state accepts data frames to populate the MAC address table in an effort to limit flooding of unknown unicast frames.

- *Forwarding*: This state is seen only in stable active topologies. Following a topology change or during synchronization, the forwarding of data frames occurs only after a proposal and agreement process.

In all port states, a port accepts and processes BPDU frames. Table 5-5 compares 802.1D and RSTP port states. Recall that the ports in the 802.1D blocking, listening, and disabled port states do not forward any frames. These port states have been merged into the RSTP discarding port state.

Table 5-5   RSTP vs. 802.1D Port States

Operational Port State	802.1D Port State	RSTP Port State
Enabled	Blocking	Discarding
Enabled	Listening	Discarding
Enabled	Learning	Learning
Enabled	Forwarding	Forwarding
Disabled	Disabled	Discarding

The port role defines the ultimate purpose of a switch port and how it handles data frames. Port roles and port states are able to transition independently of each other. Creating the additional port roles allows RSTP to define a standby switch port before a failure or topology change. The alternate port moves to the forwarding state if a failure occurs on the designated port for the segment.

Figure 5-74 displays the various RSTP port roles.

Figure 5-74   RSTP Port Roles

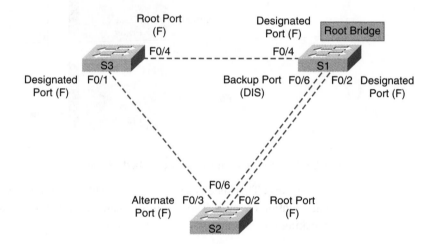

The following descriptions provide detail regarding the RSTP port roles:

- *Root Port*: This is the switch port on every nonroot bridge that is the chosen path to the root bridge. There can be only one root port on each switch. The root port assumes the forwarding state in a stable active topology. In Figure 5-74, the root port is port 0/2 on switch S2 and port F0/4 on switch S3.

- *Designated Port*: Each segment will have one switch port serving as the designated port for that segment. In Figure 5-74, port F0/1 on switch S3 and ports F0/2 and F0/4 on switch S1 are designated ports. In a stable, active topology, the switch with the designated port receives frames destined for the root bridge. The designated port assumes the forwarding state. Therefore, port F0/1 on switch S3 and ports F0/2 and F0/4 on switch S1 are in the forwarding state. All switches connected to a given segment listen to all BPDUs and determine the switch that will be the designated bridge for a particular segment.

- *Alternate*: This is a switch port that offers an alternative path toward the root bridge. Port F0/3 on switch S2 is an alternate port. The alternate port assumes a discarding state in a stable, active topology. An alternate port will be present on nondesignated bridges and will make a transition to a designated port if the current path fails.

■ *Backup:* This is a switch port on a designated bridge with a redundant link to the segment for which the switch is designated. A backup port has a higher port ID than the designated port on the designated bridge. The backup port assumes the discarding state in a stable, active topology. In Figure 5-74, port F0/6 on switch S1 is a backup port in the discarding state.

RSTP Proposal and Agreement Process

In IEEE 802.1D STP, when a port has been selected by spanning tree to be a designated port, it must wait two times the forward delay before transitioning the port to the forwarding state. RSTP significantly speeds up the recalculation process after a topology change because it converges on a link-by-link basis and does not rely on timers expiring before ports can transition. Rapid transition to the forwarding state can be achieved only on edge ports and point-to-point links. In RSTP, this condition corresponds to a designated port in the discarding state.

To see how the *proposal and agreement process* works, refer to Figure 5-75.

Figure 5-75   RSTP Proposal and Agreement Process Topology

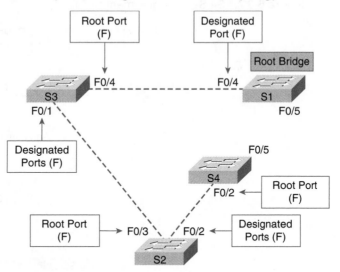

A new link is added between S1 and S4; S1 and S4 begin a proposal and agreement process. Port F0/5 on S1 and S4 assume the discarding state. S1 sends S4 a proposal BPDU, as shown in Figure 5-76.

Next, synchronization begins between S1 and S4. The proposal BPDU received from S1 on port F0/5 has a higher path cost than the cached value so all non-edge ports are blocked; Port F0/2 on S4 is blocked during the synchronization period, as illustrated in Figure 5-77. S4 sends an agreement BPDU to S1.

Figure 5-76   New Link Begins Proposal and Agreement Process

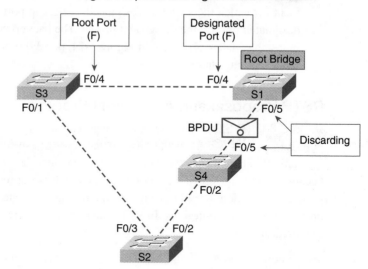

Figure 5-77   S4 Sends Agreement to S1

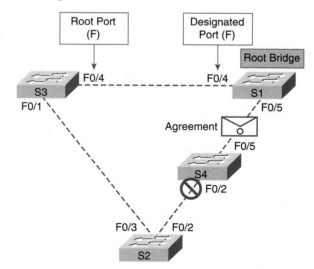

With the completion of the synchronization process, pictured in Figure 5-78, Port F0/5 on S1 becomes a designated port in the forwarding state and port F0/5 on S4 becomes a root port in the forwarding state.

Switch S4 and S2 start a proposal and agreement process. Port F0/2 on S4 and S2 assume the discarding state. Switch S4 sends S2 a proposal BPDU, as shown in Figure 5-79.

Figure 5-78   Synchronization Ends

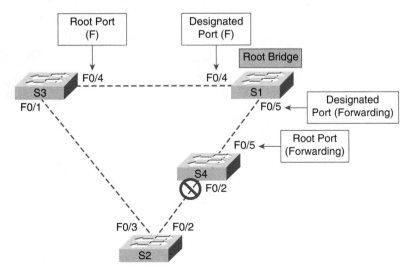

Figure 5-79   Synchronization Begins Again

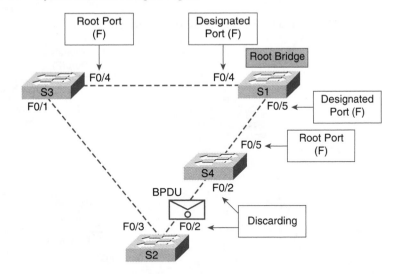

The proposal BPDU received from S4 on port F0/2 has a higher path cost than the cached value so all non-edge ports are blocked; Port F0/3 on S2 is blocked during the synchronization period. S2 sends S4 a proposal BPDU, as in Figure 5-80.

Figure 5-80   S2 Sends S4 Proposal BPDU

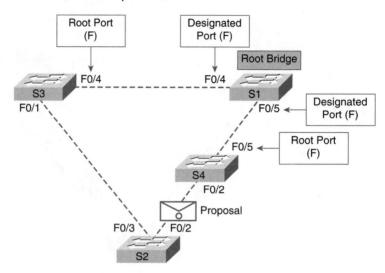

S4 sends S2 an agreement BPDU, as in Figure 5-81.

Figure 5-81   S4 Sends S2 Agreement BPDU

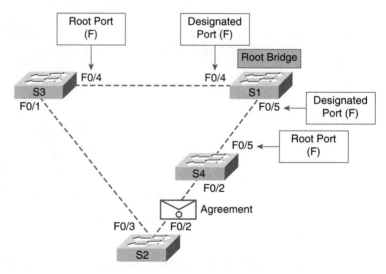

At this point, synchronization ends again and port F0/2 on S4 is a designated port in forwarding state, and port F0/2 on S2 is the root port in forwarding state, as illustrated in Figure 5-82.

Figure 5-82 Synchronization Ends Again

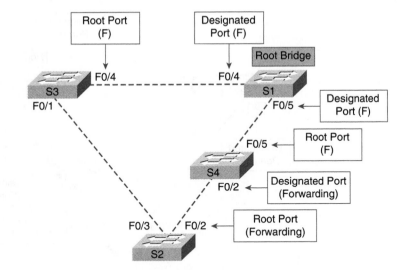

Switch S2 and S3 start a proposal and agreement process. S2 sends a proposal BPDU to S3, as seen in Figure 5-83.

Figure 5-83 Synchronization Begins Once Again

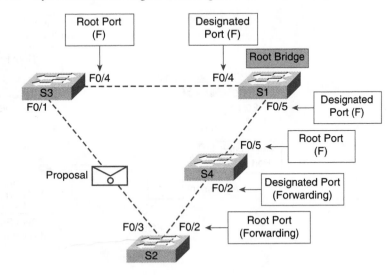

Switch S3 compares the local BID versus the BID in the proposal BPDU from S2, blocks F0/4, and F0/1 changes to a designated port in discarding state, as seen in Figure 5-84.

Figure 5-84 Designated Discarding

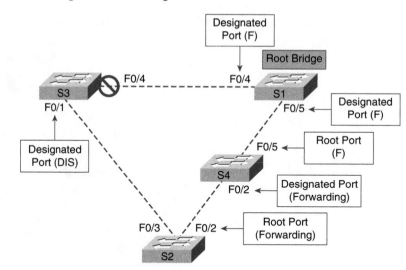

S3 determines that the BID in the proposal BPDU from S2 is higher and sends back an agreement BPDU to S2 with its lower BID, as illustrated in Figure 5-85.

Figure 5-85 S3 Sends S2 Agreement BPDU

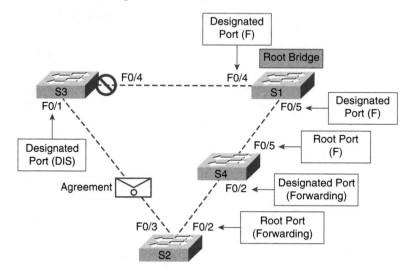

Switch S2 changes port F0/3 to an alternate port in discarding state. Switch S3 changes port F0/1 to a designated port in forwarding state; also, port F04 on S3 changes to a root port in forwarding state. All of this is illustrated in Figure 5-86.

Figure 5-86   Third Synchronization Complete

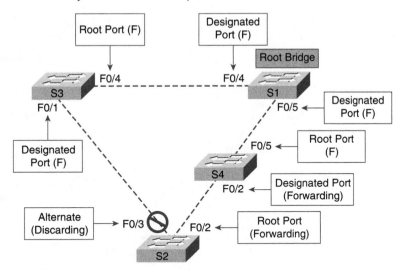

Switch S3 sends a proposal BPDU to S1, as in Figure 5-87.

Figure 5-87   S3 Sends Proposal BPDU

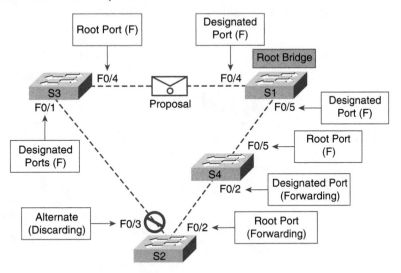

Switch S1 compares the local BID to the BID in the proposal BPDU sent from S3. Switch S1 blocks F0/5 and turns port F0/4 into a designated port in discarding state, as illustrated in Figure 5-88.

Figure 5-88   S1 Acts on Proposal BPDU

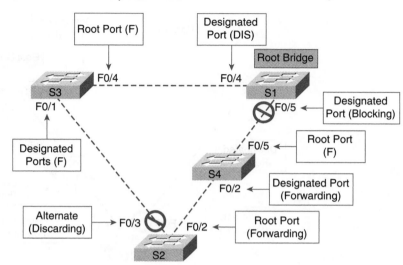

After switch S1 determines that the BID in the proposal BPDU from S3 is higher, S1 sends an agreement BPDU to S3 with its lower BID, as pictured in Figure 5-89.

Figure 5-89   S1 Sends Agreement BPDU to S3

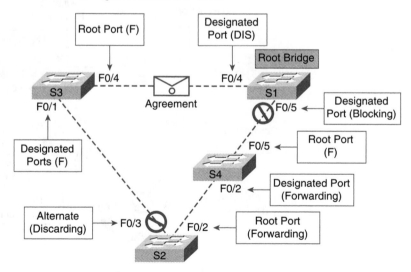

Last, switch S1 changes port F0/4 and F0/5 to designated forwarding ports, as shown in Figure 5-90.

Figure 5-90   Final Proposal-Agreement Is Complete

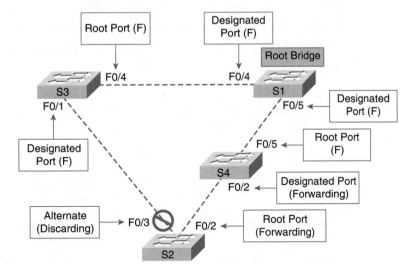

Configuring Rapid PVST+

Rapid PVST+ is a Cisco implementation of RSTP. It supports one instance of RSTP for each VLAN. This is the desired choice of STP for a modern switched LAN in a small- to medium-sized business. The topology in Figure 5-91 has two VLANs: 10 and 20. The final configuration implements rapid PVST+ on switch S1, the root bridge.

Figure 5-91   Rapid PVST+ Topology

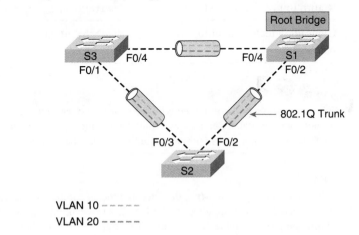

Rapid PVST+ commands control the configuration of VLAN spanning-tree instances. A spanning-tree instance is created when an interface is assigned to a VLAN and is removed when the last interface is moved to another VLAN. As well, you can configure STP switch and port parameters before a spanning-tree instance is created. These parameters are applied when a spanning-tree instance is created. However, ensure that at least one switch on each physical loop in a VLAN is running spanning tree; otherwise, a broadcast storm can result.

The Catalyst 2960 switch supports PVST+, rapid PVST+, and MSTP, but only one version can be active for the VLANs at one time.

For all the details on configuring the STP software features on a Cisco 2960 series switch, visit this Cisco site: www.cisco.com/en/US/products/ps6406/products_configuration_guide_chapter09186a0080875377.html.

Table 5-6 shows the command syntax for the rapid PVST+ commands.

Table 5-6   Cisco IOS Rapid PVST+ Command Syntax

Description	Syntax
Enter global configuration mode.	`Switch# configure terminal`
Configure rapid PVST+ spanning-tree mode.	`Switch(config)# spanning-tree mode rapid-pvst`
Specify an interface to configure, and enter interface configuration mode. The VLAN ID range is 1 to 4094. The port-channel range is 1 to 6.	`Switch(config)# interface interface-id`
Specify that the link type for this port is point-to-point.	`Switch(config-if)# spanning-tree link-type point-to-point`
Return to privileged EXEC mode.	`Switch(config-if)# end`
Clear all detected spanning tree protocols.	`Switch# clear spanning-tree detected-protocols`

Note

If you connect a port configured with the **spanning-tree link-type point-to-point** command to a remote port through a point-to-point link and the local port becomes a designated port, the switch negotiates with the remote port and rapidly changes the local port to the forwarding state.

Note

When the **clear spanning-tree detected-protocols** command is entered and one of the switch ports is connected to a port on a legacy IEEE 802.1D switch, the Cisco IOS software restarts the protocol migration process on the entire switch. This step is optional, though recommended, as standard practice.

For complete details on all the parameters associated with rapid PVST+ Cisco IOS commands, visit www.cisco.com/en/US/docs/switches/lan/catalyst2960/software/release/ 12.2_37_se/command/reference/cli3.html.

Example 5-24 shows the rapid PVST+ commands enabled on switch S1.

Example 5-24   Configure Rapid PVST+

```
S1# configure terminal
S1(config)# spanning-tree mode rapid-pvst
S1(config)# interface f0/2
S1(config-if)# spanning-tree link-type point-to-point
S1(config-if)# end
S1(config)# clear spanning-tree detected-protocols
```

The **show spanning-tree vlan** *vlan-id* command can be used to show the configuration of VLAN 10 on switch S1. Example 5-25 illustrates this command output. Notice that the BID priority is set to 4096. The BID was set using the **spanning-tree vlan** *vlan-id* **priority** *priority-number* command.

Example 5-25   Verify Rapid PVST+

```
S1# show spanning-tree vlan 20
<output omitted>
VLAN0010
  Spanning tree enabled protocol rstp
  Root ID    Priority    4106
             Address     0019.aa9e.b000
             This bridge is the root
             Hello Time   2 sec  Max Age 20 sec  Forward Delay 15 sec
  Bridge ID  Priority    4106    (priority 4096 sys-id-ext 10)
             Address     0019.aa9e.b000
             Hello Time   2 sec  Max Age 20 sec  Forward Delay 15 sec
             Aging Time 300
Interface         Role Sts Cost      Prio.Nbr Type
------------------------------------------------------------------
Fa0/2           Desg LRN 19         128.2    P2p
Fa0/4           Desg LRN 19         128.2    P2p
```

Last, the **show running-config** command can be used to verify the rapid PVST+ configuration on S1, as in Example 5-26.

Example 5-26   Verify Rapid PVST+ with **show running-config**

```
S1# show running-config
<output omitted>
!
spanning-tree mode rapid-pvst
spanning-tree extend system-id
spanning-tree vlan 1 priority 24576
spanning-tree vlan 10 priority 4096
spanning-tree vlan 20 priority 28672
!
<output omitted>
```

Design STP for Trouble Avoidance

You now know that the primary function of the STA is to break loops that redundant links create in bridged networks. STP operates at Layer 2 of the OSI model. STP can fail in some specific cases. Troubleshooting the problem can be very difficult and depends on the design of the network. That is why it is recommended that you perform the most important part of the troubleshooting before the problem occurs.

Very often, information about the location of the root is not available at troubleshooting time, as illustrated in Figure 5-92. Do not leave it up to STP to decide which bridge is root. For each VLAN, you can usually identify which switch can best serve as root. Generally, choose a powerful bridge in the middle of the network. If you put the root bridge in the center of the network with a direct connection to the servers and routers, you reduce the average distance from the clients to the servers and routers.

Figure 5-92   Know Where the Root Is

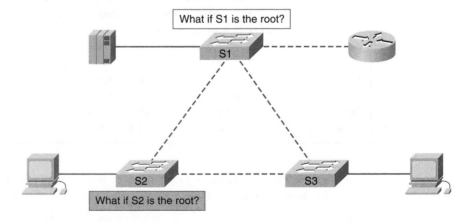

Figure 5-92 shows the following:

- If switch S2 is the root, the link from S1 to S3 is blocked on S1 or S3. In this case, hosts that connect to switch S2 can access the server and the router in two hops. Hosts that connect to bridge S3 can access the server and the router in three hops. The average distance is two and one-half hops.

- If switch S1 is the root, the router and the server are reachable in two hops for both hosts that connect on S2 and S3. The average distance is now two hops.

The logic behind this simple example transfers to more complex topologies.

To make it easier to solve STP problems, plan the organization of your redundant links. In nonhierarchical networks you might need to tune the STP cost parameter to determine which ports to block. However, this tuning is usually not necessary if you have a hierarchical design and a root bridge in a good location.

Note

For each VLAN, know which ports should be blocking in the stable network. Have a network diagram that clearly shows each physical loop in the network and which blocked ports break the loops.

Also, knowing the location of redundant links helps you to identify an accidental bridging loop and the cause. Knowing the location of blocked ports allows you to determine the location of the error.

Minimize the Number of Blocked Ports

The only critical action that STP takes is the blocking of ports. A single blocking port that mistakenly transitions to forwarding can negatively impact a large part of the network. A good way to limit the risk inherent in the use of STP is to reduce the number of blocked ports as much as possible.

You do not need more than two redundant links between two nodes in a switched network. However, a configuration shown in Figure 5-93 is common. Distribution switches are dual-attached to two core switches: switches C1 and C2. Users on switches S1 and S2, which connect via distribution switches D1 and D3, reside in only a subset of the VLANs available on the network. In the figure, users that connect on switch D1 are all in VLAN 20; switch D3 connects only users in VLAN 30. By default, trunks carry all the VLANs defined in the VTP domain. With VTP pruning, switch D1 forwards traffic for VLAN 20, but blocks unnecessary traffic for VLAN 30. There are three redundant paths between core switch C1 and core switch C2. This redundancy results in more blocked ports and a higher likelihood of a loop.

Figure 5-93 Pruning VLANs with VTP

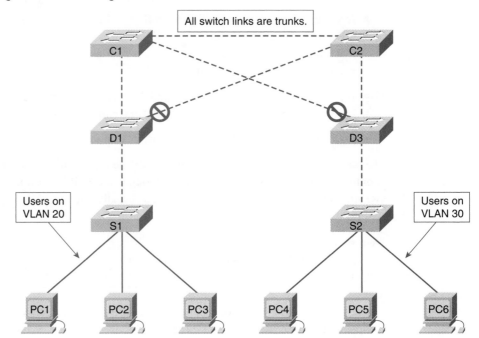

Any VLAN traffic that is unnecessary should be pruned from the appropriate trunk links. VTP pruning can help, but this feature is not necessary in the core of this network. In Figure 5-94, only an access VLAN is used to connect the distribution switches to the core. In this design, only one port is blocked per VLAN. Also, with this design, you can remove all redundant links in just one step if you shut down C1 or C2.

Use Layer 3 Switching

Layer 3 switching means routing at the speed of Layer 2 switching. A router performs two main functions:

- It builds a forwarding table. The router generally exchanges information with peers by way of routing protocols.

- It receives packets and forwards them to the correct interface based on the destination address.

Layer 3 switches are able to perform this second function at effectively the same speed as the Layer 2 switching function. In Figure 5-95

- There is no speed penalty with the routing hop and an additional segment between C1 and C2.

- Core switch C1 and core switch C2 are Layer 3 switches. VLAN 20 and VLAN 30 are now routed between C1 and C2, so no possibility exists for a loop; the Layer 3 device bounds the broadcast domains for VLAN 20 and VLAN 30.

Figure 5-94   Manual Pruning of VLANs

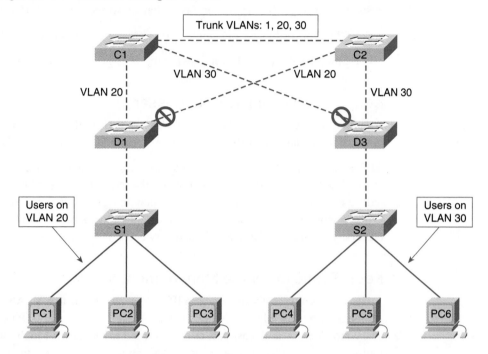

Figure 5-95   Layer 3 Switching

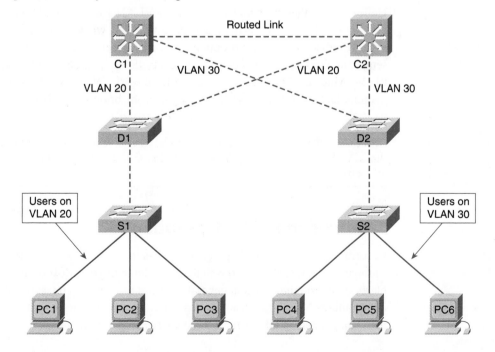

Redundancy is still present, with a reliance on Layer 3 routing protocols. The design ensures a convergence that is even faster than convergence with 802.1D STP.

- STP no longer blocks any single port, so no potential exists for a bridging loop.

- Exiting the VLAN by Layer 3 switching is as just fast as bridging within the VLAN.

Keep STP Even if It Is Unnecessary

Assuming you have removed all the blocked ports from the network and do not have any physical redundancy, it is strongly suggested that you do not disable STP.

STP is generally not very processor intensive; frame switching does not involve the CPU in most Cisco switches. Also, the few BPDUs that are sent on each link do not significantly reduce the available bandwidth. If a technician makes a connection error on a patch panel and accidentally creates a loop with STP disabled, the network will be negatively impacted. Generally, disabling STP in a switched network is not worth the risk.

Keep Traffic off of the Management VLAN

A Cisco switch typically has a single IP address that binds to a VLAN, known as the management VLAN. In this VLAN, the switch behaves like a generic IP host. In particular, every broadcast or multicast packet is forwarded to the CPU. A high rate of broadcast or multicast traffic on the management VLAN can adversely impact the CPU and its ability to process vital BPDUs. Therefore, keep user traffic off the management VLAN.

Until recently, there was no way to remove VLAN 1 from a trunk in a Cisco implementation. VLAN 1 can serve as the management VLAN, where all switches are accessible in the same IP subnet, although this option is not recommended as a security best practice. This setup can also can be dangerous because a bridging loop on VLAN 1 would affect all trunks, which could bring down the whole network. Of course, the same problem exists no matter which VLAN you use. Try to segment the bridging domains using Layer 3 switches.

Note

As of Cisco IOS Software Release 12.1(11b)E, you can remove data traffic from VLAN 1 on trunk links. VLAN 1 will still exist, but noncontrol traffic will be blocked, thus preventing any possibility of loops.

Troubleshoot STP Operation

Unfortunately, no systematic procedure exists to troubleshoot an STP issue. This section summarizes some of the actions that are available to you. Most of the steps apply to troubleshooting bridging loops in general. You can use a more conventional approach to identify other failures of STP that lead to a loss of connectivity. For example, you can explore the path being taken by the traffic that is experiencing a problem.

Before you troubleshoot a bridging loop, you need to know at least three pieces of information:

- Topology of the bridge network

- Location of the root bridge

- Location of the blocked ports and the redundant links

This knowledge is essential. To know what to fix in the network, you need to know how the network looks when it works correctly. Most of the troubleshooting steps simply use **show** commands to try to identify error conditions. Knowledge of the network helps you focus on the critical ports of the key devices.

The rest of this topic briefly looks at two common-spanning tree problems, a PortFast configuration error and network diameter issues. To learn about other STP issues, visit www.cisco.com/en/US/tech/tk389/tk621/technologies_tech_note09186a00800951ac.shtml.

PortFast Configuration Error

You typically enable PortFast only for a port or interface that connects to a host. When the link comes up on the port, the bridge skips the first stages of the STA and directly transitions to the forwarding mode.

In Figure 5-96, port F0/1 on switch S1 is already forwarding. Port F0/2 has erroneously been configured with PortFast. When a second link from switch S2 is connected to F0/2 on S1, the port automatically transitions to forwarding mode and creates a loop.

Eventually, one of the switches will forward a BPDU and one of these switches will transition a port into blocking mode.

However, a problem occurs with this kind of transient loop. If the looped traffic is very intensive, the switch can have trouble successfully transmitting the BPDU that stops the loop. This problem can delay the convergence considerably or in some extreme cases can actually bring down the network.

Figure 5-96   PortFast Troubleshooting

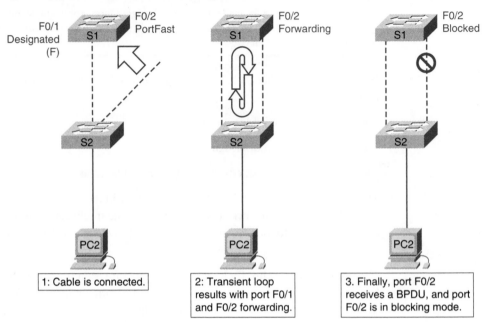

Even with a PortFast configuration, the port or interface still participates in STP. If a switch with a lower bridge priority than that of the current active root bridge attaches to a PortFast-configured port or interface, it can be elected as the root bridge. This change of root bridge can adversely affect the active STP topology and can render the network suboptimal. To prevent this situation, most Catalyst switches that run Cisco IOS software have a feature called BPDU guard. BPDU guard disables a PortFast-configured port or interface if the port or interface receives a BPDU.

For more information on using PortFast, refer to the document "Using PortFast and Other Commands to Fix Workstation Startup Connectivity Delays," available at www.cisco.com/en/US/products/hw/switches/ps700/products_tech_note09186a00800b1500.shtml.

For more information on using the BPDU guard feature on switches that run Cisco IOS software, visit www.cisco.com/en/US/tech/tk389/tk621/technologies_tech_note09186a008009482f.shtml.

Network Diameter Issues

Another STP issue relates to the diameter of the switched network. The conservative default values for the STP timers impose a maximum network diameter of seven. In Figure 5-97, the design results in a network diameter of eight. The maximum network diameter restricts how far away switches in the network can be from each other. In this case, two end stations cannot have more than seven intermediary switches between them. Part of this restriction is motivated by the age field that BPDUs propagate.

Figure 5-97   Network Diameter

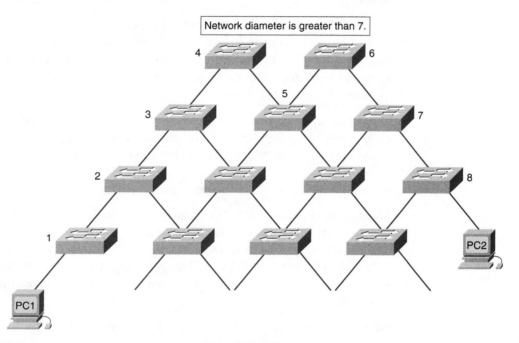

When a BPDU travels from the root bridge toward the leaves of the spanning tree, the age field increments each time the BPDU goes through a switch. Eventually, the switch discards the BPDU when the age field goes beyond the maximum *message age*. If the root is too far away from some of the switches in the network, BPDUs will be dropped. This issue affects the convergence of spanning tree.

Take special care if you plan to change STP timers from the default value. There is a danger if you try to get faster convergence in this way. An STP timer change has an impact on the diameter of the network and the stability of the STP. Alternatively, you can change the switch priority to select the root bridge, and change the port cost or priority parameter to control redundancy and load balancing.

Summary

Implementing redundancy in a hierarchical network introduces physical loops that result in Layer 2 issues, which impact network availability. To prevent problems resulting from physical loops introduced to enhance redundancy, the spanning-tree protocol was developed. The spanning-tree protocol uses the spanning-tree algorithm to compute a loop-free logical topology for a broadcast domain.

The spanning-tree process uses different port states and timers to logically prevent loops by constructing a loop-free topology. The spanning-tree topology is constructed in terms of the distance from the root bridge. The distance is communicated by the exchange of BPDUs with parameters subject to the spanning-tree algorithm. In the process, port roles are determined: designated ports, nondesignated ports, and root ports.

Using the original IEEE 802.1D spanning-tree protocol involves a convergence time of up to 50 seconds. This time delay is unacceptable in modern switched networks, so the IEEE 802.1w rapid spanning-tree protocol was developed. The per-VLAN Cisco implementation of IEEE 802.1D is called PVST+ and the per-VLAN Cisco implementation of rapid spanning-tree protocol is rapid PVST+. RSTP reduces convergence time to approximately 6 seconds or less.

We discussed point-to-point and shared link types with RSTP, as well as edge ports. We also discussed the new concepts of alternate ports and backup ports used with RSTP.

Rapid PVST+ is the preferred spanning-tree protocol implementation used in a switched network running Cisco Catalyst switches.

Labs

The labs available in the companion *LAN Switching and Wireless, CCNA Exploration Labs and Study Guide* (ISBN 1-58713-202-8) provide hands-on practice with the following topics introduced in this chapter:

Lab 5-1: Basic Spanning Tree Protocol (5.5.1)

In this lab, you are carefully guided in observing the default behavior of 802.1D spanning tree protocol, and you observe the response to a change in the spanning tree topology.

Lab 5-2: Challenge Lab—Spanning Tree Protocol (5.5.2)

In this lab, with minimal guidance you configure both 802.1D and 802.1w spanning tree protocols, including root bridge assignment.

Lab 5-3: Troubleshooting Spanning Tree Protocol (5.5.3)

In this lab, you troubleshoot increasing latency in a given switched PVST+ topology. You troubleshoot the fact that only three of six trunks are forwarding frames. The lab is complete when all wired trunks are carrying traffic and all three switches are participating in per-VLAN load balancing for the three user VLANs.

Packet Tracer
☐ Companion

Many of the hands-on labs include Packet Tracer Companion Activities, where you can use Packet Tracer to complete a simulation of the lab. Look for this icon in *LAN Switching and Wireless, CCNA Exploration Labs and Study Guide* (ISBN 1-58713-202-8) for hands-on labs that have a Packet Tracer Companion.

Check Your Understanding

Complete all the review questions listed here to test your understanding of the topics and concepts in this chapter. Answers are listed in the Appendix, "Check Your Understanding and Challenge Questions Answer Key."

1. Which are two problems associated with redundant switched Ethernet topologies? (Choose two.)

   A. Broadcast storms

   B. Routing loops

   C. Multiple frame copies

   D. Load balancing

   E. Incorrect frame addressing

   F. Unicast frame flooding

2. Refer to Figure 5-98. The network is not running spanning-tree protocol. What would be the result if an ARP request were sent by the workstation?

Figure 5-98   ARP Request

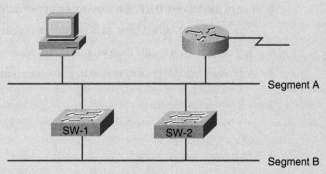

A. The frame will loop between SW-1 and SW-2 until the TTL field drops to zero.

B. The frame will loop until the TTL field reaches the default maximum value.

C. The frame will be prevented from traversing the serial network connected to the router.

D. The frame will loop between SW-1 and SW-2 repeatedly.

3. Refer to Figure 5-99. How will spanning tree prevent switching loops in the network shown if all switches have only the default VLAN configured?

Figure 5-99   Common Spanning Tree

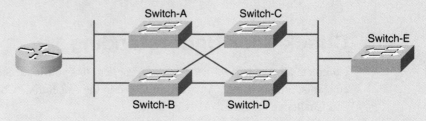

A. Traffic will be load-balanced between all switches.

B. A single switch will be elected as the root switch, and redundant paths to this switch will be blocked.

C. Two of the switches will be elected root bridges, thus blocking traffic between the other two switches.

D. Two of the switches will be elected designated switches, thus blocking traffic between the other two switches.

E. Either Switch-A or Switch-B will be elected as root switch and Switch-C or Switch-D will become the designated switch.

4. What must a switch running spanning tree do when it is first turned on?

A. Adjust its bridge priority value

B. Learn the lowest BID of all switches in the network

C. Request the MAC address of all connected hosts

D. Select the BPDU with the greatest MAC address

E. Adjust its bridge priority value to network conditions

5. Fill in the blanks.

   A. _____ is a single instance of spanning tree encompassing every VLAN in the LAN.

   B. _____ reduces the number of spanning-tree instances required to support large numbers of VLANs.

   C. _____ supports the use of ISL trunking and load balancing.

   D. _____ supports BPDU guard, root guard, and the use of IEEE 802.1Q trunking.

   E. _____ supports equivalent functionality to BackboneFast, UplinkFast, and PortFast, is based on IEEE 802.1w, and functions per-VLAN.

   F. _____ incorporated into IEEE 802.1D-2004; supports equivalent functionality to BackboneFast, UplinkFast, and PortFast.

6. Which three ports will discard data traffic during STP operation? (Choose three.)

   A. Blocking ports

   B. Disabled ports

   C. Designated ports

   D. Root ports

   E. Forwarding ports

   F. Listening ports

7. Fill in the blanks.

   A. _____ receives/processes BPDUs, populates MAC address table

   B. _____ does not process BPDUs

   C. _____ receives/processes BPDUs, populates MAC address table, sends data frames

   D. _____ receives/processes and transmits BPDUs

   E. _____ receives/processes BPDUs

8. Which three timers determine the STP performance and state changes? (Choose three.)

   A. Blocking delay

   B. Hello time

   C. Port speed

   D. Forward delay

   E. Maximum age

   F. Backward delay

9. Refer to Figure 5-100. What will be the result of the spanning tree root bridge election process in the network if each switch supports one and the same VLAN?

Figure 5-100 Root Bridge Election

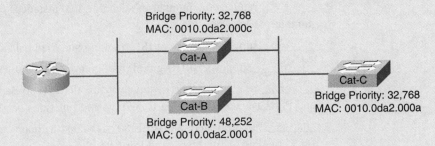

A. Cat-A will be the root bridge.

B. Cat-B will be the root bridge.

C. Cat-C will be the root bridge.

D. Cat-A and Cat-B will be the root bridges.

E. Cat-A and Cat-C will be the root bridges.

10. PVST+ provides support for which IEEE standard?

A. ISL

B. 802.1D

C. 802.1w

D. 802.1

11. Which two characteristics are associated with RSTP? (Choose two.)

A. Supports UplinkFast and BackboneFast.

B. Preferred protocol for preventing Layer 2 loops.

C. Forward delay and max age timers are unneeded.

D. Lacks backward compatibility with IEEE 802.1D.

E. Compatible with rapid PVST+.

12. What is a characteristic of an RSTP edge port?

A. It remains in learning state until it leaves a BPDU from the root bridge.

B. It goes directly from the listening state to the forwarding state.

C. Once enabled, it immediately transitions to the forwarding state.

D. It generates and propagates topology changes when it transitions to a disabled state.

13. When implementing RSTP for non-edge ports, which two categories of link types are available? (Choose two.)

    A. Shared

    B. Multipoint

    C. Redundant

    D. Point-to-point

    E. Dedicated

14. What method does RSTP use to decrease the time it takes to designate a new root port when the existing root port fails?

    A. Smaller values for forward delay and max age timers than STP

    B. Prenegotiated alternate ports for the root port

    C. TCN BPDUs originating from the affected switch

    D. An improved spanning-tree algorithm

15. A switch currently has only one VLAN configured and is running a single instance of rapid spanning tree. Which action will create a second rapid spanning tree instance?

    A. Creating a second VLAN

    B. Entering the **spanning-tree mode rapid-pvst** command

    C. Assigning a port to a VLAN other than VLAN 1

    D. Connecting to another switch

16. Refer to Figure 5-101. Spanning-tree port priorities are listed. S4 port Gi0/1 is currently in RSTP discarding state. What action would change the state to forwarding?

    A. Changing the physical connections so that Gi0/2 connects to S2 and Gi0/1 connects to S3.

    B. Using the **spanning-tree vlan priority** command to increase the priority of Gi0/2 for all VLANs.

    C. Changing the port role for Gi0/1 using the **spanning-tree port priority** command.

    D. Making S4 the root bridge by manually configuring the MAC address to a lower value than S1.

Figure 5-101 Discarding to Forwarding

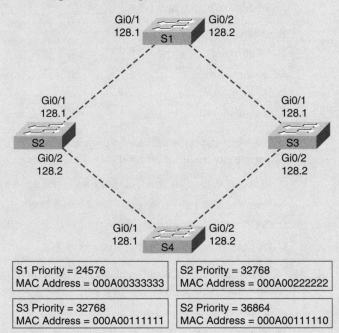

S1 Priority = 24576 MAC Address = 000A00333333	S2 Priority = 32768 MAC Address = 000A00222222
S3 Priority = 32768 MAC Address = 000A00111111	S2 Priority = 36864 MAC Address = 000A00111110

17. Refer to Example 5-27. Which two statements are true regarding the VLAN0001 spanning-tree environment in which switch SW3 is participating? (Choose two.)

Example 5-27   show spanning-tree on S3

```
S3# show spanning-tree

VLAN0001
  Spanning tree enabled protocol ieee
  Root ID    Priority    24577
             Address     0019.2f8d.d200
             Cost        27
             Port        16 (FastEthernet0/14)
             Hello Time   3 sec  Max Age 30 sec  Forward Delay 15 sec
  Bridge ID  Priority    28673  (priority 28672 sys-id-ext 1)
             Address     0019.2f94.a480
             Hello Time   2 sec  Max Age 20 sec  Forward Delay 15 sec
             Aging Time 300
```

A. Spanning tree for VLAN0001 is using the default hello time interval.

B. The root bridge was selected because of its lower MAC address.

C. The root port on SW3 is FastEthernet0/14.

D. SW3 is directly connected to port 16 on the root switch.

E. The root bridge does not have an aging time.

F. SW3 is using the timers advertised by the root switch.

18. Refer to Example 5-28. Why would interface F0/4 have spanning-tree PortFast disabled?

Example 5-28   Spanning-Tree PortFast

```
SW4(config)# interface range f0/1 - 24
SW4(config-if-range)# spanning-tree portfast
<output omitted>
SW4# show spanning-tree interface f0/1 portfast
VLAN0001     enabled
SW4# show spanning-tree interface f0/2 portfast
VLAN0001     enabled
SW4# show spanning-tree interface f0/3 portfast
VLAN0001     enabled
SW4# show spanning-tree interface f0/4 portfast
VLAN0001     enabled
```

A. Interface F0/4 is not active.

B. Interface F0/4 could not transition into forwarding mode and was thus disabled.

C. Interface F0/4 did not receive a BPDU allowing PortFast to be enabled.

D. Interfaces F0/1-3 are connected to end stations, whereas interface F0/4 is connected to another Layer 2 device.

Challenge Questions and Activities

These questions require a deeper application of the concepts covered in this chapter. You can find the answers in the Appendix.

1. Which of the following statements are true and which are false?

____   Ethernet frames do not have a time to live (TTL).

____   Broadcast frames are forwarded out all switch ports, except the ingress port.

_____ In a hierarchical design, redundancy is achieved at the distribution and core layers using additional hardware and alternate paths through the additional hardware.

_____ Layer 2 loops result in low CPU load on all switches caught in the loop.

_____ A broadcast storm results when so many broadcast frames are caught in a Layer 2 loop that all available bandwidth is consumed.

_____ Most upper-layer protocols are designed to recognize or cope with duplicate transmissions.

_____ Layer 2 loops arise as a result of multiple paths, and STP can be used to block these loops.

2. Refer to Figure 5-102. A converged STP topology is pictured with switch S1 as the root bridge. Fill in the boxes with the appropriate description: root port, designated port, or nondesignated port.

Figure 5-102 Port Roles

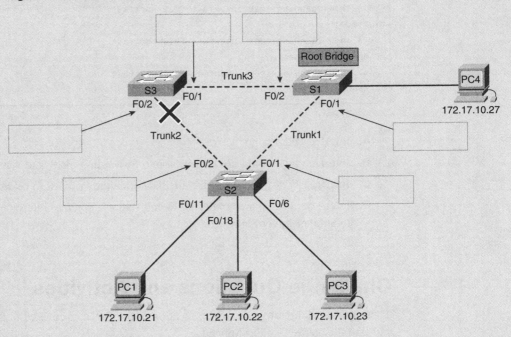

3. Refer to Example 5-29. What can be concluded about interface F0/2?

Example 5-29   show spanning-tree on S3

```
S3# show spanning-tree

VLAN0001
  Spanning tree enabled protocol ieee
  Root ID    Priority    24577
             Address     000A.0033.3333
             Hello Time   2 sec  Max Age 20 sec  Forward Delay 15 sec
  Bridge ID  Priority    32769  (priority 32768 sys-id-ext 1)
             Address     000A.0022.2222
             Aging Time 300


Interface        Role Sts Cost     Prio.Nbr Type
-------------------------------------------------------------------------
Fa0/1            Root FWD 19           128.1    Shr
Fa0/2            Altn  BLK 19      128.2    Shr
```

A. It is a designated port.

B. It is a nondesignated port.

C. It is a root port.

Explanation: Alternate ports are nondesignated ports.

4. Match the terms with the correct descriptions.

    ___   PVST

    ___   PVST+

    ___   RSTP

    ___   MSTP

    ___   802.1D

A.   Original STP.

B.   VLANs are mapped to instances.

C.   Proprietary, but supports 802.1Q trunking.

D.   Relies on ISL trunking.

E.   Faster convergence after a topology change.

Packet Tracer
☐ Challenge

Look for this icon in *LAN Switching and Wireless, CCNA Exploration Labs and Study Guide* (ISBN 1-58713-202-8) for instructions on how to perform the Packet Tracer Skills Integration Challenge for this chapter.

CHAPTER 6

Inter-VLAN Routing

Objectives

Upon completion of this chapter, you will be able to answer the following questions:

- How is network traffic routed between VLANs in a converged network?

- How are Cisco routers and switches configured to enable inter-VLAN routing?

- What are the primary troubleshooting issues related to inter-VLAN routing?

Key Terms

This chapter uses the following key terms. You can find the definitions in the Glossary.

VLANs and trunks are used to segment a switched LAN. Limiting the scope of each broadcast domain on the LAN through VLAN segmentation provides better performance and security across the network. You also learned how VTP is used to share the VLAN information across multiple switches in a LAN environment to simplify management of VLANs. Now that you have a network with many VLANs, the next question is, "How do we permit devices on separate VLANs to communicate?"

In this chapter, you learn about inter-VLAN routing and how it is used to permit devices in separate VLANs to communicate. You learn different methods for accomplishing inter-VLAN routing and the advantages and disadvantages of each. You also learn how different router interface configurations facilitate inter-VLAN routing. Finally, you explore the potential issues faced when implementing inter-VLAN routing, and how to identify and correct them.

Inter-VLAN Routing

Now that you know how to configure VLANs in a switched LAN, the next step is to allow devices connected to the various VLANs to communicate with each other. Each VLAN is a unique broadcast domain, so computers on separate VLANs are, by default, not able to communicate. A way exists to permit these end stations to communicate, called *inter-VLAN routing*. In this topic, you learn what inter-VLAN routing is and some of the different ways to accomplish inter-VLAN routing on a network.

Introducing Inter-VLAN Routing

In this chapter, we focus on one type of inter-VLAN routing using a separate router connected to the switch infrastructure, but we describe two other methods of inter-VLAN routing as well. We define inter-VLAN routing as the process of forwarding network traffic from one VLAN to another VLAN using a router or route processor. VLANs are associated with unique IP subnets on the network. This subnet-VLAN association facilitates the routing process in a multi-VLAN environment. When you use a router to enable inter-VLAN routing, the router interfaces are connected to separate VLANs. Devices on those VLANs send traffic through the router to reach the other VLANs.

As you see in Figure 6-1, traffic from PC1 on VLAN 10 is routed through router R1 to reach PC3 on VLAN 30.

One-Router-Interface-per-VLAN

Traditionally, inter-VLAN routing used routers with multiple physical interfaces. Each interface needed to be connected to a separate network and configured for a different subnet. In a traditional network that uses multiple VLANs to segment the network traffic into logical broadcast domains, routing is performed by connecting different physical router interfaces to different physical switch ports. The switch ports connect to the router in access mode. Each switch interface is assigned to a different static VLAN. Each router interface can then accept traffic from the VLAN associated with the switch interface that it is connected to, and traffic can be routed to the other VLANs connected to the other interfaces.

Figure 6-1   Inter-VLAN Routing

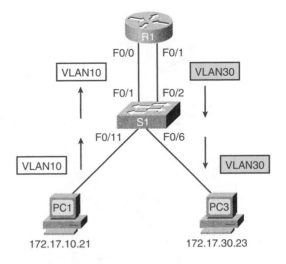

Refer to Figure 6-2. We explore the steps that occur behind the scenes to enable two hosts on different VLANs to communicate with each other through a router. PC1 in VLAN 10 initiates communication with PC3 in VLAN 30 via router R1; R1 has two connections to switch S1, one dedicated to VLAN 10 and the other dedicated to VLAN 30. Switch S1 is the root bridge for all VLANs in the network, with port F0/2 on S2 blocking and ports F0/1, F0/2, and F0/4 on switch S3 blocking (the active trunks are the one connecting port F0/1 on S1 and S2 and the one connecting port F0/3 on S1 and S3).

The exact communication process that occurs behind the scenes is as follows:

1. PC1 has IP address 172.17.10.21/24 in VLAN 10, and PC3 has IP address 172.17.30.23/24 in VLAN 30. PC1 sends unicast traffic destined for PC3 to switch S2 on VLAN 10, where it is then forwarded out the active trunk interface to switch S1.

2. Switch S1 then forwards the unicast traffic out port F0/6 to interface F0/0 on router R1.

3. The router routes the unicast traffic through to its interface F0/1, which is connected to VLAN 30.

4. The router forwards the unicast traffic to switch S1 on VLAN 30.

5. Switch S1 then forwards the unicast traffic to switch S2 through the active trunk link, after which switch S2 forwards the unicast traffic to PC3 on VLAN 30.

Figure 6-2   One-Router-Interface-per-VLAN

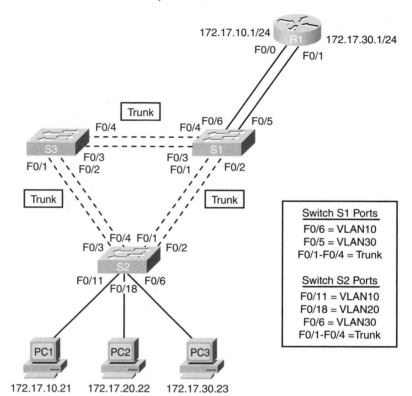

In this example, the router is configured with two separate physical interfaces to interact with the different VLANs to perform the routing.

Router-on-a-Stick

Traditional inter-VLAN routing requires multiple physical interfaces on both the router and the switch. However, not all inter-VLAN routing configurations require multiple physical interfaces. Some router software permits configuring router interfaces as trunk links. This opens up new possibilities for inter-VLAN routing.

Router-on-a-stick is a type of router configuration in which a single physical interface routes traffic between multiple VLANs on a network. As you can see in Figure 6-3, router R1 is connected to switch S1 using a single, physical network connection.

The router interface is configured to operate as a trunk link and is connected to a switch port configured in trunk mode. The router performs the inter-VLAN routing by accepting tagged VLAN traffic on the trunk interface coming from the adjacent switch and internally routing between the VLANs using *subinterfaces*. The router then forwards the routed VLAN-tagged traffic for the destination VLAN out of the same physical interface.

Figure 6-3   Router-on-a-Stick

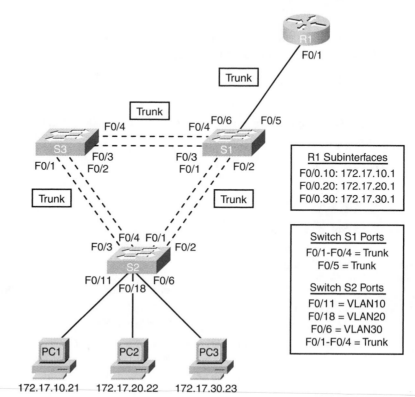

Subinterfaces are virtual interfaces associated with a physical interface. These subinterfaces are configured in software on a router and are configured independently with IP addresses and VLAN assignments. A subinterface is configured for the subnet corresponding to its VLAN assignment; this facilitates the routing process prior to data frames being tagged and sent back out the physical interface.

Refer to Figure 6-3. We explore the steps that occur behind the scenes to enable two hosts on different VLANs to communicate with each other through a router. PC1 in VLAN 10 initiates communication with PC3 in VLAN 30 via router R1; R1 has one trunk connection to switch S1. Switch S1 is the root bridge for all VLANs in the network, with port F0/2 on S2 blocking and ports F0/1, F0/2, and F0/4 on switch S3 blocking (the active trunks are the one connecting port F0/1 on S1 and S2 and the one connecting port F0/3 on S1 and S3).

The exact communication process that occurs behind the scenes is as follows:

1. PC1 has IP address 172.17.10.21/24 in VLAN 10, and PC3 has IP address 172.17.30.23/24 in VLAN 30. PC1 sends unicast traffic destined for PC3 to switch S2 on VLAN 10.

2. Switch S2 then tags the unicast traffic as originating on VLAN 10 and forwards the unicast traffic out its active trunk link to switch S1.

3. Switch S1 forwards the tagged traffic out the other trunk interface on port F0/5 to interface F0/1 on router R1.

4. Router R1 accepts the tagged unicast traffic on VLAN 10 and routes it to VLAN 30 using its configured subinterfaces.

5. The unicast traffic is tagged with VLAN 30 as it is sent out the router interface to switch S1.

6. Switch S1 forwards the tagged unicast traffic out the active trunk link to switch S2.

7. Switch S2 removes the VLAN tag of the unicast frame and forwards the frame to PC3 on port F0/6.

Layer 3 Switch

Some switches can perform Layer 3 functions, replacing the need for dedicated routers to perform basic routing on a network. Layer 3 switches are capable of performing inter-VLAN routing.

See Figure 6-4. We explore the steps that occur behind the scenes to enable two hosts on different VLANs to communicate with each other through a Layer 3 switch. PC1 in VLAN 10 initiates communication with PC3 in VLAN 30 via Layer 3 switch S1. Switch S1 is the root bridge for all VLANs in the network, with port F0/2 on S2 blocking and ports F0/1, F0/2, and F0/4 on switch S3 blocking. (The active trunks are the one connecting port F0/1 on S1 and S2 and the one connecting port F0/3 on S1 and S3.)

Figure 6-4 Layer 3 Switch

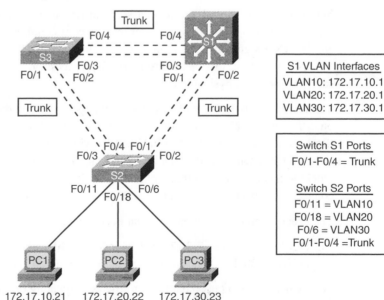

The exact communication process that occurs behind the scenes is as follows:

1. PC1 has IP address 172.17.10.21/24 in VLAN 10, and PC3 has IP address 172.17.30.23/24 in VLAN 30. PC1 sends unicast traffic destined for PC3 to switch S2 on VLAN 10.

2. Switch S2 tags the unicast traffic as originating on VLAN 10 as it forwards the unicast traffic out its active trunk link to switch S1.

3. Switch S1 removes the VLAN tag and forwards the unicast traffic to the VLAN 10 Layer 3 interface.

4. Switch S1 routes the unicast traffic to its VLAN 30 Layer 3 interface.

5. Switch S1 then retags the unicast traffic with VLAN 30 and forwards it out the active trunk link back to switch S2.

6. Switch S2 removes the VLAN tag of the unicast frame and forwards the frame out to PC3 on port F0/6.

To enable a Layer 3 switch to perform routing functions, VLAN interfaces on the switch need to be configured with the appropriate IP addresses that match the subnet that the VLAN is associated with on the network. The Layer 3 switch also must have IP routing enabled. The behind-the-scenes operation of Layer 3 switching is complex and beyond the scope of this book. For a good overview of Layer 3 switching, visit

www.cisco.com/en/US/products/ps6350/products_configuration_guide_chapter09186a0080 0ca7fc.html.

Configuring inter-VLAN routing on a Layer 3 switch is beyond the scope of this book. However, the CCNP curriculum covers the concept comprehensively. To explore additional information, you can also visit

www.cisco.com/application/pdf/en/us/guest/products/ps5023/c2001/ccmigration_09186a008 0876de7.pdf.

Interfaces and Subinterfaces

Three primary methods of inter-VLAN routing are one-router-interface-per-VLAN, router-on-a-stick, and multilayer switching. Each uses a different router configuration to accomplish the task of routing between VLANs. In this section, we look at the router interface configurations for the one-router-interface-per-VLAN method and the router-on-a-stick method of inter-VLAN routing. We then analyze the advantages and disadvantages of each method. We begin by reviewing the traditional model: one-router-interface-per-VLAN. We follow this with the router-on-a-stick model and introduce the integral concept of router subinterfaces used in this model. We then explore some considerations for the one-router-interface-per-VLAN and the router-on-a-stick inter-VLAN routing methods. The configuration of inter-VLAN routing with multilayer switches is beyond the scope of this book.

One-Router-Interface-per-VLAN

Traditional routing requires routers to have multiple physical interfaces to facilitate inter-VLAN routing. The router accomplishes the routing by having each of its physical interfaces connected to a unique VLAN. Each interface is also configured with an IP address for the subnet associated with the particular VLAN to which it is connected. By configuring the IP addresses on the physical interfaces, network devices connected to each of the VLANs can communicate with the router using the physical interface connected to the same VLAN. In this configuration, network devices can use the router as a *gateway* to access the devices connected to the other VLANs.

The routing process requires the source device to determine whether the destination device is local or remote to the local subnet. The source device accomplishes this by comparing the source and destination addresses against the subnet mask. After the destination address has been determined to be on a remote network, the source device has to identify where it needs to forward the packet to reach the destination device. The source device examines the local *routing table* to determine where it needs to send the data. Devices use their default gateway as the destination for all traffic that needs to leave the local subnet. The default gateway is the route that the device uses when it has no other explicitly defined route to the destination network. The router interface on the local subnet acts as the default gateway for the sending device.

After the source device has determined that the packet must travel through the local router interface on the connected VLAN, the source device sends out an ARP request to determine the MAC address of the local router interface. After the router sends its ARP reply back to the source device, the source device can use the MAC address to finish framing the packet before it sends it out on the network as unicast traffic.

Because the Ethernet frame has the destination MAC address of the router interface, the switch knows exactly which switch port to forward the unicast traffic out of to reach the router interface on that VLAN. When the frame arrives at the router, the router removes the Ethernet frame header, including the source and destination MAC address information, to examine the destination IP address of the packet. The router compares the destination IP address to entries in its routing table to determine where it needs to forward the data to reach its final destination. If the router determines that the destination network is a locally connected network, as would be the case in inter-VLAN routing, the router sends an ARP request out the interface physically connected to the destination VLAN. The destination device responds back to the router with its MAC address, which the router then uses to frame the packet. The router then sends the unicast traffic to the switch, which forwards it out the port where the destination device is connected.

To see this process explicitly, see Figure 6-5. Switch S1 is the root bridge for all VLANs in the network, with port F0/2 on S2 blocking and ports F0/1, F0/2, and F0/4 on switch S3 blocking. (The active trunks are the one connecting port F0/1 on S1 and S2 and the one connecting port F0/3 on S1 and S3.)

Figure 6-5   ARP with One-Router-Interface-per-VLAN

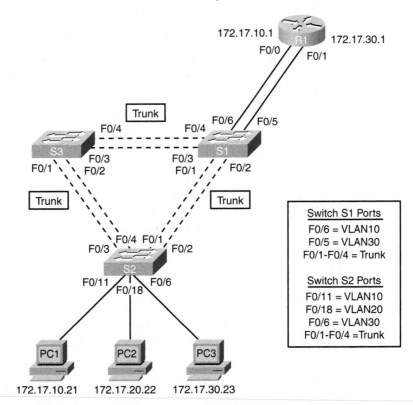

The exact communication process that occurs behind the scenes is as follows:

1. PC1 has IP address 172.17.10.21/24 in VLAN 10, and PC3 has IP address 172.17.30.23/24 in VLAN 30. PC1 sends an ARP request (broadcast) on VLAN 10 to determine the MAC address of its default gateway. The ARP request is forwarded out all active ports on S2 associated with VLAN 10, including the trunk link connecting to S1 via port F0/1.

2. Switch S2 tags, with VLAN 10, the ARP request sent out port F0/1. S1 removes the VLAN tag and forwards the frame out the ports on S1 configured for VLAN 10, including port F0/6, which connects to router R1.

3. Router R1 sends an ARP reply (unicast) with the physical MAC address of the F0/0 interface back to PC1.

4. PC1 frames the data and sends it as unicast traffic to router R1 through switches S2 and S1. After router R1 accepts the frame, it removes the Ethernet header and reads the destination IP address to determine where to forward the IP packet. R1 compares the address with the routes in its routing table and identifies that the destination network is locally connected to interface F0/1. R1 proceeds to send out an ARP request for PC3 on VLAN 30.

5. The ARP request traverses switches S1 and S2, egressing all ports configured for VLAN 30, ultimately reaching PC3.

6. PC3 sends an ARP reply back to router R1 with its MAC address as the source address.

7. Router R1 receives the ARP reply and frames the original data frame with the new source and destination MAC addresses and forwards the frame out interface F0/1 on VLAN 30. Switch S1 forwards the frame to S2 where it is forwarded out port F0/6 to PC3.

8. At this point, PC3 is aware of the MAC address of interface F0/1 on router R1, and router R1 is aware of the MAC address of PC3. PC3 responds to PC1 with a framed packet destined for PC1, using the intermediary destination MAC address of interface F0/1 on router R1.

9. Router R1 receives the frame and removes the original source and destination MAC addresses to read the destination IP address, the IP address of PC1, to determine where to forward the packet. R1 determines that interface F0/0 is connected to the correct subnet and that it should use that physical interface to send the packet back to PC1.

10. At this point, PC1 is aware of the MAC address of interface F0/0 on router R1, and router R1 is aware of the MAC address of PC1. Router R1 sends the frame through switches S1 and S2 back to PC1.

Even though many steps occur in the process of inter-VLAN routing when two devices on different VLANs communicate through a router, the entire process happens in a fraction of a second.

Router interfaces are configured similar to configuring Layer 3 VLAN interfaces on switches. In global configuration mode, first go to interface configuration mode for the specific interface you want to configure. Refer to Figure 6-5. In Example 6-1, interface F0/0 of router R1 is configured with IP address 172.17.10.1 and subnet mask 255.255.255.0 using the **ip address 172.17.10.1 255.255.255.0** command. Interface F0/1 is configured similarly.

Example 6-1 Configuring One-Router-Interface-per-VLAN

```
R1# configure terminal
Enter configuration commands, one per line.  End with CNTL/Z.
R1(config)# interface f0/0
R1(config-if)# ip address 172.17.10.1 255.255.255.0
R1(config-if)# no shutdown
%LINK-5-CHANGED: Interface FastEthernet0/0, changed state to up
%LINEPROTO-5-UPDOWN: Line protocol on Interface FastEthernet0/0, changed state to up
R1(config-if)# interface f0/1
R1(config-if)# ip address 172.17.30.1 255.255.255.0
R1(config-if)# no shutdown
%LINK-5-CHANGED: Interface FastEthernet0/1, changed state to up
%LINEPROTO-5-UPDOWN: Line protocol on Interface FastEthernet0/1, changed state to up
R1(config-if)# end
%SYS-5-CONFIG_I: Configured from console by console
```

To enable a router interface, you need to enter the **no shutdown** command on the interface. After the IP addresses are assigned to the physical interfaces, the router is capable of routing between VLAN 10 and VLAN 30.

Example 6-2 displays the routing table on router R1.

Example 6-2 Viewing the Routing Table

```
R1# show ip route
Codes: C - connected, S - static, R - RIP, M - mobile, B - BGP
       D - EIGRP, EX - EIGRP external, O - OSPF, IA - OSPF inter area
       N1 - OSPF NSSA external type 1, N2 - OSPF NSSA external type 2
       E1 - OSPF external type 1, E2 - OSPF external type 2
       i - IS-IS, su - IS-IS summary, L1 - IS-IS level-1, L2 - IS-IS level-2
       ia - IS-IS inter area, * - candidate default, U - per-user static route
       o - ODR, P - periodic downloaded static route

Gateway of last resort is not set

     172.17.0.0/24 is subnetted, 2 subnets
C       172.17.30.0 is directly connected, FastEthernet0/1
C       172.17.10.0 is directly connected, FastEthernet0/0
```

As you can see in Example 6-2, the routing table has two entries, one for network 172.17.10.0 and the other for network 172.17.30.0. Notice the letter **C** to the left of each route entry. This letter indicates that the route is associated to a connected interface, which is also identified in the route entry. Using the output in this example, if traffic were destined for the 172.17.30.0 subnet, the router would forward the traffic out interface F0/1.

Traditional inter-VLAN routing using physical interfaces does have a limitation. As the number of VLANs increases on the network, the physical approach of having one-router-interface-per-VLAN quickly becomes hindered by the physical hardware limitations of a router. Routers have a limited number of physical interfaces that they can use to connect to different VLANs. Assuming the lack of availability of Layer 3 switches, large networks with many VLANs must use VLAN trunking to assign multiple VLANs to a single router interface to work within the hardware constraints of dedicated routers.

Router-on-a-Stick

To overcome the hardware limitations of inter-VLAN routing based on physical router interfaces, virtual subinterfaces and trunk links are used. Subinterfaces are software-based virtual interfaces assigned to physical interfaces. Each subinterface is configured with its own IP address, subnet mask, and unique VLAN assignment, allowing a single physical interface to simultaneously be part of multiple logical networks. This is useful when performing inter-VLAN routing on networks with multiple VLANs and few physical router interfaces.

When you configure inter-VLAN routing using the router-on-a-stick model, the physical interface of the router must be connected to a trunk link on the adjacent switch. Subinterfaces are created for each unique VLAN/subnet on the switched LAN. Each subinterface is assigned an IP address in the appropriate subnet and configured to tag frames with the associated VLAN. This way, the router can keep the traffic from each subinterface separated as it traverses the trunk link back to the switch.

Functionally, the router-on-a-stick model for inter-VLAN routing is the same as using the traditional routing model, but instead of using the physical interfaces to perform the routing, subinterfaces of a single interface are used.

We proceed to work through an example to illustrate the details of router-on-a-stick configuration. Refer to Figure 6-6. Switch S1 is the root bridge for all VLANs in the network, with port F0/2 on S2 blocking and ports F0/1, F0/2, and F0/4 on switch S3 blocking. (The active trunks are the one connecting port F0/1 on S1 and S2 and the one connecting port F0/3 on S1 and S3.)

Figure 6-6   Router Subinterfaces

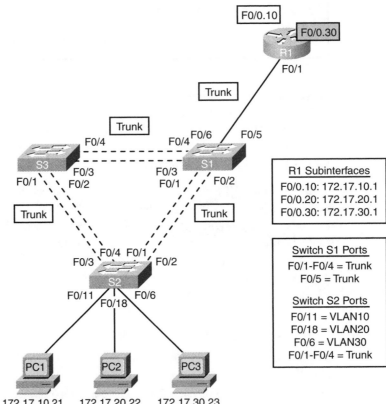

In Figure 6-6, PC1 wants to communicate with PC3. PC1 is on VLAN 10, and PC3 is on VLAN 30. For PC1 to communicate with PC3, PC1 needs to have its data routed through router R1 using the configured subinterfaces.

The exact communication process that occurs behind the scenes is as follows:

1. PC1 sends an ARP request for the MAC address of its default gateway, which is the VLAN subinterface on router R1. The ARP request is sent out for the IP address 172.17.10.1, which corresponds to the subnet to which PC1 is connected. The ARP request is sent to switch S2 on VLAN 10 and is tagged and forwarded out the active trunk link to switch S1. Switch S1 maintains the VLAN tag on the broadcast frame as it forwards it over the trunk link to router R1.

2. Router R1 reads the VLAN tag on the ARP request and recognizes that it was sent on VLAN 10. Because subinterface F0/0.10 has been configured for VLAN 10 and has been configured with the IP address specified in the ARP request, R1 responds back to PC1 with the MAC address of the *physical* interface.

3. PC1 uses the MAC address received from router R1 to frame the unicast packet before it is sent out on the network. Switch S2 tags the frame with VLAN 10 as it traverses the active trunk link to S1. Switch S1 maintains the VLAN tag as it forwards the frame on to router R1.

4. Router R1 examines the frame and sees the tag for VLAN 10. R1 reads the routing table to see if a defined route exists to use as a basis for forwarding the packet to its destination. The routing table indicates that the destination network is directly connected to subinterface F0/0.30. The router then forwards the packet to subinterface F0/0.30.

5. R1 sends an ARP request out R1's physical interface tagged with VLAN 30. PC3 receives the ARP request.

6. PC3 sends an ARP reply with its MAC address back to R1.

7. R1 receives the ARP reply and frames the original data packet with the destination MAC address of PC3 before sending it out interface F0/0, tagged with VLAN 30. Switch S1 forwards the frame to S2, which finally delivers the frame to PC3.

8. PC3 sends a unicast frame back toward PC1. The MAC addresses of PC3 and PC1 are known by R1, and the MAC address of R1 is known to PC3 and PC1.

9. R1 reads the destination IP address in the unicast frame, performs a routing table lookup, and determines that the destination IP network of PC1 is directly connected to F0/0.10.

10. R1 forwards the packet to subinterface F0/0.10 and delivers the unicast packet to PC1.

Configuring router subinterfaces is similar to configuring physical interfaces, except that you need to create the subinterface and assign it to a VLAN.

In Example 6-3, the router subinterface is created by entering the **interface f0/0.10** command in global configuration mode. The syntax for the subinterface is always the physical interface, in this case f0/0, followed by a period and a subinterface number (f0/0.10 is distinct from f0/0.1). The subinterface number is configurable, but it is almost always defined to match the VLAN number. In the example, the subinterfaces are defined with the subinterface numbers 10 and 30 to make it easier to remember the VLANs with which they are associated. The physical interface is specified because there could be multiple interfaces in the router, each of which could be configured to support many subinterfaces.

Example 6-3 Configuring Subinterfaces

```
R1# configure terminal
Enter configuration commands, one per line.  End with CNTL/Z.
R1(config)# interface f0/0.10
R1(config-subif)# encapsulation dot1q 10
R1(config-subif)# ip address 172.17.10.1 255.255.255.0
R1(config-subif)# interface f0/0.30
R1(config-subif)# encapsulation dot1q 30
R1(config-subif)# ip address 172.17.30.1 255.255.255.0
R1(config-subif)# interface f0/0
R1(config-if)# no shutdown
%LINK-5-CHANGED: Interface FastEthernet0/0, changed state to up
%LINK-5-CHANGED: Interface FastEthernet0/0.1, changed state to up
%LINK-5-CHANGED: Interface FastEthernet0/0.3, changed state to up
R1(config-if)# end
```

Before assigning an IP address to a subinterface, the subinterface needs to be configured to operate on a specific VLAN using the **encapsulation dot1q** *vlan-id* command. In the example, subinterface F0/0.10 is assigned to VLAN 10. After the VLAN has been assigned, the **ip address 172.17.10.1 255.255.255.0** command assigns the subinterface to the appropriate IP address for that VLAN.

Unlike a typical physical interface, subinterfaces are not enabled with the **no shutdown** command at the subinterface configuration mode level of the Cisco IOS Software. Instead, when the physical interface is enabled with the **no shutdown** command, all the configured subinterfaces are enabled. Likewise, if the physical interface is disabled, all subinterfaces are disabled.

In Example 6-4, the routes defined in the routing table indicate that they are associated with specific subinterfaces, rather than separate physical interfaces.

Example 6-4 show ip route Output

```
R1# show ip route
Codes: C - connected, S - static, I - IGRP, R - RIP, M - mobile, B - BGP
       D - EIGRP, EX - EIGRP external, O - OSPF, IA - OSPF inter area
       N1 - OSPF NSSA external type 1, N2 - OSPF NSSA external type 2
       E1 - OSPF external type 1, E2 - OSPF external type 2, E - EGP
       i - IS-IS, L1 - IS-IS level-1, L2 - IS-IS level-2, ia - IS-IS inter area
       * - candidate default, U - per-user static route, o - ODR
       P - periodic downloaded static route

Gateway of last resort is not set

     172.17.0.0/24 is subnetted, 2 subnets
C       172.17.10.0 is directly connected, FastEthernet0/0.10
C       172.17.30.0 is directly connected, FastEthernet0/0.30
```

One advantage of using a trunk link is that the number of router and switch ports used is reduced. Not only does this save money, it also reduces configuration complexity. Consequently, the router subinterface approach can scale to a much larger number of VLANs than a configuration with one-router-interface-per-VLAN design. However, the reality is that Layer 3 switches are now cheap enough that it is very rare for a small- or medium-sized business to employ a router-on-a-stick solution.

Considerations for Inter-VLAN Routing Methods

We know that both physical interfaces and subinterfaces are used to perform inter-VLAN routing. There are advantages and disadvantage to each method.

One method involves physical interfaces configured to have one interface per VLAN on the network. On networks with many VLANs, using a single router to perform inter-VLAN routing is not possible. Routers have physical limitations that prevent them from containing large numbers of physical interfaces. Instead, you could use multiple routers to perform inter-VLAN routing for all VLANs to avoid the use of subinterfaces.

Subinterfaces allow a router to scale to accommodate more VLANs than physical interfaces permit. Inter-VLAN routing in large environments with many VLANs is better accommodated by using a single physical interface with many subinterfaces.

Because no contention for bandwidth occurs on separate physical interfaces, physical interfaces have better performance when compared to using subinterfaces. Traffic from each connected VLAN has full access to the bandwidth of the physical interface for inter-VLAN routing.

When subinterfaces are used for inter-VLAN routing, the traffic being routed competes for bandwidth on the single physical interface. On a busy network, this could cause a bottleneck for communication. To balance the traffic load on a physical interface, subinterfaces can be configured on multiple physical interfaces, resulting in less contention between VLAN traffic.

Connecting physical interfaces for inter-VLAN routing requires that the switch ports be configured as access ports. Subinterfaces require the switch port to be configured as a trunk port so that it can accept tagged traffic on the trunk link. Using subinterfaces, many VLANs can be routed over a single trunk link rather than a single physical interface for each VLAN.

It is more cost effective to use subinterfaces than it is to use separate physical interfaces. Routers that have many physical interfaces cost more than routers with a single interface. Additionally, if you have a router with many physical interfaces, each interface is connected to a separate switch port, consuming extra switch ports on the network. Switch ports are an expensive resource on high-performance switches. By consuming additional ports for inter-VLAN routing functions, both the switch and the router drive up the overall cost of the inter-VLAN routing solution.

Using subinterfaces for inter-VLAN routing results in a less-complex physical configuration than using separate physical interfaces because fewer physical network cables interconnect the router to the switch. With fewer cables, less confusion exists about where the cable is connected on the switch. Because the VLANs are being trunked over a single link, it is easier to troubleshoot the physical connections.

On the other hand, using subinterfaces with a trunk port results in a more complex software configuration, which can be difficult to troubleshoot. In the router-on-a-stick model, only a single interface is used to accommodate all the different VLANs. If one VLAN is having trouble routing to other VLANs, you cannot simply trace the cable to see if the cable is plugged into the correct port. You need to check to see if the switch port is configured to be a trunk and verify that the VLAN is not being filtered on any of the trunk links before it reaches the router interface. You also need to check that the router subinterface is configured properly to use the correct VLAN ID and IP address for the subnet associated with that VLAN.

Table 6-1 compares the one-router-interface-per-VLAN method of inter-VLAN routing with the router-on-a-stick method.

Table 6-1   Router Interface and Subinterface Comparison

Physical Interface (One-Router-Interface-per-VLAN Method)	Subinterface (Router-on-a-Stick Method)
One physical interface per VLAN	One physical interface for many VLANs
No bandwidth contention	Bandwidth contention
Connected to access mode switch port	Connected to trunk mode switch port
More expensive	Less expensive
More complex connection configuration	Less complex connection configuration

Configuring Inter-VLAN Routing

In this topic, you learn in detail how to configure a Cisco IOS router for inter-VLAN routing, as well as the commands necessary on a Cisco Catalyst switch needed to enable inter-VLAN routing. We begin with traditional inter-VLAN routing and follow up with router-on-a-stick configuration.

Configure Inter-VLAN Routing

We proceed to work through a sample configuration with a switch and a router performing inter-VLAN routing via two distinct physical interfaces on a router. We begin with the switch configuration. As you can see in Figure 6-7, router R1 interfaces F0/0 and F0/1 are connected to switch ports F0/4 and F0/5, respectively.

Figure 6-7   Configuring Traditional Inter-VLAN Routing

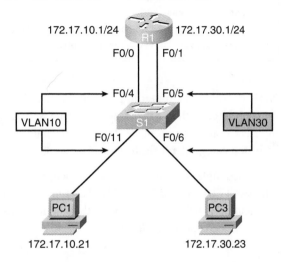

To review, VLANs are created in global configuration mode using the **vlan** *vlan-id* command. In this example, VLANs 10 and 30 are created on switch S1.

After the VLANs are created, ports F0/4 and F0/11 are assigned to VLAN 10, and ports F0/5 and F0/6 are assigned to VLAN 30. To accomplish this task, the **switchport mode access** and **switchport access vlan** *vlan-id* commands are executed from interface configuration mode on the switch for the respective interfaces.

Finally, to protect the configuration so that it is not lost after a reload of the switch, the **copy running-config startup-config** command is executed in privileged EXEC mode to back up the running configuration to the startup configuration.

These steps are all combined in Example 6-5.

Example 6-5 Configuring Traditional Inter-VLAN Routing: Switch

```
S1# configure terminal
Enter configuration commands, one per line.  End with CNTL/Z.
S1(config)# vlan 10
S1(config-vlan)# vlan 30
S1(config-vlan)# interface f0/4
S1(config-if)# switchport mode access
S1(config-if)# switchport access vlan 10
S1(config-if)# interface f0/11
S1(config-if)# switchport mode access
S1(config-if)# switchport access vlan 10
S1(config-if)# interface f0/5
S1(config-if)# switchport mode access
S1(config-if)# switchport access vlan 30
S1(config-if)# interface f0/6
S1(config-if)# switchport mode access
S1(config-if)# switchport access vlan 30
S1(config-if)# end
%SYS-5-CONFIG_I: Configured from console by console
S1# copy running-config startup-config
```

Next, configure the router to perform the inter-VLAN routing. Each router interface must be configured with an IP address using the **ip address** *ip-address subnet-mask* command in interface configuration mode. Also, router interfaces are disabled by default and need to be activated using the **no shutdown** command.

In this example, interface F0/0 is assigned the IP address of 172.17.10.1 using the **ip address 172.17.10.1 255.255.255.0** command followed by the **no shutdown** command. A notification is displayed indicating that the interface state has changed to up, indicating that the interface is now enabled.

The process is repeated for each router interface. Each router interface needs to be assigned to a unique subnet for routing to occur. In this example, the other router interface, F0/1, is configured with IP address 172.17.30.1 on a different subnet than interface F0/0.

The router commands for traditional inter-VLAN routing for the topology illustrated in Figure 6-7 are combined in Example 6-6.

Example 6-6 Configuring Traditional Inter-VLAN Routing: Router

```
R1# configure terminal
Enter configuration commands, one per line.  End with CNTL/Z.
R1(config)# interface f0/0
R1(config-if)# ip address 172.17.10.1 255.255.255.0
R1(config-if)# no shutdown
%LINK-5-CHANGED: Interface FastEthernet0/0, changed state to up
%LINEPROTO-5-UPDOWN: Line protocol on Interface FastEthernet0/0, changed state to up
R1(config-if)# interface f0/1
R1(config-if)# ip address 172.17.30.1 255.255.255.0
R1(config-if)# no shutdown
%LINK-5-CHANGED: Interface FastEthernet0/1, changed state to up
%LINEPROTO-5-UPDOWN: Line protocol on Interface FastEthernet0/1, changed state to up
R1(config-if)# end
R1# copy running-config startup-config
```

By default, Cisco routers are configured to route traffic between the local interfaces. As a result, a routing protocol does not need to be enabled. However, if multiple routers are being configured to perform inter-VLAN routing, you may want to enable a dynamic routing protocol to simplify routing table management. If you have not taken the course CCNA Exploration: Routing Protocols and Concepts, you can learn more at this Cisco site:

www.cisco.com/en/US/products/sw/iosswrel/ps1835/products_configuration_guide_chapter09186a00800ca760.html.

Next, we verify the results of our traditional inter-VLAN routing configuration. First, examine the routing table using the **show ip route** privileged EXEC mode command. In Example 6-7, there are two routes in the routing table. One route is to the 172.17.10.0 subnet, which is attached to the local interface F0/0. The other route is to the 172.17.30.0 subnet, which is attached to the local interface F0/1.

Example 6-7 Verifying Traditional Inter-VLAN Routing

```
R1# show ip route
Codes: C - connected, S - static, I - IGRP, R - RIP, M - mobile, B - BGP
       D - EIGRP, EX - EIGRP external, O - OSPF, IA - OSPF inter area
       N1 - OSPF NSSA external type 1, N2 - OSPF NSSA external type 2
```

```
        E1 - OSPF external type 1, E2 - OSPF external type 2, E - EGP
        i - IS-IS, L1 - IS-IS level-1, L2 - IS-IS level-2, ia - IS-IS inter area
        * - candidate default, U - per-user static route, o - ODR
        P - periodic downloaded static route

Gateway of last resort is not set

     172.17.0.0/24 is subnetted, 2 subnets
C       172.17.10.0 is directly connected, FastEthernet0/0
C       172.17.30.0 is directly connected, FastEthernet0/1
```

The router uses this routing table to determine where to send the traffic it receives. For example, if the router receives a packet on interface F0/0 destined for the 172.17.30.0 subnet, the router determines that it must send the packet out interface F0/1 to reach hosts on the 172.17.30.0 subnet.

To verify the router configuration, use the **show running-config** privileged EXEC mode command, as shown in Example 6-8. This command displays the current operating configuration of the router. You can see which IP addresses have been configured for each of the router interfaces.

Example 6-8 Displaying Traditional Inter-VLAN Routing Configuration

```
R1# show run
<output omitted>
!
hostname R1
!
interface FastEthernet0/0
 ip address 172.17.10.1 255.255.255.0
!
interface FastEthernet0/1
 ip address 172.17.30.1 255.255.255.0
!
<output omitted>!
end
```

In this example, notice that interface F0/0 is configured correctly with the 172.17.10.1 IP address. Also, notice the absence of the **shutdown** command following the F0/0 interface. The absence of the **shutdown** command confirms that the **no shutdown** command has been issued and that the interface is enabled.

Configure Router-on-a-Stick Inter-VLAN Routing

We next proceed to work through a sample configuration involving a router-on-a-stick topology. As before, we begin with the switch configuration and follow with the router configuration.

In Figure 6-8, you see that interface F0/0 of router R1 is connected to port F0/5 of switch S1.

Figure 6-8   Configuring Router-on-a-Stick

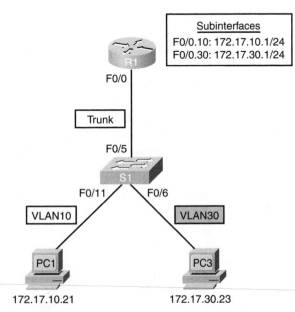

In this example, we create VLANs 10 and 30 on switch S1 using the **vlan 10** and **vlan 30** commands. Because switch port F0/5 will be configured as a trunk port, you do not have to assign any VLANs to the port. To configure switch port F0/5 as a trunk port, execute the **switchport mode trunk** command in interface configuration mode on the F0/5 interface. You cannot use the **switchport mode dynamic auto** or **switchport mode dynamic desirable** commands because the router does not support dynamic trunking protocol (DTP).

Finally, to protect the configuration so that it is not lost after a reload of the switch, the **copy running-config startup-config** command is executed in privileged EXEC mode to back up the running configuration to the startup configuration. The commands are compiled in Example 6-9.

Example 6-9 Configuring Router-on-a-Stick: Switch

```
S1# configure terminal
Enter configuration commands, one per line.  End with CNTL/Z.
S1(config)# vlan 10
S1(config-vlan)# vlan 30
```

```
S1(config-vlan)# interface f0/5
S1(config-if)# switchport mode trunk
S1(config-if)# end
S1(config-if)# copy running-config startup-config
```

Next, the router can be configured to perform the inter-VLAN routing. As you see in Figure 6-8, the configuration of multiple subinterfaces is different than when physical interfaces are used. Each subinterface is created using the **interface** *interface-id.subinterface-id* global configuration mode command. In this example, the subinterface F0/0.10 is created using the **interface f0/0.10** global configuration mode command. After the subinterface has been created, the VLAN ID is assigned using the **encapsulation dot1q** *vlan-id* subinterface configuration mode command. Then assign the IP address for the subinterface using the **ip address** *ip-address subnet-mask* subinterface configuration mode command. In this example, subinterface F0/0.10 is assigned the IP address 172.17.10.1 using the **ip address 172.17.10.1 255.255.255.0** command. You do not need to execute a **no shutdown** command at the subinterface level, because it does not enable the physical interface.

This process is repeated for all the router subinterfaces that are needed to route between the VLANs configured on the network. Each router subinterface needs to be assigned an IP address on a unique subnet for routing to occur. In this example, the other router subinterface, F0/0.30, is configured to use IP address 172.17.30.1, which is on a different subnet from subinterface F0/0.10.

After all subinterfaces have been configured on the router physical interface, the physical interface is enabled. In the example, interface F0/0 has the **no shutdown** command executed to enable the interface, which enables all the configured subinterfaces.

The router commands for traditional inter-VLAN routing for the topology illustrated in Figure 6-8 are combined in Example 6-10.

Example 6-10   Configuring Router-on-a-Stick: Router

```
R1# configure terminal
Enter configuration commands, one per line.  End with CNTL/Z.
R1(config)# interface f0/0.10
R1(config-subif)# encapsulation dot1q 10
R1(config-subif)# ip address 172.17.10.1 255.255.255.0
R1(config-subif)# interface f0/0.30
R1(config-subif)# encapsulation dot1q 30
R1(config-subif)# ip address 172.17.30.1 255.255.255.0
R1(config-subif)# interface f0/0
R1(config-if)# no shutdown
%LINK-5-CHANGED: Interface FastEthernet0/0, changed state to up
%LINEPROTO-5-UPDOWN: Line protocol on Interface FastEthernet0/0, changed state to up
```

```
%LINK-5-CHANGED: Interface FastEthernet0/0.10, changed state to up
%LINEPROTO-5-UPDOWN: Line protocol on Interface FastEthernet0/0.10, changed state
  to up
%LINK-5-CHANGED: Interface FastEthernet0/0.30, changed state to up
%LINEPROTO-5-UPDOWN: Line protocol on Interface FastEthernet0/0.30, changed state
  to up
R1(config-if)# end
```

By default, Cisco routers are configured to route traffic between the local subinterfaces. As a result, a routing protocol does not need to be enabled.

Next, we examine the routing table using the **show ip route** command. In Example 6-11, two routes are in the routing table. One is to the 172.17.10.0 subnet, which is attached to the local subinterface F0/0.10. The other route is to the 172.17.30.0 subnet, which is attached to the local subinterface F0/0.30.

Example 6-11   Verifying Router-on-a-Stick

```
R1# show ip route
Codes: C - connected, S - static, I - IGRP, R - RIP, M - mobile, B - BGP
        D - EIGRP, EX - EIGRP external, O - OSPF, IA - OSPF inter area
        N1 - OSPF NSSA external type 1, N2 - OSPF NSSA external type 2
        E1 - OSPF external type 1, E2 - OSPF external type 2, E - EGP
        i - IS-IS, L1 - IS-IS level-1, L2 - IS-IS level-2, ia - IS-IS inter area
        * - candidate default, U - per-user static route, o - ODR
        P - periodic downloaded static route


Gateway of last resort is not set

     172.17.0.0/24 is subnetted, 2 subnets
C        172.17.10.0 is directly connected, FastEthernet0/0.10
C        172.17.30.0 is directly connected, FastEthernet0/0.30
```

The router uses this routing table to determine where to send the traffic it receives. For example, if the router received a packet on subinterface F0/0.10 destined for the 172.17.30.0 subnet, the router would identify that it should send the packet out subinterface F0/0.30 to reach hosts on the 172.17.30.0 subnet.

To verify the router configuration, use the **show running-config** command, as in Example 6-12. The **show running-config** command displays the current operating configuration of the router. Notice which IP addresses have been configured for each router subinterface, as well as whether the physical interface has been left disabled or enabled using the **no shutdown** command.

Example 6-12   Displaying Router-on-a-Stick Configuration

```
Router# show running-config
<output omitted>
!
hostname R1
!
interface FastEthernet0/0
 no ip address
!
interface FastEthernet0/0.10
 encapsulation dot1Q 10
 ip address 172.17.10.1 255.255.255.0
!
interface FastEthernet0/0.30
 encapsulation dot1Q 30
 ip address 172.17.30.1 255.255.255.0
!
<output omitted>
!
end
```

Notice that interface F0/0.10 has been configured correctly with the 172.17.10.1 IP address. Also, notice the absence of the **shutdown** command following the F0/0 interface. The absence of the **shutdown** command confirms that the **no shutdown** command has been issued and the interface is enabled.

After the router and switch have been configured to perform the inter-VLAN routing, the next step is to verify that the router is functioning correctly. You can test access to devices on remote VLANs using the *ping* command.

For the topology in Figure 6-8, you initiate a **ping** and a **tracert** from PC1 to the destination address of PC3.

The **ping** command sends an *Internet Control Message Protocol (ICMP)* echo request to the destination address. When a host receives an ICMP echo request, it responds with an ICMP echo reply to confirm that it received the ICMP echo request. The **ping** command calculates the elapsed time using the difference between the time the echo reply is sent and the time the echo reply is received. This elapsed time is used to determine the latency of the connection. Successfully receiving a reply confirms that a path exists between the sending device and the receiving device.

tracert is a useful utility for confirming the routed path taken between two devices. On UNIX systems, the utility is specified by the **traceroute** command. **tracert** also uses ICMP to determine the path taken, but it uses ICMP echo requests with specific time-to-live (TTL) values defined in the IP packet header.

The TTL value determines exactly how many router hops away the ICMP echo is allowed to reach. The first ICMP echo request is sent with a TTL value set to expire at the first router en route to the destination device. When the ICMP echo request times out on the first route, a confirmation is sent back from the router to the originating device. The device records the response from the router and proceeds to send out another ICMP echo request, but this time with a greater TTL value. This allows the ICMP echo request to traverse the first router and reach the second device en route to the final destination. The process repeats until finally the ICMP echo request is sent all the way to the final destination device. After the **tracert** utility finishes running, you see a list of every router interface that the ICMP echo request reached on its way to the destination.

In Example 6-13, the **ping** utility is able to send an ICMP echo request to the IP address of PC3. Also, the **tracert** utility confirms that the path to PC3 is through the 172.17.10.1 subinterface IP address of router R1.

Example 6-13   Verifying Router-on-a-Stick

```
PC> ping 172.17.30.23


Pinging 172.17.30.23 with 32 bytes of data:


Reply from 172.17.30.23: bytes=32 time=17ms TTL=127
Reply from 172.17.30.23: bytes=32 time=15ms TTL=127
Reply from 172.17.30.23: bytes=32 time=18ms TTL=127
Reply from 172.17.30.23: bytes=32 time=19ms TTL=127


Ping statistics for 172.17.30.23:
    Packets: Sent = 4, Received = 4, Lost = 0 (0% loss),
Approximate round trip times in milli-seconds:
    Minimum = 15ms, Maximum = 19ms, Average = 17ms


PC> tracert 172.17.30.23


Tracing route to 172.17.30.23 over a maximum of 30 hops:

  1    9 ms      7 ms      9 ms       172.17.10.1
  2   16 ms     15 ms     16 ms       172.17.30.23
```

Packet Tracer
☐ Activity

Configuring Traditional Inter-VLAN Routing (6.2.2a)

In this activity, you configure traditional inter-VLAN routing by configuring two Fast Ethernet interfaces on a router. R1 has two connections to S1, one for each of the two VLANs. S1 and R1 already have basic configurations. You complete the configuration by adding VLANs to S1 and assigning ports to the correct VLANs. Then you configure R1 with IP addressing. In traditional inter-VLAN routing, no additional VLAN-related configurations are needed on R1. Use File e3-6224.pka on the CD-ROM that accompanies this book to perform this activity using Packet Tracer.

Configuring Router-on-a-Stick Inter-VLAN Routing (6.2.2b)

In this activity, you configure router-on-a-stick inter-VLAN routing. R1 has one connection to S1. S1 and R1 already have basic configurations. You complete the configuration by adding VLANs to S1 and assigning ports to the correct VLANs. Then you configure R1 with subinterfaces, 802.1Q encapsulation, and IP addressing. Use File e3-6225.pka on the CD-ROM that accompanies this book to perform this activity using Packet Tracer.

Troubleshooting Inter-VLAN Routing

There are a number of challenges associated with configuring multiple VLANs on a network. We explore common issues and describe troubleshooting methods to identify and correct these issues.

Switch Configuration Issues

When using the traditional routing model for inter-VLAN routing, ensure that the switch ports that connect to the router interfaces are configured in the correct VLANs. If a switch port is not configured in the correct VLAN, devices configured in that VLAN cannot connect to the router interface and therefore are unable to route to the other VLANs.

As you can see in Figure 6-9, PC1 and router R1 interface F0/0 are configured to be on the same logical subnet, as indicated by their IP address assignment. However, the switch port F0/4 that connects to router R1 interface F0/0 has not been configured and remains in VLAN 1. Because router R1 is on a different VLAN than PC1, they are unable to communicate.

Figure 6-9   Misconfigured VLAN Membership

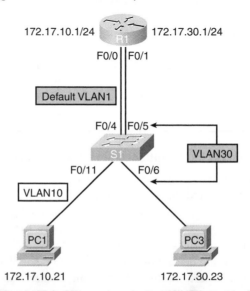

To correct this problem, execute the **switchport access vlan 10** interface configuration command on port F0/4 on switch S1. When the switch port is configured for the correct VLAN, PC1 can communicate with router R1 interface F0/0, which allows it to access the other VLANs connected to router R1.

Another issue that often occurs is a port with a misconfigured port mode. In Figure 6-10, the router-on-a-stick topology is used. However, port F0/5 on switch S1 is not configured as a trunk and hence defaults to VLAN 1. As a result, the router is not able to function correctly because each of its configured subinterfaces is unable to send or receive tagged traffic properly. This prevents all configured VLANs from routing through router R1 to reach other VLANs.

Figure 6-10   Misconfigured Switch Port Mode

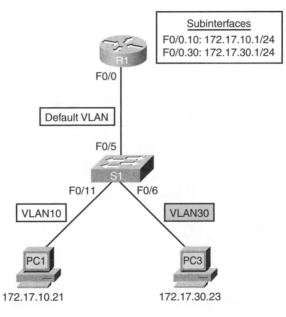

To correct this problem, enter the **switchport mode trunk** interface configuration command on port F0/5 of switch S1. This converts the interface to a trunk, allowing the trunk to successfully establish an active trunk link with router R1. When the trunk is successfully established, devices connected to each of the VLANs are able to communicate with the subinterface associated with their VLAN, allowing inter-VLAN routing to occur.

Last, an issue that can prevent inter-VLAN routing is an inactive trunk link between two switches. In Figure 6-11, the trunk link between switch S1 and switch S2 is down. Because no redundant paths exist, all devices connected to switch S2 are unable to reach router R1, hence inter-VLAN routing is precluded.

Figure 6-11   Inactive Interswitch Trunk Link

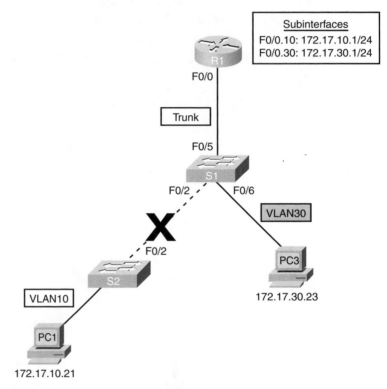

To reduce the risk of a failed interswitch link disrupting inter-VLAN routing, you should configure redundant links and alternative paths between switch S1 and switch S2. Redundant links are configured in the form of an EtherChannel that protects against a single link failure. Cisco EtherChannel technology enables you to aggregate multiple physical links into one logical link. 10 Gigabit EtherChannel can provide up to 160 Gbps of aggregate bandwidth on a Catalyst switch with 10 Gigabit Ethernet ports.

Additionally, alternative paths through other interconnected switches could be configured. This approach is dependent on STP to prevent the possibility of loops within the switch environment. A slight disruption occurs in router access while STP reconverges.

The CCNP curriculum addresses EtherChannel technology; also, to learn more about Cisco EtherChannel technology, visit

www.cisco.com/en/US/tech/tk389/tk213/technologies_white_paper09186a0080092944.shtml.

To learn more about configuring EtherChannel on a Cisco Catalyst 2960 switch, visit

www.cisco.com/en/US/products/ps6406/products_configuration_guide_chapter09186a0080
8752d9.html.

Switch Cisco IOS Commands for Troubleshooting

When you suspect a problem exists with a switch configuration, use the various verification commands to examine the configuration and identify the problem.

Example 6-14 shows the output for the **show interface** *interface-id* **switchport** command. Assume that you have issued this command because you suspect that VLAN 10 has not been assigned to port F0/11 on switch S1. The top shaded area shows that port F0/11 on switch S1 is in access mode, but it does not show that it has been directly assigned to VLAN 10. The bottom shaded area confirms that port F0/11 is still set to VLAN 1.

Example 6-14   Switch Troubleshooting

```
S1# show interface f0/11 switchport
Name: Fa0/11
Switchport: Enabled
Administrative Mode: static access
Operational Mode: up
Administrative Trunking Encapsulation: dot1q
Operational Trunking Encapsulation: native
Negotiation of Trunking: Off
Access Mode VLAN: 1 (default)
Trunking Native Mode VLAN: 1 (default)
<output omitted>
```

The configuration is corrected by entering the **switchport access vlan 10** command on interface F0/11.

A secondary issue still needs to be addressed: Communication between router R1 and switch S1 has stopped. The link between the router and the switch is supposed to be a trunk link. Example 6-15 shows the results of the **show interface** *interface-id* **switchport** and the **show running-config** commands. The top shaded area confirms that port F0/5 on switch S1 is in access mode, not trunk mode. The bottom shaded area also confirms that port F0/5 has been configured for access mode.

Example 6-15   Switch Troubleshooting Commands

```
S1# show interface f0/5 switchport
Name: Fa0/5
Switchport: Enabled
Administrative Mode: static access
```

```
Operational Mode: down
Administrative Trunking Encapsulation: dot1q
<output omitted>
S1#
S1# show run
Building configuration...

<output omitted>
!
interface FastEthernet0/5
 switchport mode access
!
<output omitted>
```

To correct the error, enter the **switchport mode trunk** command on interface F0/5.

Router Configuration Issues

As you see in Figure 6-12, interface F0/0 on router R1 is connected to port F0/9 on switch S1. Switch port F0/9 is configured for VLAN 1. This prevents PC1, in VLAN 10, from being able to communicate with router interface F0/0, and it is therefore unable to route to VLAN 30.

Figure 6-12   Switch Cabled Incorrectly

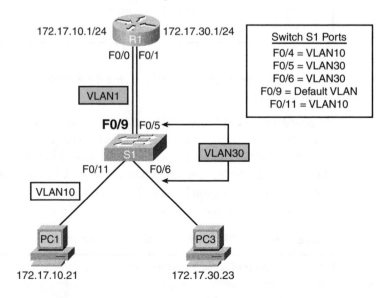

To correct this problem, physically connect R1 interface F0/0 to S1 port F0/4. This puts the router interface in the correct VLAN and allows inter-VLAN routing to function. Alternatively, you could change the VLAN assignment of switch port F0/9 to VLAN 10. This also allows PC1 to communicate with router R1 interface F0/0.

Router Cisco IOS Commands for Troubleshooting

In Figure 6-13, R1 has been configured to use the wrong VLAN on subinterface F0/0.10, preventing devices configured on VLAN 10 from communicating with subinterface F0/0.10. This prevents devices in VLAN 10 from being able to route to other VLANs.

Figure 6-13   Subinterface Configuration Error

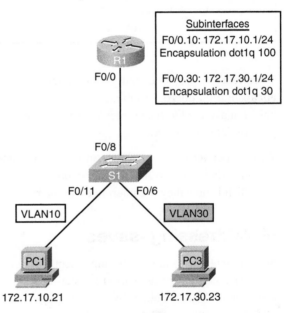

You see this error when you enter the **show interface** and **show running-config** commands on R1, as shown in Example 6-16, where you see subinterface F0/0.10 configured in VLAN 100.

Example 6-16   Router Troubleshooting Commands

```
R1# show interface
<output omitted>
FastEthernet0/0.10 is up, line protocol is down (disabled)
  Encapsulation 802.1Q Virtual LAN, Vlan ID 100
  ARP type: ARPA, ARP Timeout 04:00:00,
  Last clearing of "show interface" counters never
<output omitted>
```

```
R1#
R1# show run
Building configuration...
Current configuration : 505 bytes
<output omitted>
!
interface FastEthernet0/0.10
 encapsulation dot1Q 100
 ip address 172.17.10.1 255.255.255.0
!
interface FastEthernet0/0.30
 encapsulation dot1Q 30
 ip address 172.17.30.1 255.255.255.0
<output omitted>
```

To correct this problem, configure subinterface F0/0.10 to be in VLAN 10 using the **encapsulation dot1q 10** subinterface configuration mode command. When the subinterface has been assigned to the correct VLAN, it is accessible by devices in that VLAN and can perform inter-VLAN routing.

With proper verification, router configuration problems are quickly addressed, allowing for inter-VLAN routing to function again properly. Recall that the VLANs are directly connected, which is how they are interpreted in the routing table.

IP Addressing Issues

Subnet assignments are key to implementing inter-VLAN routing. VLANs correspond to unique subnets on the network. For inter-VLAN routing to work, a router needs to be connected to all VLANs, either by separate physical interfaces or trunked subinterfaces. Each interface, or subinterface, needs to be assigned an IP address that corresponds to the subnet for which it is connected. This permits devices on the VLAN to communicate with the router interface and enable the routing of traffic to other VLANs connected to the router. We look at some common IP addressing errors.

As you see in Figure 6-14, router R1 has been configured with an incorrect IP address on interface F0/0. This prevents PC1 from being able to communicate with router R1 on VLAN 10.

To correct this problem, assign the correct IP address to router R1 interface F0/0 using the **ip address 172.17.10.1 255.255.255.0** interface command in configuration mode. After the router interface has been assigned the correct IP address, PC1 can use the interface as a default gateway for accessing other VLANs.

Figure 6-14   Router Interface IP Addressing Error

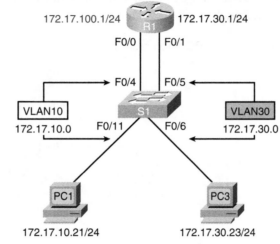

Next, refer to Figure 6-15. PC1 has been configured with an incorrect IP address for the subnet associated with VLAN 10. This prevents PC1 from being able to communicate with router R1 on VLAN 10.

Figure 6-15   PC IP Addressing Error

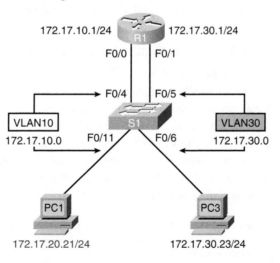

To correct this problem, assign the correct IP address to PC1. Depending on the type of PC being used, the configuration details may be different.

Finally, refer to Figure 6-16. PC1 has been configured with the incorrect subnet mask. According to the subnet mask configured for PC1, PC1 is on the 172.17.0.0/16 network.

This results in PC1 determining that PC3, with IP address 172.17.30.23, is on the local subnet. As a result, PC1 does not forward traffic destined for PC3 to router R1 interface F0/0. Therefore, the traffic never reaches PC3.

Figure 6-16 PC Subnet Error

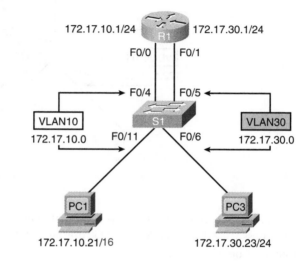

To correct this problem, change the subnet mask on PC1 to 255.255.255.0. Depending on the type of PC being used, the configuration details may be different.

IP Addressing Cisco IOS Verification Commands

Each interface or subinterface needs to be assigned an IP address that corresponds to the subnet for which it is connected. A common error is to incorrectly configure an IP address for a subinterface. Example 6-17 shows the results of the **show running-config** command. The shaded area shows that the subinterface F0/0.10 on router R1 has an IP address of 172.17.20.1. The VLAN for this subinterface should allow VLAN 10 traffic. An IP address has been incorrectly configured. The **show ip interface** is another useful command. The second shaded area shows the incorrect IP address. The router subinterface F0/0.10 IP address should be changed to 172.17.10.1.

Example 6-17 IP Addressing Verification Commands

```
R1# show run
Building configuration...
<output omitted>
!
interface FastEthernet0/0
 no ip address
 duplex auto
```

```
 speed auto
!
interface FastEthernet0/0.10
 encapsulation dot1Q 10
 ip address 172.17.20.1 255.255.255.0
!
interface FastEthernet0/0.30
<output omitted>
R1#
R1# show ip interface
<output omitted>
FastEthernet0/0.10 is up, line protocol is up
  Internet address is 172.17.20.1/24
   Broadcast address is 255.255.255.255
<output omitted>
```

Sometimes it is the end-user device, such as a personal computer, that is the culprit. In Example 6-18, you see the IP address configuration of PC1: The IP address is 172.17.20.21 with a subnet mask of 255.255.255.0. But in this scenario, PC1 should be in VLAN 10 with an address of 172.17.10.21 and a subnet mask of 255.255.255.0.

Example 6-18   PC IP Addressing Error

```
PC1>ipconfig

IP Address.........................:172.17.20.21
Subnet Mask........................:255.255.255.0
Default Gateway....................:0.0.0.0
```

This is easily corrected by changing the IP address on PC1 to 172.17.10.21. Also, double-check that the router subinterface F0/0.10 address is changed to 172.17.10.1.

Packet Tracer
☐ Activity

Troubleshooting Inter-VLAN Routing (6.3.3)

In this activity, you troubleshoot connectivity problems between PC1 and PC3. The activity is complete when the two PCs can ping each other. Any solution must conform to the topology diagram. Use file e3-6333.pka on the CD-ROM that accompanies this book to perform this activity using Packet Tracer.

Summary

Inter-VLAN routing is the process of routing traffic between different VLANs, using either a dedicated router or a multilayer switch. Inter-VLAN routing facilitates communication between devices isolated by VLAN boundaries.

The inter-VLAN routing topology using an external router with subinterfaces trunked to a Layer 2 switch is called router-on-a-stick. With this option, it is important to configure an IP address on each logical subinterface as well as the associated VLAN number.

Modern switched networks use switch virtual interfaces on multilayer switches to enable inter-VLAN routing.

Catalyst 2960 switches can be used in a router-on-a-stick scenario, whereas Catalyst 3560 switches can be used with the multilayer switching option.

Labs

The labs available in the companion *LAN Switching and Wireless, CCNA Exploration Labs and Study Guide* (ISBN 1-58713-202-8) provide hands-on practice with the following topics introduced in this chapter:

Lab 6-1: Basic Inter-VLAN Routing (6.4.1)

In this lab, you break up large broadcast domains created by the physical topology of a switched network using VLANs. Users on each VLAN must be able to communicate with users on the other VLANs—you configure inter-VLAN routing to make this possible.

Lab 6-2: Challenge Inter-VLAN Routing (6.4.2)

In this lab, with minimal guidance you configure inter-VLAN routing for the Chapter 6 topology.

Lab 6-3: Troubleshooting Inter-VLAN Routing (6.4.3)

In this lab, you troubleshoot a switched network that has been designed and configured to support five VLANs and a routed subnet just outside the LAN. Inter-VLAN routing is being provided by an external router in a router-on-a-stick configuration, and the server network is routed across a separate Fast Ethernet interface. However, the network is not working as designed and complaints from your users have not given much insight into the source of the problems. You must first define what is not working as expected, and then analyze the existing configurations to determine and correct the problems.

Packet Tracer
☐ Companion

Many of the hands-on labs include Packet Tracer Companion Activities, where you can use Packet Tracer to complete a simulation of the lab. Look for this icon in *LAN Switching and Wireless, CCNA Exploration Labs and Study Guide* (ISBN 1-58713-202-8) for hands-on labs that have a Packet Tracer Companion.

Check Your Understanding

Complete all the review questions listed here to test your understanding of the topics and concepts in this chapter. Answers are listed in the Appendix, "Check Your Understanding and Challenge Questions Answer Key."

1. Classify each item as either physical interface or subinterface.

    _____ one physical interface for many VLANs

    _____ bandwidth contention

    _____ access mode switch port connection

    _____ complex cable configuration

    _____ trunk mode switch port connection

    _____ one physical interface per VLAN

2. Refer to Figure 6-17. PC1 wants to send data to PC2, but does not know the MAC address of PC2. When PC1 sends an ARP request, which interface returns a MAC address?

Figure 6-17   ARP Request

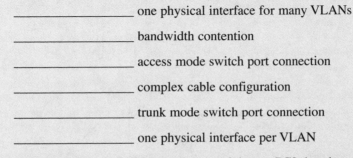
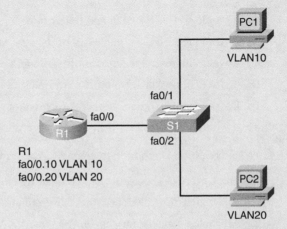

A. Because PC1 and PC2 are connected to the same switch, PC2 supplies its MAC address.

B. The switch provides the MAC address of the F0/1 interface.

C. Because the subinterfaces on the router have unique MAC addresses, subinterface F0/0.10 supplies its MAC address.

D. The router supplies the MAC address of the physical interface F0/0.

3. Refer to Figure 6-18. What are three advantages of replacing the individual VLAN links between the switch and the router with a trunk link and subinterfaces? (Choose three.)

Figure 6-18   Advantages of Router-on-a-Stick

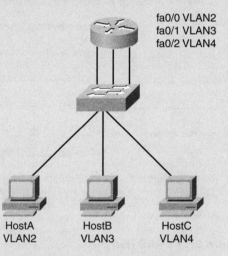

fa0/0 VLAN2
fa0/1 VLAN3
fa0/2 VLAN4

HostA   HostB   HostC
VLAN2   VLAN3   VLAN4

A. It would free two switch and router ports.

B. It would reduce the complexity of the cabling runs.

C. It would increase the amount of bandwidth available for inter-VLAN routing.

D. It would allow for less complex troubleshooting of inter-VLAN routing issues.

E. It would allow adding more VLANs without requiring more cabling or switch ports.

F. It would allow for less-complex configuration of inter-VLAN routing.

4. What condition is required to enable Layer 3 switching?

A. The Layer 3 switch must have IP routing enabled.

B. All participating switches must have unique VLAN numbers.

C. All routed subnets must be on the same VLAN.

D. Inter-VLAN portions of Layer 3 switching must use router-on-a-stick.

5. When implementing router-on-a-stick, what is necessary for establishing communication between VLANs?

   A. Multiple switch ports to connect to a single router interface

   B. Native VLAN IP address that is configured on the router physical interface

   C. All trunk ports configured in access mode

   D. Router subinterfaces

6. Which two methodologies could be employed to reduce the risk of a failed interswitch link disrupting inter-VLAN routing? (Choose two.)

   A. Configure and enable EtherChannel.

   B. Disable trunking on all switch ports.

   C. Configure and enable alternative paths between switches.

   D. Assign all switch ports to separate VLANs.

   E. Configure and enable Dynamic Tree Protocol.

7. Refer to Figure 6-19. Which three statements are true regarding this configuration? (Choose three.)

Figure 6-19   One Physical Router Interface per VLAN

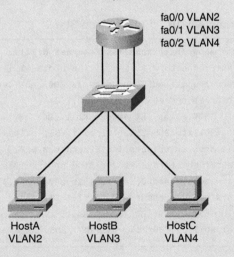

   A. This configuration will not scale easily.

   B. This configuration limits the number of VLANs because of limitations on the number of physical interfaces the router can support.

   C. The connections between the switch and router are trunk links.

   D. All traffic between the router and the switch must be tagged with its VLAN ID.

   E. This configuration is not the most scalable.

   F. The switch serves as the gateway for the hosts.

8. How does the router-on-a-stick model for inter-VLAN routing differ from traditional routing?

   A. The router-on-a-stick model uses multiple physical interfaces on the router, each configured with a different Layer 3 address.

   B. The router-on-a-stick model uses a single physical interface on the switch with only the **no shutdown** command issued.

   C. The router-on-a-stick model uses subinterfaces on the router with only the **no shutdown** command issued on the physical interface.

   D. The router-on-a-stick model uses subinterfaces on the switch with only the **no shutdown** command issued on the physical interface.

9. Which command does the network administrator use to determine whether inter-VLAN communication is functioning?

   A. **show vlan**

   B. **ping**

   C. **ipconfig**

   D. **show interface**

10. Regarding Example 6-19, which statement is true based on the displayed output?

Example 6-19   Subinterface Status

```
R1# show interfaces fastEthernet 0/0.1
FastEthernet0/0.1 is up, line protocol is up
Hardware is AmdFE, address is 0003.e36f.41e0 (bia 0003.e36f.41e0)
Internet address is 10.10.10.1/24
MTU 1500 bytes, BW 100000 Kbit, DLY 100 usec,
Reliability 255/255, txload 1/255, rxload 1/255
R1# show interfaces fastEthernet 0/0.2
FastEthernet0/0.2 is up, line protocol is up
Hardware is AmdFE, address is 0003.e36f.41e0 (bia 0003.e36f.41e0)
Internet address is 10.10.11.1/24
MTU 1500 bytes, BW 100000 Kbit, DLY 100 usec,
Reliability 255/255, txload 1/255, rxload 1/255
```

   A. Each subinterface returns a unique address in response to ARP requests.

   B. This inter-VLAN routing configuration is not the most cost effective or scalable.

   C. The router is properly configured for router-on-a-stick inter-VLAN routing between the 10.10.10.0/24 and 10.10.11.0/24 subnetworks.

   D. The trunk link was dynamically negotiated.

   E. Layer 3 addressing is not properly configured.

11. In a router-on-a-stick configuration, which two items are required to support connectivity between the router and the switch? (Choose two.)

   A. All ports on the switch must be configured as access ports.

   B. Router-to-switch physical interface must be configured with an IP address.

   C. Router subinterfaces must be configured with unique addresses in different subnets.

   D. Switch port that connects to the router must be configured as a trunk.

   E. Each subinterface must be configured with the **no shutdown** command.

12. Refer to Figure 6-20. R1 has two Fast Ethernet interfaces and is configured as a router-on-a-stick to perform all inter-VLAN routing. VLAN 10 has approximately the same amount of traffic as VLANs 20, 30, and 99 combined. Interface F0/0 on R1 is nearing capacity and funds are limited for additional equipment. The company expects to add more VLANs in the future. R1 has an unused Fast Ethernet interface, F0/1. What configuration change will reduce the traffic on R1 F0/0, maintain routing between VLANs, and improve fault tolerance for the network in the event of switch failure?

Figure 6-20   Scaling Router-on-a-Stick

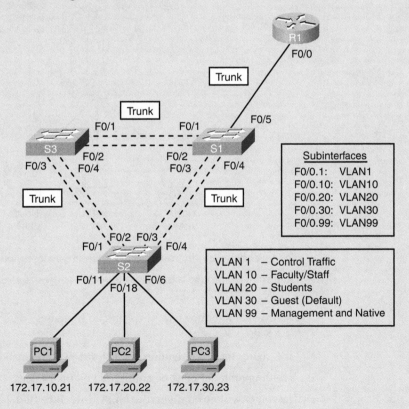

A. Connect F0/1 on R1 to S3 configured as a trunk link with all VLANs. Load balance between F0/0 and F0/1 to reduce the traffic load. The two links back each other up in the case of a single switch failure. Add any new VLAN additions to both links.

B. Remove the F0/0.10 subinterface from R1. Connect F0/1 on R1 to S3 configured as a trunk link with only VLAN 10 as subinterface F0/1.10. Alternate any new VLAN additions on the two links to balance traffic.

C. Remove the link to R1. Implement Layer 2 inter-VLAN routing on each switch. The switches jointly back each other up.

D. Remove the subinterfaces from R1. Add a primary IP address to F0/0 in VLAN 99 on R1. Add secondary addresses on F0/0 for all other VLANs. Connect F0/1 on R1 to S3. Configure F0/1 as the same as F0/0, but with different host addresses. The two links back each other up in case of a switch failure.

13. Refer to Figure 6-21. Which three statements are true regarding the configuration shown in the exhibit? (Choose three.)

Figure 6-21   One-Interface-per-VLAN: Implications

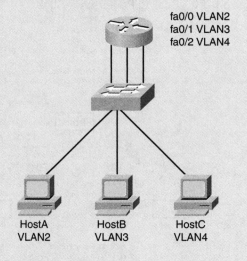

A. The links between the router and switch are access mode links.

B. Each router interface requires a unique IP address on separate subnets for each VLAN.

C. Each switch interface requires a unique IP address on separate subnets for each VLAN.

D. Each router interface requires a **no shutdown** command.

E. A routing protocol must be configured on the router.

F. The router will be configured with the **interface f0/0.2** command.

14. Which three options are valid inter-VLAN routing methods? (Choose three.)

   A. Traditional routing

   B. Spanning-tree routing

   C. Router-on-a-stick

   D. 802.1Q routing

   E. Multilayer-switch-based routing

15. A network technician is configuring a router to support inter-VLAN routing. After entering interface F0/0/1 configuration mode, the network administrator attempts to enter the command **encapsulation dot1q 10**. The router refuses to accept this command. What could account for this failure?

   A. Router port F0/0/1 is not physically connected to the switch.

   B. VLAN0001 has been renamed.

   C. R1 interface F0/0/1 was configured for subinterface operation.

   D. This command can be configured only on router subinterfaces.

   E. Interface F0/0/1 on the switch is shut down.

Challenge Questions and Activities

These questions require a deeper application of the concepts covered in this chapter. You can find the answers in the aappendix.

1. How many physical interfaces are required to perform inter-VLAN routing with each method indicated?

   Traditional inter-VLAN routing: _____

   Router-on-a-stick: _____

   Multilayer switching: _____

2. Refer to Figure 6-22. Assume that VLANs 10 and 30 are instantiated on switch S1. To enable inter-VLAN routing for VLANs 10 and 30, list the appropriate configurations for interface F0/0 on router R1 and interface F0/5 on switch S1.

Figure 6-22   Router-on-a-Stick Topology

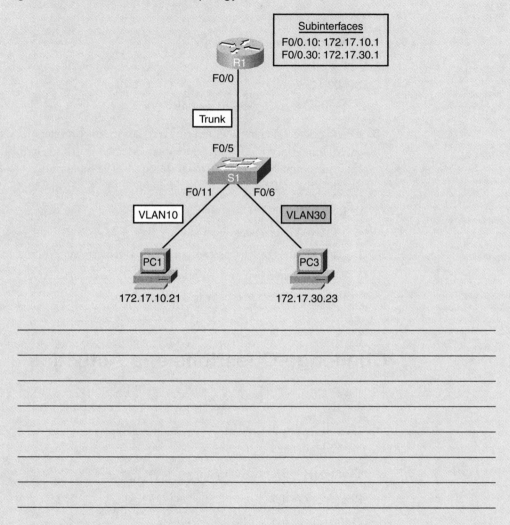

3. Refer to Figure 6-23. PC1 cannot communicate with PC3. List four issues that may be causing the lack of communication.

Figure 6-23   Router-on-a-Stick Issues

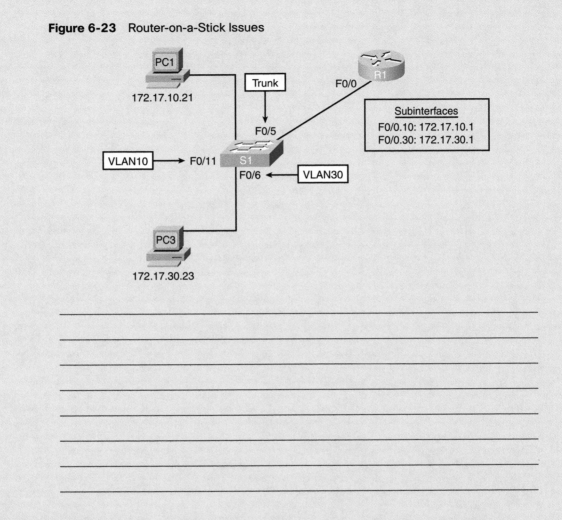

Look for this icon in *LAN Switching and Wireless, CCNA Exploration Labs and Study Guide* (ISBN 1-58713-202-8) for instructions on how to perform the Packet Tracer Skills Integration Challenge for this chapter.

Packet Tracer
☐ Challenge

CHAPTER 7

Basic Wireless Concepts and Configuration

Objectives

Upon completion of this chapter, you will be able to answer the following questions:

- What are the components of a wireless LAN?

- How does a WLAN operate?

- How do you configure and verify WLAN functionality?

- How do you troubleshoot client WLAN access?

Key Terms

This chapter uses the following key terms. You can find the definitions in the Glossary.

wireless LAN (WLAN)   page 380

global positioning system (GPS)   page 380

IEEE 802.11   page 381

radio frequency (RF)   page 382

access point (AP)   page 382

industrial, scientific, and medical (ISM)   page 383

IEEE 802.11a   page 384

IEEE 802.11b   page 384

IEEE 802.11g   page 384

IEEE 802.11n (draft)   page 384

modulation   page 384

direct-sequence spread spectrum (DSSS)   page 384

orthogonal frequency division multiplexing (OFDM)   page 384

interference   page 384

multiple input/multiple output (MIMO)   page 385

International Telecommunications Union-Radio communication sector (ITU-R)   page 386

Wi-Fi Alliance   page 386

IEEE 802 LAN/MAN Standards Committee (LMSC)   page 386

IEEE 802.11i   page 387

wireless NIC   page 387

distributed coordination function (DCF)   page 388

Carrier Sense Multiple Access with Collision Avoidance (CSMA/CA)   page 388

attenuation   page 389

hidden node problem   page 389

request to send/clear to send (RTS/CTS)   page 389

channel   page 389

service set identifier (SSID)   page 392

basic service set (BSS)   page 393

ad hoc   page 394

independent BSS (IBSS)   page 394

basic service area (BSA)   page 394

common distribution system (CDS)   page 394

Switches interconnect devices on a wired network. Typical business networks make extensive use of wired networks. Physical connections are made between computer systems, phone systems, and other peripheral devices to switches located in the wiring closets.

Managing a wired infrastructure can be challenging. Consider what happens when workers decide that they prefer their computer system in a different location in their office, or when a manager wants to bring a notebook to a meeting room and connect to the network there. In a wired network, you need to move the network connection cable to a new location in the worker's office and make sure there is a network connection available in the meeting room. To avoid these physical changes, wireless networks are becoming more and more common.

In this chapter, you learn how wireless local area networks (WLANs) offer businesses a flexible networking environment. You learn the different wireless standards available today and the features that each standard offers. You also learn which hardware components are typically necessary in a wireless infrastructure, how WLANs operate, and how to secure them. Finally, you will learn how to configure a wireless access point and a wireless client.

The Wireless LAN

Business networks today are evolving to support people who are on the move. Employees and employers, students and faculty, government agents and those they serve, sports fans and shoppers, all are mobile and many of them are connected. Perhaps you have a mobile phone that you route instant messages to when you are away from your computer. This is the vision of mobility—an environment where people can take their connection to the network along with them on the road. We continue this motivation for wireless technology as a first step in our wireless exploration.

Why Use Wireless?

Many different infrastructures, such as wired LANs and service provider networks, allow for some degree of mobility, but in a business environment, the most important network solution is the WLAN.

Productivity is no longer restricted to a fixed work location or a defined time period. People now expect to be connected at any time and any place, from the office to the airport and even the home. Twenty years ago, traveling employees used to be restricted to pay phones for checking messages and returning a few phone calls between flights. Now employees can check e-mail, voice mail, and the status of products on personal digital assistants (PDAs) while at temporary locations.

At home, people have changed the way they live and learn. The Internet is a standard service in many homes, along with TV and phone service. It is now fairly common to watch streaming movies on high definition televisions connected to the Internet. Even the method of accessing the Internet has quickly moved from temporary modem dial-up service to dedicated DSL, cable service, and fiber to the home. Home users are seeking many of the same flexible wireless solutions as office workers. In 2005, for the first time, more Wi-Fi-enabled mobile laptops were purchased than fixed desktops.

In addition to the flexibility that WLANs offer, another important benefit is reduced costs. For example, with a wireless infrastructure already in place, savings are realized when moving a person within a building, reorganizing a lab, or moving to temporary locations or project sites. On average, the IT cost of moving an employee to a new location within a site is US$375.

Another example is when a company moves into a new building that does not have a wired infrastructure. In this case, the savings that result from using WLANs can be even more significant, because the cost of running cables through walls, ceilings, and floors is largely avoided.

Although harder to measure, WLANs can result in higher worker productivity and give employees more freedom of movement, leading to improved results for customers and increased profits.

Wireless LANs

Current business networks rely on switch-based LANs for day-to-day operation inside the office. However, workers are becoming more mobile and want to maintain access to their business LAN resources from locations other than their desks. Workers in the office want to take their laptops to meetings or to a co-worker's office. When using a laptop in another location, it is inconvenient to rely on a wired connection. In this chapter, you learn about *wireless LANs (WLANs)* and how they benefit a business. You also explore the security concerns associated with WLANs.

Portable communications have become an expectation in many countries around the world. You can see portability and mobility in everything from cordless keyboards and headsets to satellite phones and *global positioning systems (GPS)*. A range of wireless technologies and standards can be applied to different network applications, as shown in Figure 7-1. This chapter focuses on the application of wireless technologies to extend the LAN with wireless LANs.

WLANs are extensions of Ethernet LANs. Figure 7-2 illustrates a WLAN topology that we use as a reference topology throughout the chapter. We explore WLAN technology and the standards behind the mobility that allows people to participate in meetings while walking, while riding in a taxi, and while waiting for a flight at the airport.

Figure 7-1   Wireless Technologies and Standards

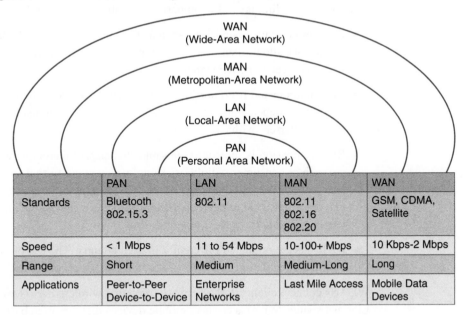

	PAN	LAN	MAN	WAN
Standards	Bluetooth 802.15.3	802.11	802.11 802.16 802.20	GSM, CDMA, Satellite
Speed	< 1 Mbps	11 to 54 Mbps	10-100+ Mbps	10 Kbps-2 Mbps
Range	Short	Medium	Medium-Long	Long
Applications	Peer-to-Peer Device-to-Device	Enterprise Networks	Last Mile Access	Mobile Data Devices

Figure 7-2   Wireless LAN Topology

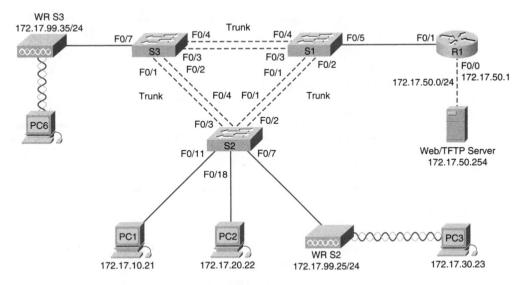

Comparing a WLAN to a LAN

Wireless LANs share a similar origin with Ethernet LANs. The IEEE adopted the 802 LAN/MAN portfolio of computer network architecture standards. The two dominant 802 working groups are IEEE 802.3 Ethernet and *IEEE 802.11* wireless LAN. However, important differences exist between the two.

WLANs use *radio frequencies (RF)* instead of cables at the physical layer and MAC sublayer of the data link layer. In comparison to cable, RF has the following characteristics:

- RF does not have boundaries, such as the limits of a wire in a sheath. The lack of such a boundary allows data frames traveling over the RF media to be available to anyone who can receive the RF signal.

- RF is unprotected from outside signals, whereas cable is in an insulating sheath. Radios operating independently in the same geographic area but using the same or a similar RF can interfere with each other.

- RF transmission is subject to the same challenges inherent in any wave-based technology, such as consumer radio. For example, as you get further from the source, you may hear stations playing over each other or hear static in the transmission. Eventually, you may lose the signal altogether. Wired LANs have cables that are of an appropriate length to maintain signal strength.

- RF bands are regulated differently in each country. The use of WLANs is subject to additional regulations and sets of standards that are not applied to wired LANs.

WLANs connect clients to the network through a wireless *access point (AP)* instead of an Ethernet switch. WLANs connect mobile devices that are often battery powered, in contrast to plugged-in LAN devices. Wireless network interface cards (NICs) tend to reduce the battery life of a mobile device.

WLANs support hosts that contend for access on the RF media via frequency bands. Refer to Table 7-1. 802.11 prescribes collision avoidance instead of collision detection for media access to proactively avoid collisions within the media (which is primarily air).

Table 7-1   Comparing a Wireless LAN to a Wired LAN

Characteristic	802.11 Wireless LAN	802.3 Ethernet LAN	802.3 Switched LAN
Physical Layer	Radio Frequency (RF)	Cable	Cable
Connection	Access Point	Hub	Switch
Media Access	Collision Avoidance	Collision Detection	No collision domain between host and switch
Availability	Anyone with a radio NIC in range of an access pointrequired	Cable connection required	Cable connection
Signal Interference	Yes	Inconsequential	Inconsequential
Regulation	Additional regulation by local authorities	IEEE standard dictates	IEEE standard dictates

WLANs use a different frame format than wired Ethernet LANs. WLANs require additional information in the Layer 2 header of the frame. Also, WLANs raise more privacy issues because radio frequencies can reach outside the respective facility.

Wireless LAN Components

802.11 wireless LANs extend the 802.3 Ethernet LAN infrastructure to provide additional connectivity options. Additional components and protocols are used to complete wireless connections.

In an 802.3 Ethernet LAN, each client has a cable that connects the client NIC to a switch. The switch is the point where the client gains access to the network, as shown in Figure 7-3.

In a wireless LAN, each client uses a wireless adapter to gain access to the network through a wireless device such as a wireless router or access point, as in Figure 7-3.

Figure 7-3   Wireless LAN Components

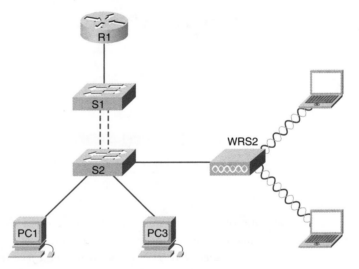

The wireless adapter in the client communicates with the wireless router or access point using RF signals. After they connect to the network, wireless clients can access network resources the same as if they were wired to the network.

Wireless LAN Standards

IEEE 802.11 is a standard that defines how radio frequencies in the unlicensed *industrial, scientific, and medical (ISM)* frequency bands are used for the physical layer and the MAC sublayer of wireless links.

When 802.11 was first released, it prescribed 1–2 Mbps data rates in the 2.4 GHz band. At that time, wired LANs were operating at 10 Mbps, so the new wireless technology was not overwhelmingly adopted. Since then, wireless LAN standards have continuously improved with the release of *IEEE 802.11a*, *IEEE 802.11b*, *IEEE 802.11g*, and *draft 802.11n*.

Typically, the choice of which WLAN standard to use is based on data rates. For instance, 802.11a and g can support up to 54 Mbps, whereas 802.11b supports up to a maximum of 11 Mbps, making 802.11b the slower standard, and 802.11a and 802.11g the preferred ones. A fourth WLAN draft, 802.11n, exceeds the currently available data rates. IEEE 802.11n should be ratified by November 2008. Figure 7-4 compares the ratified IEEE 802.11a, b, and g standards, as well as the draft 802.11n standard.

Figure 7-4   Wireless LAN Standards

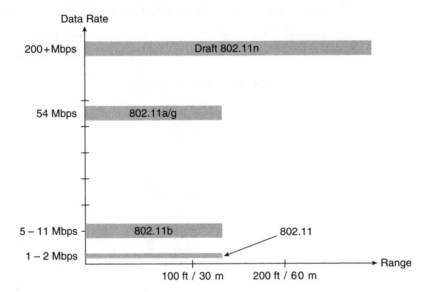

The data rates of different wireless LAN standards are affected by something called a *modulation* technique. The two modulation techniques that you will see in this book are *direct-sequence spread spectrum (DSSS)* and *orthogonal frequency division multiplexing (OFDM)*. You do not need to know how these techniques work for this book, but you should be aware that when a standard uses OFDM, it has faster data rates. Also, DSSS is simpler than OFDM, so it is less expensive to implement.

IEEE 802.11a adopted the OFDM modulation technique and uses the 5 GHz band. 802.11a devices operating in the 5 GHz band are less likely to experience *interference* than devices that operate in the 2.4 GHz band, because fewer consumer devices use the 5 GHz band. Also, higher frequencies allow for the use of smaller antennas.

There are some important disadvantages to using the 5 GHz band. The first is that higher frequency radio waves are more easily absorbed by obstacles such as walls, making 802.11a susceptible to poor performance due to obstructions. The second is that this higher frequency band has slightly poorer range than either 802.11b or g. Also, some countries, including Russia, do not permit the use of the 5 GHz band, which may continue to curtail its deployment.

802.11b specifies data rates of 1, 2, 5.5, and 11 Mbps in the 2.4 GHz ISM band using DSSS. 802.11g achieves higher data rates in that band by using the OFDM modulation technique. IEEE 802.11g also specifies the use of DSSS for backward compatibility with IEEE 802.11b systems. DSSS data rates of 1, 2, 5.5, and 11 Mbps are supported, as are OFDM data rates of 6, 9, 12, 18, 24, 48, and 54 Mbps.

Advantages exist to using the 2.4 GHz band. Devices in the 2.4 GHz band will have better range than those in the 5 GHz band. Also, transmissions in this band are not as easily obstructed as 802.11a. The main disadvantage is the competition with other consumer devices in this frequency range.

The IEEE 802.11n draft standard is intended to improve WLAN data rates and range without requiring additional power or RF band allocation. 802.11n uses multiple radios and antennae at endpoints, each broadcasting on the same frequency to establish multiple streams. The *multiple input/multiple output (MIMO)* technology splits a high data-rate stream into multiple lower rate streams and broadcasts them simultaneously over the available radios and antennae. This allows for a theoretical maximum data rate of 248 Mbps using two streams. The standard is expected to be ratified by November 2008.

Table 7-2 summarizes the wireless LAN standards.

Table 7-2   Wireless LAN Standards

	802.11a	802.11b	802.11g	802.11n
Band	5.7 Ghz	2.4 GHz	2.4 GHz	Possibly 2.4 and 5 GHz
Channels*	Up to 23	3	3	
Modulation	OFDM	DSSS	DSSS/OFDM	MIMO-OFDM
Data Rates	Up to 54 Mbps	Up to 11 Mbps	Up to 11 Mbps/ 54 Mbps	Up to 248 Mbps for two MIMO streams
Pros	Up to 35 meters Fast, less prone to interference	Up to 35 meters Low cost, good range	Up to 35 meters Fast, good range, not easily obstructed	Up to 70 meters Very high data rates, improved range
Cons	Higher cost, shorter range	Slow, prone to interference	Prone to interference from appliances operating on 2.4 GHz band	

Note

RF bands are allocated by the *International Telecommunications Union-Radio communication sector (ITU-R)*. The ITU-R designates the 900 MHz, 2.4 GHz, and 5 GHz frequency bands as unlicensed for ISM communities. Although the ISM bands are globally unlicensed, they are still subject to local regulations. The use of these bands is administered by the FCC in the United States and by the ETSI in Europe. These issues may impact your selection of wireless components in a wireless implementation.

Wi-Fi Certification

Wi-Fi certification is provided by the *Wi-Fi Alliance* (http://www.wi-fi.org), a global, non-profit, industry trade association devoted to promoting the growth and acceptance of wireless technology. You will better appreciate the importance of Wi-Fi certification if you consider the role of the Wi-Fi Alliance in the context of WLAN standards. Wi-Fi–certified products are stamped with the contents of Figure 7-5.

Figure 7-5   Wi-Fi Certified

Standards ensure interoperability between devices made by different manufacturers. Internationally, the three key organizations influencing WLAN standards are

- ITU-R

- IEEE

- Wi-Fi Alliance

The ITU-R regulates the allocation of the RF spectrum and satellite orbits. These are described as finite natural resources that are in demand from such consumers as fixed wireless networks, mobile wireless networks, and global positioning systems.

The IEEE develops and maintains the standards for local and metropolitan area networks with the IEEE 802 LAN/MAN family of standards. IEEE 802 is managed by the *IEEE 802 LAN/MAN Standards Committee (LMSC)*, which oversees multiple working groups. The dominant standards in the IEEE 802 family are 802.3 Ethernet and 802.11 Wireless LAN.

Although the IEEE has specified standards for RF modulation devices, it has not specified manufacturing standards, so interpretations of the 802.11 standards by different vendors can cause interoperability problems between their devices.

The Wi-Fi Alliance is an association of vendors whose objective is to improve the interoperability of products that are based on the 802.11 standard by certifying vendors for conformance to industry norms and adherence to standards. Certification includes all three IEEE 802.11 RF technologies, as well as early adoption of pending IEEE drafts, such as 802.11n, and the WPA and WPA2 security standards based on *IEEE 802.11i*.

The roles of these three organizations can be summarized as follows:

- ITU-R regulates allocation of RF bands.

- IEEE specifies how RF is modulated to carry information.

- Wi-Fi ensures that vendors make devices that are interoperable.

Wireless Infrastructure Components

You may already use a wireless network at home, in a local coffee shop, at work, or at a school that you or one of your family members attends. Have you ever wondered what hardware components are involved in allowing you to wirelessly access the local network or Internet? Here we discuss the components available to implement WLANs and how each is used in the wireless infrastructure.

Wireless NICs

The building block components of a WLAN are client stations that connect to access points that in turn connect to the network infrastructure. The device that makes a client station capable of sending and receiving RF signals is the *wireless NIC*. Figure 7-6 shows some examples of wireless NICs.

Like an Ethernet NIC, the wireless NIC, using the modulation technique it is configured to use, encodes a data stream onto an RF signal. Wireless NICs are most often associated with mobile devices, such as laptop computers. In the 1990s, wireless NICs for laptops were cards that slipped into the PCMCIA slot. PCMCIA wireless NICs are still available, but manufacturers now build wireless NICs right into the laptop. Unlike 802.3 Ethernet interfaces built into PCs, the wireless NIC is not visible, because there is no requirement to connect a cable to it.

Other options have emerged over the years as well. Desktops located in an existing, non-wired facility can have a wireless PCI NIC installed. To quickly set up a PC, mobile or desktop, with a wireless NIC, many USB options are available.

Figure 7-6   Wireless NICs

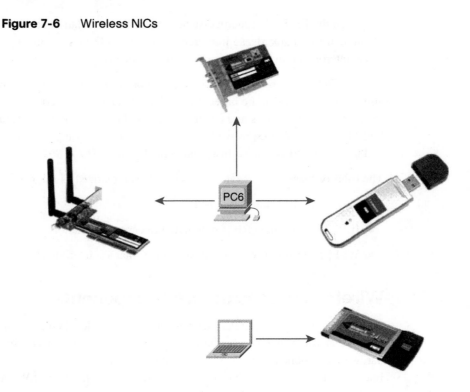

Wireless Access Points

An access point (AP) connects wireless clients (or stations) to the wired LAN. Client devices do not typically communicate directly with each other; they communicate through the AP. In essence, an AP converts the TCP/IP data packets from their 802.11 frame encapsulation format in the air to the 802.3 Ethernet frame format on the wired Ethernet network, and vice versa. Figure 7-7 illustrates wireless access points being used in a production environment.

In an infrastructure network, clients must associate with an access point to obtain network services. Association is the process by which a client joins an 802.11 network. It is similar to plugging into a wired LAN. Association is discussed in more detail later in the chapter.

An access point is a Layer 2 device that functions like an 802.3 Ethernet hub. RF is a shared medium and access points hear all radio traffic. Just as with 802.3 Ethernet, the devices that want to use the medium contend for it. Unlike Ethernet NICs, though, it is expensive to make wireless NICs that can transmit and receive at the same time, so radio devices do not detect collisions. Instead, WLAN devices are designed to avoid them.

Access points oversee a *distributed coordination function (DCF)* called *Carrier Sense Multiple Access with Collision Avoidance (CSMA/CA)*. This means that devices on a WLAN must sense the medium for energy levels and wait until the medium is free before sending. Because all devices are required to do this, the function of coordinating access to the medium is distributed. If an AP receives data from a client station, it sends an acknowledgement to the client that the data has been received. This acknowledgement keeps the client from assuming that a collision occurred and prevents a data retransmission by the client.

Figure 7-7   Wireless Access Points

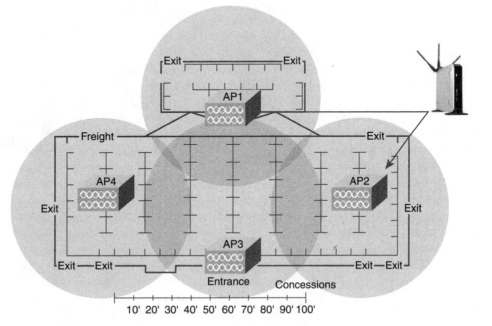

RF signals attenuate. That means that they lose their energy as they move away from their point of origin. Think about driving out of range of a radio station. This signal *attenuation* can be a problem in a WLAN where stations contend for the medium.

Imagine two client stations that both connect to the access point, but are at opposite sides of its reach. If they are at the maximum range to reach the AP, they will not be able to reach each other. So neither of those stations sense the other on the medium, and they may end up transmitting simultaneously. This is known as the *hidden node problem*, illustrated in Figure 7-8. Here, Vivian might be unable to access the medium because of another station that is within range of the AP, yet out of range of her station. Vivian and George are in range of each other and in range of the AP. Yet neither of them is in range of Tony. Tony is in range of the AP and attempts to transmit on the medium as well. Tony is hidden to Vivian and George.

One means of resolving the hidden node problem is a CSMA/CA feature called *request to send/clear to send (RTS/CTS)*. RTS/CTS was developed to allow a negotiation between a client and an access point. When RTS/CTS is enabled in a network, access points allocate the medium to the requesting station for as long as is required to complete the transmission. When the transmission is complete, other stations can request the *channel* in a similar fashion. Otherwise, normal collision avoidance function is resumed.

Figure 7-8   Hidden Node Problem

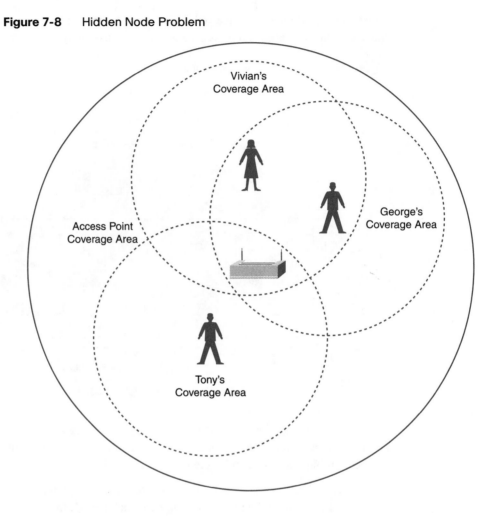

Wireless Routers

Wireless routers perform the roles of access point, Ethernet switch, and router. For example, the Linksys WRT300N shown in Figure 7-9 is really three devices in one box. First is the wireless access point, which performs the typical functions of an access point. A built-in four-port, full-duplex, 10/100 switch provides connectivity to wired devices. Finally, the router function provides a gateway for connecting to other network infrastructures.

The WRT300N is commonly used as a small business or residential wireless access device. The expected load on the device is low enough that it should be able to manage the WLAN requirements, the 802.3 Ethernet requirements, and connect to an ISP.

Figure 7-9   Wireless Routers

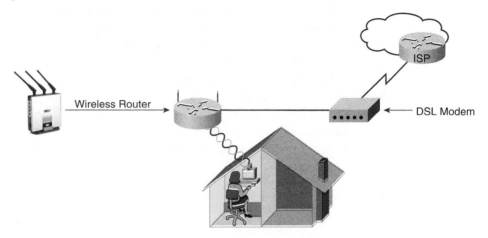

Wireless Operation

Wireless operation entails configurable parameters for wireless access points (a/b/g/n, SSIDs, and channels), 802.11 topologies (ad hoc, BSS, and ESS), authentication (open, shared), and association (beacons, probes). Next we explore these core functions of wireless operation.

Configurable Wireless Parameters

Figure 7-10 shows the initial screen for wireless configuration on a Linksys wireless router. Several processes take place in creating a connection between a client and an access point. To this end, you need to configure parameters on the access point and on the client device.

Figure 7-10   Configurable Wireless Parameters

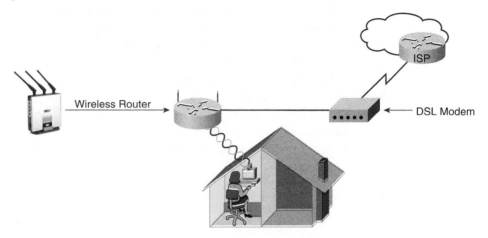

The wireless network mode refers to the WLAN protocols: 802.11a, b, g, or n. Because 802.11g is backward compatible with 802.11b, access points support both standards. Remember that if all the clients connect to an access point with 802.11g, they all enjoy the better data rates provided. When 802.11b clients associate with the access point, all the faster clients contending for the channel have to wait on 802.11b clients to clear the channel before transmitting, thus effectively reducing the 802.11g clients to 802.11b speeds (11 Mbps maximum). When a Linksys access point is configured to allow both 802.11b and 802.11g clients, as in Figure 7-11, it is configured to operate in mixed mode. An access point can simultaneously operate in both 2.4 and 5 GHz frequency ranges if two separate radio interfaces and antennas are provided; this capability is typically found only on enterprise access points.

Figure 7-11   Mixed Mode

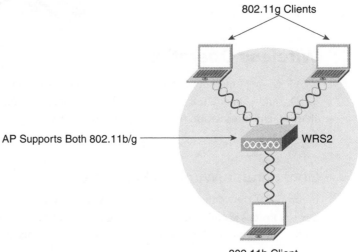

A shared *service set identifier (SSID)* is a unique identifier that client devices use to distinguish between multiple wireless networks in the same vicinity. An SSID is an alphanumeric, case-sensitive string from 2 to 32 characters in length. Several access points on a network can share the same SSID to enable roaming by clients. Figure 7-12 shows an example of a list of wireless LANs detected by a wireless NIC and defined by their SSIDs.

The radio transmitters and receivers on WLAN devices operate over a range of frequencies, also known as frequency bands. The IEEE 802.11 standard establishes the channelization scheme for the use of the unlicensed ISM RF bands in WLANs. Figure 7-13 illustrates a range of frequencies between 2.4 and 2.483 GHz. The 2.4 GHz band is broken down into 11 channels for North America and 13 channels for Europe. These channels have a center frequency separation of only 5 MHz and an overall channel bandwidth (or frequency occupation) of 22 MHz. The 22 MHz channel bandwidth combined with the 5 MHz separation between center frequencies means an overlap exists between successive channels.

Figure 7-12   SSID

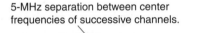

Figure 7-13   2.4 GHz Channels

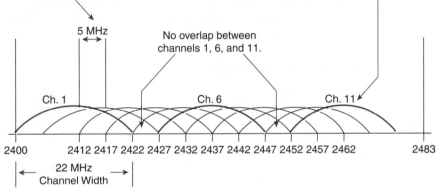

A best practices for WLANs requiring multiple access points is to use nonoverlapping channels. For example, if there are three adjacent access points, use channels 1, 6, and 11. If there are just two, select any two that are five channels apart, such as channels 5 and 10. Many access points can automatically select a channel based on adjacent channel use. Some products continuously monitor the radio space to adjust the channel settings dynamically in response to environmental changes.

Wireless Topologies

Wireless LANs can accommodate various network topologies. When describing these topologies, the fundamental building block of the IEEE 802.11 WLAN architecture is the *basic service set (BSS)*. The standard defines a BSS as a group of stations that communicate with each other.

Wireless networks can operate without access points; this is called an *ad hoc* topology, illustrated in Figure 7-14. Client stations that are configured to operate in ad hoc mode configure the wireless parameters between themselves. The IEEE 802.11 standard refers to an ad hoc network as an *independent BSS (IBSS)*.

Figure 7-14   Ad Hoc

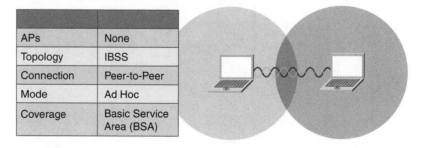

APs	None
Topology	IBSS
Connection	Peer-to-Peer
Mode	Ad Hoc
Coverage	Basic Service Area (BSA)

Access points provide an infrastructure that adds services and improves the range for clients. A single access point in infrastructure mode manages the wireless parameters, and the topology is simply a BSS, pictured in Figure 7-15. The coverage area for both an IBSS and a BSS is the *basic service area (BSA)*.

Figure 7-15   Basic Service Set

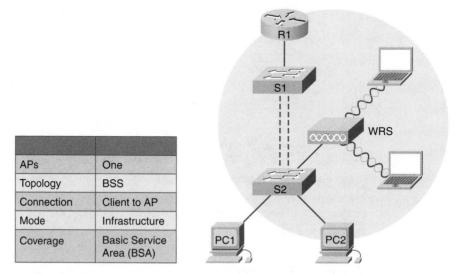

APs	One
Topology	BSS
Connection	Client to AP
Mode	Infrastructure
Coverage	Basic Service Area (BSA)

When a single BSS provides insufficient RF coverage, one or more can be joined through a *common distribution system* into an *extended service set (ESS)*, pictured in Figure 7-16. In an ESS, one BSS is differentiated from another by the *BSS identifier (BSSID)*, which is the MAC address of the access point serving the BSS. The coverage area is the *extended service area (ESA)*.

Figure 7-16   Extended Service Set

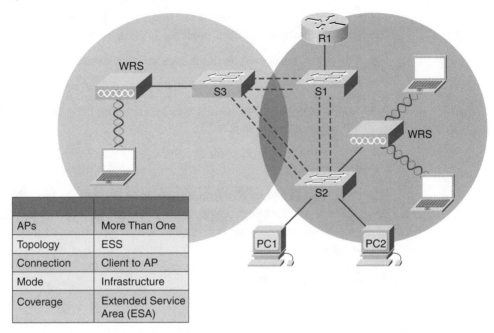

APs	More Than One
Topology	ESS
Connection	Client to AP
Mode	Infrastructure
Coverage	Extended Service Area (ESA)

The common distribution system allows multiple access points in an ESS to appear to be a single BSS. An ESS generally includes a common SSID to allow a user to roam from access point to access point. Table 7-3 summarizes the 802.11 topologies.

Table 7-3   IEEE 802.11 Topologies

Wireless Devices	Topology Mode	Topology Building Block	Coverage Area
No access points	Ad Hoc	Independent Basic Service Set (IBSS)	Basic Service Area (BSA)
One access point	Infrastructure	Basic Service Set (BSS)	Basic Service Area (BSA)
More than one access point	Infrastructure	Extended Service Set (ESS)	Extended Service Area (ESA)

Cells represent the coverage area provided by a single channel. An ESS should have 10 to 15 percent overlap between cells in an extended service area. With a 15 percent overlap between cells, an SSID, and nonoverlapping channels (one cell on channel 1 and the other on channel 6), roaming capability is facilitated.

Wireless Association

A key part of the 802.11 process is discovering a WLAN and subsequently connecting to it. The primary components of this process are as follows:

- *Beacons*: Frames used by the WLAN network to advertise its presence.

- *Probes*: Frames used by WLAN clients to find their networks.

- *Authentication*: A process that is an artifact from the original 802.11 standard, but is still required by the standard.

- *Association*: The process for establishing the data link between an access point and a WLAN client.

The primary purpose of the beacon, shown in Figure 7-17, is to allow WLAN clients to learn which networks and access points are available in a given area, thereby allowing them to choose which network and access point to use. Access points may broadcast beacons periodically.

Figure 7-17   Beacons

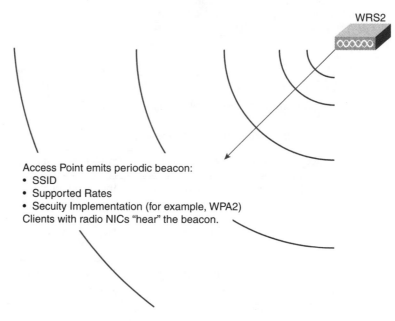

Access Point emits periodic beacon:
- SSID
- Supported Rates
- Secuity Implementation (for example, WPA2)
Clients with radio NICs "hear" the beacon.

Although beacons may regularly be broadcast by an access point, the frames for probing, authentication, and association are used only during the association (or reassociation) process.

Before an 802.11 client can send data over a WLAN network, it goes through the following three-stage process:

Stage 1.   802.11 probing

Clients search for a specific network by sending a probe request out on multiple channels. The probe request, pictured in Figure 7-18, specifies the network name (SSID) and bit rates. A typical WLAN client is configured with a desired SSID, so probe requests from the WLAN client contain the SSID of the desired WLAN network.

Figure 7-18   Probes

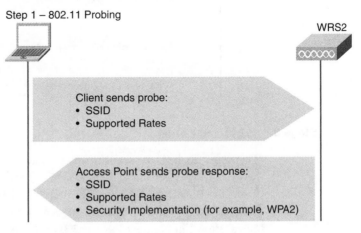

Step 1 – 802.11 Probing

WRS2

Client sends probe:
• SSID
• Supported Rates

Access Point sends probe response:
• SSID
• Supported Rates
• Security Implementation (for example, WPA2)

 Quiz?

If the WLAN client is trying to discover the available WLAN networks, it can send out a probe request with no SSID, and all access points that are configured to respond to this type of query respond. WLANs with the broadcast SSID feature disabled do not respond.

Stage 2.   802.11 authentication

IEEE 802.11 was originally developed with two authentication mechanisms. The first one, called open authentication, is fundamentally a NULL authentication where the client says "authenticate me," and the access point responds with "yes." This is the mechanism used in almost all 802.11 deployments and is illustrated in Figure 7-19.

A second authentication mechanism is based on a key that is shared between the client station and the access point called the *Wired Equivalent Privacy (WEP)* key. The idea of the shared WEP key is that it gives a wireless link the equivalent privacy of a wired link, but the original implementation of this authentication method was flawed. Although shared key authentication needs to be included in client and access point implementations for overall standards compliance, it is not used or recommended.

Figure 7-19   Authentication

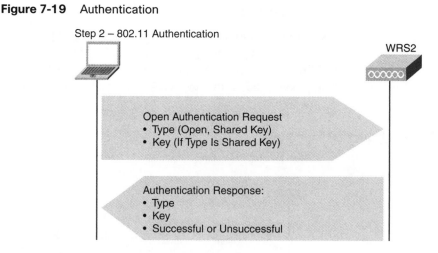

Step 2 – 802.11 Authentication

WRS2

Open Authentication Request
• Type (Open, Shared Key)
• Key (If Type Is Shared Key)

Authentication Response:
• Type
• Key
• Successful or Unsuccessful

Stage 3.   802.11 association

This stage finalizes the security and bit-rate options, and establishes the data link between the WLAN client and the access point. As part of this stage, the client learns the BSSID, which is the access point MAC address, and the access point maps a logical port known as the *association identifier (AID)* to the WLAN client, shown in Figure 7-20. The AID is equivalent to a port on a switch. The association process allows the infrastructure switch to keep track of frames destined for the WLAN client so that they can be forwarded.

Figure 7-20   Association

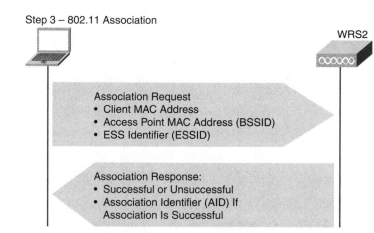

Step 3 – 802.11 Association

WRS2

Association Request
• Client MAC Address
• Access Point MAC Address (BSSID)
• ESS Identifier (ESSID)

Association Response:
• Successful or Unsuccessful
• Association Identifier (AID) If
  Association Is Successful

After a WLAN client has associated with an access point, traffic can travel back and forth between the two devices.

Planning the Wireless LAN

Implementing a WLAN that takes the best advantage of resources and delivers the best service requires careful planning. WLANs can range from relatively simple installations to very complex and intricate designs. A well-documented plan must be in place before a wireless network can be implemented. Here we introduce what considerations go into the design and planning of a wireless LAN.

The number of users a WLAN can support is not a straightforward calculation. The number or users depends on the geographical layout of your facility (how many people and devices fit in a space), the data rates users expect (because RF is a shared medium and the more users there are the greater the contention for RF), the use of nonoverlapping channels by multiple access points in an ESS, and *transmit power* settings (which are limited by local regulation). You will have sufficient wireless support for your clients if you plan your network for proper RF coverage in an ESS. Detailed consideration of how to plan for specific numbers of users is beyond the scope of this book.

You begin with a map of the area that will be supported with the wireless solution, as shown in Figure 7-21. When planning the location of access points, you may not be able to simply draw coverage area circles and drop them over a plan. The approximate circular coverage area is important, but there are some additional recommendations.

Figure 7-21   Wireless Design Map

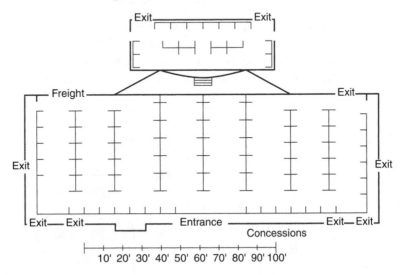

If access points are to use existing wiring or if there are locations where access points cannot be placed, note these locations on the map.

■ Position access points above obstructions.

- Position access points vertically near the ceiling in the center of each coverage area, if possible.

- Position access points in locations where users are expected to be. For example, conference rooms are typically a better location for access points than a hallway.

When these points have been addressed, estimate the expected coverage area of an access point. This value varies depending on the WLAN standard or mix of standards that you are deploying, the nature of the facility, the transmit power for which the access point is configured, and so on. Always consult the specifications for the access point when planning for coverage areas. Based on your plan, place access points on the floor plan so that coverage circles are overlapping.

Let us look at a sample calculation. The open auditorium (a warehouse/manufacturing building type) shown in Figure 7-21 is approximately 20,000 square feet.

Network requirements specify that there must be a minimum of 6 Mbps 802.11b throughput in each BSA, because there is a wireless voice over WLAN implementation on the network. With access points, 6 Mbps can be achieved in open areas like those on the map, with a coverage area of 5,000 square feet in many environments.

Note

The 5,000 square foot coverage area is for a square. The BSA takes its radius diagonally from the center of this square.

We determine where to place the access points using the breakdown in Figure 7-22. The facility is 20,000 square feet; dividing 20,000 square feet by a coverage area of 5,000 square feet per access point results in at least four access points required for the auditorium. Next, determine the dimension of the coverage areas and arrange them on the floor plan.

Figure 7-22   Coverage Area

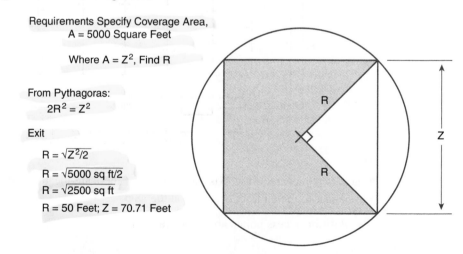

Requirements Specify Coverage Area,
A = 5000 Square Feet

Where $A = Z^2$, Find R

From Pythagoras:
$$2R^2 = Z^2$$

Exit

$R = \sqrt{Z^2/2}$
$R = \sqrt{5000\ sq\ ft/2}$
$R = \sqrt{2500\ sq\ ft}$
$R = 50$ Feet; $Z = 70.71$ Feet

Because the coverage area is a square with side length Z, the circle that circumscribes the square has a radius of 50 feet, as derived in the calculations. When the dimensions of the coverage area have been determined, you arrange them in a manner similar to those shown in Figure 7-23.

Figure 7-23   Aligning Coverage Area

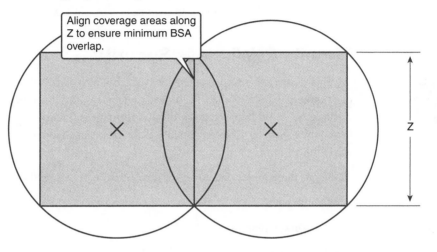

On your floorplan map, arrange four 50-foot radius coverage circles so that they overlap, as shown in Figure 7-24.

Figure 7-24   Wireless Plan

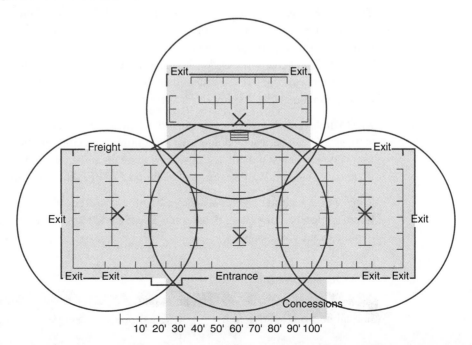

Wireless LAN Security

Security should be a priority for anyone who uses or administers networks. The difficulties in keeping a wired network secure are amplified with a wireless network. A WLAN is open to anyone within range of an access point and the appropriate credentials to associate to it. With a wireless NIC and knowledge of cracking techniques, an attacker may not have to physically enter the workplace to gain access to a WLAN.

Threats to Wireless Security

We first describe how wireless security threats have evolved. These security concerns are even more significant when dealing with business networks, because the livelihood of the business relies on the protection of its information. Security breaches for a business can have major repercussions, especially if the business maintains financial information associated with its customers.

There are three major categories of threat that lead to unauthorized access:

- War drivers
- Hackers (Crackers)
- Employees

War driving originally referred to using a scanning device to find cellular phone numbers to exploit. War driving now also means driving around a neighborhood with a laptop and an 802.11 client card looking for an unsecured 802.11 system to exploit.

The term *hacker* originally meant someone who delved deeply into computer systems to understand, and perhaps exploit for creative purposes, the structure and complexity of a system. The term *ethical hacker* is now used to differentiate a well-intentioned hacker from a criminal. Today, the terms hacker and *cracker* have come to mean malicious intruders who enter systems as criminals and steal data or deliberately harm systems. Hackers intent on doing harm are able to exploit weak security measures.

Most wireless devices sold today are WLAN-ready. In other words, the devices have default settings and can be installed and used with little or no configuration by users. Often, end users do not change default settings, leaving client authentication open, or they may implement only standard WEP security. Unfortunately, WEP keys are broken relatively easily.

Tools with a legitimate purpose, such as wireless sniffers, allow network engineers to capture data packets for system debugging. These same tools can be used by intruders to exploit security weaknesses.

Rogue Access Points

A *rogue access point* is an access point placed on a WLAN that is used to interfere with normal network operation. If a rogue access point is configured with the correct security settings, client data can be captured. A rogue access point can also be configured to provide unauthorized users with information such as the MAC addresses of clients (both wireless and wired), or to capture and disguise data packets, or even to gain access to servers and files.

A simple and common version of a rogue access point is one installed by employees without authorization. Employees install access points intended for home use on the enterprise network. These access points typically do not have the necessary security configuration, so the network ends up with a security hole.

Man-in-the-Middle Attacks

One of the more sophisticated attacks an unauthorized user can make is a *man-in-the-middle (MITM)* attack, pictured in Figure 7-25. Attackers select a host as a target and position themselves logically between the target and the router or gateway of the target. In a wired LAN environment, the attacker needs to be able to physically access the LAN to insert a device logically into the topology. With a WLAN, the radio waves emitted by access points can provide the connection.

Figure 7-25   Man-in-the-Middle Attack

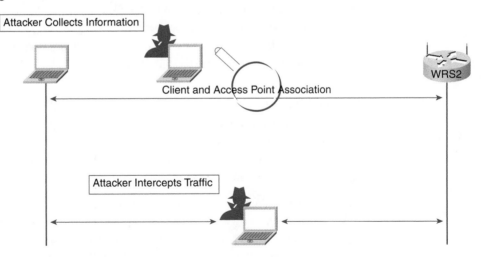

Radio signals from stations and access points are audible by anyone in a BSS with the proper equipment, such as a laptop with a NIC. Because access points act like Ethernet hubs, each NIC in a BSS hears all the traffic. A device discards any traffic not addressed to it. Attackers can modify the NIC of their laptop with special software so that it accepts all traffic. With this modification, the attacker can carry out wireless MITM attacks, using the laptop NIC acts as an access point.

To carry out this attack, a hacker selects a station as a target and uses packet-sniffing software, such as Wireshark, to observe the client station connecting to an access point. The hacker might be able to read and copy the target username, server name, client and server IP address, the ID used to compute the response, and the challenge and associate response, which is passed in clear text between station and access point.

If an attacker is able to compromise an access point, the attacker can potentially compromise all users in the BSS. The attacker can monitor an entire wireless network segment and wreak havoc on any users connected to it.

Defeating an attack such as a MITM attack depends on the sophistication of your WLAN infrastructure and your vigilance in monitoring activity on the network. The process begins with identifying legitimate devices on your WLAN. To do this, you must authenticate users on your WLAN.

When all legitimate users are known, you then monitor the network for devices and traffic that is not supposed to be there. Enterprise WLANs that use state-of-the-art WLAN devices provide administrators with tools that work together as a wireless *intrusion prevention system (IPS)*. These tools include scanners that identify rogue access points and ad hoc networks, and *radio resource management (RRM),* which monitors the RF band for activity and access point load. An access point that is busier than normal alerts the administrator of possible unauthorized traffic.

Further explanation of these mitigation techniques is beyond the scope of this book. For more information, refer to the Cisco paper "Addressing Wireless Threats with Integrated Wireless IDS and IPS" available at www.cisco.com/en/US/products/ps6521/products_white_paper0900aecd804f155b.shtml.

Denial of Service

802.11b and 802.11g WLANs use the unlicensed 2.4 GHz ISM band. This is the same band used by most wireless consumer products, including baby monitors, cordless phones, and microwave ovens. With these devices crowding the RF band, attackers can create noise on all the channels in the band with commonly available devices, as illustrated in Figure 7-26.

An attacker can turn a NIC into an access point. This can in turn be used to create a DoS attack. The attacker, using a PC as an access point, can flood the BSS with *clear-to-send (CTS)* messages, which defeat the CSMA/CA function used by the stations. The access points, in turn, flood the BSS with simultaneous traffic, causing a constant stream of collisions.

Another DoS attack that can be launched in a BSS occurs when an attacker sends a series of disassociate commands that cause all stations in the BSS to disconnect. When the stations are disconnected, they immediately try to reassociate, which creates a burst of traffic. The attacker sends another disassociate command and the cycle repeats itself. This process is illustrated in Figure 7-27.

Figure 7-26   Unorchestrated Denial of Service

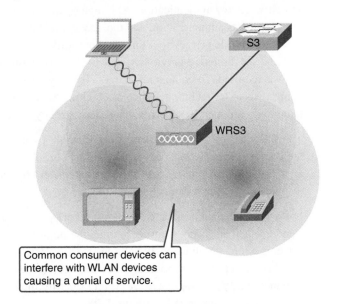

Figure 7-27   Orchestrated Denial of Service

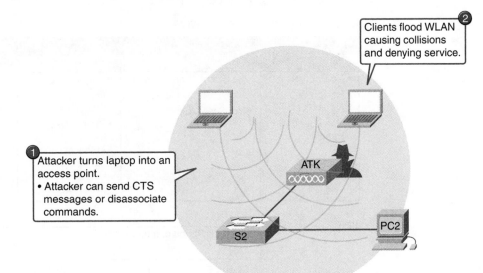

Wireless Security Protocols

We now have sufficient background to begin our exploration of the common wireless protocols and the level of security each provides.

Two types of authentication were introduced with the original 802.11 standard: open and shared WEP key authentication. Although open authentication is really no authentication (a client requests authentication and the access point grants it), WEP authentication was supposed to provide privacy to a link, making it like a cable connecting a PC to an Ethernet wall jack. As we discussed previously, shared WEP keys proved to be flawed and something better was required. To counteract shared WEP key weaknesses, the very first approach by companies was to try techniques such as cloaking SSIDs and filtering MAC addresses; these two techniques are merely superficial and do not really qualify as valid security measures.

The flaws with WEP shared-key encryption are twofold. First, the algorithm used to encrypt the data is crackable. Second, scalability is a problem. The 32-bit WEP keys must be managed individually, one-by-one, so users enter them by hand, often incorrectly, resulting in trouble calls to the technical support desk.

Following the weakness of WEP-based security was a period of interim security measures. Vendors such as Cisco, wanting to meet the demand for better security, developed their own systems while simultaneously helping to evolve the 802.11i standard. On the way to 802.11i, the TKIP encryption algorithm was created, which was linked to the Wi-Fi Alliance *Wi-Fi Protected Access (WPA)* security method. The evolving wireless security solutions are summarized in Figure 7-28.

Figure 7-28   Wireless Protocol Overview

Major Stepping Stones to Secure WLAN

Open Access	First Generation Encryption	Interim	Present
SSID	WEP	WPA	802.11i/WPA2
• No Encryption • Basic Authentication • Not a Security Handle	• No Strong Authentication • Static, Breakable Keys • Not Scalable	• Standardized • Improved Encryption • Strong, User-Based Authentication (for Example, LEAP, PEAP, EAP-FAST)	• AES Encryption • Authentication: 802.1x • Dynamic Key Management • WPA2 Is the Wi-Fi Alliance Implementation of 802.11i

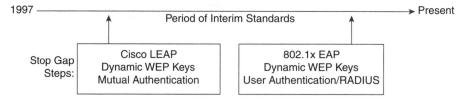

Today, the standard that is followed in most enterprise networks is the 802.11i standard. This is similar to the Wi-Fi Alliance *WPA2* standard. For enterprises, WPA2 includes a connection to a *Remote Authentication Dial In User Service (RADIUS)* database. RADIUS will be described later in the chapter.

For more about the WEP security weakness, see the paper "Security of the WEP Algorithm" available at www.isaac.cs.berkeley.edu/isaac/wep-faq.html.

Authenticating the Wireless LAN

In an open network, such as a home network, association may be all that is required to grant a client access to devices and services on the WLAN. In networks that have stricter security requirements, an additional authentication or login is required to grant clients such access. This login process is managed by the *Extensible Authentication Protocol (EAP)*. EAP is a framework for authenticating network access. IEEE developed the 802.11i standard for WLAN authentication and authorization to use *IEEE 802.1x*.

The enterprise WLAN authentication process is summarized as follows:

- The 802.11 association process creates a virtual port for each WLAN client at the access point.

- The access point blocks all data frames, except for 802.1x-based traffic, as shown in Figure 7-29.

Figure 7-29   Enterprise WLAN Association

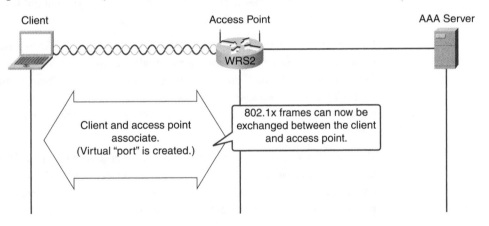

- The 802.1x frames carry the EAP authentication packets via the access point to a server that maintains authentication credentials. This server is an *Authentication, Authorization, and Accounting (AAA)* server running the RADIUS protocol.

- If the EAP authentication is successful, the AAA server sends an EAP success message to the access point, as shown in Figure 7-30, which then allows data traffic from the WLAN client to pass through the virtual port.

- Before opening the virtual port, data link encryption between the WLAN client and the access point is established to ensure that no other WLAN client can access the port that has been established for a given authenticated client.

Figure 7-30   EAP Authentication

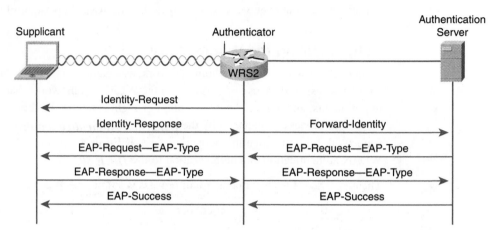

Before WPA2 was in use, some companies tried to secure their WLANs by filtering MAC addresses and not broadcasting SSIDs. Today, it is easy to use software to modify MAC addresses attached to adapters, so MAC address filtering is easily hacked. It does not mean you should not do it, but if you are using this method, you should back it up with additional security measures, such as WPA2.

Even if an SSID is not broadcast by an access point, the traffic that passes back and forth between the client and access point eventually reveals the SSID. If an attacker is passively monitoring the RF band, the SSID can be sniffed in one of these transactions because it is sent in clear text. The ease of discovering SSIDs has led some people to leave SSID broadcasting turned on. If so, that should probably be an organizational decision recorded in the security policy.

The idea that you can secure your WLAN with nothing more than MAC filtering and turning off SSID broadcasts leads to a completely insecure WLAN. The best way to ensure that end users are supposed to be on the WLAN is to use a security method that incorporates port-based network access control, such as WPA2.

Wireless Encryption

Two enterprise-level encryption mechanisms specified by 802.11i are certified as WPA and WPA2 by the Wi-Fi Alliance: *Temporal Key Integrity Protocol (TKIP)* and *Advanced Encryption Standard (AES)*.

TKIP is the encryption method certified as WPA. It provides support for legacy WLAN equipment by addressing the original flaws associated with the 802.11 WEP encryption method. It makes use of the original encryption algorithm used by WEP.

TKIP has two primary functions:

- It encrypts the Layer 2 payload.

- It carries out a *message integrity check (MIC)* in the encrypted packet. This helps ensure against a message being tampered with.

Although TKIP addresses all the known weaknesses of WEP, the AES encryption of WPA2 is the preferred method because it brings the WLAN encryption standards into alignment with broader IT industry standards and best practices, most notably IEEE 802.11i.

AES has the same functions as TKIP, but it uses additional data from the MAC header that allows destination hosts to recognize if the nonencrypted bits have been tampered with. It also adds a sequence number to the encrypted data header.

When you configure Linksys access points or wireless routers, such as the WRT300N, you may not see WPA or WPA2; instead, you may see references to something called *pre-shared key (PSK)*. Various types of PSKs are as follows:

- PSK or PSK2 with TKIP is the same as WPA.

- PSK or PSK2 with AES is the same as WPA2.

- PSK2, without an encryption method specified, is the same as WPA2.

Controlling Access to the WLAN

The concept of depth means having multiple solutions available. It is analogous to having a security system in your house, but still locking all the doors and windows and asking the neighbors to keep an eye on your house. The security methods you have seen, especially WPA2, are similar to having a security system. If you want to do something extra to secure access to your WLAN, you can add depth, as shown in Figure 7-31, by implementing this three-step approach:

- **SSID cloaking:** Disable SSID broadcasts from the access points.

- **MAC address filtering**: Tables are manually constructed on the access point to allow or disallow clients based on their physical hardware address.

- **WLAN security implementation**: WPA or WPA2 are available.

An additional consideration for a vigilant network administrator is to configure access points that are near outside walls of buildings to transmit on a lower power setting than other access points closer to the middle of the building. This is merely to reduce the RF signature on the outside of the building where anyone running an application such as Netstumbler (www.netstumbler.com), Wireshark, or even Windows Vista, can map WLANs.

Neither SSID cloaking nor MAC address filtering are considered a valid means of securing a WLAN for the following reasons:

- MAC addresses are easily spoofed.

- SSIDs are easily discovered even if access points do not broadcast them.

Figure 7-31   Controlling Access to the WLAN

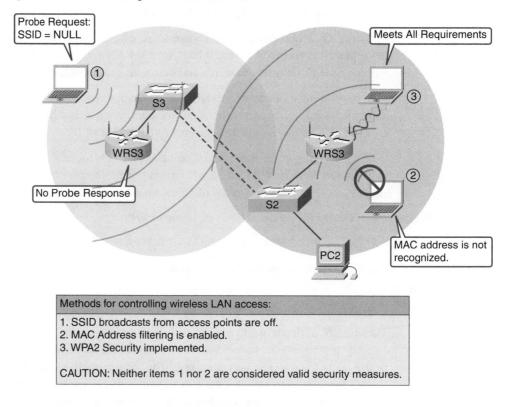

Configure Wireless LAN Access

With a solid foundation of basic wireless LAN theory in place, we move forward to configuring wireless access points. You will learn how to set the SSID, enable security, configure the channel, and adjust the power settings for a wireless access point. You also learn how to back up and restore the configuration of a typical wireless access point.

Configuring the Wireless Access Point

The basic approach to wireless implementation, as with any basic networking, is to configure and test incrementally. Before implementing any wireless devices, verify the existing network and Internet access for the wired hosts. Start the WLAN implementation process with a single access point and a single client, without enabling wireless security. Verify that the wireless client has received a DHCP IP address and can ping the local wired default router and then browse to the Internet. Finally, configure wireless security with WPA2. Use WEP only if the hardware does not support WPA.

Most access points have been designed to be functional right out of the box with the default settings. It is good practice to change initial default configurations. Many access points can be configured through a GUI web interface.

With a plan for implementation in mind, wired network connectivity confirmed, and the access point installed, you will now configure it. The following example uses the Linksys WRT300N multifunction device.

First, ensure that your PC is connected to the access point via a wired connection, and access the web utility with a web browser. To access the web-based utility of the access point, launch Internet Explorer (for example) and enter the WRT300N default IP address, 192.168.1.1, into the address field. Press the Enter key.

A screen appears, prompting you for your username and password. Leave the Username field blank. Enter **admin** in the Password field. These are the default settings for a Linksys WRT300N. If the device has already been configured, the username and password may have been changed. Click **OK** to continue.

For a basic network setup use the **Setup**, **Management**, and **Wireless** options in the web-based utility:

- **Setup:** Enter your basic network settings, as in Figure 7-32.

Figure 7-32   Linksys Basic Setup

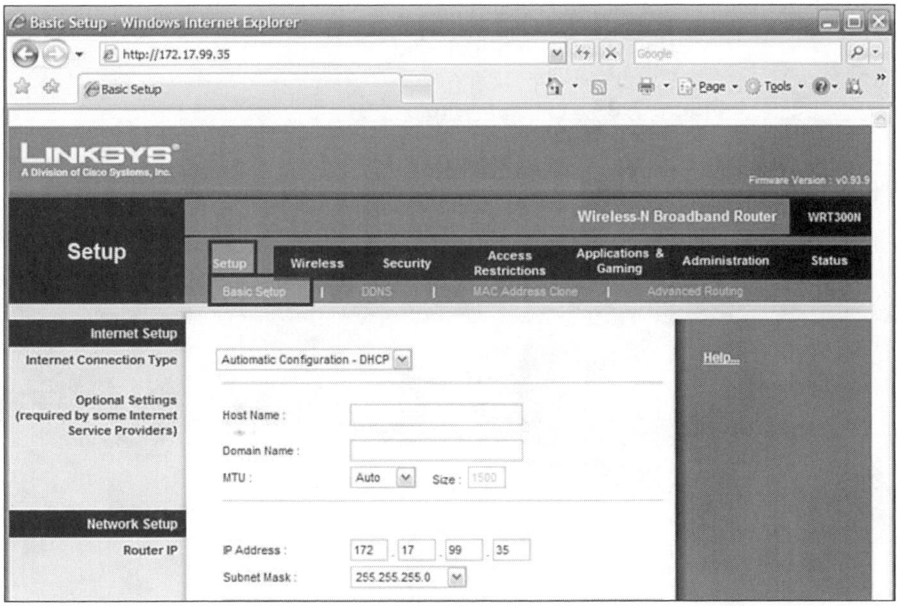

- **Management**: Click the **Administration** tab and then select the **Management** screen. The default password is **admin**. To secure the access point, change the password from its default, as in Figure 7-33.

Figure 7-33   Linksys Administration Setup

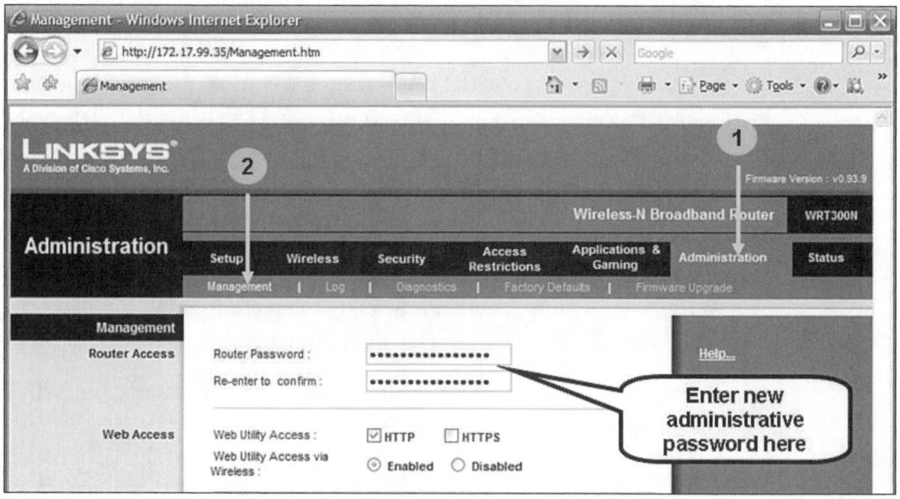

■ **Wireless**: Change the default SSID in the **Basic Wireless Settings** tab. Select the level of security in the **Wireless Security** tab and complete the options for the selected security mode, as in Figure 7-34.

Figure 7-34   Linksys Wireless Setup

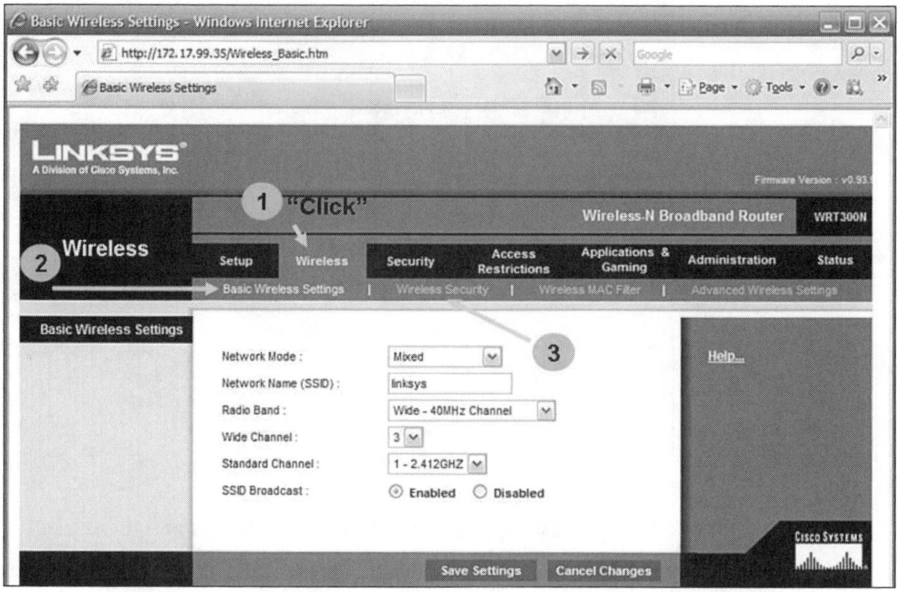

Make the necessary changes through the utility. When you have finished making changes to a screen, click the **Save Settings** button, or click the **Cancel Changes** button to undo your changes. For information on a tab, click Help.

Configuring Basic Wireless Settings

The Basic Setup screen is the first screen you see when you access the web-based utility. Click the **Wireless** tab and then select the **Basic Wireless Settings** tab, as in Figure 7-35. Several configuration options are available.

Figure 7-35   Basic Wireless Settings

- **Network Mode:** If you have Wireless-N, Wireless-G, and Wireless-B devices in your network, keep **Mixed**, the default setting. If you have Wireless-G and Wireless-B devices, select **BG-Mixed**. If you have only Wireless-N devices, select **Wireless-N Only**. If you have only Wireless-G devices, select **Wireless-G Only**. If you have only Wireless-B devices, select **Wireless-B Only**. If you want to disable wireless networking, select **Disable**. These modes are illustrated in Figure 7-36.

Figure 7-36   Network Mode

- **Network Name (SSID):** The SSID is the network name shared among all points in a wireless network. The SSID must be identical for all devices in the wireless network. It is case-sensitive and must not exceed 32 characters (use any of the characters on the keyboard). For added security, you should change the default SSID (*linksys*) to a unique name. The SSID field is shown in Figure 7-37.

Figure 7-37   Network Name

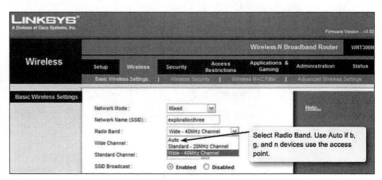

- **SSID Broadcast:** When wireless clients survey the local area for wireless networks to associate with, they detect the SSID broadcast by the access point. To broadcast the SSID, keep **Enabled**, the default setting, as in Figure 7-37. If you do not want to broadcast the SSID, select **Disabled**. When you have finished making changes to this screen, click the **Save Settings** button, or click the **Cancel Changes** button to undo your changes. For more information, click Help.

- **Radio Band:** For best performance in a network using Wireless-N, Wireless-G, and Wireless-B devices, keep the default **Auto**. For Wireless-N devices only, select **Wide—40MHz Channel**. For Wireless-G and Wireless-B networking only, select **Standard—20MHz Channel**. The selection of frequency band granularity is illustrated in Figure 7-38.

Figure 7-38   Radio Band

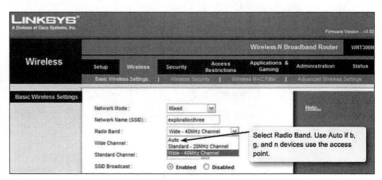

- **Wide Channel:** If you selected **Wide—40MHz Channel** for the **Radio Band** setting, this setting is available for your primary Wireless-N channel. Select any channel from the drop-down menu. The wide channel options are shown in Figure 7-39.

Figure 7-39   Wide Channel

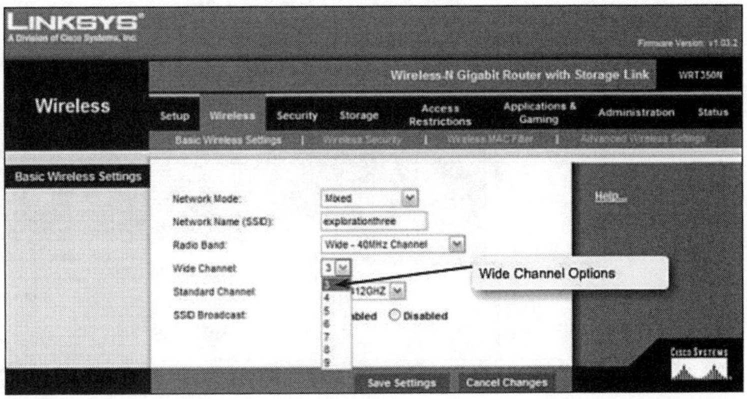

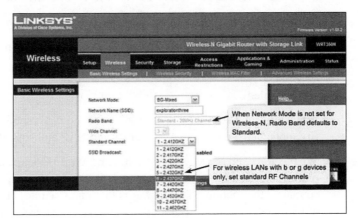

■ **Standard Channel:** Select the channel for Wireless-N, Wireless-G, and Wireless-B networking. If you selected **Wide—40MHz Channel** for the **Radio Band** setting, the standard channel is a secondary channel for Wireless-N. The standard channel settings are illustrated in Figure 7-40.

Figure 7-40   Standard Channel

Configuring Wireless Security

The security configuration is absolutely critical to the security of your wireless network. Refer to Figure 7-41.

Figure 7-41   Wireless Security Configuration Overview

Seven wireless security modes are supported by the WRT300N, listed here in the order you see them in the GUI, from weakest to strongest, except for the last option, which is disabled:

- WEP

- PSK-Personal, or WPA-Personal in v0.93.9 *firmware* or older

- PSK2-Personal, or WPA2-Personal in v0.93.9 firmware or older

- PSK-Enterprise, or WPA-Enterprise in v0.93.9 firmware or older

- PSK2-Enterprise, or WPA2-Enterprise in v0.93.9 firmware or older

- RADIUS

- Disabled

When you see **Personal** in a security mode, no AAA server is used. **Enterprise** in the security mode name means an AAA server and EAP authentication are used.

WEP is a flawed security mode. PSK2, which is the same as WPA2 or IEEE 802.11i, is the preferred option for the best security. If WPA2 is the best, you may wonder why there are so many other options. The answer is that many wireless LANs are partially composed of old wireless devices. Because all client devices that associate to an access point must be running the same security mode that the access point is running, the access point has to be set to support the device running the weakest security mode. All wireless LAN devices manufactured after March 2006 must be able to support WPA2, or in the case of Linksys routers, PSK2; in time, as devices are upgraded, you will be able to switch your network security mode over to PSK2. It is strongly recommended that hardware and firmware in the wireless infrastructure of any business support WPA2.

To configure security, do the following:

- **Security Mode:** Select the mode you want to use: **PSK-Personal**, **PSK2-Personal**, **PSK-Enterprise**, **PSK2-Enterprise**, **RADIUS**, or **WEP**. These options are shown in Figure 7-42.

Figure 7-42   Security Mode

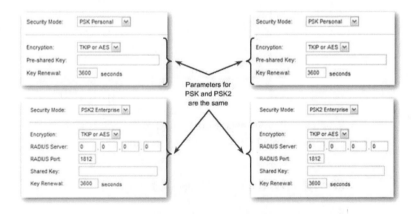

- **Mode Parameters:** Each of the PSK and PSK2 modes have parameters that you can configure, as shown in Figure 7-43. If you select the PSK2-Enterprise security version, you must have a RADIUS server attached to your access point. If you have this configuration, you need to configure the access point to point to the RADIUS server. For **RADIUS Server** enter the IP address of the RADIUS server. For **RADIUS Port** enter the port number used by the RADIUS server. The default is 1812.

Figure 7-43   Mode Parameters

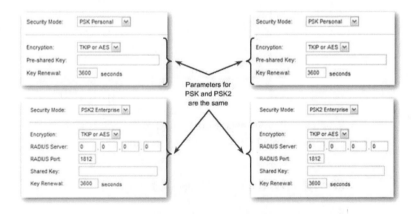

- **Encryption:** Select the algorithm you want to use, **AES** or **TKIP**. AES is a stronger encryption method than TKIP. The options are shown in Figure 7-44.

- **Preshared Key:** Enter the key shared by the router and your other network devices. It must have 8 to 63 characters. For **Key Renewal** enter the key renewal period, which tells the router how often it should change encryption keys. The key is typed into the field illustrated in Figure 7-45.

Figure 7-44   Encryption

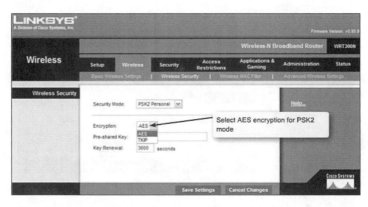

Figure 7-45   Preshared Key

When you have finished making changes to this screen, click the **Save Settings** button, or click the **Cancel Changes** button to undo your changes.

Configuring a Wireless NIC

When the access point has been configured, you need to configure the wireless NIC on a client device to allow it to connect to the wireless network. You also should verify that the wireless client has successfully connected to the correct wireless network, especially because many WLANs may be available to connect with.

Scan for SSIDs

If your PC is equipped with a wireless NIC, you should be ready to scan for wireless networks. PCs running Microsoft Windows XP have a built-in wireless networks monitor and client utility. You very well may have a different wireless utility installed as the default rather than the one native to Microsoft Windows XP.

The following steps describe the use of the View Wireless Networks feature in Microsoft Windows XP.

Step 1. On the Microsoft Windows XP toolbar system tray, find the network connection icon that looks similar to the one shown in Figure 7-46. Double-click the icon to open the Network Connections dialog box.

Figure 7-46 View Wireless Networks

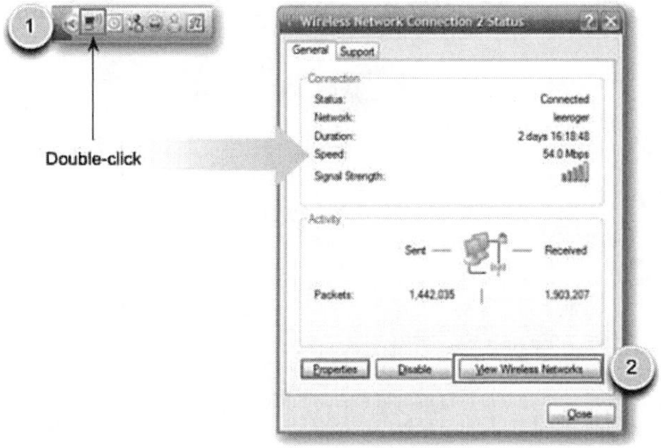

Step 2. Click the **View Wireless Networks** button in the dialog box.

Step 3. Observe the wireless networks that your wireless NIC has been able to detect, as shown Figure 7-47.

Figure 7-47 Choose Wireless Network

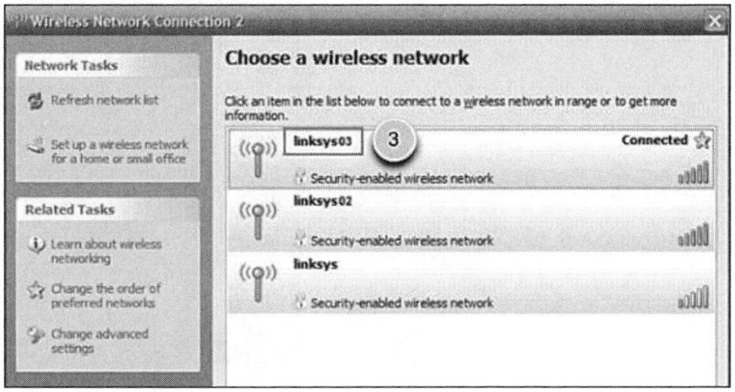

If you have a WLAN that is not showing up on the list of networks, you may have disabled SSID broadcast on the access point. If this is the case, you must enter the SSID manually.

Select the Wireless Security Protocol

After having configured your access point to authenticate clients with a strong security type, you must match your client configuration to the access point parameters. The following steps describe how to configure your wireless network security parameters on the client:

How To

Step 1.   Double-click the network connections icon in the Microsoft Windows XP system tray, as in Figure 7-48.

Figure 7-48   Wireless Network Connection Status Dialog Box

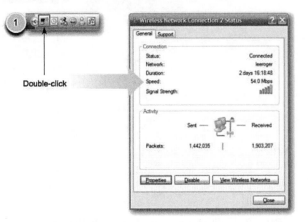

Step 2.   Click the **Properties** button in the Wireless Network Connections Status dialog box, as in Figure 7-49.

Figure 7-49   Wireless Network Properties

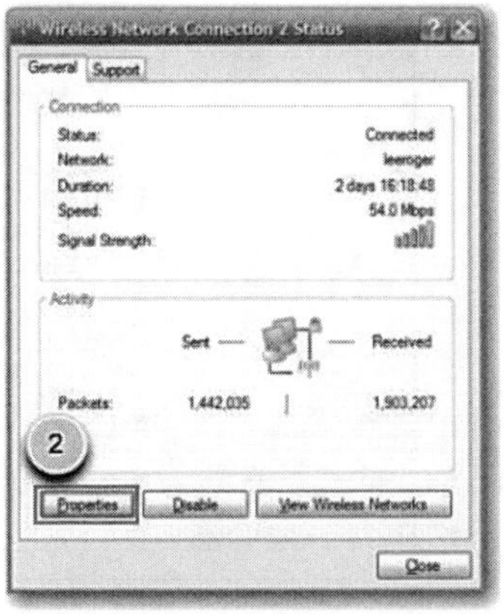

Step 3.   In the Properties dialog box, click the **Wireless Networks** tab, as in Figure 7-50.

Figure 7-50   Wireless Networks Tab

Step 4.   In the **Wireless Networks** tab, click the **Add** button, as in Figure 7-51. Also, you can save multiple wireless profiles with different security parameters allowing you to quickly connect to the WLANs you may use regularly.

Figure 7-51   Add Wireless Network

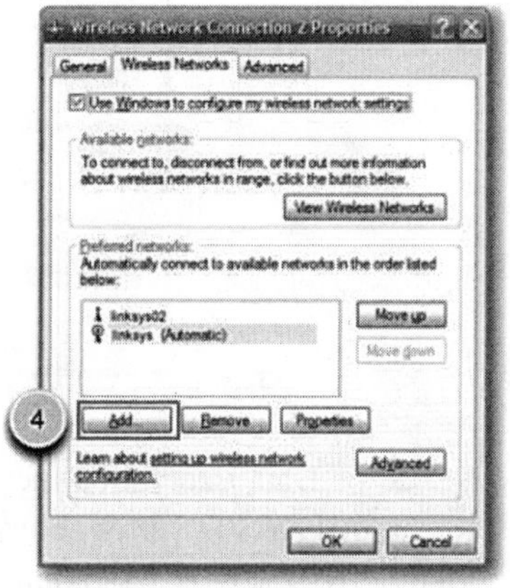

Step 5.   In the Wireless Network Properties dialog box, enter the SSID of the WLAN you want to configure, as in Figure 7-52.

Step 6.   In the Wireless Network Key box, select your preferred authentication method from the **Network Authentication** drop-down menu, as in Figure 7-53. WPA2 and PSK2 are preferred because of their strength.

Figure 7-52   SSID Box

Figure 7-53   **Network Authentication** Drop-Down Menu

Step 7.   Select the Data Encryption method from the drop-down menu, as in Figure 7-54. Recall that AES is a stronger *cipher* than TKIP, but you should match the configuration from your access point here on your PC.

After selecting the encryption method, enter and confirm the network key. Again, this is a value that you have entered into the access point.

Step 8.   Click **OK**, as in Figure 7-55.

Figure 7-54   Data Encryption

Figure 7-55   Click **OK**

Verify Connectivity to the WLAN

With configurations set for both the access point and the client, the next step is to confirm connectivity by pinging devices in the network.

Try to ping a known IP address for a device in the network. In Figure 7-56, the IP address is 192.168.1.254. The ping is successful, indicating a successful connection.

Configuring Wireless LAN Access (7.3.2)

Use the Packet Tracer Activity to configure a Linksys wireless router, allowing for remote access from PCs as well as wireless connectivity with WEP security. Use File e3-7324.pka on the CD-ROM that accompanies this book to perform this activity using Packet Tracer.

Figure 7-56   Verify Connectivity with Ping

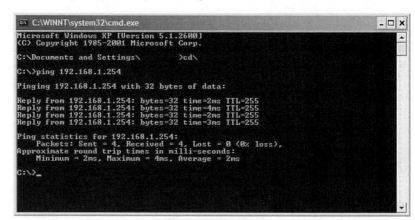

Troubleshooting Simple WLAN Problems

Troubleshooting any sort of network problem should follow a systematic approach, working up the TCP/IP stack from the physical layer to the application layer. This helps to eliminate any issues that you may be able to resolve yourself. The major troubleshooting considerations concern access point radio and firmware issues, channel settings, RF interference, access point placement, authentication, and encryption.

A Systematic Approach to WLAN Troubleshooting

Before delving into specific WLAN troubleshooting issues, it is useful to set out a systematic approach to troubleshooting WLANs. Refer to Figure 7-57.

Figure 7-57   Loss of WLAN Connectivity

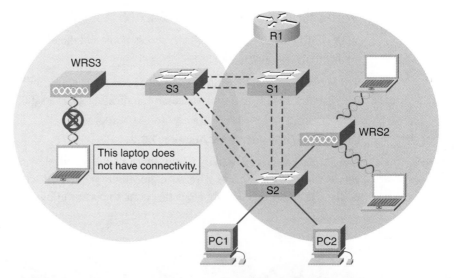

The following is a three-step approach to troubleshooting for WLANs:

How To

Step 1.   Eliminate the user PC as the source of the problem. Try to determine the severity of the problem. If there is no connectivity, check the following:

- Confirm the network configuration on the PC using the **ipconfig** command. Verify that the PC has received an IP address via DHCP or is configured with a static IP address.

- Confirm that the device can connect to the wired network. Connect the device to the wired LAN and ping a known IP address.

- It may be necessary to try a different wireless NIC. If necessary, reload drivers and firmware as appropriate for the client device.

- If the wireless NIC of the client is working, check the security mode and encryption settings on the client. If the security settings do not match, the client cannot get access to the WLAN.

If the connectivity is functional but performing poorly, check the following:

- How far is the PC from an access point? Is the PC out of the planned basic service area?

- Check the channel settings on the client. The client software should detect the appropriate channel as long as the SSID is correct.

- Check for the presence of other devices in the area that operate on the 2.4 GHz band. Examples of other devices are cordless phones, baby monitors, microwave ovens, wireless security systems, and rogue access points. Data from these devices can cause interference in the WLAN and intermittent connection problems between a client and an access point.

Step 2.   Confirm the physical status of devices.

- Are all the devices actually in place? Consider a possible physical security issue.

- Is there power to all devices and are they powered on?

Step 3.   Inspect links.

- Inspect links between cabled devices looking for bad connectors or damaged or missing cables.

- If the physical plant is in place, use the wired LAN to see if you can ping devices, including the access point.

If connectivity still fails at this point, it may be that something is wrong with the access point or its configuration.

As you troubleshoot a WLAN, a process of elimination is recommended, working from physical possibilities to application-related ones. When you have reached the point where you have eliminated the user PC as the problem and also confirmed the physical status of devices, begin investigating the performance of the access point. Check the power status of the access point.

When the access point settings have been confirmed, if the radio continues to fail, try to connect to a different access point. You may try to install new radio drivers and firmware, which is part of our next discussion.

Solve Access Point Radio and Firmware Issues

The firmware for a Linksys device is upgraded using the web-based utility. Follow these instructions:

How To Q

Step 1. Download the firmware from the web. For a Linksys WRT300N, go to www.linksys.com, as illustrated in Figure 7-58.

Figure 7-58   Download Firmware

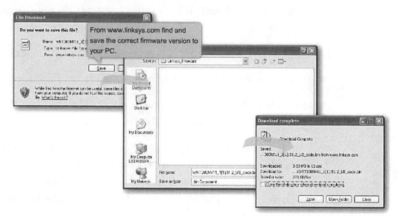

Step 2. Extract the firmware file on your computer.

Step 3. Open the web-based utility, and click the **Administration** tab.

Step 4. Select the **Firmware Upgrade** tab.

Step 5. Enter the location of the firmware file, or click the Browse button to find the file, as illustrated in Figure 7-59.

Step 6. Click the **Start to Upgrade** button and follow the instructions, as in Figure 7-60.

Channel Settings

If users report connectivity issues in the area between access points in an extended service set WLAN, as in Figure 7-61, a channel setting issue could exist.

Figure 7-59   Select Downloaded Firmware File

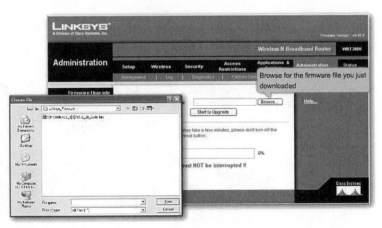

Figure 7-60   Run Firmware Upgrade

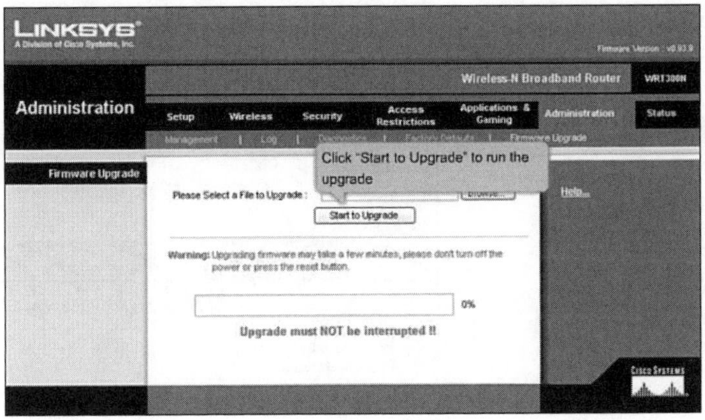

Many WLANs today operate in the 2.4 GHz band, which can have as many as 14 channels, each occupying 22 MHz of bandwidth. Energy is not spread evenly over the entire 22 MHz; rather the channel is strongest at its center frequency, and the energy diminishes toward the edges of the channel. The concept of the waning energy in a channel is shown in Figure 7-62 by the curved line used to indicate each channel. The high point in the middle of each channel is the point of highest energy. Figure 7-62 provides a graphical representation of the channels in the 2.4 GHz band.

A full explanation of the way energy is spread across the frequencies in a channel is beyond the scope of this book.

Interference can occur when an overlap of channels occurs. It is worse if the channels overlap close to the center frequencies, but even if a minor overlap occurs, signals interfere with each other. Set the channels at spaces of five or more channels, such as channel 1, channel 6, and channel 11. This is illustrated in Figure 7-63.

Figure 7-61   Incorrect Channel Settings

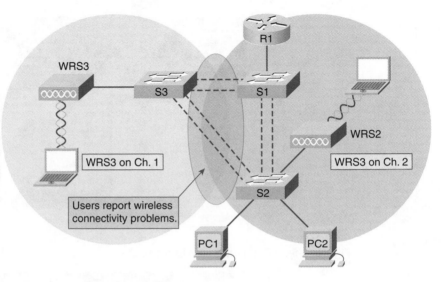

Figure 7-62   Channels and Frequency Overlap

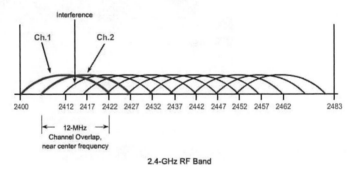

Figure 7-63   Configure Nonoverlapping Channels

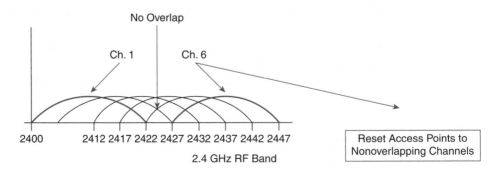

Incorrect channel settings are actually a subset of the set of RF interference problems. WLAN administrators can control interference caused by channel settings with good planning, including proper channel spacing.

RF Interference

Outside of RF interference resulting from incorrect channel settings, other sources of RF interference can be found all around the workplace or in the home. Perhaps you have experienced the snowy disruption of a television signal when someone nearby runs a vacuum cleaner. Such interference can be moderated with good planning. For instance, plan to place microwave ovens away from access points and potential clients. Unfortunately, the entire range of possible RF interference issues cannot be planned for because there are just too many.

The problem with devices such as cordless phones, baby monitors, and microwave ovens is that they are not part of a BSS, so they do not contend for the channel, they just use it, as pictured in Figure 7-64. How can you find out which channels in an area are most crowded?

Figure 7-64   RF Interference from Non-Networking Devices

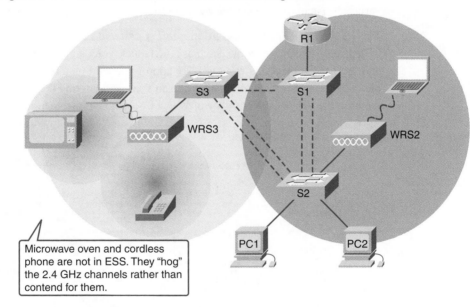

In a small WLAN environment, try setting your WLAN access point to channel 1 or channel 11. Many consumer items, such as cordless phones, operate on channel 6, as in Figure 7-65.

In more crowded environments, a site survey might be needed. Although you do not learn how to conduct *site surveys* in this book, you should know that there are two categories of site surveys: manual and utility-assisted.

Figure 7-65   Channel 6 Interference

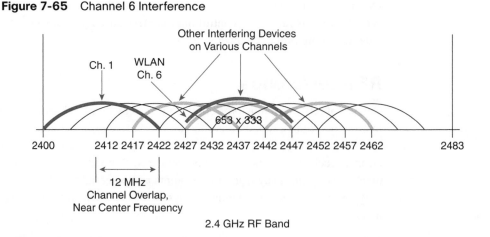

2.4 GHz RF Band

Manual site surveys can include a site evaluation to be followed by a more thorough utility-assisted site survey. A site evaluation involves inspecting the area with the goal of identifying potential issues that could impact the network. Specifically, look for the presence of multiple WLANs, unique building structures, such as open floors and atriums, and high client usage variances, such as those caused by differences in day- or night-shift staffing levels.

There are several approaches to doing *utility-assisted site surveys*. If you do not have access to dedicated site survey tools, such as AirMagnet, you can mount access points on tripods and set them in locations you think are appropriate and in accordance with the projected site plan. With access points mounted, you can then walk around the facility using a site survey meter in the WLAN client utility of your PC, as shown in screenshot 1 of Figure 7-66.

Figure 7-66   Site Surveys

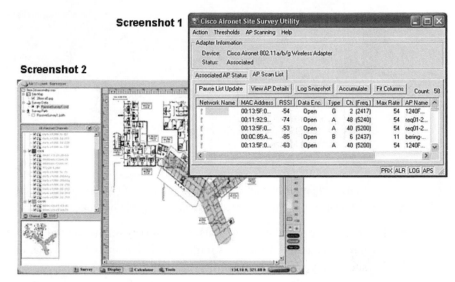

Alternatively, sophisticated tools are available that allow you to enter a facility floor plan. You can then begin a recording of the RF characteristics of the site, which are then shown on the floor plan as you move about the facility with your wireless laptop. An example of an AirMagnet site survey output is shown in screenshot 2 of Figure 7-66.

Part of the advantage to utility-assisted site surveys is that RF activity on the various channels in the various unlicensed bands (900 MHz, 2.4 GHz, and 5 GHz) is documented, and you are then able to choose channels for your WLAN, or at the very least to identify areas of high RF activity, and then make provisions for them.

Access Point Placement

It is important to be able to identify when an access point is incorrectly placed and how to correctly place the access point in a small- or medium-sized business.

You may have experienced a WLAN that just did not seem to perform like it should. Assume that such a WLAN is represented in Figure 7-67. Perhaps you keep losing association with an access point, or your data rates are much slower than they should be. You may even have done a quick walk-through in the facility to confirm that you could actually see the access points. Having confirmed that they are there, you wonder why you continue to get poor service.

Figure 7-67   Access Point Placement

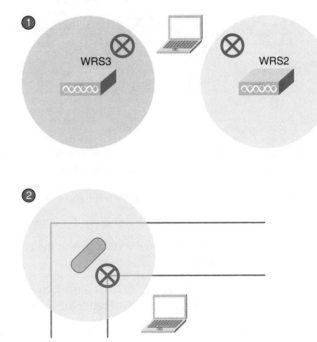

Two major deployment issues, illustrated in Figure 7-68, may occur with the placement of access points:

■ The distance separating access points is too far to allow overlapping coverage.

■ The orientation of access point antennae in hallways and corners diminishes coverage.

Figure 7-68   Access Point Misplacement Issues

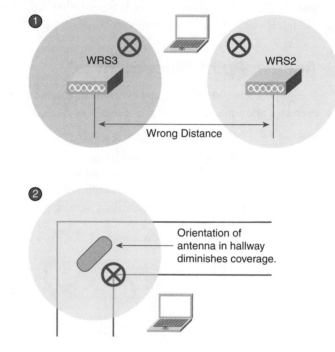

Fix access point placement as follows:

■ Confirm the power settings and operational ranges of access points and place them for a minimum of 10 to 15% cell overlap, as you learned earlier this chapter.

■ Change the orientation and positioning of access points:

   ■ Position access points above obstructions.

   ■ Position access points vertically near the ceiling in the center of each coverage area, if possible.

   ■ Position access points in locations where users are expected to be. For example, large rooms are typically a better location for access points than a hallway.

Figure 7-69 illustrates solutions to the access point misplacement issues.

Figure 7-69   Access Point Misplacement Solutions

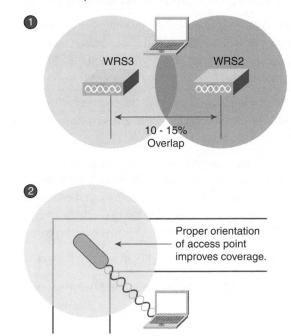

Some additional specific details concerning access point and antenna placement are as follows:

- Ensure that access points are not mounted closer than 7.9 inches (20 cm) from the body of all persons.

- Do not mount the access point within 3 feet (91.4 cm) of metal obstructions.

- Install the access point away from microwave ovens. Microwave ovens operate on the same frequency as the access point and can cause signal interference.

- Always mount the access point vertically (standing up or hanging down).

- Do not mount the access point outside of buildings.

- Do not mount the access point on building perimeter walls, unless outside coverage is desired.

- When mounting an access point in the corner of a right-angle hallway intersection, mount it at a 45-degree angle to the two hallways, as illustrated in Figure 7-69. The access point internal antennas are not omnidirectional, and they cover a larger area when mounted this way.

Authentication and Encryption

The WLAN authentication and encryption problems you are most likely to encounter, and that you will be able to solve, are caused by incorrect client settings. If an access point is expecting one type of encryption, and the client offers a different type, the authentication process fails.

Encryption issues involving the creation of dynamic keys and the conversations between an authentication server, such as a RADIUS server, and a client through an access point are beyond the scope of this book.

All devices connecting to an access point must use the same security type as the one configured on the access point. Therefore, if an access point is configured for WEP, both the type of encryption (WEP, for example) and the shared key must match between the client and the access point. If WPA is being used, the encryption algorithm is TKIP. Similarly, if WPA2 or 802.11i is used, AES is the encryption algorithm.

In Figure 7-70, a client is not able to authenticate with the access point.

Figure 7-70   Authentication and Encryption Issues

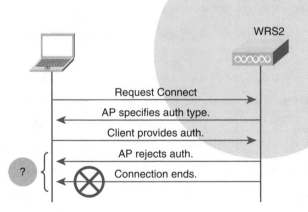

The network administrator troubleshooting the problem discovers that the client security settings are incorrect, as shown in Figure 7-71.

To correct the problem, the network administrator changes the encryption setting to PSK2/AES and reenters the network key, as shown in Figure 7-72.

Figure 7-71   Incorrect Client Security Settings

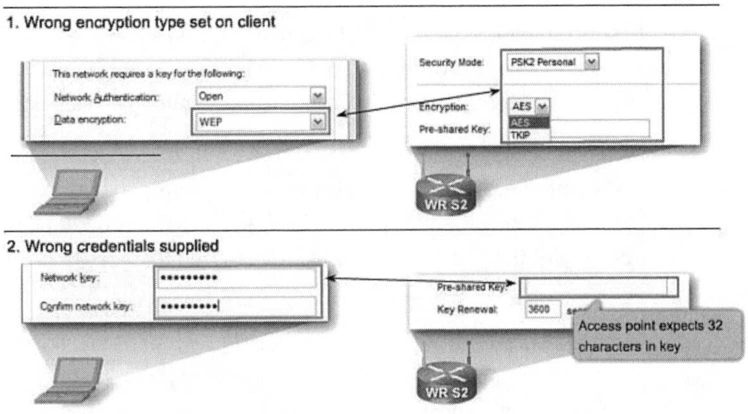

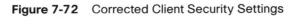

Figure 7-72   Corrected Client Security Settings

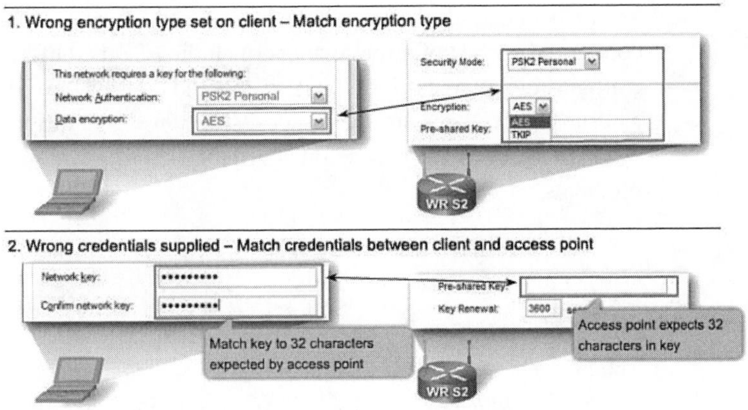

Summary

In this chapter, we discussed the evolving wireless LAN standards, including IEEE 802.11a, 802.11b, 802.11g, and now, draft 802.11n. Newer standards take into account the need to support voice and video and the requisite quality of service.

A single access point connected to the wired LAN provides a basic service set to client stations that associate to it. Multiple access points that share a service set identifier combine to form an extended service set. Wireless LANs can be detected by any radio-enabled client device and therefore may enable access by attackers that do not have access to a wired-only network.

Methods such as MAC address filtering and SSID masking can be part of a security best practice implementation, but these methods alone are easily overcome by a determined attacker. WPA2 and 802.1x authentication provide very secure wireless LAN access in an enterprise network.

End users have to configure wireless NICs on their client stations that communicate with and associate to a wireless access point. Both the access point and wireless NICs must be configured with similar parameters, including SSID, before association is possible. When configuring a wireless LAN, ensure that the devices have the latest firmware so that they can support the most stringent security options. In addition to ensuring compatible configuration of wireless security settings, troubleshooting wireless LANs involves resolving RF problems.

Labs

The labs available in the companion *LAN Switching and Wireless, CCNA Exploration Labs and Study Guide* (ISBN 1-58713-202-8) provide hands-on practice with the following topics introduced in this chapter:

Lab 7-1: Basic Wireless Configuration (7.5.1)

In this lab, you configure a Linksys WRT300N, including WEP. Make note of the procedures involved in connecting to a wireless network because some changes involve disconnecting clients, which may then have to reconnect after making changes to the configuration.

Lab 7-2: Challenge Wireless WRT300N (7.5.2)

In this lab, you configure a Linksys WRT300N in the Chapter 7 LAN/WLAN topology. You configure port security on a Cisco switch, as well as static routes on multiple devices. You also configure frequency channels, MAC filters, password management, logging, and a firmware upgrade.

Lab 7-3: Troubleshooting Wireless Configuration (7.5.3)

In this lab, the Chapter 7 LAN/WLAN topology has been configured improperly. You must find and correct the misconfigurations based on the minimum network specifications provided by your company.

Many of the hands-on labs include Packet Tracer Companion Activities, where you can use Packet Tracer to complete a simulation of the lab. Look for this icon in *LAN Switching and Wireless, CCNA Exploration Labs and Study Guide* (ISBN 1-58713-202-8) for hands-on labs that have a Packet Tracer Companion.

Check Your Understanding

Complete all the review questions listed here to test your understanding of the topics and concepts in this chapter. Answers are listed in the Appendix, "Check Your Understanding and Challenge Questions Answer Key."

1. Fill in IEEE 802.11b, 802.11g, 802.11a, or 802.11n in the blank to match the description.

   _____ specifies data rates of 1, 2, 5.5, and 11 Mbps due to differently sized spreading sequences specified in the DSSS modulation technique.

   _____ uses the 802.11 MAC, but with higher data rates in the 2.4 GHz ISM band by using the OFDM modulation technique.

   _____ uses the 5.7 GHz band with less interference, but obstructions can affect performance and limit range.

   _____ uses multiple radios and antennae at endpoints, each broadcasting on the same frequency to establish multiple streams.

2. Fill in the term for the wireless networking device in the blank to match the description.

   _____ encodes a data stream onto an RF signal using the configured modulation technique.

   _____ connects multiple wireless clients or stations to the wired LAN.

   _____ connects two separated, isolated wired networks together.

3. At which layer of the OSI model do wireless access points operate?

   A. Physical

   B. Data link

   C. Network

   D. Application

4. Which two steps are required for a wireless client to associate with an access point? (Choose two.)

    A. IP addressing

    B. Wireless address translation

    C. Wireless client authentication

    D. Channel identification

    E. Wireless client association

5. Which three WLAN client authentication types require a preprogrammed network key to be set on the client? (Choose three.)

    A. OPEN with data encryption disabled

    B. SHARED with data encryption algorithm WEP

    C. WPA with data encryption algorithm TKIP

    D. WPA-PSK with data encryption algorithm TKIP

    E. WPA2-PSK with data encryption algorithm AES

6. Which two items contribute to the security of a WLAN? (Choose two.)

    A. WPA2

    B. Use of multiple channels

    C. Hiding the SSID

    D. Open authentication

    E. AES

7. Which term is used for products that are tested to be interoperable in both PSK and 802.1x EAP operation for authentication?

    A. Personal mode

    B. WPA2 compatible

    C. RADIUS authenticated

    D. Enterprise mode

    E. Preshared key authenticated

8. To help ensure a secure wireless network, most enterprise networks should follow which IEEE standard?

    A. 802.11a

    B. 802.11b

    C. 802.11c

    D. 802.11i

9. Refer to Figure 7-73. The authentication and encryption menu options are displayed. Which wireless settings provide the highest level of security?

Figure 7-73   Wireless Security Settings

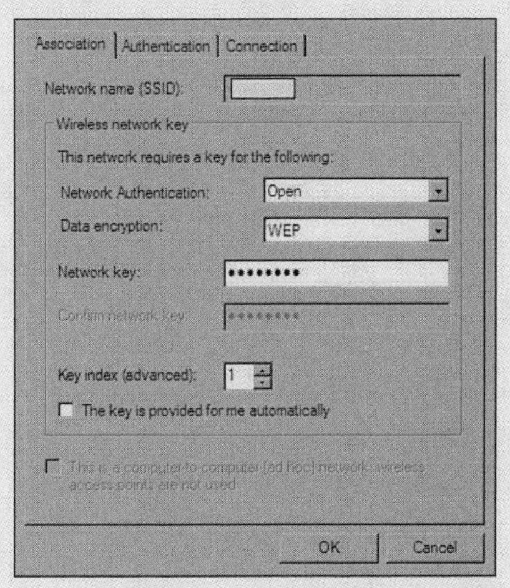

A. Open

B. Shared

C. WPA

D. WPA-PSK

10. Which two combinations of 802.11b RF channels would allow two wireless APs to operate simultaneously in the same room with no channel overlap? (Choose two.)

A. Channels 10 and 6

B. Channels 9 and 6

C. Channels 8 and 5

D. Channels 7 and 2

E. Channels 6 and 2

F. Channels 6 and 11

11. Why do cordless devices, such as cordless telephones, sometimes interfere with wireless access points?

A. These devices operate at similar frequencies.

B. These devices operate at the same frequencies and have higher RF power settings.

C. These devices flood the entire frequency spectrum with low power noise, which may cause loss of signal for wireless devices trying to connect with an access point.

D. The signal from the cordless device is nonpolarized and combines with the access point polarized signal, thus reducing the overall signal strength.

12. Refer to Figure 7-74. What is the recommended overlap between the two wireless access points to provide proper connectivity for users?

Figure 7-74   Wireless Channel Overlap

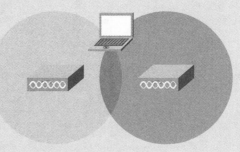

A. 5–10%

B. 10–15%

C. 15–20%

D. 20–25%

13. Fill in the authentication method in the blank that best matches the encryption algorithm or security protocol listed.

_____ Disabled

_____ RC4

_____ TKIP

_____ AES

14. Which WLAN client settings would be reviewed to resolve problems accessing the network?

A. Wireless mode (802.11a, 802.11b, 802.11g, 802.11n)

B. Wireless network card drivers

C. Channel selection for ad hoc networks

D. TCP/IP properties

E. Wireless association properties

Challenge Questions and Activities

These questions require a deeper application of the concepts covered in this chapter. You can find the answers in the Appendix.

1. Match the terms with the correct descriptions.

    ___ Wireless bridge

    ___ Wireless router

    ___ Wireless NIC

    ___ Wireless AP

    A. Connects two separated, isolated wired networks together

    B. Performs the role of a switch, a router, and an AP

    C. Encodes a data stream onto an RF signal

    D. Not required for RF communication between two devices

2. Refer to Table 7-4. Fill in the abbreviation for each of the wireless technologies described.

Table 7-4   Wireless Technologies

Open Access	First Generation Encryption	Interim	Present
___	___	___	___
No encryption	No strong authentication	Standardized	AES Encryption
Basic authentication	Static, breakable keys	Improved encryption	Authentication: 802.1X
Not a security handle	Not scalable	Strong, user-based authentication (for example, LEAP, PEAP, EAP-FAST)	Dynamic key management WPA2 is the Wi-Fi Alliance implementation of 802.11i

3. Refer to Figure 7-75. For the most rudimentary wireless scurity, which two of the displayed settings should be changed?

Figure 7-75   Linksys Basic Wireless Settings

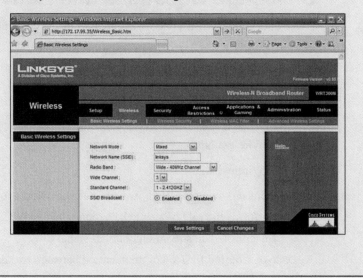

4. Refer to Figure 7-76. The laptop on the left is unable to communicate with the rest of the network. What are three possible problems? (Choose all that apply.)

Figure 7-76   Linksys Basic Wireless Settings

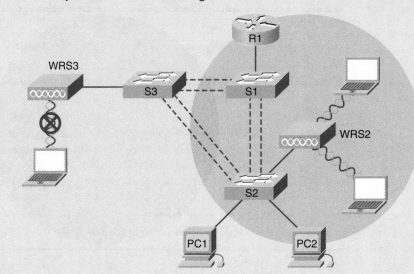

A. The SSID does not match the SSID of WRS3.

B. The security mode does not match that of WRS3 (for example, WEP, WPA, WPA2).

C. The security key does not match that of WRS3.

D. The channel setting does not match that of WRS3.

E. There is RF interference or the distance to WSR3 is too great.

F. The drivers on the laptop need to be upgraded to support the appropriate wireless protocol.

G. The firmware on WSR3 needs to be upgraded to support the appropriate wireless protocol.

H. The laptop user is unable to authenticate to obtain network access.

Packet Tracer
☐ Challenge

Look for this icon in *LAN Switching and Wireless, CCNA Exploration Labs and Study Guide* (ISBN 1-58713-202-8) for instructions on how to perform the Packet Tracer Skills Integration Challenge for this chapter.

Check Your Understanding and Challenge Questions Answer Key

Chapter 1

Check Your Understanding

1. **B**, **C**, and **E**. These are the principal characterizations of the respective design layers.

2. **D**. This is how network engineers understand convergence.

3. **B**, **C**, and **E**. Convergence does not simplify data network configuration; if anything, it becomes more complex. Similarly, maintenance of a hierarchical network will not be simplified with convergence. Finally, QoS becomes absolutely critical in a converged network—to a large extent, QoS technologies exist as a result of convergence.

4. **B**, **D**, **F**, and **G**. Workstation ports required for a department, intensity of use of a department application server, and anticipated department port growth are user community analysis actions.

5. **C**. Intensity of use of a department application server is associated with user community analysis, but the application usage is not bound by geography.

6. **B** and **D**. Port density is the number of ports available on a single switch and link aggregation relates to using multiple switch ports concurrently.

7. **C**. 1 Gbps = 1000 Mbps.

8. **B**. MAC addresses are associated with Ethernet frames, which are associated with Layer 2 of the OSI model.

9. **B**. Port numbers vary among stackable switch models. Some stackable switches are Fast Ethernet. The interswitch communication is high speed. PoE capability is not associated with stackable switches.

10. **C**. Inter-VLAN support, routing, and link aggregation are associated with distribution and core layer switches.

11. **B**, **C**, and **E**. PoE, VLANs, and port security are associated with access layer switches.

12. **A** and **E**. B reflects the distribution layer. C and D reflect the access layer.

Challenge Questions and Activities

1.

- **Access Layer**: The access layer interfaces with end devices, such as PCs, printers, and IP phones, to provide access to the rest of the network. The access layer can include routers, switches, bridges, hubs, and wireless access points. The main purpose of the access layer is to provide a means of connecting devices to the network and controlling which devices are allowed to communicate on the network.

- **Distribution Layer**: The distribution layer aggregates the data received from the access layer switches before it is transmitted to the core layer for routing to its final destination. The distribution layer controls the flow of network traffic using policies and delineates broadcast domains by performing routing functions between virtual LANs (VLANs) defined at the access layer. Distribution layer switches are typically high-performance devices that have high availability and redundancy to ensure reliability.

- **Core Layer**: The core layer of the hierarchical design is the high-speed backbone of the internetwork. The core layer is critical for interconnectivity between distribution layer devices, so it is important for the core to be highly available and redundant. The core area also connects to Internet resources. The core aggregates the traffic from all the distribution layer devices, so it must be capable of forwarding large amounts of data quickly.

2. _D_   Fixed Configuration Switch

   _B_   Forwarding Rate

   _I_   Quality of Service

   _G_   Power over Ethernet

   _F_   Modular Switch

   _E_   Link Aggregation

   _A_   Port Density

   _C_   Stackable Switch

   _H_   Redundancy

Chapter 2

Check Your Understanding

1. **C**. The caret points to the first character in the line where the command syntax is incorrect.

2. **D**. Explanation: D describes the prescribed behavior for the login banner.

3. **C, D**, and **E**. The descriptions in A and B are permuted.

4. **D**. The table indicates that the MAC address associated with the destination indicated in the Ethernet frame is paired with Interface1.

5. **A**. The last line of the output gives the quantity of nonvolatile RAM.

6. **A**. SSH enables remote administration with the benefit of encryption.

7. **C**. The serial link does not count as a collision or broadcast domain.

8. **D**. The description in A goes with DHCP starvation, in B goes with CDP attack, in C goes with MAC address flooding.

9. **A**, **B**, and **D**. Priorities are not assigned in CSMA/CD.

10. **A**. With incoming traffic, queueing is obviously linked to incoming ports.

11. **A** and **E**. Multicast traffic management is not a feature of Layer 2 switches; similarly for ACLs, Layer 3 functions, and NAT.

12. **C**. A Layer 2 switch is allotted a single Layer 3 logical address in the form of a switch virtual interface (SVI) used for managing the switch.

13. **D**. The default gateway provides a means for the administrator of the switch to access networks not directly connected to the switch.

14. **A** and **C**. Autonegotiation sets duplex and speed.

15. **C**. The switch will connect with full duplex when autonegotiating with a peer device.

16. **B**. Latency describes the cumulative delays involved in moving a frame from source to destination.

17. **F**. Following left-to-right, option F is the only logical solution.

18. **D**, **E**, and **G**. Options D, E, and G delineate the sequence for securing the console line.

Challenge Questions and Activities

1. ___4____ The intended destination device replies to the broadcast with a unicast frame addressed to PC 1.

   ___2____ The switch enters the source MAC address and the switch port that received the frame into the address table.

   ___5____ The switch enters the source MAC address of PC 2 and the port number of the switch port that received the frame into the address table. The destination address of the frame and its associated port is found in the MAC address table.

   ___6____ The switch can now forward frames between source and destination devices without flooding because it has entries in the address table that identify the associated ports.

   ___3____ Because the destination address is a broadcast, the switch floods the frame to all ports, except the port on which it received the frame.

   ___1____ The switch receives an ARP broadcast frame from PC 1 on Port 1.

   This is standard operating procedure for switches populating MAC address tables.

2. Store-and-forward switching and cut-through switching

   Port-based memory buffering and shared memory buffering

   These are the major classifications of switch forwarding methods and memory buffering.

3. There are no active physical interfaces associated with VLAN 99.

   VLAN 99 will not appear active until there is an active port assigned to VLAN 99.

4. The **ip ssh version 2** and **transport input SSH** commands are not required to provide remote access.

   Version 2 is the default and **transport input all** is also a default.

5. **protect**: When the number of secure MAC addresses reaches the limit allowed on the port, packets with unknown source addresses are dropped until you remove a sufficient number of secure MAC addresses or increase the number of maximum allowable addresses. You are not notified that a security violation has occurred.

   restrict: When the number of secure MAC addresses reaches the limit allowed on the port, packets with unknown source addresses are dropped until you remove a sufficient number of secure MAC addresses or increase the number of maximum allowable addresses. In this mode, you are notified that a security violation has occurred. Specifically, an SNMP trap is sent, a syslog message is logged, and the violation counter increments.

   shutdown: In this mode, a port security violation causes the interface to immediately become error-disabled and turns off the port LED. It also sends an SNMP trap, logs a syslog message, and increments the violation counter. When a secure port is in the error-disabled state, you can bring it out of this state by entering the **shutdown** followed by the **no shutdown** interface configuration commands. This is the default mode.

   These descriptions are provided in the "Configuring Port Security" section.

Chapter 3

Check Your Understanding

1. **C**. There are four VLANs, hence four subnets.

2. **A**. 802.1p is used for prioritization, multiplexing is a telecommunications term, and the native VLAN is not used to differentiate between VLANs on a trunk (it is associated with untagged traffic on a trunk link).

3. **B** and **C**. Port security is used only on access ports. The native VLAN must be the same on both ends of an 802.1Q trunk.

4. **A** and **D**. Ports are administratively disabled only with the **no shutdown** command. Access ports never default to trunk ports. Ports do not automatically get reassigned to another VLAN upon deletion of their respective VLAN.

5. **A, C,** and **E**. A router is needed for inter-VLAN communication. Each port on a switch is associated with a separate collision domain. Hosts on the same VLAN can all be on distinct physical segments.

6. **B**. The ARP request is a broadcast and is heard only by devices within the same VLAN.

7. __S__ Each port associated with specific VLAN.

    __S__ Manual configuration of port assignment required.

    __D__ Ports work out their own configuration.

    __D__ Less administrative overhead when users moved.

    __S__ Requires administrator interaction when users moved.

    __D__ Configured based on database.

    These solutions exactly reflect the definitions of static and dynamic VLANs.

8. __N__ 1–1001

    __E__ 1006–4094

    __E__ Not learned by VTP

    __N__ Stored in vlan.dat

    __1__ Default management VLAN

    __1__ Default native VLAN

    __1__ All ports are a member of by default

    Only normal range VLANs are propagated by VTP and stored in the vlan.dat file.

9. **D**. Although the frame will be flooded to all VLAN 10 hosts connected to SW1, the best answer is D because the point of the question is how the frame gets to Host B.

10. **B, C,** and **F**. Basically, all intra-VLAN connectivity is successful and no inter-VLAN connectivity is successful.

11. **A, B,** and **D**. **show vlan brief** gives only summary information about each VLAN; **show interface f0/1** does not show VLAN information.

12. __C__ **switchport mode trunk**

    __A__ **switchport mode dynamic desirable**

    __B__ **switchport nonegotiate**

__D__ **switchport mode access**

These descriptions match the definitions of the trunking behavior associated with the respective commands. DTP is active in option A.

13. __D__ Native VLAN mismatch

__A__ Trunk mode mismatch

__B__ Incorrect VLAN list

__C__ VLAN subnet conflict

Untagged frames are associated with the native VLAN. Two dynamic auto ports will not negotiate a trunk link.

14. **B**, **D**, and **F**. Static VLANs cannot change dynamically. VMPS is based on source MAC address. Voice-enabled ports are connected to IP phones.

Challenge Questions and Activities

1. **E**. This is standard design for how modern switched LANs map VLANs to subnets.

2. **B** and **C**. There is no router to enable inter-VLAN connectivity. S1 and S2 are on the same VLAN, so they can ping each other.

3. **D**. Addition and deletion of VLANs is performed in global configuration mode. Assignment of ports to VLANs and native VLAN assignment are carried out in interface configuration mode.

4. **A**, **B**, **C**, **D**, and **E**. All these are possible causes for the lack of connectivity.

Chapter 4

Check Your Understanding

1. **E**. VTP propagates VLAN names.

2. **B**. VTP transparent mode allows for deletion and addition of VLANs, but does not propagate the information throughout the VTP domain.

3. **D**. Transparent mode switches forward (multicast) VTP messages but do not alter their configurations based on information within VTP messages.

4. **C**. The switches need not be in the same VTP mode, nor share the same VTP configuration revision number (which may be the case when the VTP domain names do not match).

5. **C**. There is no such thing as a configuration status reply, nor a three-way handshake associated with VTP. The revision number would never be set to zero based on receipt of VTP messages.

6. **C**. This is the exact function of VTP pruning.

7. **A**, **E**, and **F**. VTP requires trunk links, the same VTP version, and the same VTP domain name to operate. Pruning settings do not have to agree and passwords would have to match (not be unique). VTP version 3 is not relevant to Token Ring.

8. VTP client specifies that the switch cannot create or delete VLANs shared in VTP advertisements.

    vtp domain *domain-name* configures the name used to determine which switches belong to the same management group.

    VTP pruning restricts flooded traffic to trunk links that the traffic must use to reach destination devices.

    VTP server mode allows for creation of VLANs. VTP version 2 is not directly related to flooding traffic or domain association.

9. **A**. VTP does not route or tag frames or distribute BPDUs.

10. **C**. Explanation: VTP passwords and VTP domain names are case sensitive.

11. **B**. Changing the VTP domain name twice resets the revision number to zero. VTP pruning is not applicable here. VTP server mode switches *do* accept VTP updates, depending on the associated revision number.

12. VTP transparent mode forwards VTP advertisements that are received out the trunk ports, but cannot advertise and synchronize the VLAN configuration based on received advertisements.

    VTP client mode advertises and synchronizes the VLAN configuration to other switches in the same VTP domain, but cannot create, change, or delete VLANs.

    VTP server mode creates, modifies, and deletes VLANs and specifies other configuration parameters, such as VTP version and VTP pruning for the entire VTP domain.

    VTP clients cannot advertise VTP pruning information. VTP transparent mode switches *can* forward VTP advertisements.

13. **A**, **B**, and **C**. The VTP transparent mode switch forwards the VTP multicast messages. Switch4 does receive the update and will update its database. Switch3 will not add the VLAN to its database.

Challenge Questions and Activities

1. _E_ VTP domain

   _F_ VTP advertisements

   _A_ VTP modes

   _G_ VTP server

   _D_ VTP client

   _B_ VTP transparent

   _C_ VTP pruning

   VTP servers can alter VLAN information, but clients are able to synchronize only with servers. Pruning regulates VLAN propagation. Transparent switches forward VTP messages but do not act on them.

2. VTP Version = 1

   VTP Domain Name = null

   VTP Mode = Server

   Config Revision = 0

   VLANs = 1 (VLAN 1)

   VLANs 1002, 1003, 1004, and 1005 are default reserved VLANs on a Catalyst 2960 switch, but we count VLAN 1 as only a default VLAN. The null VTP domain name means no VTP domain name has been configured; a neighbor switch with a configured VTP domain name will automatically propagate it over a trunk link.

3. **A**, **B**, and **C**. The addition of switch S4 deletes VLANs 10 and 20 from the VTP domain, so the switch ports connected to the six PCs are associated with inactive VLANs.

Chapter 5

Check Your Understanding

1. **A** and **C**. Unicast frame flooding does not require redundant links. Routing loops are layer 3 constructs. Load balancing is not a problem. Incorrect frame addressing is spurious.

2. **D**. Ethernet frames have no TTL. ARP requests are local to the broadcast domain.

3. **B**. The diagram is symmetric and no inferences can be made about which switch will be the root switch for the common VLAN. At least three switches will be designated switches.

4. **B**. Priority values are not dynamically adjusted. MAC addresses may be learned during STP convergence, but that is not required.

5. **A**.   __CST__ is a single instance of spanning tree encompassing every VLAN in the LAN.

   B.   __MSTP__ reduces the number of spanning-tree instances required to support large numbers of VLANs.

   C.   __PVST__ supports the use of ISL trunking and load balancing.

   D.   __PVST+__ supports BPDU guard, root guard, and the use of IEEE 802.1Q trunking.

   E.   __Rapid PVST+__ supports equivalent functionality to BackboneFast, UplinkFast, and PortFast, is based on IEEE 802.1w, and functions per-VLAN.

   F.   __RSTP__ incorporated into IEEE 802.1D-2004; supports equivalent functionality to BackboneFast, UplinkFast, and PortFast.

   PVST can work ISL. PVST+ can work with 802.1Q and supports BPDU guard and root guard.

6. **A**, **B**, and **F**. Designated is not a port state. Forwarding means exactly that. Root ports are forwarding ports.

7. **A**.   __Learning__ receives/processes BPDUs, populates MAC address table

   B.   __Disabled__ does not process BPDUs

   C.   __Forwarding__ receives/processes BPDUs, populates MAC address table, sends data frames

   D.   __Listening__ receives/processes and transmits BPDUs

   E.   __Blocking__ receives/processes BPDUs

   The listening state permits BPDU transmission. Disabled state does not process frames, whereas blocking does.

8. **B**, **D**, and **E**. The default settings are 2 seconds for hello time, 15 seconds for forward delay, and 20 seconds for max age.

9. **C**. Cat-C has the lowest BID, based on its bridge priority and MAC address.

10. **A**. ISL is not an IEEE standard. 802.1w is RSTP. 802.1 is a superset of 802.1D, 802.1w, 802.1s, and 802.1Q, dealing with LAN/MAN architecture.

11. **B** and **C**. RSTP does not imply per-VLAN support. RSTP is compatible with 802.1D. RSTP does not support UplinkFast and BackboneFast proper, verbatim, but supports equivalent functionality.

12. **C.** An RSTP edge port acts just like a PVST+ PortFast port with respect to the speed of transition to forwarding state.

13. **A** and **D.** There are no multipoint, redundant, or dedicated RSTP link types.

14. **B.** Alternate ports provide an alternate path to the root, giving immediate reconvergence when the primary path fails.

15. **C.** Assigning a port to an uninstantiated VLAN will create the VLAN.

16. **C.** A would work but is not the best answer. B is specific to a VLAN. C works. Changing the MAC address would not make S4 the root bridge.

17. **D** and **F.** SW3 uses the timers advertised from the root bridge, shown on the top half of the output. The root bridge was selected based on bridge priority. Port 16 is an internal label for FastEthernet0/14. Of course the root bridge has an aging time, but you don't see it in the output.

18. **D.** PortFast is configured only on ports connected to end stations.

Challenge Questions and Activities

1. _T_   Ethernet frames do not have a time to live (TTL).

   _T_   Broadcast frames are forwarded out all switch ports, except the ingress port.

   _T_   In a hierarchical design, redundancy is achieved at the distribution and core layers by using additional hardware and alternate paths through the additional hardware.

   _F_   Layer 2 loops result in low CPU load on all switches caught in the loop.

   _T_   A broadcast storm results when so many broadcast frames are caught in a Layer 2 loop that all available bandwidth is consumed.

   _F_   Most upper-layer protocols are designed to recognize or cope with duplicate transmissions.

   _T_   Layer 2 loops arise as a result of multiple paths, and STP can be used to block these loops.

   Layer 2 loops result in high CPU load on switches in the loop. Most upper-layer protocols do not have a mechanism to handle multiple transmissions.

2. Figure 5-103 shows the answers. The X is a giveaway for the nondesignated port.

Figure 5-103 Port Roles Answers

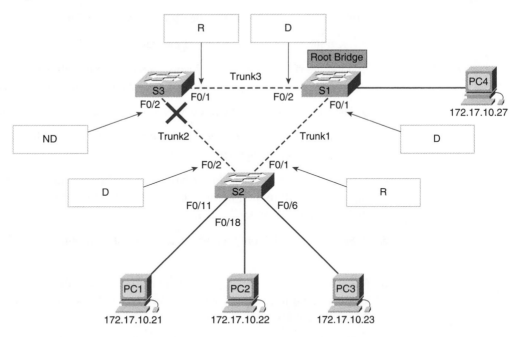

3. **B**. Alternate ports are nondesignated ports.

4. _D_ PVST

   _C_ PVST+

   _E_ RSTP

   _B_ MSTP

   _A_ 802.1D

   RSTP converges faster, MSTP uses instances, PVST relies on ISL, 802.1D is the original STP, and PVST+ supports 802.1Q.

Chapter 6

Check Your Understanding

1. subinterface   one physical interface for many VLANs

   subinterface   bandwidth contention

   physical   interface access mode switch port connection

physical interface	complex cable configuration
subinterface	trunk mode switch port connection
physical interface	one physical interface per VLAN
physical interface	solutions involve more complex cabling, access port switch configurations, and one physical router interface per VLAN.

2. **D**. The MAC address of the physical interface is used for all its subinterfaces.

3. **A**, **B**, and **E**. The solution decreases available bandwidth and increases troubleshooting and configuration complexity.

4. **A**. Some Layer 3 switches do not have an image loaded that supports Layer 3 switching; if it does, IP routing needs to be enabled (it is by default). Layer 3 switches preclude the need for router-on-a-stick.

5. **D**. Router-on-a-stick only requires a single trunk port with a native VLAN assigned to one subinterface.

6. **A and C**. Disabling switch ports would not help. Separate switch ports to separate VLANs would limit connectivity relative to trunk links. There is no such thing as Dynamic Tree Protocol.

7. **A**, **B**, and **E**. The links are access links, traffic is untagged, and the router interfaces are the gateways.

8. **C**. Router-on-a-stick uses subinterfaces on the participating router.

9. **B**. **Ping** tests the connectivity between the source and destination devices.

10. **C**. The configuration is correct.

11. **C** and **D**. Subinterfaces of a physical router interface (which trunks to the opposing switch port) correspond to VLANs, which in turn correspond to distinct subnets.

12. **B**. There is no such thing as Layer 2 inter-VLAN routing. The first option works but does not take into account that VLAN 10 traffic balances the remaining VLAN traffic. Secondary addresses are a legacy solution no longer recommended for Cisco routers.

13. **A**, **B**, and **D**. Switch interfaces are Layer 2 and do not require IP addresses. Routing protocols are unnecessary because all routes are directly connected. No subinterfaces are needed here.

14. **A**, **C**, and **E**. Traditional routing means one physical router interface per VLAN. There is no such thing as spanning-tree routing or 802.1Q routing.

15. **D**. F0/0/1 is a physical interface and the command given is configured only on subinterfaces.

Challenge Questions and Activities

1. Traditional inter-VLAN routing: one port per VLAN

   Router-on-a-stick: one trunk port

   Multilayer switching: no physical interfaces

   Router-on-a-stick requires only one physical interface. Multilayer switching requires one SVI per VLAN.

2. The following is a correct configuration:

```
R1(config)# interface f0/0.10
R1(config-subif)# encapsulation dot1q 10
R1(config-subif)# ip address 172.17.10.1 255.255.255.0
R1(config-subif)# interface f0/0.30
R1(config-subif)# encapsulation dot1q 30
R1(config-subif)# ip address 172.17.30.1 255.255.255.0
S1(config)# interface f0/5
S1(config-if)# switchport mode trunk
```

   This is an absolutely minimal functional configuration.

3. This is a fairly exhaustive list of the most common causes of communication failure in such a scenario/topology:

   - There is a native VLAN mismatch on the trunk link.

   - The wrong IP address is configured on a particular subinterface on interface F0/0 on router R1.

   - Trunking is not enabled on interface F0/1 of switch S1.

   - The TCP/IP settings on PC1 or PC3 are wrong.

   - Interface F0/11 or F0/6 is assigned to the wrong VLAN on switch S1.

   - The **encapsulation** command is missing on one of the subinterfaces of F0/0 on router R1.

   - Interface VLAN 1 is not configured as a subinterface on interface F0/0 of router R1.

Chapter 7

Check Your Understanding

1. __802.11b__ specifies data rates of 1, 2, 5.5, and 11 Mbps due to differently sized spreading sequences specified in the DSSS modulation technique.

   __802.11g__ uses the 802.11 MAC, but with higher data rates in the 2.4 GHz ISM band by using the OFDM modulation technique.

   __802.11a__ uses the 5.7 GHz band with less interference, but obstructions can affect performance and limit range.

   __802.11n__ uses multiple radios and antennae at endpoints, each broadcasting on the same frequency to establish multiple streams.

   Multiple antennae and multiple streams are key descriptors for 802.11n. The rates of 1/2/5.5/11 match the 802.11b standard. The 5.7 GHz is consistent with 802.11a.

2. __wireless NIC__ encodes a data stream onto an RF signal using the configured modulation technique.

   __access point__ connects multiple wireless clients or stations to the wired LAN.

   __wireless router__ connects two separated, isolated wired networks together.

   Routers connect networks. APs connect clients.

3. **B**. APs use MAC addresses in their operation.

4. **C and E**. Authentication is a precursor to association (if it is configured).

5. **B, D, and E**. PSK is an acronym for pre-shared key. WEP always uses a key.

6. **A and E**. Channel selection, SSID broadcast disabling, and open authentication provide no security.

7. **D**. Authentication is used in enterprise implementations.

8. **D**. IEEE 802.11i is a protocol specifying wireless security implementations.

9. **D**. WPA-PSK requires a key, unlike open and WPA; shared requires a WEP key but is breakable.

10. **D and F**. Five degrees of separation are required.

11. **A**. Microwaves and baby monitors are common culprits for frequency overlap with 2.4 MHz wireless devices.

12. **B**. 10–15% is the recommended optimal overlap.

13. __OPEN__   Disabled

__WEP__   RC4

__WPA__   TKIP

__WPA2__   AES

RC4 matches WEP by elimination. 104-bit RC4 is used in 128-bit WEP.

14. **A**. Wireless mode (802.11a, 802.11b, 802.11g, 802.11n)

B. Wireless network card drivers

C. Channel selection for ad hoc networks

D. TCP/IP properties

E. Wireless association properties

All these options may affect wireless access to the network.

Challenge Questions and Activities

1. _A_   Wireless bridge

_B_   Wireless router

_C_   Wireless NIC

_D_   Wireless AP

An AP is not needed for two wireless clients to communicate with each other.

2.

Table 7-4   Wireless Technologies

Open Access	First Generation Encryption	Interim	Present
SSID	_WEP_	_WPA_	_802.11i/WPA2_
No encryption	No strong authentication	Standardized	AES Encryption
Basic authentication	Static, breakable keys	Improved encryption	Authentication: 802.1X
Not a security handle	Not scalable	Strong, user-based authentication (for example, LEAP, PEAP, EAP-FAST)	Dynamic key management WPA2 is the Wi-Fi Alliance implementation of 802.11i

AES is used in WPA2, WEP uses breakable keys, and SSID is not a security handle.

3. Change the SSID to something other than linksys.

Change the SSID broadcast setting to Disabled.

These are the absolute minimal security settings. Most network administrators do not consider these to actually provide meaningful security beyond no security.

4. A. The SSID does not match the SSID of WRS3.

   B. The security mode does not match that of WRS3 (for example, WEP, WPA, WPA2).

   C. The security key does not match that of WRS3.

   D. The channel setting does not match that of WRS3.

   E. There is RF interference or the distance to WSR3 is too great.

   F. The drivers on the laptop need to be upgraded to support the appropriate wireless protocol.

   G. The firmware on WSR3 needs to be upgraded to support the appropriate wireless protocol.

   H. The laptop user is unable to authenticate to obtain network access.

Each of the listed problems could be the cause of the laptop not gaining access to the network.

access layer The access layer in the three-layer hierarchical network model describes the portion of the network where devices connect to the network and includes controls for allowing devices to communicate on the network.

access point (AP) A device that connects wireless communication devices to form a wireless network, analogous to a hub connecting wired devices to form a LAN. The AP usually connects to a wired network and can relay data between wireless devices and wired devices. Several APs can link together to form a larger network that allows roaming.

ad hoc A WLAN topology, also called independent basic service set, where mobile clients connect directly without an intermediate access point. Referred to as IBSS by IEEE.

Advanced Encryption Standard (AES) AES replaced WEP as the most secure method of encrypting data. AES is an option for WPA2.

allowed VLAN Each VLAN trunk supports a set of allowed VLANs. Data associated with these VLANs is transmitted over the respective trunk link; remaining data is not transmitted over the link.

alternate port A switch port in an RSTP topology that offers an alternate path toward the root bridge. An alternate port assumes a discarding state in a stable, active topology. An alternate port will be present on nondesignated bridges and will make a transition to a designated port if the current path fails.

association The state achieved when a properly configured wireless client is able to wirelessly communicate with an access point.

association identifier (AID) An access point maps a logical port, known as the association identifier (AID) to the WLAN client. The AID is equivalent to a port on a switch.

attenuation Loss of communication signal energy.

authentication In network security, authentication is the verification of the identity of a person or process. Authentication is also used to describe the process a client device goes through before it can join a WLAN.

Authentication, Authorization, and Accounting (AAA) A protocol, specified in RFC 2903 and several other RFCs, for specifying who can access a system or network, how they can access it, and what they did while they were connected.

auto-MDIX An optional feature of Catalyst switches. When the auto-MDIX feature is enabled, the switch detects the required cable type for copper Ethernet connections and configures the interface pin-outs accordingly, enabling the use of either a crossover cable or a straight-through cable for connections to a 10/100/1000 port on the switch, regardless of the type of device on the other end of the connection.

backup port In an RSTP topology, this is a switch port on a designated bridge with a redundant link to the segment for which the switch is designated. A backup port has a higher port ID than the designated port on the designated bridge. The backup port assumes the discarding state in a stable, active topology.

basic service area (BSA)   The area of radio frequency coverage provided by an access point. This area is also referred to as a microcell.

basic service set (BSS)   A WLAN infrastructure mode whereby mobile clients use a single access point for connectivity to each other or to wired network resources.

basic service set identifier (BSSID)   The MAC address of the access point serving the BSS.

beacon   A wireless LAN packet that signals the availability and presence of the wireless device. Beacon packets are sent by access points and base stations; however, client radio cards send beacons when operating in computer-to-computer (ad hoc) mode.

black hole VLAN   The black hole VLAN for a switch or switched infrastructure is defined by the switch administrator as a dummy VLAN distinct from all other VLANs. All unused switch ports are assigned to the black hole VLAN so that any device connecting to an unused switch port will be assigned to the black hole VLAN. Any traffic associated with the black hole VLAN is not allowed on trunk links, thus preventing any device associated with the black hole VLAN from communicating beyond the switch to which it is connected.

blocking state   A port is in blocking state if it is a nondesignated port and does not participate in frame forwarding. The port continues to process received BPDU frames to determine the location and root ID of the root bridge and what port role the switch port should assume in the final active STP topology.

bridge ID (BID)   The bridge ID is composed of a priority value, an extended system ID, and the reserved MAC address from the switch. The BID is used by the spanning-tree algorithm; in particular, the BID is used for root bridge election.

bridge priority   The first parameter used in building a spanning-tree topology. The switch with the lowest bridge ID will be elected as the root bridge.

bridge protocol data unit (BPDU)   A spanning-tree protocol Ethernet frame that is sent out at regular intervals to exchange information among bridges in the network relating to spanning-tree topology formation.

Canonical Format Identifier (CFI)   A single bit flag value in the IEEE 802.1Q header. The CFI bit set indicates that all MAC address information present in the MAC address data carried by the frame is in canonical format.

Carrier Sense Multiple Access with Collision Avoidance (CSMA/CA)   This media access method requires WLAN devices to sense the medium for energy levels and wait until the medium is free before sending.

channel   A channel consists of a range of frequencies. Channels are used by wireless devices to hone in on a particular signal to differentiate it from wireless communications taking place at other frequencies. For example, the 2.4 GHz band is broken down into 11 channels in North America and 13 channels in Europe.

cipher   An algorithm for performing encryption and decryption. It consists of a series of well-defined steps that can be followed as a procedure.

Cisco Discovery Protocol (CDP)   A media- and protocol-independent device-discovery protocol that runs on all Cisco-manufactured equipment, including routers, access servers, bridges, and switches. Using CDP, a device can advertise its existence to other devices and receive information about other devices on the same LAN or on the remote side of a WAN.

clear-to-send (CTS)   A mechanism used in wireless technology to indicate that a wireless device is ready to accept data. RTS/CTS is used to resolve device access to avoid the hidden node problem.

common distribution system (CDS)   Allows multiple access points in an ESS to appear to be a single BSS. An ESS generally includes a common SSID to allow a user to roam from access point to access point.

configuration BPDU   Used by STP to build a loop-free topology. In normal STP operation, a switch receives configuration BPDU frames from the root bridge on its root port; however, it never sends a configuration BPDU toward the root bridge, in contrast to topology change notification BPDUs.

convergence   The speed and capability of a group of switches running STP to agree on a loop-free Layer 2 topology for a switched LAN.

core layer   The backbone of a switched LAN. All traffic to and from peripheral networks must pass through the core layer. It includes high-speed switching devices that can handle relatively large amounts of traffic.

cracker   One who breaks security on a system.

cut-through switching   An Ethernet frame switching approach that streams data through a switch so that the leading edge of a packet exits the switch at the egress port before the packet finishes entering the ingress port. A device using cut-through packet switching reads, processes, and forwards packets as soon as the destination address is read and the egress port determined.

data VLAN   A VLAN that is configured to carry only user-generated traffic. In particular, a data VLAN does not carry voice-based traffic or traffic used to manage a switch.

default gateway   The route that the device uses when it has no other explicitly defined route to the destination network. The router interface on the local subnet acts as the default gateway for the sending device.

default VLAN   The VLAN that all the ports on a switch are members of when a switch is reset to factory defaults. All switch ports are members of the default VLAN after the initial boot of the switch. On a Catalyst switch, VLAN 1 is the default VLAN.

designated bridge   The bridge that incurs the lowest path cost when forwarding a frame from a segment to the root bridge. Exactly one end of each trunk link in a spanning-tree topology is the designated bridge for that link.

designated port   In spanning tree, a nonroot switch port that is permitted to forward traffic on the network. For a trunk link connecting two switches, one end connects to the designated bridge via the designated port. One and only one end of every trunk link in a switched LAN (with spanning tree enabled) connects to a designated port. The selection of designated ports is the last step in the spanning-tree algorithm.

direct-sequence spread spectrum (DSSS)   One of the modulation techniques set out in IEEE 802.11 and the one chosen by the 802.11 Working Group for IEEE 802.11b devices.

disabled port   A port that is administratively shut down.

disabled state   A switch port is in the spanning-tree disabled state if it is administratively shut down. A disabled port does not function in the spanning-tree process.

discarding state   An RSTP port state seen in both a stable active topology and during topology synchronization changes. The discarding state prevents the forwarding of data frames, thus breaking the continuity of a Layer 2 loop.

distributed coordination function (DCF)   All wireless devices in a WLAN use CSMA/CA—the function of coordinating access to the medium is distributed. If an access point receives data from a client station, it sends an acknowledgement to the client that the data has been received. This acknowledgement keeps the client from assuming that a collision occurred and prevents data retransmission by the client. Access to the network is a coordinated process with an access control function that uses assigned wait times to distribute access to the network, thus limiting collisions.

distribution layer   In the three-layer hierarchical network design model, the distribution layer is the layer that invokes policy and routing control. Typically, VLANs are defined at this layer.

dynamic auto   A DTP setting whereby the local switch port advertises to the remote switch port that it is able to trunk but does not request to go to the trunking state. After a negotiation, the local port ends up in trunking state only if the remote port trunk mode has been configured to be on or desirable. If both ports on the switches are set to auto, they do not negotiate to be in the trunking state; they negotiate to be in the access (nontrunk) mode state. This is the default setting on Catalyst 2960 and 3560 switches.

dynamic desirable   A DTP setting whereby the local switch port advertises to the remote switch port that it is able to trunk and asks the remote switch port to go to the trunking state. If the local port detects that the remote has been configured in on, desirable, or auto mode, the local port ends up in trunking state. If the remote switch port is in the nonegotiate mode, the local switch port remains a nontrunking port. This is the default setting on Catalyst 2950 and 3550 switches.

Dynamic Trunking Protocol (DTP)   A Cisco-proprietary protocol that negotiates both the status and encapsulation of trunk ports.

dynamic VLAN   VLAN port membership modes are either static or dynamic. Dynamic VLANs are not widely used in production networks. Dynamic port VLAN membership is configured using a special server called a VLAN Membership Policy Server (VMPS).

edge port   An RSTP edge port is a switch port that is never intended to be connected to another switch device. It immediately transitions to the forwarding state when enabled. Edge ports are conceptually similar to PortFast enabled ports in the Cisco implementation of IEEE 802.1D.

encryption   The application of a specific algorithm to data so as to alter the appearance of the data, making it incomprehensible to those who are not authorized to see the information.

enterprise network   A large and diverse network connecting major sites within a company or other organization. An enterprise network differs from a WAN in that it is privately owned and maintained.

ethical hacker   A computer and network expert who attacks a security system on behalf of its owners, seeking vulnerabilities that a malicious **hacker** could exploit.

extended service area (ESA)   The coverage area of an ESS.

extended service set (ESS)   A WLAN infrastructure mode whereby two or more basic service sets are connected by a common distribution system. An ESS generally includes a common SSID to allow roaming from access point to access point without requiring client configuration.

extended system ID   Constitutes 12 bits of the 8-byte BID and contains the ID of the VLAN with which an STP BPDU is associated. The presence of the extended system ID results in bridge priority values incrementing in multiples of 4096.

Extensible Authentication Protocol (EAP)   A universal authentication framework frequently used in wireless networks defined by RFC 3748. Although the EAP protocol is not limited to WLANs and can be used for wired LAN authentication, it is most often used in WLANs. The WPA and WPA2 standards have adopted five EAP types as their official authentication mechanism.

firmware   Software instructions set permanently or semipermanently in ROM. On Cisco Catalyst switches, the firmware provides a means of booting the switch with these instructions, which are unaffected by a power loss.

Flash   Technology developed by Intel and licensed to other semiconductor companies. Flash memory is nonvolatile storage that can be electrically erased and reprogrammed. Flash allows software images to be stored, booted, and rewritten as necessary.

flooding   A data-trafficking technique used by switches in which traffic received on an interface is sent out all the other interfaces of the switch.

forward delay   The time a switch port spends in the STP listening state after the port is activated for bridging and before forwarding begins.

forwarding state   An STP port in forwarding state is considered part of the active topology and forwards data frames as well as sending and receiving BPDU frames.

full duplex   The capability of a port for simultaneous data transmission and reception.

gateway   A special-purpose device that performs an application-layer conversion of information from one protocol stack to another. The term *gateway* also is used to refer to a router or an interface on a router that enables users in an organization to connect to the Internet.

global positioning system (GPS)   Enables a receiver to determine its location, speed, direction, and time.

graphical user interface (GUI)   An environment that uses pictorial as well as textual representations of the input and output of applications and the data structure in which information is stored. Conventions such as buttons, icons, and windows are typical, and many actions are performed using a pointing device (such as a mouse). Microsoft Windows and the Apple Macintosh are prominent examples of platforms utilizing a GUI.

hacker   A malicious intruder who enters systems as a criminal and steals data or deliberately harms systems. Hackers are intent on doing harm and are able to exploit weak security measures.

half duplex   Refers to the transmission of data in just one direction at a time. At any given instant, the device can transmit or receive, but not both simultaneously.

hello time   The value of a field in a BPDU frame that specifies how frequently BPDUs are transmitted. The default is 2 seconds.

hidden node problem   The hidden node problem occurs when two client stations connect to the same access point, but are on opposing ends of the range of the AP, resulting in simultaneous transmissions by the clients as a result of the incapability of one client to sense the presence of the other.

IEEE 802 LAN/MAN Standards Committee (LMSC)   Chartered to oversee the various IEEE 802 working groups.

IEEE 802.1p   A standard that provides traffic class expediting. It provides a mechanism for implementing QoS at the MAC sublayer. Eight classes of service are available, expressed through the 3-bit user priority field in the IEEE 802.1Q header.

IEEE 802.1Q   A project in the IEEE 802 standards process to develop a mechanism to allow multiple bridged networks to transparently share the same physical network link without leaking information between networks. IEEE 802.1Q is also the name of the encapsulation protocol used to implement this mechanism over Ethernet networks.

IEEE 802.1x   A standard for port-based network access control. It provides authentication to devices attached to a LAN port, establishing a point-to-point connection or preventing access from that port if authentication fails. It is used for wireless access points and is based on EAP.

IEEE 802.11   A standard that defines how radio frequency in the ISM frequency bands is used for the physical layer and the MAC sublayer of wireless links.

IEEE 802.11a   A standard specifying wireless data communication at up to 54 Mbps at the 5 GHz range using OFDM.

IEEE 802.11b   A standard specifying wireless data communication at up to 11 Mbps at the 2.4 GHz range using DSSS.

IEEE 802.11g   A standard specifying wireless data communication at up to 54 Mbps at the 2.4 GHz range using DSSS and OFDM.

IEEE 802.11i   A standard specifying security mechanisms for wireless networks.

IEEE 802.11n (draft)   A draft standard specifying wireless data communication at up to 248 Mbps at an unspecified frequency range and using MIMO.

independent BSS (IBSS)   The IEEE terminology for an ad hoc topology.

industrial, scientific, and medical (ISM)   The ISM radio bands were originally reserved internationally for the use of RF electromagnetic fields for industrial, scientific, and medical purposes other than communications. Communications equipment must accept any interference generated by ISM equipment.

interference   Unwanted communication noise.

International Telecommunications Union-Radiocommunication Sector (ITU-R)   One of the three sectors (divisions or units) of the International Telecommunication Union (ITU), and is responsible for radio communication.

Internet Control Message Protocol (ICMP)   Chiefly used by TCP/IP network operating systems to send error messages indicating, for instance, that a requested service is not available or that a host or router could not be reached.

inter-switch link (ISL)   A Cisco-proprietary protocol that maintains VLAN information as traffic flows between switches and routers, or switches and switches. ISL is used by trunk ports to encapsulate Ethernet frames between network devices.

inter-VLAN routing   The process of routing data between VLANs within a switched LAN.

intrusion prevention system (IPS)   A device that monitors network activities for malicious behavior and can react in real-time to block those activities.

IP multicast   Enables single packets to be copied by the network and sent to a specific subset of network addresses. These receivers subscribe to the multicast group, which correlates to the destination multicast address in the transmission from the source.

learning state   The IEEE 802.1D learning state is seen in both a stable active topology and during topology synchronization changes. During the learning state a port accepts data frames to populate the MAC address table in an effort to limit flooding of unknown unicast frames.

listening state   The IEEE 802.1D listening state is seen in both a stable active topology and during topology synchronization changes. In the listening state, the port cannot send or receive data frames; however, the port is allowed to receive and send BPDUs.

load balance   The capability of a networking device to distribute traffic over some of its network ports on the path to the destination. Load balancing increases the utilization of network segments, thus increasing effective network bandwidth.

maintainability   A measure of the lack of difficulty in keeping network devices and associated software in working order.

man-in-the-middle (MITM)   An attack in which the attacker is able to read, insert, and modify at will messages between two endpoints without either party being aware that the data path has been compromised.

manageability   A measure of the lack of difficulty in managing network devices using network management software and protocols.

management VLAN   A VLAN defined by the switch administrator as a means of accessing the management capabilities of a switch. On a Catalyst switch, VLAN 1 would serve as the management

VLAN if you did not proactively define a unique VLAN to serve as the management VLAN. You assign the management VLAN an IP address and subnet mask. A switch can be managed via HTTP, Telnet, SSH, or SNMP. It is a security best practice to define the management VLAN to be a VLAN distinct from all other VLANs defined in the switched LAN.

manual site survey   A site evaluation that involves inspecting the area with the goal of identifying potential issues that could impact the network. Specifically, it involves the search for the presence of multiple WLANs, unique building structures, and high client usage variances.

maximum age   An STP timer that controls the maximum length of time a switch port saves configuration BPDU information. The default is 20 seconds, but can be tuned between 6 and 40 seconds.

MD5 algorithm   Message digest 5 is an algorithm used for message authentication in SNMPv2 and several other network protocols. MD5 verifies the integrity of the communication, authenticates the origin, and checks for timeliness.

message age   A field in a BPDU that specifies a metric for distance from the root bridge. The root bridge sends all its BPDUs with a message age value of 0, and all subsequent switches add 1 to this value. Effectively, this value contains the information on how far you are from the root bridge when you receive a BPDU.

message integrity check (MIC)   Part of the IEEE 802.11i standard. MIC is an 8-byte field placed between the data portion of an IEEE802.11 frame and the 4-byte ICV (Integrity Check Value). The algorithm that implements MIC is known as *Michael*; Michael also implements a frame counter, which discourages replay attacks.

modulation A technique for combining user information with a transmitter's carrier signal. It is a process by which the characteristics of electrical signals are transformed to represent information. Types of modulation include AM, FM, and PAM.

multilayer switch A multilayer switch filters and forwards packets based on OSI Layer 2 through Layer 7 information at wire-speed by utilizing dedicated hardware that stores data structures mirroring routing table, ARP table, and ACL information.

multiple input/multiple output (MIMO) MIMO technology, used in IEEE 802.11n wireless devices, splits a high data-rate stream into multiple lower-rate streams and broadcasts them simultaneously over the available radios and antennae. This allows for a theoretical maximum data rate of 248 Mbps.

Multiple Instance Spanning Tree Protocol (MISTP) A prestandard version of MSTP used on Catalyst 6000 Family switches running CatOS.

Multiple Spanning Tree Protocol (MSTP) MSTP, introduced as IEEE 802.1s, is an evolution of IEEE 802.1D STP and IEEE 802.1w (RSTP). MSTP enables multiple VLANs to be mapped to the same spanning-tree instance, reducing the number of instances needed to support a large number of VLANs.

native VLAN A native VLAN is assigned to an IEEE 802.1Q trunk port. An IEEE 802.1Q trunk port supports tagged and untagged traffic coming from many VLANs. The 802.1Q trunk port places untagged traffic on the native VLAN. Native VLANs are set out in the IEEE 802.1Q specification to maintain backward compatibility with untagged traffic common to legacy LAN scenarios. A native VLAN serves as a common identifier on opposing ends of a trunk link. It is a security best practice to define a native VLAN to be a dummy VLAN distinct from all other VLANs defined in the switched LAN. The native VLAN is not used for any traffic in the switched network.

nondesignated port An STP port dynamically configured to be in a blocking state to prevent loops.

nonegotiate The nonegotiate trunking option sets the local port to be in an unconditional trunking state with DTP disabled. Use this feature when you need to configure a trunk with a switch from another switch vendor.

nonvolatile RAM (NVRAM) RAM that retains its contents when a device is powered off. In Cisco products, NVRAM is used to store configuration information.

organizational unique identifier (OUI) A 3-byte hexadecimal number that the IEEE Registration Authority assigns to any company that manufactures components under the ISO/IEC 8802 standard. The OUI is used to generate universal LAN MAC addresses and protocol identifiers for use in local and metropolitan area network applications. For example, an OUI for Cisco Systems is 00-03-6B.

orthogonal frequency division multiplexing (OFDM) A modulation technique used with IEEE 802.11g and IEEE 802.11a.

out-of-band Refers to any type of access of a networking device operating system by means other than the network itself; with Cisco devices, out-of-band almost always refers to console access.

path cost The cumulative STP cost from a device to the root bridge; it is a function of the bandwidths of the individual links connecting the device to the root bridge.

Per-VLAN Spanning Tree (PVST) A Cisco-proprietary STP implementation that maintains a spanning-tree instance for each VLAN configured in the network. PVST relies on ISL for VLAN trunk encapsulation.

Per-VLAN Spanning Tree Plus (PVST+)   PVST+ provides the same functionality as PVST, including PortFast, and adds support for IEEE 802.1Q. PVST+ is not supported on non-Cisco devices.

performance   A loosely defined networking measure based on throughput and error rates.

ping   A command used to verify Layer 3 connectivity. Ping sends an ICMP echo request to the destination address. When a host receives an ICMP echo request, it responds with an ICMP echo reply to confirm that it received the request.

point-to-point link type   In an RSTP topology, nonedge ports are categorized into two link types: point-to-point and shared. The link type is automatically determined, but can be overwritten with an explicit port configuration. Point-to-point link types are used except on links connected to a shared multi-access half-duplex environment.

port cost   The spanning-tree port cost is a measure assigned on a per-link basis in a switched LAN; it is determined by the link bandwidth, with a higher bandwidth giving a lower port cost.

port ID   The spanning-tree port priority coupled with the port number of the switch port.

port number   A numerical value associated with switch ports and used to break ties in spanning-tree calculations. For example, on a Catalyst 2960 switch, interface F0/1 has port number 1.

port priority   A configurable spanning-tree parameter assigned to a switch port. The default setting is 128.

PortFast   A Cisco Catalyst switch technology. When a switch port configured as an access port is configured with PortFast, the port transitions from blocking to forwarding state immediately, bypassing the usual STP listening and learning states. PortFast is used on ports that are connected to end devices, such as workstations, servers, and printers. If an interface configured with PortFast receives a BPDU frame, spanning-tree can put the port into the blocking state using a feature called BPDU guard.

Power over Ethernet (PoE)   The powering of network devices over Ethernet cable. IEEE 802.3af and Cisco specify two different PoE methods. Cisco power sourcing equipment (PSE) and powered devices (PDs) support both PoE methods.

preshared key (PSK)   A key used in various encryption schemes whereby the opposing ends of a connection share the knowledge of a secret key used to encrypt and decrypt the data. PSK is also an alternative method for authentication in a network that does not have a RADIUS server.

private branch exchange (PBX)   A digital or analog telephone switchboard located on the subscriber premises and used to connect private and public telephone networks.

probe   IEEE 802.11 frames used by WLAN clients to find the networks they can associate with.

propagation delay   The time lag between the departure of a signal from the source and the arrival of the signal at the destination.

proposal and agreement process   RSTP dramatically speeds up convergence relative to IEEE 802.1D STP implementations by functioning on a link-by-link basis without relying on timers expiring before ports can transition between states. The link-by-link process consists of a proposal and agreement process.

quality of service (QoS)   A measure of performance for a transmission system that reflects its transmission quality and service available.

radio frequency (RF)   A generic term referring to frequencies that correspond to radio transmissions. Cable TV, WLANs, and broadband networks use RF technology.

radio resource management (RRM)   RRM monitors the RF band for activity and access point load. An access point that is busier than normal alerts the administrator of possible unauthorized traffic.

Rapid Per-VLAN Spanning Tree Plus (Rapid PVST+)   A Cisco implementation of RSTP. It supports one instance of RSTP for each VLAN.

Rapid Spanning Tree Protocol (RSTP)   RSTP, specified by IEEE 802.1w, is a dramatic improvement to IEEE 802.1D, providing very fast spanning-tree convergence on a link-by-link basis using a proposal and agreement process independent of timers.

read-only memory (ROM)   Nonvolatile memory that can be read, but not written to, by the microprocessor.

redundancy   The duplication of devices, services, or connections so that, in the event of a failure, the redundant devices, services, or connections can perform the work of those that failed.

Remote Authentication Dial In User Service (RADIUS)   An authentication protocol for controlling access to network resources within an IEEE 802.1x framework. RADIUS is commonly used by ISPs, enterprise networks, and corporations managing access to Internet or internal networks across an array of access technologies, including modems, DSL, wireless, and VPNs.

request to send/clear to send (RTS/CTS)   A feature used in the CSMA/CA media access method of WLANs to allow a negotiation between a client and an access point without collisions.

rogue access point   An access point, placed on a WLAN, which is used to interfere with normal network operation, capture client data, or gain access to servers. A rogue access point is an unauthorized AP accessing the WLAN.

root bridge   The root of a spanning-tree topology. A root bridge exchanges topology information with other bridges in a spanning-tree topology to notify all other bridges in the network when topology changes are required; this prevents loops and provides a measure of defense against link failure.

root ID   The bridge ID of the root bridge in a spanning-tree topology.

root port   The unique port on a nonroot bridge that has the lowest path cost to the root bridge. Every nonroot bridge in an STP topology must elect a root port. The root port on a switch is used for communication between the switch and the root bridge.

router-on-a-stick   A term used to describe the topology of a Layer 2 switch trunked to an interface on a router for the purposes of inter-VLAN routing. In this topology, the router interface is configured with one logical subinterface for each VLAN.

routing table   The table, stored in a router or other internetworking device, which keeps track of routes of network destinations and metrics associated with those routes.

scalability   A desirable property of a network to handle growing amounts of traffic in a graceful manner. A scalable network is readily enlarged.

security   An encompassing term describing the prevention and means of prevention of unauthorized access to an entity, location, or system.

service set identifier (SSID)   A code attached to all packets on a wireless network to identify each packet as part of that network. The code is a case-sensitive text string that consists of a maximum of 32 alphanumeric characters. All wireless devices attempting to communicate with each other must share the same SSID. Apart from identifying each packet, the SSID also serves to uniquely identify a group of wireless network devices used in a given service set.

shared link type   Nonedge ports are categorized into two link types: point-to-point and shared. The link type is automatically determined, but can be overwritten with an explicit port configuration. The shared link type is associated with ports connecting to a shared multi-access half-duplex environment.

signaling traffic   IP telephony traffic responsible for call setup, progress, and teardown, traversing the network end-to-end.

Simple Network Management Protocol (SNMP) Used to monitor and control network devices, and to manage configurations, statistics collection, performance, and security.

site survey   The process of planning and designing a wireless network to provide a solution that will deliver the required coverage, data rates, network capacity, roaming capability, and QoS.

spanning-tree algorithm (STA)   Used by STP to create a spanning tree.

Spanning Tree Protocol (STP)   Bridge protocol that utilizes the spanning-tree algorithm, enabling a learning bridge to dynamically work around loops in a network topology by creating a spanning tree. Bridges exchange BPDU messages with other bridges to detect loops, and then remove the loops by shutting down selected bridge interfaces. Refers to both the IEEE 802.1 Spanning-Tree Protocol standard and the earlier Digital Equipment Corporation Spanning-Tree Protocol on which it is based. The IEEE version supports bridge domains and allows the bridge to construct a loop-free topology across an extended LAN. The IEEE version is generally preferred over the Digital Equipment Corporation version. Sometimes abbreviated STP. *See also* BPDU and spanning-tree algorithm.

spoofing   The act of a packet or frame being represented with a false source address to mask its true source. Spoofing is designed to foil network security mechanisms such as filters and access lists.

static VLAN   One in which ports on the switch are manually assigned. A convenient feature of the Catalyst CLI is that if you assign an interface to a VLAN that does not exist, the new VLAN is created for you.

store-and-forward switching   A technique in which frames are completely processed before being forwarded out the appropriate port. This processing includes calculating the CRC and checking the destination address. In addition, frames must be temporarily stored until network resources are available to forward the message.

subinterface   A virtual interface associated with a single physical interface on a router.

switch diameter   The number of intermediary switches between two endpoints.

switch virtual interface (SVI)   A Layer 3 logical interface associated with a specific VLAN. You need to configure an SVI for a VLAN if you want to route between VLANs or to provide IP host connectivity to the switch. By default, an SVI is created for VLAN 1 on a Catalyst switch.

Temporal Key Integrity Protocol (TKIP)   Also referred to as Temporary Key Integrity Protocol, TKIP was designed by the IEEE 802.11i task group and the Wi-Fi Alliance as a solution to replace WEP without requiring the replacement of legacy hardware. This was necessary because the breaking of

WEP had left Wi-Fi networks without viable link-layer security, and a solution was required for already deployed hardware. The Wi-Fi Alliance endorsed TKIP under the name Wi-Fi Protected Access (WPA). The IEEE also endorsed TKIP.

time-to-live (TTL)   The field in an IP header that indicates how long a packet is considered valid; each routing device that an IP packet passes through decrements the TTL by 1.

topology change acknowledgement (TCA)   A BPDU with the TC bit set to 1. When the TC bit is set to 1, it indicates that a switch has received a TCN BPDU. This process is repeated until the root bridge receives and responds to the TCN BPDU.

topology change (TC) bit   A bit in a configuration BPDU that is used only when a switch is acknowledging the receipt of a TCN BPDU. The TC bit is set by the root bridge for a period of 35 seconds, by default.

topology change notification (TCN)   A special BPDU used when a switch needs to signal a topology change. A switch sends TCNs out of its root port, toward the root bridge. The TCN is a very simple BPDU that contains no information and is sent out at the hello time interval.

tracert   A Microsoft implementation of the trace-route program, which traces the path a packet takes to a destination. It is mostly used to debug routing problems between hosts.

transmit power   A measure of the strength of the radio transmissions emanating from a wireless networking device.

Trivial File Transfer Protocol (TFTP)   A simplified version of FTP that allows files to be transferred from one computer to another over a network in clear text without authentication.

trunking mode   Catalyst switches support a variety of trunking modes used by DTP to negotiate the status of a trunk port. The options are desirable, auto, on, and nonegotiate.

untagged frame   A normal Ethernet frame in a switched LAN. There is no IEEE 802.1Q tag associated with an untagged frame.

utility-assisted site survey   A sophisticated site survey carried out with a dedicated survey tool, such as AirMagnet. It often involves mounting access points on tripods and setting them in appropriate locations and in accordance with the projected site plan; with access points mounted, a walkaround of the facility using a site survey meter in the WLAN client utility of a PC is carried out.

virtual LAN (VLAN)   A group of hosts with a common set of requirements that communicate as if they were attached to the same wire, regardless of their physical location. A VLAN has the same attributes as a physical LAN, but it allows for end stations to be grouped together even if they are not located on the same LAN segment. Network reconfiguration can be done through software instead of physically relocating devices.

VLAN ID (VID)   The parameter in the IEEE 802.1Q tag that indicates the VLAN the frame is associated with. A Catalyst 2960 switch supports up to 4096 VLAN IDs.

VLAN trunk   An Ethernet point-to-point link between an Ethernet switch interface and an Ethernet interface on another networking device, such as a router or a switch, carrying the traffic of multiple VLANs over the singular link. A VLAN trunk allows you to extend the VLANs across an entire switched LAN.

VLAN Trunking Protocol (VTP)   A Cisco-proprietary Layer 2 protocol that enables a network manager to configure a single switch so that it propagates VLAN configuration information to other switches in the network, as well as synchronizes the information with the switches in the VTP domain.

vlan.dat   Catalyst switch VLAN configuration information is stored within a VLAN database file, called vlan.dat. The vlan.dat file is located in the Flash memory of the switch.

voice over IP (VoIP)   The capability to carry voice traffic over an IP-based network with POTS-like functionality, reliability, and voice quality. VoIP enables a router to carry voice traffic (for example, telephone calls and faxes) over an IP network. Voice packets are transported using IP in compliance with ITU-T specification H.323.

voice VLAN   Specialized Catalyst switch VLANs with an accompanying Catalyst CLI command set. Voice VLANs are designed for and dedicated to the transmission of voice traffic involving Cisco IP phones or Cisco softphones. QoS configurations are applied to voice VLANs to prioritize voice traffic.

VTP advertisements   VTP advertisements are messages transmitted between Catalyst switches to share and synchronize VLAN configuration details in the switched LAN.

VTP client   VTP clients participate in VTP operation, but do not permit creating, changing, or deleting of VLANs on the client itself. A VTP client stores VLAN information for the VTP domain only while the switch is powered on. A switch reset deletes the VLAN information. A switch must be manually configured to change its mode from VTP server to VTP client.

VTP configuration revision number   A number that indicates the current state of the VLAN information on the switch. The number enables the synchronization of VLAN information within the VTP domain.

VTP domain   A set of Catalyst switches with the same VTP domain name; all switches in a VTP domain share the same synchronized VLAN information.

VTP modes   VTP has three operating modes: server, client, and transparent. The operating mode determines how the switch uses and shares VLAN information within the VTP domain.

VTP password   The VTP password must match on all switches in a VTP domain. The password secures the information in the VTP domain and prevents a rogue switch added to a network from compromising VLAN information.

VTP pruning   Prevents unnecessary transmission of VLAN information from one VLAN across all trunks in a VTP domain. VTP pruning permits switches to negotiate which VLANs have active associations with ports on the portion of the network connected to the opposing end of a trunk link and, hence, prune the VLANs that are not actively associated with ports on that portion of the network. VTP pruning is disabled by default.

VTP request advertisement   Sent with a VTP server as the intended recipient of the VTP message. When a request advertisement is sent to a VTP server in the same VTP domain, the VTP server responds by sending a summary advertisement and then one or more subset advertisements.

VTP server   VTP servers advertise the VTP domain VLAN information to other VTP-enabled switches in the same VTP domain. VTP servers store the VLAN information for the entire domain in NVRAM. The server is where VLANs can be created, deleted, or renamed for the domain. It may take multiple subset advertisements to fully update the VLAN information.

VTP subset advertisement   A subset advertisement contains VLAN information. Subset advertisements are sent when a VLAN is created or deleted, after a VLAN is suspended of activated, when a VLAN name is changed, and when the MTU for a VLAN is changed.

VTP summary advertisement   VTP summary advertisements compose the majority of VTP advertisement traffic. A summary advertisement contains the VTP domain name, the current revision number, and some other VTP configuration details.

VTP transparent   VTP transparent mode switches forward VTP advertisements to VTP clients and VTP servers, but does not originate or otherwise process VTP advertisements. VLANs that are created, renamed, or deleted on a VTP transparent mode switch are local to that switch only.

VTP version   VTP has three versions: version 1, version 2, and version 3. Catalyst 2960 and 3560 switches support versions 1 and 2.

war driving   The act of searching for Wi-Fi wireless networks by a person in a moving vehicle using a Wi-Fi-equipped computer, such as a laptop or a PDA. Software for war driving is freely available on the Internet, and includes applications such as NetStumbler for Windows or Kismet for Linux.

Wi-Fi Alliance   The Wi-Fi Alliance owns the trademark to Wi-Fi. The Wi-Fi Alliance is a global, non-profit, industry trade association devoted to promoting the growth and acceptance of wireless technology.

Wi-Fi Protected Access (WPA and WPA2)   A class of systems to secure wireless LANs. It was created in response to several serious weaknesses researchers had found in the previous system, Wired Equivalent Privacy (WEP). WPA implements the majority of the IEEE 802.11i standard and was intended as an intermediate measure to take the place of WEP while IEEE 802.11i was prepared. WPA is specifically designed to also work with pre-WPA wireless network interface cards (through firmware upgrades), but not necessarily with first generation wireless access points. WPA2 implements the full standard and supports AES encryption (WPA does not support AES).

Wired Equivalent Privacy (WEP)   An algorithm to secure IEEE 802.11 wireless networks. Wireless networks broadcast messages using radio frequencies and are more susceptible to eavesdropping than wired networks. WEP, introduced in 1999, was intended to provide confidentiality comparable to that of a traditional wired network.

wireless LAN (WLAN)   A LAN with access points, together with the devices supporting them and supported by them.

wireless NIC   The device that makes a client station capable of sending and receiving RF signals is a wireless NIC. Some access points also have removable wireless NICs.

Index

Numbers

2.4 GHz channels, 392

3DES (Triple DES) algorithm, 94

802.1Q support website, 151

A

AAA (Authentication, Authorization, and Accounting) server, 76, 407

access

console, 85-86

distribution path failures, 232

ports

configuring with PortFast, 271-272

VTP, configuration, 211

privileged EXEC, 88-89

spoofing attacks, 100-101

virtual terminal, 87-88

WLANs, 410

access points, configuring, 410-417

protocols, 409

access layer (hierarchical network design model), 2, 28-29

access mode (VLAN trunks), 150

access points. *See* **APs**

ad hoc topologies, 394

addresses

dynamic, 77

IP, 362-365

MAC

address tables, 77-78, 236

determining root bridges, 260

Ethernet, 49

flooding, 96-99

port security, 105-106, 109

sticky secure MAC addresses, 106

switch configuration, 77-78

switch tables, 51-52

static, 77, 105

advertisements (VTP), 185, 190-192

802.1Q frame encapsulation, 191

configuration revision numbers, 192-193

frame structure, 191

header/message fields, 190

types, 193-196

AES (Advanced Encryption Standard), 408

AID (association identifier), 398

algorithms

3DES (Triple DES), 94

STA, 244

best paths, 249-252

port types, 247-248

root bridges, 248

allowed VLANs list issues, 169-171

alternate ports (RSTP), 300

APs (access points), 382

configuring, 410-412

basic wireless settings, 413-415

security, 415-417

placement, 431-433

radio/firmware, troubleshooting, 426

rogue, 402-403

wireless, 388-389

WLANs, 382

assigning port roles, 264

association, 396-398

association identifier (AID), 398

asymmetric switching, 60

attacks (security), 96

CDP, 101

MAC address flooding, 96-99

spoofing, 100-101

Telnet, 102-103

attenuation, 389

authentication, 396

AAA, 76

TACAS, 76

WLANs, 397

open, 406

protocols, 407-408

troubleshooting, 434

WEP, 406

Authentication, Authorization, and Accounting (AAA) server, 76, 407

auto-MDIX feature, 51

W-X-Y-Z

war driving, 402

websites

802.1Q support, 151

AAA authentication, 77

BackboneFast STP extension, 287

BPDU guards, 271, 287, 318

Catalyst switches

2960, 35

3560, 36

3750, 36

4500, 37

4900, 38

6500, 39

Express 500, 34

CCNA Exploration: Routing Protocols and Concepts, 349

Cisco

Device Manager, 66

EtherChannel, 8, 242, 358

Network Assistant, 65

CiscoView, 65

disaster recovery, 10

DTP support, 150-151

EtherChannels, 8, 242, 358

high availability discussion, 9

HP OpenView, 68

ISL support, 151

Layer 3 switches, 337

MSTP, 288

Netstumbler, 409

password recovery procedures, 92

port security, 108

PortFast, 318

rapid PVST+ commands, 311

reload command, 82

RSA technology, 96

show interfaces command output fields, 158

show spanning-tree command parameters, 294

show vlan command output fields, 158

SSH, 96

STP

configuration on Cisco 2960 series switch, 310

troubleshooting, 317

switches comparison, 39

switchport mode command parameters, 162

TACAS authentication, 77

TFTP server, 83

traffic flow analysis tools, 17

UplinkFast STP extension, 287

voice VLAN configuration, 138

VTP pruning, 204

WEP keys, 407

Wi-Fi Alliance, 386

WLAN security threats, 404

WEP (Wired Equivalent Privacy) key, 397, 406-407

Wi-Fi Alliance, 386-387

Wi-Fi Protected Access (WPA), 406

wireless

access points, 388-389

association

association, 398

authentication, 397

beacons, 396

probes, 397

design map, 399

NICs, 387, 418

connectivity, verifying, 423

security protocols, 420-422

SSIDs, scanning, 418-419

operation

configurable parameters, 391-393

discovery/connection, 396-398

topologies, 393-395

parameters, configuring, 391-393

routers, 390

security protocols, 405-406

access control, 409

authentication, 407-408

encryption, 408-409

technologies, 380

topologies, 380, 393-395

ad hoc, 394

BSS, 394

ESS, 394

IEEE 802.11, 395

wireless LANs. *See* WLANs

Wireless Network Connection Status dialog box, 420

Wireless Network Properties dialog box, 420-421

wiring closet loops, 242-243

WLANs (wireless LANs), 379

access, 409-410

access points, 382, 388-389, 410-412

basic wireless settings, 413-415

security, 415-417

authentication

open, 406

protocols, 407-408

WEP, 406